COMPUTER SOCIETY PRESS TECHNOLOGY SERIES

NEURAL NETWORKS

Artificial Neural Networks: Theoretical Concepts

V. Vemuri

Computer Society Order Number 855
Library of Congress Number 88-71053
IEEE Catalog Number EH0279-0
ISBN 0-8186-0855-2

THE COMPUTER SOCIETY OF THE IEEE

IEEE THE INSTITUTE OF ELECTRICAL AND ELECTRONICS ENGINEERS, INC.

IEEE COMPUTER SOCIETY PRESS

Published by

IEEE Computer Society Press
10662 Los Vaqueros Circle
P.O. Box 3014
Los Alamitos, CA 90720-1264

Cover designed by Jack I. Ballestero

Printed in United States of America

IEEE Computer Society Press Order Number 855
Library of Congress Number 88-71053
IEEE Catalog Number EH0279-0
ISBN 0-8186-0855-2 (paper)
ISBN 0-8186-4855-4 (microfiche)
SAN 264-620X

Additional copies can be ordered from:

IEEE Computer Society Press
Customer Service Center
10662 Los Vaqueros Circle
P.O. Box 3014
Los Alamitos, CA 90720-1264

IEEE Computer Society
13, Avenue de l'Aquilon
B-1200 Brussels
BELGIUM

IEEE Computer Society
Ooshima Building
2-19-1 Minami-Aoyama,
Minato-Ku
Tokyo 107, JAPAN

IEEE Service Center
445 Hoes Lane
P.O. Box 1331
Piscataway, NJ 08855-1331

THE INSTITUTE OF ELECTRICAL AND ELECTRONICS ENGINEERS, INC.

ARTIFICIAL NEURAL NETWORKS: THEORETICAL CONCEPTS

Preface

This volume provides an introduction to the exciting field of artificial neural networks and their potential role in the emerging field of neurocomputing. Although the genesis of this subject can be traced back to the 1940s, the present interest is largely due to the recent developments in theoretical models, technologies, and algorithms.

As this subject caught the imagination of a number of people working in a wide variety of areas with varying motivations, material on artificial neural networks appeared in a variety of journals — from commercial to popular and all the way to the archival. The level of treatment, the terminology used, and the perspective varied accordingly. To maintain uniformity in the level of presentation, we decided to select papers that were reviewed and published primarily in IEEE journals. For a balanced presentation of the various facets of this material, one has to touch topics on neurobiology, network architectures, associative memory, self-organization, adaptive resonance, learning algorithms, combinatorial optimization, technology issues (e.g., electronic and optical implementations, simulations, computerized tools), applications (e.g., vision, speech, image processing, robotics), and implementations. Even a sampling of these topics will take us too far afield from our modest goal of producing a small volume devoted to introductory and theoretical concepts. This constraint was responsible for our decision to put some emphasis on network architectures, learning, associative memories, and a glimpse of the application areas and implementation experiences. The introductory remarks by this editor and the paper by Hecht-Nielsen should provide the necessary motivational background to a novice exploring this subject. The paper by Anderson provides some biological perspective to the theoretical underpinnings. Lippman's paper is a concise tutorial on various learning algorithms. These four papers constitute a unit and are deemed adequate to introduce the subject to the serious student. The next four papers provide a perspective of the Amari, Grossberg, and Hopfield schools. The next two papers respectively by Abu-Mostafa *et al.* and McEliece *et al.* address the important question of information capacity of a neural network. The following two papers on associative memory address two different aspects of the problem. Finally, the paper on Neocognitron was selected to impress upon the reader that the ANNs are no longer a theoretical speculation. As opportunities arise, some of the future issues in this Technology Series will be devoted to explore other aspects of ANNs and neurocomputing.

V. Vemuri, Editor

Technology Series

Artificial Neural Networks: Theoretical Concepts

Table of Contents

Artificial Neural Networks: An Introduction

by

V. Vemuri
Department of Applied Science
University of California, Davis/Livermore
and
Lawrence Livermore National Laboratories

1. Introduction

Neurons are living nerve cells and neural networks are networks of these cells. The cerebral cortex of the brain is an example of a *natural* neural network. Somehow, such a network of neurons thinks, feels, learns and remembers. In the past, many investigators attempted to build models to study neural networks. These models fall into two categories. In ***biological modeling*** the goal is to study the structure and function of real brains in order to explain biological data on aspects such as behavior. In ***technological modeling*** the goal is to study brains in order to extract concepts to be used in new computational methodologies. There are points of contention on which of these two branches should constitute the true focus of research in neural network modeling. If the goal is to advance our understanding of biological intelligence, then the validity of the models should be corroborated with experimental evidence. However, many scientists and engineers (as opposed to biologists and psychologists) are usually content with models inspired by brain function. Although this controversy continues, the latter viewpoint is taken by several investigators working in the area of *artificial* neural networks (hereafter referred to as ANNs) and neurocomputers.

The objectives of research in ANNs may be paraphrased as follows. The first objective is to understand how the brain imparts abilities like perceptual interpretation, associative recall, common sense reasoning and learning to humans. Toward this goal, it is necessary to understand how "computations" are organized and carried out in the brain. These computations are of a different kind than the formal manipulation of symbolic expressions. The second objective is to understand the subclass of neural network models that emphasize "computational power" rather than their biological fidelity. To achieve this objective, it is admissible to incorporate features in a model even if those features are not neurobiologically possible. There is some controversy about this narrow viewpoint. For example, according to Grossberg, some of the features in the popular ***back propagation*** learning model are not supported, so far, by experimental evidence [1].

The restricted view taken by technological modelers also has a turbulent history. In the early days of computers, two philosophically opposing views of what computers could be emerged and struggled for recognition. One school believed that both minds and digital computers are symbol-manipulating systems. Symbolic logic and programming became the tools of their trade. The opposing school felt that the ultimate goal of computation is better achieved by modeling the brain itself rather than manipulating the mind's symbolic representation of the external world [2]. Stated differently, the symbol-manipulating school believed that the problem-solving process is essentially *algorithmic*. Although initial demonstrations proved the viability of both these approaches, the brain modelers lost some ground when digital computers were successfully used in 1956 by A. Newell and H. Simon to solve puzzles and prove theorems. By this time F. Rosenblatt also succeded in building a device, called the *perceptron*, and demonstrated the viability of the opposing school. In the decade that followed, this *holistic* school received a severe blow when in 1965 Minsky and Papert claimed [3] that the perceptron approach is fundamentally flawed. Reference [2] contains a brief but informative account of this intriguing interlude and its impact on the progress of research in the field of ANNs.

2. Motivations for ANN Research

The recent renewal of interest in ANNs is prompted by advances in technology as well as a deeper understanding of how the brain works. One motivation is a desire to build a new breed of powerful computers (already being touted as the *sixth* generation computers) to solve a variety of problems that are proving to be very difficult with conventional digital computers. Cognitive tasks such as recognizing a familiar face, learning to speak and understand a natural language, retrieving contextually appropriate information from memory, and guiding a mechanical hand to grasp objects of different shapes and consistencies are some examples that come quickly to mind. Problems of this kind typically involve pattern recognition under real-world conditions, fuzzy pattern matching, nonlinear discrimination, or combinatorial optimization. That is, these tasks are analogous to those typically performed naturally by the brain, and are beyond the reach of conventionally programmed computers as well as the rule-based expert systems. For example, we can usually recognize a familiar face in only about 200 milliseconds. The human eye can adjust to light intensity levels over 7 orders of magnitude. No man-made image processing system can come even close to this in performance. It is remarkable that this performance is obtained by a system whose individual components are larger, slower, and noisier than state-of-the-art electronic components.

Another motivation behind the spurt of activity in this area is a desire to develop cognitive models that can serve as a foundation for artificial intelligence. Although it is well known that the brain is not as good at performing arithmetic operations as a digital computer, there are several aspects of brain function that we are not able to duplicate with conventional computers. Some of these are association, categorization, generalization, classification, feature extraction, and optimization. These capabilities fall under three broad categories: searching, representation, and learning. These aspects are closely related to the associative property and self-organizing capability of the brain. By associative property, we mean the capability of recalling an entire complex of information by using a small part of it as a key to a search process. The brain does this remarkably well. By self-organizing, we mean the ability to acquire knowledge through a trial-and-error learning process involving organizing and reorganizing in response to external stimuli.

The computational process envisioned with ANNs is as follows: An "artificial neuron" (AN) receives its inputs from a number of other ANs or from the external world. A weighted sum of these inputs constitutes the argument of an *activation function*. This activation function g is assumed to be nonlinear. Hard limiting (i.e., either the step or the signum function), threshold, and soft limiting (i.e., the sigmoidal) are the three most often used forms of nonlinearities. The resulting value of the activation function is the output of the AN. This output is distributed along weighted connections to other ANs. The notion of memory in a conventional computer is analogous to the concept of the weight settings. As these weighted connections play an important role, these ANNs are also called the *connectionist* models of computation. It should be emphasized that models of this kind have only a metaphorical resemblance to natural neural networks.

A device that is familiar to electrical engineers and that behaves somewhat like a neuron is the *electronic analog operational amplifier*, or simply the *op amp*, configured as an *integrator*. If one can visualize hundreds of these integrators interconnected together through potentiometers (the potentiometer settings representing the synaptic strengths of real neurons), then what we have is a crude model of an ANN. Several researchers in the sixties attempted to simulate ANNs by using operational amplifiers and potentiometers. Most of those efforts proved the concept but were of little practical use because of the limitations imposed by the analog computers of that pre-VLSI era. With the advent of VLSI technology and the availability of electronic implementations based on novel thin film materials, it is now possible to build high-density custom circuits to represent the neurons (via thresholding amplifiers) as well as the synapses (from a matrix of passive circuit elements). Recent work at many institutions demonstrated the feasibility of fabricating binary as well as variable strength synapses. Recent advances in charge-coupled devices (CCDs) may now make it possible to fabricate dynamically reprogrammable synapses. Practical limitations of VLSI technology may impose constraints on the density of interconnectivity but advances in optical, opto-electronic, and holographic technologies may eventually help overcome this constraint also.

Aside from technological challenges, there are a number of problems of theoretical nature (e.g., representation, learning, and self-organizing procedures) that need to be addressed and solved if ANNs are to become a viable force in the computational arena. Although more than a dozen ANNs have been built, each with a different "architecture" and each aimed at solving a different problem (see Hecht-Nielsen's paper in this volume), there seems to be a lack of commonality in their theoretical basis. It is not yet clear whether or when such a common theoretical basis will emerge. Similarly much remains to be learned about learning paradigms. In spite of these uncertainities, a forceful motive behind the current enthusiasm for artificial neural networks is in the promise they hold in solving the diversity of "hard" problems.

3. Evolution of ANN Models

Models of ANNs are specified by three basic entities: models of the neurons themselves (i.e., the node characteristics), models of synaptic interconnections and structures (i.e., net topology and weights), and the training or learning rules (i.e., the method of adjusting the weights or how the network interprets the information it is receiving). The nodes themselves can be characterized by analog (continuous) or digital (discrete) summing elements exhibiting either nonlinear or threshold behavior.

To understand the essence of the issues involved it is sufficient to inspect a handful of models and their underlying philosophies. One of the first abstract models of a neuron was introduced in 1943 by McCulloch and Pitts [4]. This "M-P neuron" is characterized by a finite number of excitatory (i.e., weight $w_i = +1$) and inhibitory (i.e., weight $w_i = -1$) inputs, x_i, $(i = 1, 2, \cdots, n)$, a threshold level L, and an output, y. The inputs and ouputs can assume the binary values 0 or 1. The threshold can be any positive integer. Expressed mathematically, the output of an "isolated" M-P neuron can be described in terms of its inputs by

$$y = g(\sum w_i x_i - L) \tag{1a}$$

where $g(p) = 0$ if $p < 0$, and $+1$ if $p \geq 0$. Stated in words, this means that a neuron can "fire" if the total excitation it receives reaches or exceeds the threshold value.

The threshold term L can be eliminated from the equation by adding an extra input connection from a node whose output is always 1 and whose weight is the negative of the threshold value, L. The advantage of this approach is that L can now be adjusted along with the other weights. Similarly, an external input can be supplied to the network either by clamping the outputs of some units or by adding an extra term, I, to the sum of the inputs of some units.

Groups of AN can be interconnected in a variety of ways to form ANNs. Over the years, many topological configurations for these ANNs were proposed. Networks comprising only a single layer of ANs as well as many layers have been tried. Many layered networks comprise two or more rows of ANs. In *feed-forward* networks the signal flow from one layer to the next is unidirectional. In *feedback* networks, both forward and backward connections exist. Among the feedback networks, another modification is to explicitly allow feedback paths within the same layer as well as from one layer to an "earlier" layer. Even a cursory discussion of these topics will take us too far afield. The following paragraphs survey some of the simple configurations.

A simple ANN consisting of a single layer of M-P neurons can be created from an array of n neurons. Each of these receives inputs from m sources, $x_1, x_2, \cdots, x_m$, via weights w_{ij}, and having outputs $y_1, y_2, \cdots, y_n$. Note that no mention is made at this time about the nature of the sources. In such a *network*, Equation (1a) for the output of the jth neuron can be rewritten as

$$y_j = g(\sum w_{ij} x_i - L_j) \tag{1b}$$

Although not stated explicitly, the above network comprising of M-P neurons works synchronously at discrete instants of time.

To understand what such a network can do, consider an M-P network consisting of only one ($n = 1$) neuron, two inputs X_1 and X_2 and an output Y. If the weights associated with the two inputs are set at $+1$ and the threshold set at 2, the output Y would be the logical AND of the two inputs. If the threshold is set, instead, at 1, the output would be the logical OR of the two inputs. If there is only one input with a weight -1 and the threshold is 0, then the output would be a logical NOT of the input.

McCulloch and Pitts not only demonstrated the capability of their model in performing simple logical tasks, but they also recognized that the problem of pattern classification is central to any theory of intelligent behavior. They proceeded to construct two neural networks that addressed this problem [5].

In 1949 D.O. Hebb proposed [6] that the connectivity of the brain is continually changing as an organism learns. Hebb further postulated that repeated activation of one neuron by another through a particular synapse increases its conductance. This implies that groups of weakly connected neurons, if activated synchronously, tend to organize themselves into more strongly connected assemblies. This influential postulation triggered many investigations of learning and launched much work on adaptive neural networks.

In 1958, F. Rosenblatt published a paper [7] in which he showed how an M-P network with adjustable synapses can be "trained" to classify certain sets of patterns. Rosenblatt called these networks *perceptrons*. A typical *elementary perceptron* consists of three "layers." The first layer consists of a set of "sensory" units. The second or middle layer, composed of a set of M-P neurons, receives its inputs from the first layer via weighted connections and provides outputs to the third layer. The third is called the "motor" layer. Initially the weight settings are arbitrary, so that any stimulation of the network produces an arbitrary response. To obtain the desired response, the weights are to be adjusted. The adjustment procedure is *training*.

A variant of the perceptron is the *adaline* (for adaptive linear neuron), proposed by Widrow and Hoff [8]. For the purposes of this introduction, the differences between perceptrons and adalines are not significant enough to merit further discussion of adalines.

At this point Minsky and Papert proved that elementary perceptrons cannot distinguish between such simple patterns as T and C. The problem lies with the M-P neurons. For example, it turns out that one M-P neuron is not sufficient to implement the EXCLUSIVE OR function. The significance is that a single M-P neuron cannot act as a computationally universal element in the Turing sense. To implement an EXCLUSIVE OR, for example, one has to use two *threshold* units and two M-P neurons. The output of one of these M-P units is not connected to the motor layer and is therefore called the "hidden" unit. Although the M-P neuron is important as a basis for (a) the logical analysis of "neural computability," and (b) the design of some currently available neural devices, it is no longer considered a useful model in explaining actually observed neurophysiological data.

There were some attempts to replace the M-P neuron with a more realistic model. One attempt to bring realism to neuron modeling resulted in the treatment of time as a continuous variable. Now the *firing rate* (viz., the number of spikes traversing the axon in the most recent 20 milliseconds) and the *membrane potential* (viz., the total instantaneous input received by a neuron) are important parameters. This membrane potential, denoted by u, is also called the *state* (a term borrowed from control theory) of the neuron. With this notation, the time evolution of the membrane potential of the jth neuron can be described by

$$\frac{du_j}{dt} = -u_j + \sum_{i=1}^{n} w_{ij}x_i - L_j \tag{2a}$$

where the output y_j is related to the state u_j via the relation

$$u_j = h(y_j) \tag{2b}$$

If the inputs x_i are held stationary, or if the inputs vary slowly, we can set $du_j/dt \approx 0$. For this case, Equations (2a) and (2b) reduce to

$$y_j = h^{-1}[\sum_{i=1}^{n} w_{ij}x_i - L_j] \tag{2c}$$

If h^{-1} is identified with g, this equation is analogous to Equation (1). Neural network literature contains several mathematical models which may be construed as variations of Equation (2).

Equation (2) represents a point of departure from the discrete to the continuous models. That is, instead of treating an ANN as a finite-state, discrete system, one treats it as a collection of continuous-state (e.g., analog) devices modeled as systems of ordinary differential equations. Proponents of this approach argue that real neurons have graded, continuous outputs rather than step-wise, two-state response curves. Furthermore, a number of theoretical issues can conveniently be addressed in the continuous domain by bringing in the knowledge from dynamic systems to bear upon this problem of characterizing artificial neurons. Although no modeling approach is automatically appropriate for all circumstances, we seek to find the simplest model that (a) is adequate to address the task at hand, and (b) opens the doors for new lines of investigation. For example, the concept of storing information in the stable configurations of dynamical systems, introduced by Hopfield, is rather profound.

In 1984, J.J. Hopfield observed some analogies between the behavior of collections of neurons and collections of atoms. The excitatory and inhibitory forces exerted by real neurons on one another are somewhat like the forces exerted by atoms on their neighbors. Then he proceeded to establish a formal analogy between the so-called *Hopfield nets* (namely, a network of neuronlike elements with symmetric connections) and a new class of magnetic materials called spin glasses. Expanding upon the earlier work of Steinbuch, Amari and others, Hopfield and his colleagues start off with [9]

$$C_i \frac{du_i}{dt} = -\frac{1}{R_i} u_i + \sum_{j=1}^{n} T_{ij} v_j + I_i \tag{3a}$$

where u_i is the state of the ith neuron, T_{ij} are the weights, and the I_i represent external inputs (or forcing functions). The output v_j of neuron j is assumed to be of the form $g(u_j)$ where g is sigmoidal. In biological systems, the instantaneous input u_i lags behind the outputs v_j of other neurons because of the input capacitance C_i and the transmembrane resistance R_i. Then they defined an energy-like function

$$E = -\frac{1}{2} \sum_{i=1}^{n} \sum_{j=1}^{n} T_{ij} v_i v_j + \sum_{i=1}^{n} \frac{1}{R_i} \int_0^{v_i} g_i^{-1}(\lambda) d\lambda + \sum_{i=1}^{n} I_i v_i \tag{3b}$$

Hopfield and his colleagues then proceeded to prove that the above system evolves toward a stable configuration if the T_{ij} are symmetric. These stable configurations can be used to store information.

4. Learning in Neural Networks

That learning is central to ANN research was recognized early. The perceptron convergence procedure used by Rosenblatt and Hebb's rule are two examples of classical learning procedures. Rosenblatt's procedure is applicable only if the desired solution is specified in advance. Hebb's learning procedure states that changes in the synaptic weight connecting the ith and the jth neurons is directly proportional to the activities (measured, say, in terms of the magnitudes of the outputs) of the ith and the jth neurons.

Modern learning procedures fall into two broad categories: *Supervised* methods which require a teacher to specify the desired output, and *unsupervised* procedures which construct internal models that capture regularities in input signals. Grossberg's school argues that only unsupervised learning is biologically plausible. However, many supervised learning procedures give excellent results while solving technological problems and are therefore in widespread use. Salient features of some simple learning procedures are outlined below.

A simple supervised learning procedure works as follows. Suppose we wish to train a network to produce certain desired states at the output for each member of a set of input vectors. A measure of how poorly the network is performing with the current set of weights is

$$Error = \frac{1}{2}\sum(y_{j,c} - d_{j,c})^2 \tag{4}$$

where $y_{j,c}$ is the actual output of unit j in input-output case c, and $d_{j,c}$ is the desired output. Methods, such as the above, that strive to minimize the sum of the squares of the error are called LMS (for least mean square) procedures.

The above error can be minimized by starting with an arbitrary set of weights and systematically changing them by a value equal to $\Delta W_{i,j}$. The actual calculation of $\Delta W_{i,j}$ can be done in a variety of ways. For example, Hebb's procedure uses an equation like (the subscript c is suppressed, for convenience),

$$\Delta W_{i,j} = k y_i y_j \tag{5}$$

where k is a constant of proportionality.

Grossberg, for example, suggested a modification to this scheme in which changes in weights are proportional to the activation function g evaluated at the difference between y_j and $W_{i,j}$. That is,

$$\Delta W_{i,j} = k g(y_j - W_{i,j}) \tag{6}$$

Both these schemes are inspired by knowledge about biological phenomena.

An obvious mathematical approach to minimizing E is by a gradient descent procedure which changes the weights by an amount proportional to $\partial E/\partial W$. That is

$$\Delta W_{i,j} = k\partial E/\partial W \tag{7}$$

One of the major drawbacks of the above class of LMS procedures is that many "interesting" mappings between input and output cannot be captured by any combination of weights. Furthermore, gradient descent procedures converge very slowly as one approaches stable points.

A popular generalization of the LMS procedure is the *back propagation* method. To understand the training procedure based on back propagation, one has to look at the steps involved in calculating the derivatives $\partial E/\partial Wi, j$. One of these steps requires computation of $\partial E/\partial y_j$. This quantity is hard to compute in networks with hidden units. The central idea of back propagation is the recognition that these calculations are simpler if one starts the evaluations at the output layer and works backwards. The method is implemented in two stages. During the forward pass, the activity levels y_j of all units are calculated. Then, starting at the output layer, the derivatives are evaluated in a backward sweep. Multilayer networks with hidden units have been trained with the back propagation method to "solve" the EXCLUSIVE OR problem alluded to earlier in this paper. Nevertheless, back propagation suffers from several drawbacks. It was found to be slow, temporally unstable ("forgets" previously learned patterns), and tends to get stuck at local minima. The major objection is that this is biologically not plausible; there is no evidence that synapses can be used in the reverse direction.

Another method, apparantly suggested independently by A. H. Klopf and B. Kosco, appears to be gaining some ground. This new rule has two important features: (a) unlike Hebb's rule, the change in strength of an interconnection is proportional, not to the product of the magnitudes of the input and output, but to the product of *changes* in input and output, and (b) the present output depends only upon the previous inputs, not the current input. Other possibilities abound. For example, one can try *lateral inhibition* (a phenomenon found in natural neural networks) as a vehicle to prevent a first experience from "taking over." Some other possibilities lead to the so-called *Boltzmann machines* and *Cauchy machines*. Both these machines are really ANNs with a *stochastic* learning procedure. Both these machines attempt to resolve the dilemma of what to do when a gradient descent procedure gets stuck at a local minimum. Researchers often use *simulated annealing* to solve this problem [10]. To apply simulated annealing, one draws an analogy between the system under study and a thermodynamical system at temperature T. In order to gain some insight into this analogy, consider a system of atoms. At high temperatures, they gain energy, move about freely, and find equilibrium states rapidly, but the atoms occupy high and low energy equilibrium states with roughly equal probability.

At low temperatures, they approach the equilibrium states relatively slowly, but they tend to occupy low energy states with much higher probability than high energy states. The best way to approach low energy equilibrium states is to first heat the system to a high temperature and gradually cool it. This process is called *annealing*. This idea when applied to an optimization problem is called *simulated annealing*. Application of this idea to ANN learning procedures yields the *Boltzmann machine*.

In a Boltzmann machine, each AN updates its state according to a *stochastic* decision rule. An example of this rule is: the probability that a unit j adopts the state 1 (the other state being 0) is

$$p_j = \frac{1}{1 + e^{-\Delta E_j / T}} \tag{8}$$

where ΔE_j is the total input received by the jth AN and T is the absolute temperature. If Cauchy distribution, rather than Boltzmann distribution, is used, the resulting machine is called a *Cauchy machine*. Lippman's paper included in this volume is a good starting point for exploring learning algorithms.

5. Computing with ANNs

Although the emphasis of this volume is on theoretical issues, the discussion would be sterile without some mention of what is happening in the realization of these theoretical efforts. At the time of this writing, not less than 50 research groups in industry, universities, defense agencies, and national laboratories are engaged in the actual design and implementations of some kind of ANN-based computer system. For example, TRW's Mark III and Mark IV machines are probably the world's first commercially available computers of this kind. These machines are digital implementations of the discretized versions of a set of differential equations derived from Grossberg's work. The original Mark III had 8 microprocessors, implementing 8,000 neurons with up to 400,000 interconnections. Both these machines were designed to function in a *backend* configuration and have been used to solve signal and speech processing problems. There are many more and some of them would be the subject of a future issue of this series.

ACKNOWLEDGMENTS

I am indebted to Bruce D. Shriver, Jon T. Butler, and Ez Nahouraii for their critique on this effort and to Lee Blue and the staff at the Computer Society publications office for their help in launching this Technology Series.

References

1. Grossberg, S. 1988. Neural networks research: From a personal perspective, *Electronic Engineering Times*, (March 7):A12-A40.

2. Dreyfus, H.L. and S.E. Dreyfus. 1988. Making a mind versus modeling a mind: Artificial intelligence back at a branch point, *Daedalus*, 117(1):15-43.

3. Minsky, M. and S. Papert. 1969. *Perceptrons: An Introduction to Computational geometry*, Cambridge: MIT Press.

4. McCulloch, W.S. and W.H. Pitts. 1943. A logical calculus for the ideas immanent in nervous activity. *Bulletin of Mathematical Biophysics* 5:115-133.

5. Pitts, W.H. and W.S. McCulloch. 1947. How we know universals: The perception of auditory and visual forms. *Bulletin of Mathematical Biophysics*. 9:127ff.

6. Hebb, D.O. 1949 *The Organization of Behavior*, New York: John Wiley.

7. Rosenblatt, F. 1958. The Perceptron, a probabilistic model for information storage and organization in the brain. *Psychological Review* 62:559ff.

8. Widrow, B. and M.E. Hoff. 1960. Adaptive Switching Circuits. *WESCON Convention Record* 4:96-104.

9. Hopfield, J.J. 1984. Neurons with graded response have collective computational properties like those of two-state neurons. *Proc. Natl. Acad. Sci.*, (USA) 81:3088-3092.

10. Kirkpatrick, C., D. Gelat, Jr., and M.P. Vecchi. 1983. Optimization by simulated annealing. *Science* 220:681ff.

For More Information

In addition to the articles included in this volume, the following constitute a good initial source of recommended reading.

1. Rumelhart, D.E. and J.L. McCleland (Eds.). 1986. *Parallel Distributed Processing* I & II, Cambridge: MIT Press.

2. Denker, J. (Ed.). 1986. *Computing with Neural Networks*. American Institute of Physics.

3. *Daedalus* 117(1) Winter 1988. Special Issue on Artificial Intelligence.

4. Abu-Mostafa, Y.S. and D. Psaltis. 1987. Optical neural computers. *Scientific American* 256:88-95.

5. *IEEE Computer* 21(3) March 1988. Special Issue on Artificial Neural Systems.

Reprinted from IEEE Spectrum 25(3), March 1988, pp. 36-41.

Neurocomputing: picking the human brain

Borrowing from biology, researchers are exploring neural networks—a new, nonalgorithmic approach to information processing

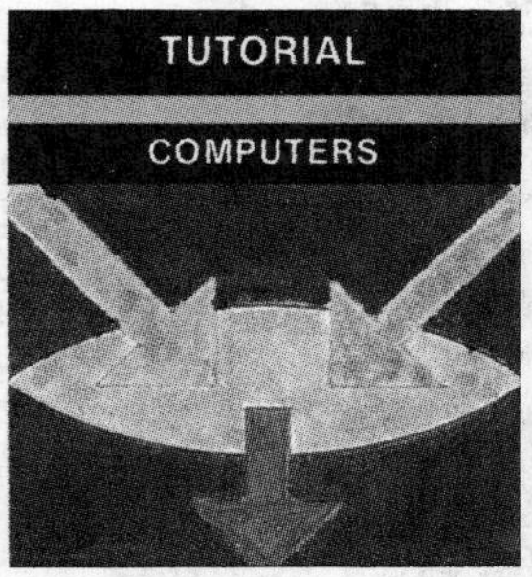

Imagine a computer that learns. Information is fed into it, along with examples of the conclusions it should be reaching or feedback on how it is doing—or the machine may even be left to its own devices. The computer simply runs through the material again and again, making myriads of mistakes but learning from them, until finally it gets itself into proper shape to carry out the task successfully. Such behavior is quite human, and naturally so; for the design of the machine's information-processing system, a neural network, was inspired by the structure of the human brain—its nerve cells, their interconnections, and their interactions—and by envy of what the brain can do.

As an alternative form of information processing, neurocomputing is fast becoming an established discipline, and some neural networks are already on the market. Neural networks are good at some things that conventional computers are bad at. They do well, for instance, at solving complex pattern-recognition problems implicit in understanding continuous speech, identifying handwritten characters, and determining that a target seen from different angles is in fact one and the same object.

Neural networks parallel-process immense quantities of information. Yet for a long time the only way to implement them was by simulating them laboriously, inefficiently, and at great expense on standard, serial computers. That situation is changing. Neurocomputers—hardware on which neural networks can be implemented efficiently—have reached the prototype stage at several companies, and some are already commercially available. All are coprocessor boards that plug into conventional machines. Developers include Hecht-Nielsen Neurocomputer Corp. (HNC), IBM Corp., Science Applications International Corp. (SAIC), Texas Instruments Corp., and TRW Inc.

Meanwhile, researchers at Boston University, the California Institute of Technology, the Helsinki University of Technology, Johns Hopkins University, the University of California at San Diego, and other universities have been investigating the theory behind neural networks and exploring their potential to solve problems that have stumped algorithmic computing for decades.

What is neurocomputing?

Nearly all automated information processing is at present based upon John von Neumann's "glorified adding machine" concept. But before such a computer can be programmed to carry out an information-processing function, some person has both to understand that function and to devise an algorithm for implementing it. For complex functions, such as computed axial tomography, development waits on the birth of geniuses capable of propounding the needed algorithm—in this case, Johan Radon and Alan Cormack.

Even worse, there may be tasks for which algorithms do not yet exist, or for which it is virtually impossible to write down a series of logical or arithmetic steps that will arrive at the answer. Yet in some of these cases it is possible to specify the tasks exactly and even develop an endless set of examples of the function being carried out. Many such tasks exist. There is no algorithmic software as yet for an automobile autopilot, a handwritten-character reader, a spoken-language translator, a system that can identify enemy airplanes or ships, or a system capable of recognizing continuous speech, regardless of who is speaking.

These tasks do have three important characteristics in common, however: humans know how to do them; large sets of examples of the tasks being carried out can be generated; and each task involves associating objects in one set with objects in another set. Such associations are known as mappings or transformations. For example, a computer that can read aloud must somehow associate groups of written letters, spaces, and punctuation with specific sounds, pauses, and intonations.

Robert Hecht-Nielsen
Hecht-Nielsen Neurocomputer Corp.

Defining terms

Adaptive coefficients: values of the previous computations (weights) of a processing element stored in its local memory, which modify subsequent computations.
Connection: a signal transmission pathway between processing elements, corresponding to the axons and synapses of neurons in a human brain, that connects the processing elements into a network.
Learning law: an equation that modifies all or some of the adaptive coefficients (weights) in a processing element's local memory in response to input signals and the values supplied by the transfer function. The equation enables the network to adapt itself to examples of what it should be doing and to organize information within itself, and thereby learn.
Processing element: an artificial neuron in a neural network, consisting of a small amount of local memory and processing power. The output from a processing element is fanned out and becomes the input to many other elements.
Scheduling function: a function that determines if and how often a processing element is to apply its transfer function.
Transfer function: a mathematical formula that, among other things, determines a processing element's output signal as a function of the most recent input signals and the adaptive coefficients (weights) in local memory. The transfer function includes the learning law of the processing element.
Transformations: mappings or associations of objects or representations in one set (such as written words) with objects or representations in another set (such as spoken sounds) according to some rule, which is typically not known to a human programmer, but is implicit in the training data.
Weight: within a processing element, an adaptive coefficient associated with a single input connection. The weight determines the intensity of the connection, depending on the network's design and the information it has learned.

EH0279-0/88/0000/0013$01.00 © 1983 IEEE

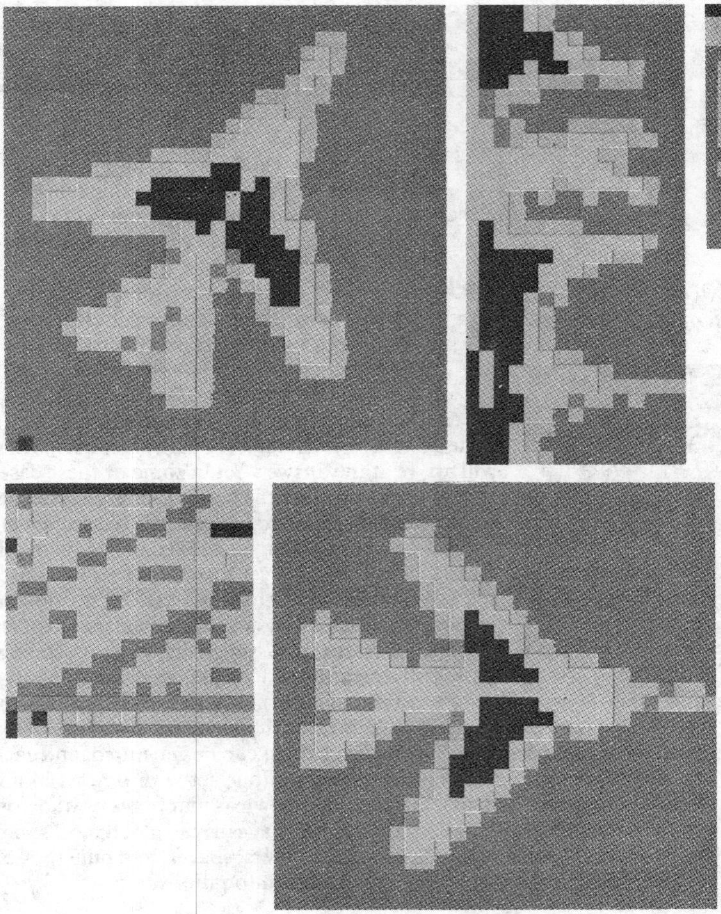
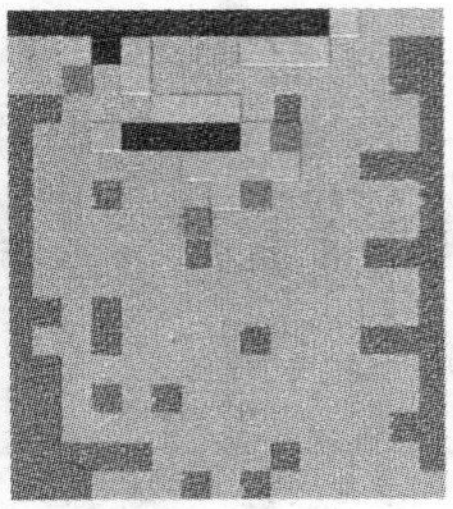

Michael Myers, TRW Inc.

Types of aircraft can be identified with 95-percent accuracy by the TRW Mark IV neurocomputer. The input image of an airplane taken from directly overhead with the nose at any angle (top left), *is digitized into picture elements (pixels), and their brightness is color coded. A neural network takes each pixel from the image, calculates its radius from the center and its angular coordinate on a polar scale, and enters this information on a graph* (top middle). *Next, the network does a Fourier transform on each vertical column, giving a processed image* (top right) *that is independent of the rotation of the plane in the input image. The processed image is fed into a second neural network, one trained to recognize images and classify them; this network mulls the problem* (bottom left), *picks a category for the new image, and produces one of the training images of a plane in that category* (bottom right). *(All the training images had the aircraft noses at the 3 o'clock position.)*

In formal terminology, neurocomputing is the engineering discipline concerned with nonprogrammed adaptive information-processing systems—neural networks—that develop associations (transformations or mappings) between objects in response to their environment. Instead of being given a step-by-step procedure for carrying out the desired transformation, the neural network itself generates its own internal rules governing the association, and refines those rules by comparing its results to the examples. Through trial and error, the network literally teaches itself how to do the task.

Neurocomputing is a fundamentally new and different information-processing paradigm—the first alternative to algorithmic programming. Wherever it is applicable, totally new information-processing capabilities can be developed, and development costs and time often shrink by an order of magnitude.

Neurocomputing does not, however, replace algorithmic programming. For one thing, neurocomputing is still in its infancy and is currently applicable to only certain classes of problems. More important, on a philosophical level, it is now suspected that neurocomputing and algorithmic programming may be conceptually incompatible. Transformations often prove impossible to describe satisfactorily in terms of an algorithm, and vice versa. This fact often unsettles people who think solely in procedural terms, since it means that neurocomputing may solve important information-processing problems without disclosing the rules used in the solution (at least in terms of present-day information-processing concepts). Neuroscience itself may run into this same problem in the future: an accurate understanding of how individual nerve cells interact in the brain may reveal virtually nothing about how brains process information.

How a neural network works

A neural network is modeled on the gross structure of the brain: a collection of nerve cells, or neurons, each of which is connected to as many as 10 000 others, from which it receives stimuli—inputs and feedback—and to which it sends stimuli. Some of those connections are strong; others are weak. The brain accepts inputs and generates responses to them, partly in accordance with its genetically programmed structure, but mainly through learning, organizing itself in reaction to input rather than by doing only by rote what it is told.

The neural networks used by engineers are only loosely based upon biology. At best, the only fair comparison is that they behave in a vaguely similar way. Since we have almost no idea how brains work, it will be a long time before we can re-create in a machine all the capabilities of the brain. Even so, neurocomputing is already offering some valuable, specialized, brain-like capabilities that in all likelihood lie beyond the reach of algorithmic programming.

A neural network consists of a collection of processing elements. Each processing element has many input signals, but only

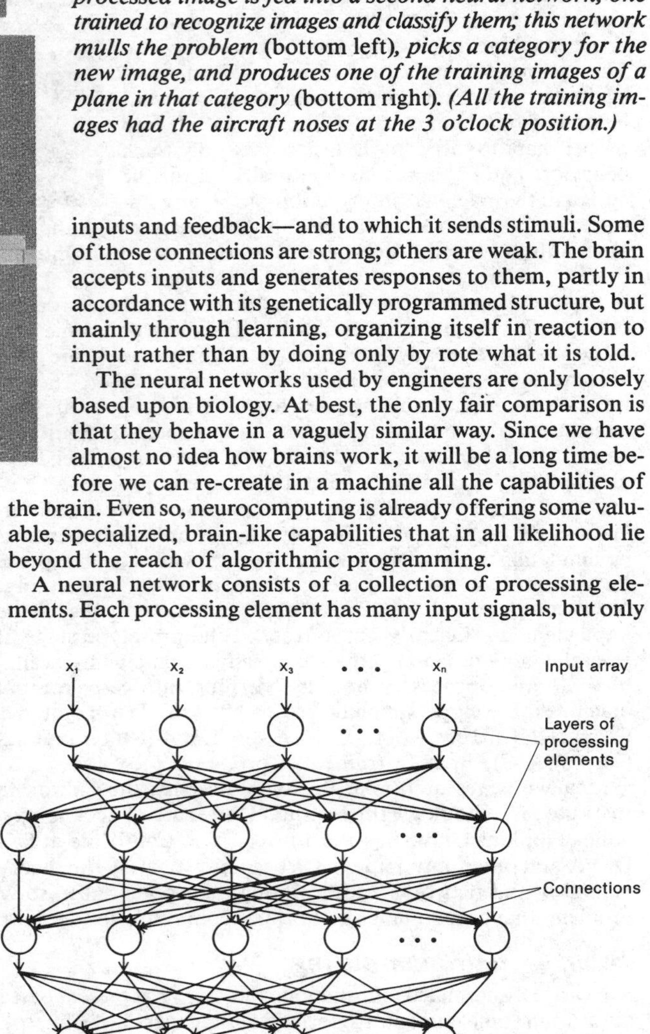

Conceptually, a neural network consists of many processing elements (circles), *each connected to many others. An input array, or sequence of numbers, is entered into the network. Each processing element in the first layer takes a component of the input array, operates on it in parallel with the other processing elements in the layer according to the transfer function, and delivers a single output to processing elements in a layer below. The result is an output array representing some characteristic associated with the input. Since inputs and adaptive coefficients (weights) can change over time, the network adapts and learns.*

a single output signal. The output signal fans out along many pathways to provide input signals to other processing elements. These pathways connect the processing elements into a network [see figure, lower right, p. 37].

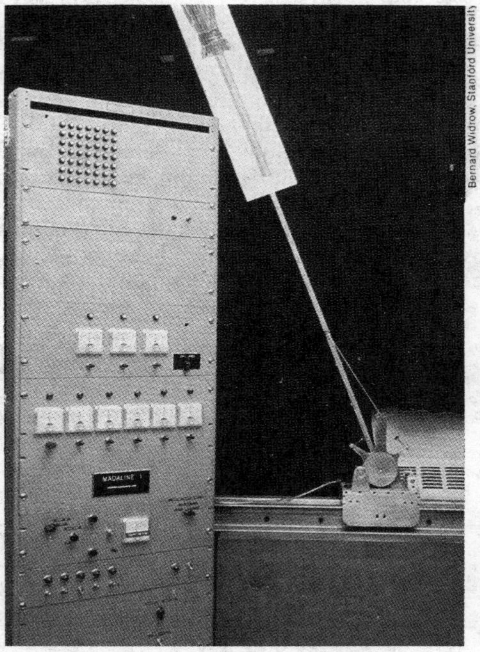

Bernard Widrow, Stanford University

Broomstick balancing has become a classic test of a neural network's performance in adaptive control. The original experiment, conducted in 1962 by Bernard Widrow at Stanford University (now professor of electrical engineering), used his Madaline (Multiple ADAptive LINear Elements) neurocomputer (left), *with sensors on the broomstick and cart indicating position, angle, velocity, and acceleration.*

Each processing element typically has its own small local memory, which stores the values of some previous computations along with the adaptive coefficients basic to neural-network learning. The processing that each element does is determined by a transfer function—a mathematical formula that defines the element's output signal as a function of whatever input signals have just arrived and the adaptive coefficients present in the local memory. Often a neural network is divided into layers—groups of processing elements all having the same transfer function.

Depending on the design of the neural network, the processing elements either operate continuously or are updated episodically. A scheduling function determines in which way and how often each processing element is to apply its transfer function.

Each processing element is completely self-sufficient and works away in total disregard of the processing going on inside its neighbors. In any neural network a great deal of independent parallel computation is usually under way.

At the same time, all the processing elements intimately affect the behavior of the entire network, since each element's output becomes the input to many others. The topology of the connections among processing elements influences what information-processing functions a neural network can carry out, as it determines what data each processing element receives and therefore the information on which it can act.

By and large, every connection entering a processing element has an adaptive coefficient called a weight assigned to it. This weight, which is stored in the local memory of the processing element, is generally used to amplify, attenuate, and possibly change the sign of the signal in the incoming connection. Often, the transfer function sums this and other weighted input signals to determine the value of the processing element's next output signal. Thus the weights determine the strength of the connections from neighboring processing elements.

Learning without programming

The weights, moreover, are not fixed but may change. Most transfer functions include a learning law—an equation that modifies all or some of the weights in the local memory in response to the input signals and the values supplied by the transfer function. In effect, the learning law allows the processing element's response to change with time, depending on the nature of the input signals. It is the means by which the network adapts itself to the answers desired and so organizes information within itself—in short, learns.

A neural network learns how to process information usually by being given either supervised training or graded training. In both, it runs through a series of trials. In supervised training, the network is supplied with both input data and desired output data (correct answers as examples). After each trial, the network compares its own output with the right answers, corrects any differences, and tries again, iterating until the output error reaches an acceptable level. In graded training, the network is given input data but no desired output data; instead, after each trial or series of trials it is given a grade or performance score that tells it how well it is doing.

In either case, after training, the network is ready to process genuine inputs. At this point, depending upon the task to be done, a human operator may disable the learning law and "freeze the weights" of the connections, so that the network will stop adapting itself to new data and speed up its processing. For example, if the network has been well trained to read aloud from written text, it need not continue to learn on real data. On the other hand, if the network is to control the attitude of an orbiting spacecraft whose mass will decrease as fuel is spent, it should continue to adapt itself to changing conditions.

From concept to hardware

Neural networks are varied. At least 50 different types are being explored in research or being developed for applications. Of these, 13 are in common use [Table I]. Although all consist of processing elements joined by a multiplicity of connections, they differ in the learning laws incorporated into their transfer functions, the topology of their connections, and the weights assigned to their connections. In fact, some neural networks that learn may not be trained (self-organizing map) and some do not even learn at all (Hopfield network). The result: a host of networks, each suited to different types of tasks.

Any neural-network architecture can take different physical forms: electronic (in which everything consists of electronic devices and circuitry), electrooptical (in which optical signals link electronic processing elements), or entirely optical (in which light signals link optical processing elements made out of some nonlinear optical material). Experimenters at various institutions are working on all of these approaches. But problems with materials make the physical hardware of a network less straightforward than the conceptual architecture ["Neural networks: the physical reality," p. 40].

A number of neurocomputers—specialized machines able to efficiently and cost-effectively implement neural networks—have been built, and a few are now becoming commercially available [Table II]. All of them are configured as coprocessors to a standard serial computer, which acts as the host. The neurocomputer coprocessor, usually a board that looks much like any other circuit board, is connected to the host through a shared data bus or through a standard peripheral interconnection—PC-bus, Ethernet, or DRV-11.

As coprocessors, neurocomputers can be thought of as just another type of peripheral, like a printer or external disk drive. Data are shuffled into and out of the neurocomputer by the host computer through software routines supplied by the neurocomputer's manufacturer, even though the neurocomputer does its actual work on the data nonalgorithmically. No one has proposed a stand-alone neurocomputer—mainly because present networks do not handle input-output processing, and host computers already do that very well.

Most of the neurocomputer coprocessors built so far have been hard-wired designs optimized for implementing one type of neural network or a small selection of types. A few neurocomputers—notably those developed at IBM, Texas Instruments, and TRW—can implement several classes of networks, and a very few—such as those developed at HNC and SAIC—can implement essentially any neural network.

Such flexibility is valuable because the ability to quickly modify the neural network being used is critically important in research, application studies, and early applications. As with von Neumann machines, though, the more general-purpose a neurocomputer is, the slower it is. After the applications of neural networks are understood more fully, it may be possible to substitute specialized neurocomputers in those applications where only a particular network, or small range of networks, is needed.

For those who wish to get deeply involved in altering the structure and thus the behavior of a network, there are languages designed expressly for describing neural networks in a high-level, machine-independent way. The field is very new, and so far only four neurosoftware languages have been introduced: P3, Panspec, AnSpec, and Axon.

Neural networks applied

Several organizations are trying to apply neural networks to information-processing problems in commerce and industry that have proved intractable or far too expensive with algorithmic computers. Preliminary results have been encouraging.

Behavioristics Inc., Silver Spring, Md., has demonstrated a neural network for scheduling airline flights. Airlines sell seats at

I. Thirteen best-known neural networks

Name of network	Inventors and developers	Years introduced	Primary applications	Limitations	Comments
Adaptive resonance theory	Gail Carpenter, Northeastern U.; Stephen Grossberg, Boston U.	1978–86	Pattern recognition, especially when pattern is complicated or unfamiliar to humans (radar or sonar readouts, voiceprints)	Sensitive to translation, distortion, changes in scale	Very sophisticated; not yet applied to many problems
Avalanche	Stephen Grossberg, Boston U.	1967	Continuous-speech recognition; teaching motor commands to robotic arms	Literal playback of motor sequences—no simple way to alter speed or interpolate movements	Class of networks—no single network can do all these tasks
Back propagation	Paul Werbos, Harvard U.; David Parker, Stanford U.; David Rumelhart, Stanford U.	1974–85	Speech synthesis from text; adaptive control of robotic arms; scoring of bank loan applications	Supervised training only—correct input-output examples must be abundant	The most popular network today—works well, simple to learn
Bidirectional associative memory	Bart Kosko, U. of Southern California	1985	Content-addressable associative memory	Low storage density; data must be properly coded	Easiest network to learn—good educational tool; associates fragmented pairs of objects with complete pairs
Boltzmann and Cauchy machines	Jeffrey Hinton, U. of Toronto; Terry Sejnowsky, Johns Hopkins U.; Harold Szu, Naval Research Lab	1985–6	Pattern recognition for images, sonar, radar	Boltzmann machine: long training time. Cauchy machine: generating noise in proper statistical distribution	Simple networks in which noise function is used to find a global minimum
Brain state in a box	James Anderson, Brown U.	1977	Extraction of knowledge from data bases	One-shot decision making—no iterative reasoning	Similar to bidirectional associative memory in completing fragmented inputs
Cerebellatron	David Mar, MIT; James Albus, NBS; Andres Pellionez, NYU	1969–82	Controlling motor action of robotic arms	Requires complicated control input	Similar to avalanche network; can blend several command sequences with different weights to interpolate motions smoothly as needed
Counterpropagation	Robert Hecht-Nielsen, Hecht-Nielsen Neurocomputer Corp.	1986	Image compression; statistical analysis; loan application scoring	Large number of processing elements and connections required for high accuracy for any size of problem	Functions as a self-programming look-up table; similar to back propagation only simpler, although also less powerful
Hopfield	John Hopfield, California Inst. of Technology and AT&T Bell Labs	1982	Retrieval of complete data or images from fragments	Does not learn—weights must be set in advance	Can be implemented on a large scale
Madaline	Bernard Widrow, Stanford U.	1960–62	Adaptive nulling of radar jammers; adaptive modems; adaptive equalizers (echo cancellers) in telephone lines	Assumes a linear relationship between input and output	Acronym stands for multiple adaptive linear elements; powerful learning law; in commercial use for more than 20 years
Neocognitron	Kunihiko Fukushima, NHK Labs	1978–84	Handprinted-character recognition	Requires unusually large number of processing elements and connections	Most complicated network ever developed; insensitive to differences in scale, translation, rotation; able to identify complex characters (such as Chinese)
Perceptron	Frank Rosenblatt, Cornell U.	1957	Typed-character recognition	Cannot recognize complex characters (such as Chinese); sensitive to difference in scale, translation, distortion	The oldest neural network known; was built in hardware; rarely used today
Self-organizing map	Teuvo Kohonen, Helsinki U. of Technology	1980	Maps one geometrical region (such as a rectangular grid) onto another (such as an aircraft)	Requires extensive training	More effective than many algorithmic techniques for numerical aerodynamic flow calculations

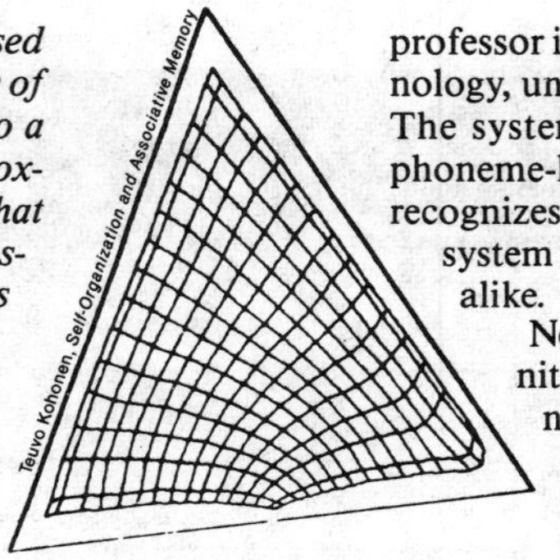

Self-organizing map, a neural network devised by Teuvo Kohonen of the Helsinki University of Technology, can map a rectangular grid onto a nonrectangular shape. Here, the map is approximating a triangle, having arranged itself so that the squares remain equal in area so far as is possible. In modeling three-dimensional shapes (such as airframes) for numerical analysis, the network performs the mappings more accurately than most algorithmic techniques.

different fares depending how far in advance a reservation is made. The system, called the Airline Marketing Tactician, optimizes over time the allocation of seats between discount and standard fare classes to maximize the airline's profits. At present, several major airlines are considering the system.

Murray Smith, president of Adaptive Decision Systems Inc., Andover, Mass., has shown how accurately neural networks can score applications for bank loans. The network is given relevant data from a loan application form, and judges the applicant as a good or bad credit risk in terms of the examples on which it has been trained. The scoring system based on neurocomputing performed much more accurately than an existing operational point-scoring system based upon a combination of an expert system and a statistical model. A neurocomputer loan-scoring application has been developed for a major finance company, which plans to install it in the field around midyear.

A great challenge has been to get a computer to recognize human speech and translate it into written text—especially when a person speaks naturally, running words together in a continuous stream rather than articulating every syllable and pausing between individual words. Jeffrey Elman, associate professor of linguistics of the University of California at San Diego, has shown that neural networks can pick individual words out of connected streams and devise representations for them. The neural-network speech-recognition system with the highest accuracy and largest vocabulary was developed by Teuvo Kohonen, research professor in technical physics at the Helsinki University of Technology, under contract to Asahi Chemical Co. of Tokyo, Japan. The system has a front-end network that recognizes short, phoneme-like fragments of speech and a back-end network that recognizes strings of the fragments as words. A post-processing system uses context to distinguish between words that sound alike.

Neural networks have also broken ground in image recognition. Kohonen has shown that an associative memory network can take the image of a partially obscured face, complete it, and identify it with an image in a memory of 500 different people's faces. Kunihiko Fukushima, senior research scientist of NHK Laboratories in Tokyo, and Sei Miyake, a research director at the Automated Telecommunications Research Center in Osaka, have demonstrated a network, the neocognitron, that can identify hand-printed characters with 95-percent accuracy, regardless of shifts in position, changes in scale, and even small distortions.

Adaptive-control problems have been solved by neural networks for more than 25 years [see photograph, p. 38]. The early demonstrations have prompted efforts to apply neural networks to the practical "eye-hand coordination" of robot arms moving in response to feedback from camera images. Remarkable progress has been made by Andres Pellionez, research associate professor of physiology and biophysics of New York University, New York City, who has demonstrated the ability to move a finger of a robot arm in a beautifully coordinated perfect straight line at any angle.

Complementary to algorithmic computing

Algorithmic computing and neurocomputing complement each other nicely. The first is ideal for accounting, aerodynamic and hydrodynamic modeling, and the like. The second is ideal for pattern recognition, fuzzy knowledge processing, and adaptive control. Neurocomputers should not be used to balance checkbooks. Algorithmic computers should not be used to recognize speech. The two can also be integrated easily in hardware.

A technology succeeds, it seems, if it fits smoothly into an existing infrastructure and important applications are developed quickly. Neurocomputing appears to fill the bill. And if the his-

Neural networks: the physical reality

A neural network should in principle be simple to build. In the most basic networks, a processing element needs only to take all its incoming signals, multiply them by the weights of the connections over which they entered, add up the intermediate answers, and multiply the total by a nonlinear function to give its single output. If the incoming signals are voltages, then the weights can be represented by resistors, and by Ohm's law the intermediate answers are currents; by Kirchoff's law, all these currents can be summed by connecting the currents together at one terminal to give the output. Seemingly, then, that processing elements in the simplest neural networks should be resistors at the intersections of connecting wires.

A number of investigators—notably John Hopfield and others at AT&T Bell Laboratories—have indeed built neural networks of wires and resistors. But translating them into chips has proven difficult because it is virtually impossible to build accurate resistors on silicon wafers.

As a result, some neural-network engineers have resorted to "faking" accurate resistances on silicon. For example, Hans Peter Graf, member of the technical staff, and Larry Jackel, head of the device structure research department, at AT&T Bell Laboratories at Holmdel, N.J., have designed a combination analog-and-digital chip in which a digital gate at the crosspoint of the conductors acts in effect like a resistor with a value appropriate to the processing element. Carver Mead, the Gordon and Eddy Moore professor of computer science at the California Institute of Technology in Pasadena, has designed a neurocomputing chip on which each accurate linear "resistor" is simulated by a group of seven digital transistors. Jay Sage, staff member of the analog device technology group at MIT Lincoln Laboratory, Lexington, Mass., has designed a chip in which the same kind of field-effect transistor used in electrically erasable programmable ROMs acts as a resistor whose value is determined by charge buried under the gate.

Other neural network researchers have gotten around the problem by abandoning traditional VLSI processing materials. For example, Satish Khanna, technical group supervisor of advanced materials and devices section, and his colleagues at Jet Propulsion Laboratory, Pasadena, Calif., have devised resistors out of silicon hydride compounds, which are deposited on the spots where the rows and columns of connections meet. For any given network, current pulses sent along the pairs of vertical and horizontal conductors heat the spots of silicon hydride and drive off hydrogen, tailoring the resistance by up to three orders of magnitude.

Still other researchers have circumvented the problem by creative computation techniques. For example, in the Anza Plus neurocomputer manufactured by the Hecht-Nielsen Neurocomputer Corp., a processing element is not a physical entity at all. Instead, it is a slice of time on a VLSI digital arithmetic processing chip: its values are computed in a few microseconds, and then those values are stored in memory until needed again. Thus many processing elements share the same physical hardware, creating a "virtual network"—an approach that has proven to be economic, since VLSI is so fast and powerful. —*R.H.-N.*

II. Neurocomputers built to date*

Neurocomputer	Year introduced	Technology	Capacity: Number of processing elements	Capacity: Number of connections	Capacity: Number of networks†	Speed: Connections per second‡	Developers	Status§
Perceptron	1957	Electromechanical and electronic	8	512	1	10^3	Frank Rosenblatt, Charles Wightman, Cornell Aeronautical Laboratory	Experimental
Adaline/Madaline	1960/62	Electrochemical (now electronic)||	1/8	16/128	1	10^4	Bernard Widrow, Stanford U.	Commercial
Electro-optic crossbar	1984	Electro-optic	32	10^3	1	10^5	Demitri Psaltis, California Inst. of Technology	Experimental
Mark III	1985	Electronic	8×10^3	4×10^5	1	3×10^5	Robert Hecht-Nielsen, Todd Gutschow, Michael Myers, Robert Kuczewski, TRW	Commercial
Neural emulation processor	1985	Electronic	4×10^3	1.6×10^4	1	4.9×10^5	Claude Cruz, IBM	Experimental
Optical resonator	1985	Optical	6.4×10^3	1.6×10^7	1	1.6×10^5	Bernard Soffer, Yuri Owechko, Gilbert Dunning, Hughes Malibu Research Labs	Experimental
Mark IV	1986	Electronic	2.5×10^5	5×10^6	1	5×10^6	Robert Hecht-Nielsen, Todd Gutschow, Michael Myers, Robert Kuczewski, TRW	Experimental
Odyssey	1986	Electronic	8×10^3	2.5×10^5	1	2×10^6	Andrew Penz, Richard Wiggins, Texas Instruments Central Research Labs	Commercial
Crossbar chip	1986	Electronic	256	6.4×10^4	1	6×10^9	Larry Jackel, John Denker and others, AT&T Bell Labs	Experimental
Optical novelty filter	1986	Optical	1.6×10^4	2×10^6	1	2×10^7	Dana Anderson, U. of Colorado	Experimental
Anza	1987	Electronic	3×10^4	5×10^5	No limit	2.5×10^4 (1.4×10^5)	Robert Hecht-Nielsen, Todd Gutschow, Hecht-Nielsen Neurocomputer Corp.	Commercial
Parallon 2	1987	Electronic	10^4	5.2×10^4	No limit	1.5×10^4 (3×10^4)	Sam Bogoch, Oren Clark, Iain Bason, Human Devices	Commercial
Parallon 2x	1987	Electronic	9.1×10^4	3×10^5	No limit	1.5×10^4 (3×10^4)		Commercial
Delta floating-point processor	1987	Electronic	10^6	10^6	No limit	2×10^6 (10^7)	George A. Works, William L. Hicks, Stephen Deiss, Richard Kasbo, Science Applications Int'l Corp.	Commercial
Anza plus	1988	Electronic	10^6	1.5×10^6	No limit	1.5×10^6 (6×10^6)	Robert Hecht-Nielsen, Todd Gutschow, Hecht-Nielsen Neurocomputer Corp.	Commercial

*Numbers given pertain to individual boards or chips. More than one board may be used to build an individual machine.
†Number of networks that can be simultaneously resident on the board, without going to an outside memory peripheral.
‡Speed outside parentheses is with learning; speed inside parentheses is without learning.
§"Experimental" describes a one-of-a-kind device or machine built to explore an idea or prove a point; "commercial" describes a device or machine that has been offered for sale.
||Early versions required continuous electroplating lasting about a minute for full-scale change.

tory of computing is any guide, the capabilities of neural networks are likely to grow with every successive generation.

To probe further

An excellent review of neurocomputing in the 1950s and 1960s can be found in *Learning Machines* by Nils Nilsson, McGraw-Hill, N.Y., 1965. James Anderson and Edward Rosenfeld have collected classic papers about neural networks in their book *Neurocomputing*, MIT Press, Cambridge, Mass., 1988.

David Tank and John Hopfield review their work in neurocomputing in "Collective Computation in Neuronlike Circuits," *Scientific American*, December 1987, pp. 104–114.

The IEEE 1988 International Conference on Neural Networks, cosponsored by half a dozen IEEE societies, will be held July 24–27 in San Diego. Contact Nomi Feldman, IEEE ICNN-88 Conference Secretariat, 3770 Tansy St., San Diego, Calif. 92121.

A new quarterly journal, *Neural Networks*, began publication in January 1988. A subscription to it is included in the annual membership fee ($45 regular, $35 student) of the International Neural Network Society, founded last year; for information, write to the society's secretary-treasurer Harold Szu, Naval Research Laboratory, Code 5756, Washington, D.C. 20375. The society will hold its 1988 annual meeting in Boston, Sept. 6–10.

The state of the art in neurocomputing is detailed in the four-volume *Proceedings of the IEEE First International Conference on Neural Networks*, held in San Diego, Calif., June 21–24, 1987. The set, IEEE Catalog No. 87TH0191-7, is available from the IEEE Service Center, 445 Hoes Lane, Piscataway, N.J. 08854.

About the author

Robert Hecht-Nielsen [M] is chair of the board of the Hecht-Nielsen Neurocomputer Corp. in San Diego, Calif. Before cofounding HNC with Todd Gutschow in October 1986, he founded and ran the neurocomputing programs from 1979 to 1983 at the Motorola Government Electronics Group in Tempe, Ariz., and from 1983 to 1986 at the TRW Electronics Systems Group in San Diego. He has B.S. and Ph.D. degrees in mathematics (1971 and 1974) from Arizona State University in Tempe. He teaches neurocomputing at the University of California at San Diego and is a member of the Del Mar Surf Club. ◆

Cognitive and Psychological Computation with Neural Models

JAMES A. ANDERSON

Abstract—**Biological support exists for the idea that large-scale models of the brain should be parallel, distributed, and associative. Some of this neurobiology is reviewed. It is then assumed that state vectors, large patterns of activity of groups of individual somewhat selective neurons, are the appropriate elementary entities to use for cognitive computation. Simple neural models using this approach are presented that will associate and will respond to prototypes of sets of related inputs. Some experimental evidence supporting the latter model is discussed. A model for categorization is then discussed. Educating the resulting systems and the use of error correcting techniques are discussed, and an example is presented of the behavior of the system when diffuse damage occurs to the memory, with and without compensatory learning. Finally, a simulation is presented which can learn partial information, integrate it with other material, and use that information to reconstruct missing information.**

> The object of science is the connection of phenomena; but the theories are like dry leaves which fall away when they have ceased to be the lungs of the tree of science.
>
> Ernst Mach (1872)

I. Introduction

THE DESIRE to build artificial systems that do the kinds of interesting things that we do has long existed. From mechanical automata in past centuries to electronic devices now, we have tried to make hardware and software that acts like us, or at least some significant part of us. Much of the current work in this tradition now tries to model with computers various aspects of human cognition. The things that make us most interesting to each other and which seem to be the most highly developed in humans as opposed to other animals are the faculties that are usually called cognitive, that is, our abilities to speak, to perceive, to reason, and to speculate.

There are many ways to understand cognition, in particular, to understand it well enough to mimic it with models or gadgets. We have access to a number of examples of a cognizing organism (i.e., us). We can study us in detail, both in terms of our system performance (psychology) and in terms of our hardware (neuroscience). We can also study us in the abstract, asking essentially, how we would (preferably from first principles) build a system that performs the cognitive functions that we can. The result of such a design process may bear little or no relationship to the system that nature has evolved, though it has been claimed that there are powerful constraints on intelligence, so that all systems that can do the same intelligent things are somehow related since they have solved the same problems.

My own bias, however, based more on faith than concrete accomplishment, is that the best approach to understanding and constructing intelligent devices is to study carefully the one that we know works. The limitations of this approach are obvious: birds fly. Airplanes are neither feathered nor flap their wings. Studying flying from first principles might have given rise to hot air balloons and rockets, but it is unlikely that studying birds in order to fly would have done so.

This paper will discuss some of the hardware of real nervous systems. We will then develop some simple neural models for cognition that try to work within the constraints that nature has had to work with. At the end of this paper we show the beginnings of an approach to cognitive computation: that is, how it is possible to use these distributed parallel associative models to compute and what they can be used for.

II. Biological Assumptions

State Vectors

Our claim is that biology places severe restrictions on the kinds of computations done by our brains. A great deal is currently known about neuroscience that bears on this point. A particularly good introduction to neuroscience for nonbiologists is an issue of *Scientific American* now available as a book [16]. An excellent textbook has also recently appeared [55].

Two key conclusions must be mentioned. First, neurons are analog devices. That is, they take their synaptic inputs, perform a computation on these inputs, and generate an output which is almost always a continuous valued firing frequency, represented as the time between discrete pulses called action potentials. A weighted integration of the synaptic inputs over a brief period of time is an oversimplified but useful first approximation of a neuron model. The neuron typically does not act like a digital device such as a McCulloch–Pitts neural logic element, but as a pulse-code modulation system.

Manuscript received August 1, 1982; revised April 4, 1983. This work was supported in part by the National Science Foundation under Grants BNS-79-23900 and BNS-82-14728, administered by the Memory and Cognitive Processes section, in part by the Alfred P. Sloan Foundation, in part by the Digital Equipment Corporation, and in part by Contract N-00014-81-K-0136 from the U.S. Office of Naval Research.

The author is with the Department of Psychology and Center for Neural Science, Brown University, Providence, RI 02912.

Reprinted from IEEE Transactions on Systems, Man, and Cybernetics 13(5), September/October 1983, pp. 799-815.

EH0279-0/88/0000/0019$01.00 © 1983 IEEE

Second, ten billion or more individual neurons exist in the mammalian nervous system. This means that the computational strategies used by the nervous system can take advantage of the presence of very large numbers of elements. However, since neurons are slow devices, operating with integration times in the millisecond or tens of milliseconds range, no time exists for the long strings of elementary computations that characterize digital computers. A highly parallel strategy is employed. The brain's "machine operations" must be of a very powerful kind since not many of them will have time to execute during a single "program."

When a stimulus of any complexity is presented, many neurons respond. (Not all of them, but not a single one either.) When a motor action of any significant kind is made, many motor neurons respond. Therefore, a pattern of activity of many neurons represents response to the input and many neurons respond as the output of the system. Internal communication between brain areas has the same many-to-many architecture. Therefore, we become interested in elementary operations involving the simultaneous activities of many individual neurons which give rise to the activities of many neurons. In the models to be presented, we represent these activities as state vectors of simultaneous neuron activities, and we claim that elementary operations involving transformations of state vectors form a useful approach to nervous system models.

This approximation is one way of avoiding the "homunculus" problem. No internal CPU (a high-tech homunculus) abstractly processes information. Activity pattern may follow activity pattern in lawful sequence, but information is not represented in a form other than as neuron activities or as connection strengths between neurons.

Neurons

Large state vectors are a biologically justifiable way to represent information in the human nervous system. The elements of these vectors correspond with something of the size and properties of single neurons.

At the lowest level, single neurons devote great care to analyzing what is important to the organism. In primary visual cortex, many cells analyze orientation, binocular interactions, movement, color, spatial frequency, and spatial location. Less or no analysis is made of absolute light intensity, large areas with no change in intensity, and stationary stimuli in general. The implication of this is that interesting things potentially affect a number of cells strongly though only a small number are actually excited or inhibited by a stimulus. The cells not affected are also contributing information of a kind. Interesting aspects of the stimulus are "richly coded" in that they may make profound effects on potentially very many elements of the state vectors.

As one example, higher mammals are born with what are apparently inbuilt orientation detectors in their visual system whose properties can be modified (usually for the worse) by environmental manipulation. However, these orientation selective units are also affected by other physical aspects of the stimulus such as binocularity, spatial frequency, wavelength, or movement. The biological approach taken seems to be to have many cells responding somewhat selectively to important aspects of the environment. An alternative design would be to have a few high-quality feature detectors, but this design does not seem to be used by mammals, though it is by invertebrates and perhaps by some nonmammalian vertebrates. The equivalents of the exquisitely selective neural responses to pheromones, say, or to particular patterns and frequencies of sound found in invertebrate species may also exist in mammals, but they seem to be outnumbered by less selective cells, where the emphasis has shifted to developing processing selectivity at the group level.

The question of specificity and distribution in the nervous system is important for neuroscientists and for theoreticians as well. As a recent example, Feldman and Ballard [18] have suggested that information is represented in the nervous system by a very small number of active neurons. Each potential value of a stimulus parameter (say size, brightness, color) is represented by a single neuron. Combinations of parameters may be represented by single cells also, though Feldman and Ballard devote some time to discussing ways of avoiding the obvious combinatorial explosion of the required number of units. They develop the nice idea of "winner take all" networks where only one of a number of contending values is excited and the rest are inhibited. The final representation is that stable coalitions are formed: they give as an example of a stable coalition one containing three active units.

Interestingly, Barlow [8], a neurophysiologist, suggested a similar idea: very selective cells ("on the order of selectivity of a word") are present in the nervous system, and most cells are quiet most of the time. However, Barlow came to the same conclusion as Feldman and Ballard that, to represent information of any complexity, more than one active cell was necessary. Barlow concluded there were no "pontifical" cells, but there was a distributed "college of cardinals."

The physiology supports a degree of selectivity in neural coding. Suppose one percent of cells were active in a complex concept or perception. This would correspond to many millions of cells, yet a microelectrode would reveal very little electrical activity in such a brain. The conclusions that representation of information in the nervous system is contained in simultaneous discharge of a number of neurons and that information is distributed in this sense are difficult to avoid.

Cerebral Cortex

The cerebral cortex is a flat thin two-dimensional structure on the order of a fifth of a square meter in area [12]. It is extensively folded in higher mammals to fit inside a skull of reasonable size. The neocortex is relatively homogeneous; the similarities of cell type and circuitry between different areas are more striking than the differences. (See the collection of essays on cortical organization edited by

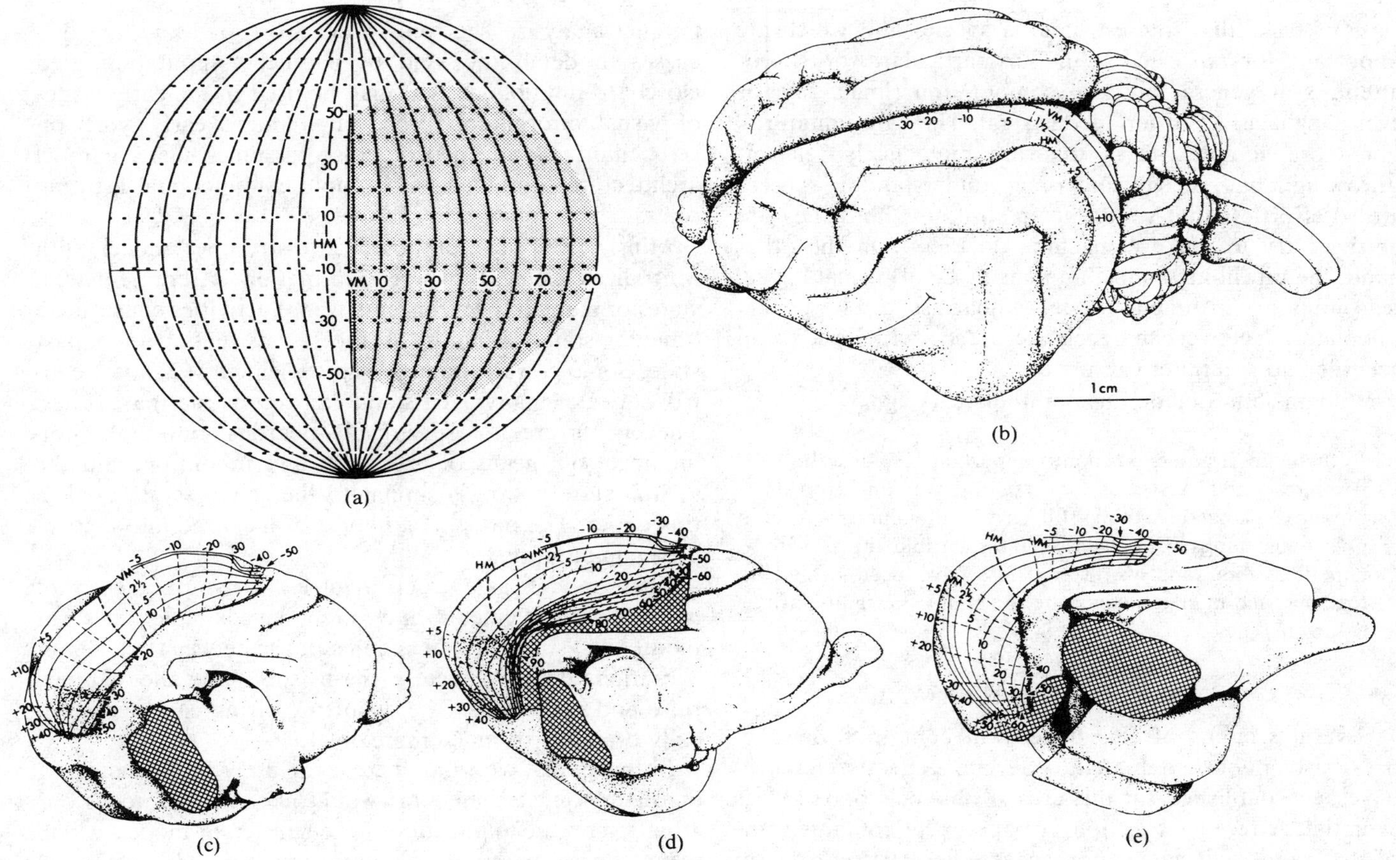

Fig. 1. Diagram of representation of visual field in area 17 (primary visual cortex) of cat. (a) Perimeter chart showing extent of visual field represented in area 17. (b)–(e) Location of visual field in area 17 of cat brain. From Tusa *et al.* [60], reprinted by permission.

Schmitt *et al.* [52]). The already two-dimensional cortex is strongly layered. There are numerous subareas (perhaps 50 or so) of cerebral cortex, which seem to be functional areas, though details of organization and function are often quite obscure. Thus Area 17 (located in humans at the back of the head) is the primary cortical receiving area for visual inputs. Area 3 receives somatic sensory inputs (skin senses). The cortex is exquisitely structured. Areas associated with a sensory system have topographic organization, that is, the visual field in area 17 is represented as a distorted map of visual space. Fig. 1 shows a diagram of the topography of the map of visual space onto the surface of cortex. If the location of a cell is known, its general area of maximum visual responsiveness can be inferred. The body surface is represented in the somatosensory areas, frequency is loosely plotted on the surface of the auditory cortex, and so on. Although the overall outlines of the map are lawful in the large, individual cells may show local variability.

The maps show striking distortions. The human retina has an area of greatest optical quality called the fovea. The fovea has a higher receptor density than other regions of the retina and is correspondingly overrepresented in the cortex. It is possible to get a good first impression of the relative importance of a structure in the life of a mammal by looking at its cortical map: in our own somatosensory system we have a very large cortical area devoted to our fingers and a small area devoted to the toes. A rhesus monkey has more equal representation of toes and fingers. Any model of the cortex must be consistent with this "more is better" philosophy because it is not immediately obvious why it should be so. The brain could have simply paid more attention to input signals from the fovea, for example and not had more of them. Nervous tissue is very costly in terms of its biological overhead: it consumes enormous amounts of energy, it is very sensitive mechanically and biochemically and is generally more of a burden than other tissue types. Therefore, if it physically expands to the extent it has in us, it must earn its keep in enhanced processing power. Whatever organizational scheme is used in the cortex must be such as to add on power by expansion in a simple way, without requiring too much in the way of detailed interconnection specifications.

Connections between sensory receptors and cortex, and between one cortical area and another are physically parallel. One sheet of cells projects to another, with very many fibers and considerable convergence and divergence in the projections. This striking parallelism in the anatomy has led to interest in parallel models for brain function over the past decades, from the Perceptron onward.

These points are worth briefly mentioning here, because I feel that our minds are much less of a general purpose cognitive device than we might like to think. What we seem to be is a somewhat flexible analog processor with enormous memory capacity, which is good at performing a class of tasks that interest us as a species and which are important for our success in our particular world. Our attempts at general purpose computation (logic, say, or even language) are often inconsistent. They are unnatural. Far more complex tasks that are biologically relevant (throwing a ball, recognizing a face, understanding speech) are so effortless that we do not realize how hard they are until we try to make a machine do them. On the other hand, the pitiful mess most humans make of formal logical reasoning or arithmetic would embarrass a $10 pocket calculator. Yet we can recognize a face with speed and accuracy no computer can match.

William James made this point 90 years ago.

> In the main, if a phenomenon is important for our welfare, it interests and excites us the first time we come into its presence. Dangerous things fill us with involuntary fear; poisonous things with distaste; indispensible things with appetite. Mind and world in short have been evolved together, and in consequence are something of a mutual fit [27, p. 17].

III. Associative Models

Several sections of this paper will contain reviews of previously published material. Several general references have been published for this area. Kohonen's book [30] is essential. A recent collection of papers [26] contains some related and alternate approaches. The Perceptron of Rosenblatt and related models in the late 1950's and early 1960's pioneered the use of models for cognition inspired by parallel nervous system architecture. Nilsson [42] summarizes this literature. Minsky and Papert [40] pointed out the considerable limitations in processing ability of simple Perceptrons. (We argue later that limitations in ability are to be expected from brainlike models and allow the strongest experimental tests of such models.) McCulloch and Pitts, after their immensely influential paper on neurons as discrete logical devices [38], published a paper [44] proposing a parallel model for eye movements using continuous mathematics and based on the topographic organization of the superior colliculus.

A recent paper by Sutton and Barto [57] contains a fine review of work in the area along with an application of a learning model to psychological classical conditioning. A specifically parallel model using state vectors and tensors to model the cerebellum has been described by Pellionisz and Llinas [43]. Papers by Bienenstock *et al.* [9] and by Cooper [13] deal with application of the learning rule used in this paper and extensions of it to plasticity in the visual cortex, with careful fitting of neurophysiological data to theoretical predictions.

A somewhat different approach to cognitive questions is taken by Grossberg [21] but with significant similarities in direction. Arbib's book [6] and his work with Szentagothai [59] contain many valuable insights and interesting material. These sources will provide more detailed references to the journal literature, as will many of the papers in this journal. The visual system lends itself in a very obvious way to parallel analysis. The well-known work of Marr [36] discusses in detail the kind of parallel computation, tied closely to physiology, that may be used in the early stages of visual information processing. Marr's early work on cerebellum [34] and neocortex [35] assumes highly parallel architecture combined with simple conjunctional learning rules.

Minsky [39] has proposed a distributed model with centralized elements where information is represented in states of many low-level agents whose activities constitute a "mental state." Memory is the reconstruction of a past state. Some powerful and selective elements (*K*-lines) control states of many agents and can reconstruct past states. The agents are not specifically neurons, but they communicate by means of excitation and inhibition, and the mental state notion is similar to the state vectors used in this paper. The model is a hybrid of localized and distributed computation.

These models as a group involve massive parallelism of many simple elements and often have simple rules for modifying strengths of connections between elements. Variations between them come in specifying the assumed rules and operations. The details of wiring can be specifically brainlike or much more abstract.

In this paper, we will adhere less closely to the details of the neuroscience than some would like. We will focus our attention on the implications for cognition of models which seem to us to capture the appropriate parallel, distributed essence of most of the models proposed to date, yet which are simple enough to analyze and simulate in some detail. This means we will start with a linear model which demonstrates how associative learning can arise naturally in parallel neural models. We will show that even this simple, rather unrealistic model is capable of some striking psychological predictions. Then we will introduce simple nonlinearities as we need them to make a first step at curing some of the obvious defects of the linear model, always hoping that each increase in complexity pays for itself in explaining a new psychological phenomenon or giving us more cognitive computing power. Such successive refinement seems to us to be one valid way of approaching a system with the complexity of the brain.

Synaptic Connectivity

Neurons talk to one another. The connections between neurons are called synapses. We have argued that many neurons talk to many neurons. The connectivity of cortical neurons is extensive; a single large cortical pyramidal cell is estimated to have thousands of synapses. The exact value is a function of the type and location of the cell. Although competing hypotheses have been seriously considered, almost every neuroscientist believes that changes in synaptic strength are the location of memory. In some cases, it has been possible to demonstrate convincingly that synaptic changes occur in learning-related contexts: the best studied example of this is the marine mollusk *Aplysia* which has been studied by Kandel and coworkers for a number of years [28].

One might first think that learning is simply a matter of strengthening synapses by use: the more a synapse is used (or not used) the stronger (or weaker) it gets. Indeed, the *Aplysia* has an inverted version of this in the habituation paradigm, where recurrent stimulation causes a diminution (habituation) of the resulting response. However, this kind of learning, though interesting, present, and important, seems to be inadequate for most complex and cognitively interesting kinds of learning. For millenia, since Aristotle, those interested in memory recognized its associative aspect. That is, events tended to become linked together because, "... one (event) is of a nature to occur after another." [7, p. 54]. Association of a sufficiently flexible kind seems not to be possible with a simple stimulus directed change-by-use rule such as habituation. A close connection with the response is required.

The rule that seems to be the starting point for virtually every recent model of associative memory seems to have first been formulated by Hebb [22]. Hebb's proposal for cellular learning was

> When an axon of cell A is near enough to excite a cell B and repeatedly or persistently takes part in firing it, some growth process or metabolic change takes place in one or both cells such that A's efficiency as one of the cells firing B, is increased [22, p. 62].

This rule suggests that a correlation between pre- and postsynaptic cell will develop, and such a synapse is called a correlational synapse. Such a rule is indeed adequate to build an associative memory that does a number of quite interesting things. The rest of this paper will be devoted to exploring some of the specifically psychological and cognitive implications of networks using correlational synapses.

Simple Association

The basic system that we shall discuss in one variant or another throughout this review is shown in Fig. 2. We assume one set of simple model neurons projects to another set (or to the same set, a special case). This architecture is specifically inspired by projection systems in the brain, where one set of elements projects to another over highly parallel pathways.

Suppose we have two sets of N neurons, called alpha and beta, where every neuron in beta projects to every neuron in alpha. A neuron j in alpha is connected to neuron i in beta by way of a modifiable synapses with strength $A(i, j)$, forming an $N \times N$ connectivity matrix A. We are interested in the set of simultaneous individual neuron activities in a group of neurons. We represent these large patterns as state vectors. We assume these components can have positive or negative values. This could occur if we build inhibition as well as excitation into the system and if we assume that the nervous system is concerned with deviations from spontaneous level, positive as well as negative.

If pattern f occurs in alpha and pattern g occurs in beta, we can associate these two patterns using a simple learning

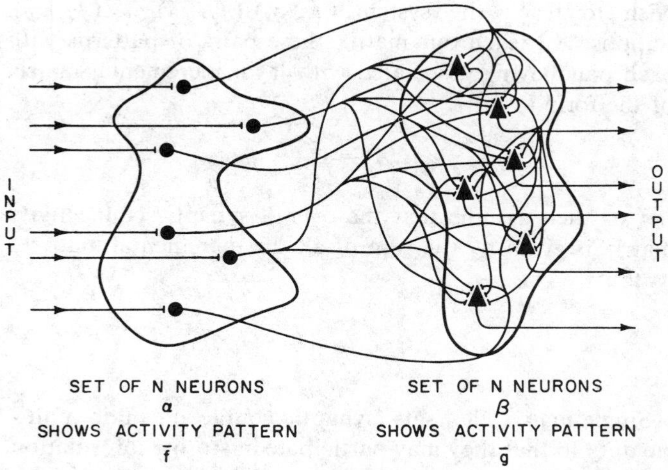

Fig. 2. Models assume two sets of N neurons, alpha projecting to beta. Every neuron in alpha projects to every neuron in beta. This drawing has $N = 6$. From Anderson *et al.* [4], reprinted by permission.

rule, a generalization of a Hebb synapse. We need to change the connectivity matrix according to the rule,

$$\Delta A(i, j) = \eta f(j) g(i).$$

We have introduced a learning parameter η. Note that this is information locally available to the junction: it is proportional to the product of pre- and postsynaptic activity. This defines the matrix ΔA to be of the form

$$\Delta A = \eta g f^T.$$

This matrix now acts like an associator. Consider the simplest case: Initially, $A = 0$, $\eta = 1$, and f and g are normalized. If now

$$A = g f^T,$$

we have established connections between the first and second set of neurons. Now, if an input pattern of activation is impressed on f, a pattern will appear on g. If we assume as an initial approximation a simple linear integrator model for the way neurons respond to their inputs, we can calculate the output pattern as the product of the connectivity matrix A, and the input pattern. Suppose the pattern is f. Then the output pattern will be g, since

$$g = g f^T f.$$

The classic neural system showing simple linearity of this kind is the Limulus eye, where the approximation is quite accurate [10], [11]. Other systems show various nonlinearities, but often (referring to communication from one neuron to another) a simple linear model is quite good as a first approximation. Sensory transduction of the physical stimulus can be quite nonlinear, however, masking what may be a simpler relationship at the neuron level. Linearity is an adequate approximation only up to a point. The relationship of linearity and the nervous system is a complex one; see Anderson and Silverstein [5] for a few examples and caveats. For a fuller discussion of this issue in the visual system, see Ratliff [47].

In general, we want to couple more than one set of patterns. Suppose we have a set of associations that we wish to teach the system $(f_1, g_1), (f_2, g_2), \cdots, (f_k, g_k)$. Suppose we teach our matrix these pairs of patterns with each pair having associated with it an incremental matrix of the form

$$\Delta A_i = g_i f_i^T.$$

Let us then assume that the overall synaptic connectivity matrix is given by the sum of all the incremental matrices so that

$$A = \sum_i g_i f_i^T.$$

Single matrix elements (synaptic contacts) can do multiple duty in that they may participate in storing information about associations between any pairs of statea vectors. This means information may not be localized or localizable, and the joint operation of many synapses is required for function. Information is distributed in the state vectors (since the simultaneous pattern of many cells is required for meaning) and also in the actual locus of memory. This is a holographic property, though these models are not Fourier transform holograms.

Suppose that the input vectors are orthonormal. Then, if one of the stored items is impressed on alpha, we have

$$\begin{aligned}(\text{pattern on beta}) &= Af_i \\ &= gf_i^T f_i + g\left(\sum_{i \neq j} f_j^T f_i\right) \\ &= g.\end{aligned}$$

This means that vector g_i can be generated at the output if vector f_i is presented at the input. Note that the state vectors are large, and if components are statistically independent, then the resulting vectors will be close to orthogonal. We assume as a fundamental coding assumption that stimuli very different from each other have uncorrelated state vectors, that is, orthogonal to each other on the average.

Many intriguing properties emerge from the interaction between learned vectors. Two recent psychological papers [41], [17] use a vector approach similar to the foregoing to explain a good many psychological phenomena. The model they both use stores associations by a convolution operation and retrieves them by correlation, extensions of a model of Liepa [31]. The memory vectors are "superimposed in a composite memory trace" [17, p. 627]. Murdock and Eich discuss, simulate, and suggest explanations for some classic list learning experiments, some short-term memory phenomena, the qualitative effects found during the learning of lists of associations, and prototype formation. Many of the most interesting effects in their model arise because "... the events stored in such a memory combine and interfere with one another ..." [17, p. 657]. As Eich comments, "... it is precisely because CHARM [Eich's model] transforms and combines events that the model is psychologically interesting" [17, p. 654].

General Properties

Matrix and vector associative models have some pronounced strengths and limitations. Their strengths are, first, that they are intrinsically parallel. Second, they are very tolerant of noise and partial connectivity. Since they contain correlational and averaging elements, the resulting systems are often optimal or close to optimal in a signal processing sense. (See the section on error correction.) They tend to be computationally robust. Third, they work better in the sense of better discrimination and signal-to-noise ratio as the state vectors increase in size. Since the models are parallel, this can be done with no increase in processing time if the hardware is also parallel.

Their primary limitation is their limited storage capacity relative to the size of the system. Clearly, only N orthogonal vectors can exist. Second, they can generate noise and inappropriate behavior of an unpredictable nature since things mix together in storage. (This can be a virtue or a problem, depending on context.) Third, they are poorly suited to rapid computation using traditional digital computers. Fourth, they tend to be rather ponderous and inflexible. Fifth, as linear models, they are subject to a host of essential limitations. As Sejnowski comments, "The matrix model resembles memory in the way a toy glider resembles a bird. It does fly, in a rigid sort of way, but it lacks dynamics and grace" [53, p. 203]. However, if it flies even crudely, let us see if it takes us anywhere interesting.

III. Categorization

Concepts and Prototypes

The nervous system is faced with the problem of using information from many moderately selective analyzers. Another problem is intrinsic to the functions of a cognitive system: analysis of the world cannot be too precise. It is necessary to form equivalence classes of events and things of a convenient size. For example, many real things are described by the words "dog" or "bird." Not only are particular individuals different from each other, but the same individual at different times is quite different in its exact physical description. A simple change in lighting can cause great changes in the physical properties of the reflections from the object. We are constructed to ignore these differences, a photocell is not. This process is so basic that we arc often not aware of its operation.

A malfunction of this mechanism described in the psychological literature is the subject burdened with an exceptional memory described by Luria [32]. Luria's mnemonist had difficulty recognizing people because, as Luria commented:

> S. often complained that he had a poor memory for faces: "They're so changeable," he had said. "A person's expression depends on his mood and on the circumstances under which you happen to meet him. People's faces are constantly changing; it's the different shades of expression that confuse me and make it so hard to remember faces." [32, p. 64]

We are faced with the problem of forming equivalence classes in a natural way. A tremendous amount of biology is involved in this. We discriminate what we are built to be good at discriminating.

In cognitive science and cognitive psychology, the equivalence classes that result are usually called concepts. The study of concepts is difficult because different kinds exists and because concepts, by their nature, are not consistent or totally stable entities. Good introductions to the modern study of concepts are contained in books by Rosch and Lloyd [50] and by Smith and Medin [56]. One idea supported by a good deal of evidence is that humans will normally operate at a "natural" level of concept complexity, often related to sensory aspects of the stimulus. We will say in normal speech, "Look at that bird on the lawn," as opposed to, "Look at that organism on the flat area of Kentucky bluegrass, clover, and creeping red fescue." We can say the last, but a default level exists which seems to correspond to a natural concept level. The second sentence is both too general and too specific.

We will be concerned in the next sections with two particular aspects of simple concept formation: prototypes and categories. We make the fundamental assumption that items that belong in the same natural categories will have similar neural codings. Their state vectors will be correlated in terms of our models. The study of natural psychological categories does suggest this: many familiar birds look and behave similarly to each other; birds that do not (penguins or ostriches) are often handled as concepts by themselves. One will say, "There is a bird on the lawn," if the bird is a sparrow, pigeon, or robin but, "There is a penguin on the lawn." This observation is related to the model of concepts usually associated with the work of Rosch, which holds that many natural concepts (dogs, birds, vegetables, etc.) are represented by prototypical members, i.e., best examples of the class. People agree on how close objects are to the prototype. There are "good" birds (robins, sparrows, etc.) and birds which are not good examples, such as turkeys, ostriches, and buzzards. To use one of Rosch's more picturesque examples, one would not be bothered in the least by the occurrence in a novel of a sentence such as, "Twenty or so birds often perch on the telephone wires outside my window and twitter in the morning" [49, p. 39] until one replaces the word "birds" with "turkeys."

Prototype Formation in a Neural Model

Suppose we have a number of examples of a category. Suppose we call the category name the state vector g and the different example vectors $f_1, f_2, \cdots, f_k$. Each incremental matrix is generated as before, and we arrive at an overall connectivity matrix given by

$$A = g\sum_i f_i^T.$$

This expression contains the sum of the f's. This term acts like an average response computer. The central tendency of the f's will emerge. The amplitude of response to a new state vector will give a measure of distance from the central tendency. (See [2,], [17], [29] for further discussions of this effect and its implications from a psychological perspective.)

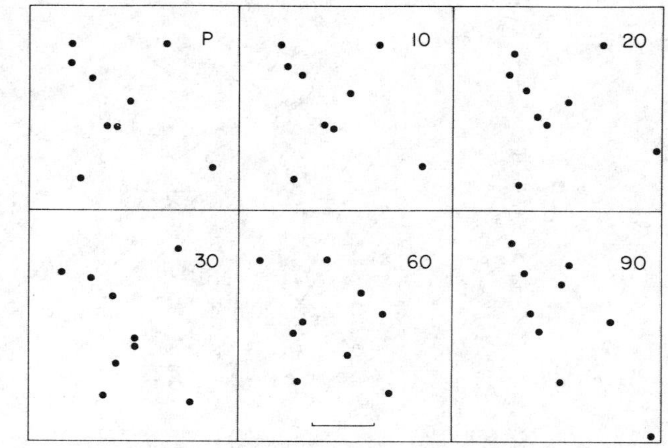

Fig. 3. Prototype dot pattern (P), followed by five examples at various degrees of distortion. Dots were generated on 512 × 512 array and presented to subjects on CRT screen. Number refers to average number of locations moved on the array. Distance of 100 array locations is indicated. In experiments distortions of about 24 units were used. From Knapp and Anderson [29], reprinted by permission.

Posner–Keele Experiments

Psychologists Posner and Keele have demonstrated what might be a simple example of this process [45], [46]. These experiments, extensions of them, and a theoretical discussion, of which the following is a summary, can be found in Knapp and Anderson [29].

A pattern of nine random dots is generated on an oscilloscope screen. These initial patterns are denoted "prototypes." Then examples of the prototypes are made by moving the dots random directions and distances. Fig. 3 shows a prototype and different examples of the prototype, as the average distance a dot moved is increased. Subjects classify examples of a prototype together in the learning phase of the experiment by pressing one of several buttons, each button associated arbitrarily with distortions of a particular prototype by the experimenter. After the response, they are told whether their classification was correct. They do not see the prototype. They are then given a test where they are asked to classify a set of patterns. Classification is correct if a new example is associated with the same response as old distortions of the same prototype. In the testing phase, they can be given 1) the examples they saw, 2) the prototypes, and 3) new examples of the prototypes. Depending on experimental conditions, the prototype (which subjects never saw) may be the best classified, both in terms of reaction time, percent correct classification, and confidence the pattern had been seen before.

In our experiments, patterns of nine random dots were used. Distortions were generated in such a way as to ensure the prototype was extremely unlikely to occur as a stimulus, yet the prototype was often categorized most accurately. This is a common result in the concept literature.

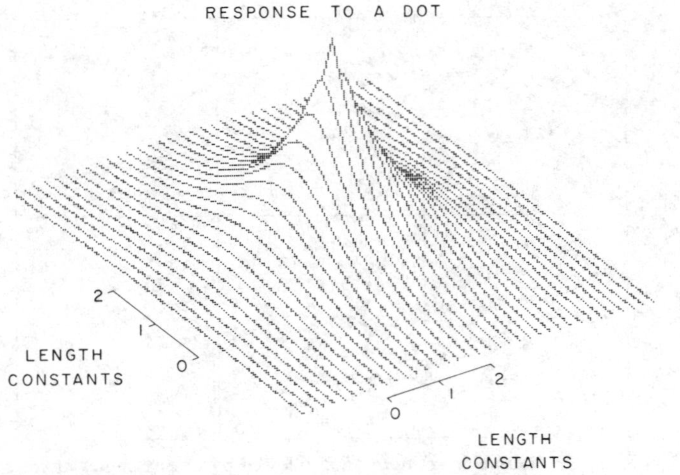

Fig. 4. Activity pattern on hypothetical cortex from single dot in the real world. This is exponential falloff of activity from a single location. From Knapp and Anderson [29], reprinted by permission.

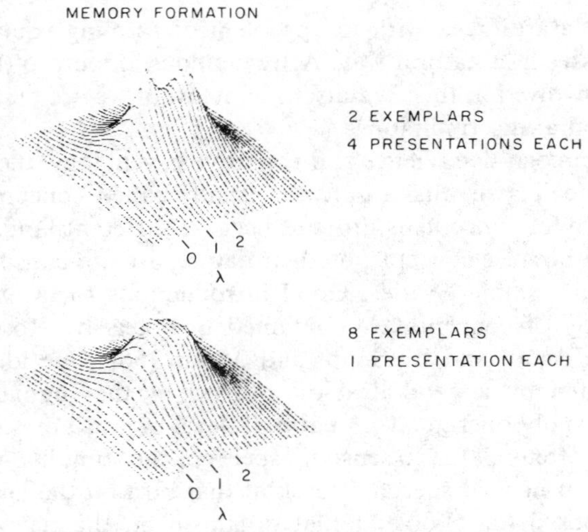

Fig. 5. Sum of eight activity patterns. In one case, two exemplars (presented four times each) form memory; in other case, eight different exemplars are used. In both cases, significant representation is seen at prototype location, but in two exemplar case is also stronger representation of patterns actually seen ("old" patterns). From Knapp and Anderson [29], reprinted by permission.

Application of our concept abstraction model is straightforward. Suppose the neural representation of a dot in the visual system is somewhat localized. (The spectacular map of the visual field shown in Fig. 1 would certainly suggest this.) Suppose that the amount of activity in a two-dimensional representation of visual space falls off exponentially from a central location on the topographic map. Fig. 4 shows the activity pattern due to a single dot on a hypothetical flat cortex. The model predicts that we should sum activities due to different examples of the same prototype, since they are associated with the same response. Fig. 5 shows activity patterns of a single dot in eight patterns when added together. In one case, there were eight different dot locations, in the other only two different dot locations. Note that the first case has "averaged out," few irregularities appear on the resulting summed activity; the second case has strong representations at the locations of the two presented examples. Both have strong representations at the location of the prototype, even though the prototype had never actually been seen.

It is convenient to simplify our calculations. Since we do not know and are not really interested in the details of the output of the system, we want to compute interactions between the stimuli (the vector f's). These will be the coefficients multiplying the g's in the vector model. We assume the output pattern with the largest coefficient will be the categorization made. This is a nonlinear decision rule.

Ultimately, we could use a nonlinear classification model to generate a model response directly, but for initial studies this seemed premature. We want to know the strength of response to different patterns given a memory constructed from the activities. These will be given by dot products of the stored vectors with the input vectors, that is, if similarity of f_1 and f_2 are to be judged.

$$(\text{output strength}) = f_1^T f_2.$$

These are interactions at the level of the rows of the connectivity matrix. A memory composed of K items, $f_1 \cdots f_K$ associated with the same response would have, in response to input f,

$$(\text{output strength}) = \sum_i f_i^T f.$$

A series of experiments was done to collect similarities between dot patterns generated with different degrees of distortion. The prediction is that subjective similarity should be proportional to the inner product between one pattern of activity and the other pattern. The fit using the model, assuming an exponential falloff of activity as shown in Fig. 4, is quite good (0.97 correlation between theory and prediction) and allows determination of the spatial falloff length constant of the activity.

We can see that a number of different examples learned and average displacement of examples from prototype should be powerful determiners of the classification ability of the system. One experimental manipulation was to change the number of different examples learned and study the resulting behavior.

The experimental results are shown in Fig. 6 for an experiment where prototypes were formed from nine random dots presented on a CRT screen. One, six, and 24 different examples were learned. In any given experiment three different prototypes were used. Results show a pronounced change in behavior. If 24 examples are used, pronounced prototype enhancement occurs. With one example, the example presented gives the largest correct classification as would be expected. Of course, a one-example category does not, strictly speaking, show prototype averaging but similarity between one pattern and a different one, since the resulting memory representation will be a multiple of activity at a single dot location.

A direct computer simulation of this experiment using the model presented is possible using this length constant determined from the similarity experiment. The resulting

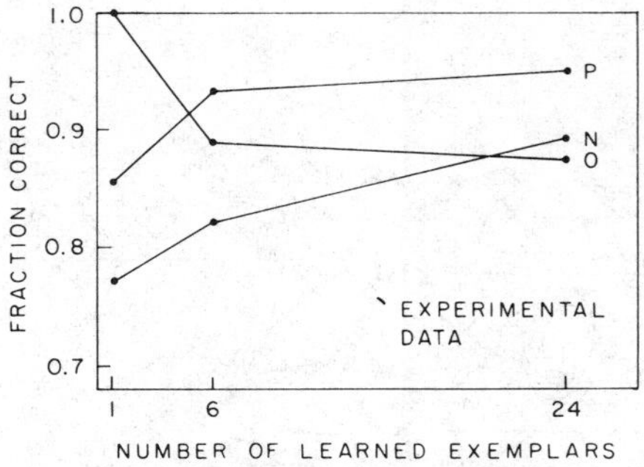

Fig. 6. Experimental results from categorization experiment using dot patterns like those in Fig. 3. Subjects received during learning part same total number of patterns, but generated from one, six, or 24 different exemplars. Three prototypes were used during each experiment. Subjects were taught to classify distortions of given prototype together. During test phase, percent correct categorization was measured for old, new, and prototype patterns. From Knapp and Anderson [29], reprinted by permission.

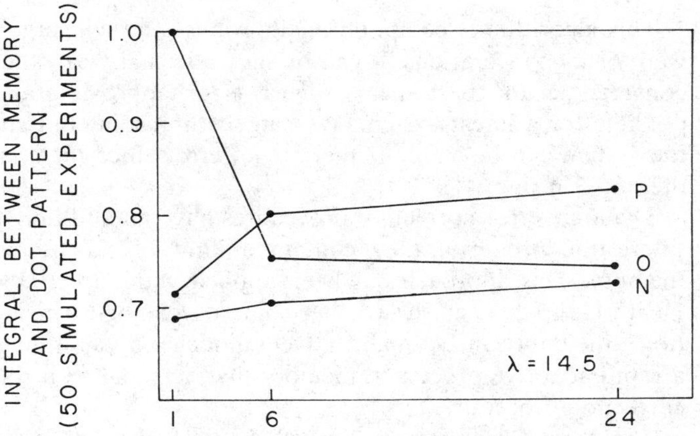

Fig. 7. Simulation of experimental results for prototype experiments. Dot patterns were generated exactly as in experiment, length constant of exponential falloff was measured in similarity judgment experiment, and model computed integral between resulting memory and input pattern (old, new, or prototype, as in experiments). Simulation was repeated 50 times; averages are plotted. Percent correct does not map directly into this integral, but qualitative agreement is quite good. From Knapp and Anderson [29], reprinted by permission.

activity patterns for all conditions of the experiment are generated, summed, and theoretical similarities between memory and the prototype, new examples, and old examples, are computed. These computations are shown in Fig. 7. A very strong qualitative similarity exists between the two figures. There is not necessarily a simple relationship between computed similarity and percent correct classification, but we should expect relative relationships to be maintained. Since we have accounted for the similarity data with the same constants and model, we find that a reasonably powerful model for actual data can be evolved essentially from the first principles of the associative model.

Teaching Methods

Cognitively oriented neural models become problems in teaching. We assume that when an input state vector is presented, an output state vector appears. The problem is how to arrange synaptic interactions to ensure that the output state vector is the one we want. Many of the difficult problems in distribution systems arise in a context that can only be called educational. Putting information into the system is tricky. Once the system works correctly, however, information retrieval is easy, since only simple operations need be performed independent of what other or how much information has been put into the system. Since the system is parallel, everything is searched at once. The combinatorially growing search trees, common in some information retrieval methods, do not occur.

This leads to a difficult problem for distributed systems: how to debug an incorrectly functioning system. In a complex computer program that malfunctions there is faith that the cause is reasonable, discoverable, and correctable. In a distributed system, the error is also distributed and is no more localizable than the correct information. There are some ways around this problem; the error correction procedures discussed next are one example. In general, this is a major difficulty for distributed systems because stored information interacts in so many unpredictable and subtle ways. This problem will not yield to a quick fix—first, since it is fundamental, and second, since some of the more desirable features of distributed systems (such as inference, prototype extraction, and concept formation) are due to the same interactions in a constructive role.

Error Correction

The state vector models presented up to now can learn arbitrary associations in a few favorable cases. Correct operation of the system consists of generating the proper output paired with the input during learning. Suppose due to the nonorthogonality of the learned inputs, or noise, the correct output does not appear. That is, if g is the correct association, what can be done if Af does not equal g?

We have described a classical statistical problem. Because of the correlational nature of the synaptic modification scheme we have assumed, it has been pointed out [30], [19], [20] that the associative model discussed and simple variants are often optimal in the least mean squares sense: the output is often the best linear estimator of what the completely correct response pattern would be, and many useful neural models realize known statistical techniques.

How can we modify our system to converge to the correct, or nearly correct, association? As Sutton and Barto [57] have pointed out, a slight modification of the association model implements the well-known Widrow–Hoff procedure (see, for example, Duda and Hart [15]). Suppose that, instead of incrementing the connectivity matrix with the outer product gf^T, we use the error signal

$$\Delta A = \eta(g - Af)f^T.$$

Here, we learn the difference between what the output of the system ought to be (g) and what it actually is (Af). We assume the learning system has access to both patterns: trying to match a pronunciation during foreign language learning could be one example of such a situation.

This algorithm is computationally robust and converges well for many situations. It can be shown in many cases to converge to the best mean square error approximation possible for a linear system. We can see immediately that the system can be stable if there is no error since there is then no learning.

Dynamic error correction procedures have an additional interesting property: they contain a kind of short-term memory. This approach has been applied with success by Heath [23], who has shown that some psychological reaction time data can be quantitatively modeled by assuming a rapid adaptive process in memory that acts like an error correction procedure.

The short-term memory aspect arises in the following way. If we consider the foregoing formula when a sequence of associated inputs and outputs that are not orthogonal are learned, the immediately last pair learned will (with appropriate parameters) have small or no error. As more pairs are learned, pairs further in the past will develop an error because of the later material stored in the system. In situations where perfect association does not occur, the system gives its most accurate response to items presented in the immediate past: a recency effect. Fig. 8 shows a computational example of this as a demonstration. Interestingly, the amount of recency is powerfully affected by the nature of the learned vectors. The top trace is the correlation between desired and actual output vectors for random vectors as the last presentation of the pair recedes into the past. The bottom trace plots the same thing for a highly structured set of vectors generated for a cognitive example, where a number of the input vectors were highly correlated in parts, causing interference between associations. The qualitative prediction is that a correlated group of inputs should be more difficult to keep straight in short-term memory and should show a relatively stronger recency effect than uncorrelated inputs. This is consistent with much psychological data.

A Nonlinear Algorithm for Categorization

Throughout this review, the emphasis has been on state vectors; nothing is analysed or represented, but one state vector is transformed into another, eventually to become a pattern of motor neuron discharges. When psychologists or linguists describe the component parts of a complex stimulus, the word most frequently used is "feature." To claim the existence of "feature detectors" in the nervous system (single elements) that respond to psychological or linguistic features is then only a small step.

Neurons, though selective, do not show this kind of extreme selectivity. Features, a very useful concept, must correspond to more complex and abstract aspects of the stimulus. We have argued elsewhere [4] that it is possible to discriminate two different kinds of featurelike entities in a way that seems consistent with single neuron properties. We differentiate microfeatures (selective single units) and macrofeatures (vector valued activity patterns that act in a featurelike manner).

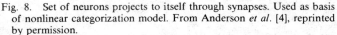

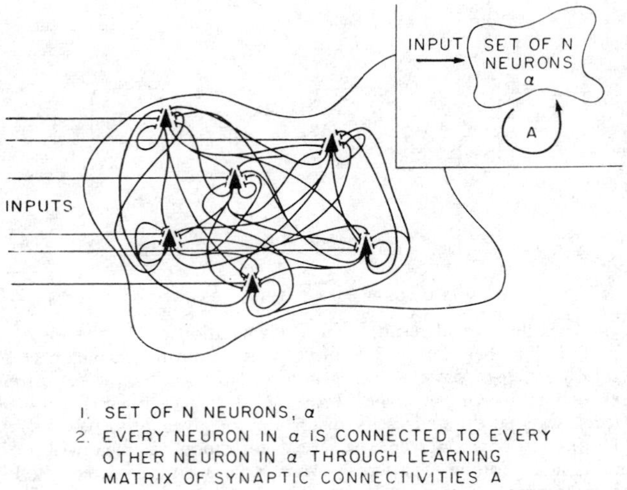
INPUT
SET OF N NEURONS α
A
INPUTS
1. SET OF N NEURONS, α
2. EVERY NEURON IN α IS CONNECTED TO EVERY OTHER NEURON IN α THROUGH LEARNING MATRIX OF SYNAPTIC CONNECTIVITIES A

Fig. 8. Set of neurons projects to itself through synapses. Used as basis of nonlinear categorization model. From Anderson *et al.* [4], reprinted by permission.

The engineering literature on features sometimes defines features as vector valued quantities: the chapter in [63] on feature extraction was influential in developing the categorization model described next. Having features to be more than single elements in the vectors (i.e., selective single neurons) is neither the terminology or the tradition in psychology or neuroscience, hence the attempt on our part to emphasize this distinction with the microfeature versus macrofeature dichotomy.

We can develop a vector feature model quite easily if we assume a kind of connection known to exist in the cerebral cortex. The cortex contains an extensive set of collateral connections so that one pyramidal cell can influence another over a distance of millimeters. These collateral connections are not inhibitory (i.e., they are not "lateral inhibition," though this exists also) but probably excitatory, as indicated by the shape of the neurotransmitter containing vesicles in the collateral synapses. (For more details of the relevant anatomy see Szentagothai [58] or Shepherd [54].) Note that the system of extensive lateral interconnections forces the system to become closely related to many relaxation type models, models which give a generally good account of themselves on the types of problems that concern us here [48], [24].

Feedback Models

Let us assume that we have a single set of neurons and that this set of neurons projects to itself over a set of modifiable synapses. This anatomy is shown in Fig. 9. Let us assume that this set of lateral interconnections shows the same kind of Hebbian modification discussed earlier. When a pattern of activity learns itself, the synaptic incremental matrix is given by

$$A(i, j) = f(i)f(j).$$

The form of the resulting matrix is essentially that of the sample covariance matrix. This means that the kinds of

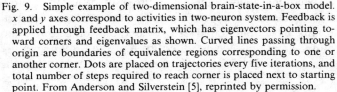

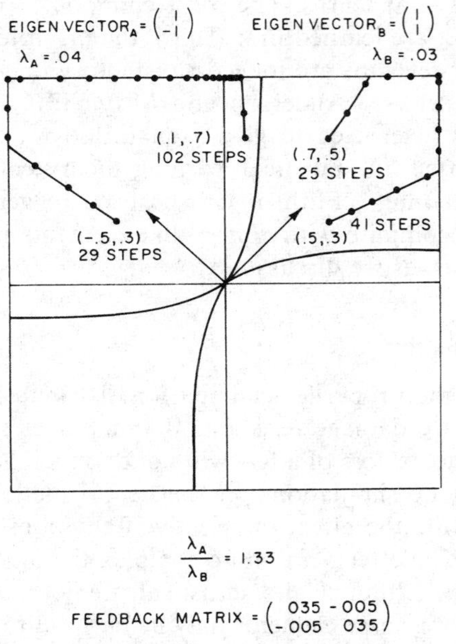

Fig. 9. Simple example of two-dimensional brain-state-in-a-box model. x and y axes correspond to activities in two-neuron system. Feedback is applied through feedback matrix, which has eigenvectors pointing toward corners and eigenvalues as shown. Curved lines passing through origin are boundaries of equivalence regions corresponding to one or another corner. Dots are placed on trajectories every five iterations, and total number of steps required to reach corner is placed next to starting point. From Anderson and Silverstein [5], reprinted by permission.

results obtained in principal component analysis (factor analysis) hold, and the eigenvectors, with the largest positive eigenvectors of the resulting matrix, contain the largest amount of the variance of the system. This is another example of the correlation synapse giving us a statistically useful result. The cognitive importance of these eigenvectors is that if we wish to discriminate members of a stimulus set, these particular eigenvectors are the ones to use.

However, this is also a feedback system. The coefficient of feedback of a pattern corresponding to an eigenvector is a function of the eigenvalue of that eigenvector. This positive feedback will cause a relative enhancement of eigenvectors with large positive eigenvalue over the others. We have created a system with differential weighting of a useful set of eigenvectors. This looks something like feature analysis (representation is a better word), but at no point was the stimulus actually analyzed into its component parts.

Nonlinearities

We should discriminate two aspects of this model: learning and performance. Feedback, eigenvector enhancement, takes place in real time. Learning takes place on a different time scale and may or may not affect feedback, depending on the learning time constant.

Let us consider a particular example of such a system. Suppose we have a feedback system which has generated a feedback matrix A. An input $x(0)$ is presented to the system. Suppose decay of activity is quite long (i.e., the membrane time constants are long, say). Left to itself, the activity pattern would be unchanged. When feedback through the matrix enters the system, then we have, assuming linear addition of activities again, after t time periods,

$$x(t+1) = x(t) + Ax(t) = (I + A)x(t)$$

as a convenient discrete representation of the underlying continuous system.

This is positive feedback system, and any nonzero eigenvector with a positive eigenvalue will increase its activity without bound. Such instability is undesirable and untypical of the nervous system which is normally exceedingly stable under almost all conditions. The simplest (traditional) way of stabilizing the system is simply to put limits on element activity. This is quite consistent with physiology where cells can fire no slower than zero or faster than a limiting rate. This has the effect of putting the state vector in a hypercube, leading to the nickname for this model of the "brain-state-in-a-box."

Qualitative Dynamics

Once the system has learned, the qualitative dynamics of this nonlinear system are quite intuitive (and easy to simulate on a computer). If we start with an activity pattern inside the box, it receives positive feedback on certain components which have the effect of forcing it outward. When its elements start to limit (i.e., when it hits the walls of the box), it moves into a corner of the box where it remains for eternity. The corners then become particularly salient aspects of the system, and the elements take on a hybrid aspect, being partially continuous (when within the box) and partly discrete (when limited).

Fig. 10 shows a simple two-dimensional system of this kind. The connectivity matrix has two eigenvectors pointing toward corners. The box becomes divided into regions, where the final state of every point in the region is the same corner. This system forms a categorizer in a strict sense. All information about the starting point is lost, and the final state only contains the category information.

This is a classification algorithm. Its novelty is that it actually constructs the classification rather than represents the classification. We have suggested that such a system might perform a useful function as a preprocessor of noisy data, since moderate noise in the starting point is supressed in the final state.

Simulations

We have done a large number of simulations of this system over the past few years, experimenting with parameters, learning assumptions, etc. As might be expected, because of powerful feedback coupled with a limiting nonlinearity, the system is robust, and most variants work similarly. (A detailed analysis of a simulation is given in [3] and another in [2].)

A typical simulation would start with a set of vectors to be discriminated, say codings of letters, or whatever. This

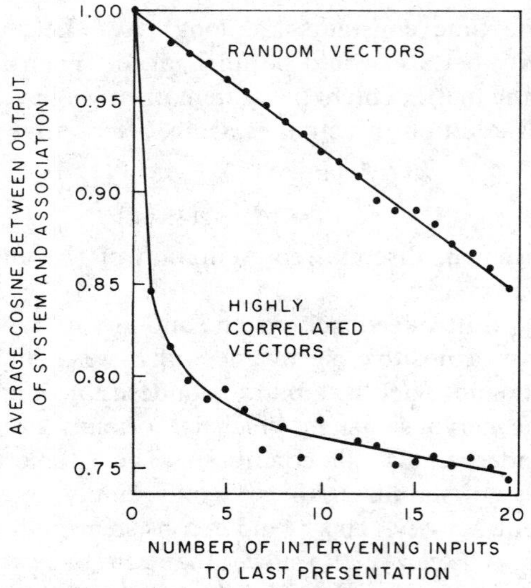

Fig. 10. Short-term changes in response can be seen when error correction techniques is used. Here input is presented, and as additional inputs from set are learned in error correction procedure, response to first input becomes less and less accurate as last presentation recedes in time. Loss of accuracy with time is function of nature of input set. Random, nearly orthogonal vectors gradually lose accuracy; highly correlated input set shows more rapid dropoff.

starting state vector $x(t)$ would change under the influence of feedback according to the rule given earlier, so that

$$x(t+1) = (I + A)x(t).$$

After seven iterations (seven is chosen arbitrarily as being large enough to approximate a continuous system and small enough to compute quickly), the process is stopped. The final state is then learned according to the rule

$$\Delta A = \eta x x^T.$$

The main technical problem is making learning "turn off" when the synapses have learned enough. The simplest assumption is that no synapse associated with a cell learns when the cell limits. (This means the corresponding row and column of the incremental matrix are set to zero.) Limitation rules related to error correction models work somewhat better. The matrix is no longer the sample covariance matrix, but often is closely related to it, sufficiently enough to have many of the same desirable properties.

In the first few presentations very few elements saturate, and the matrix learns rapidly. Typically, all members of the input set finish in the same corner if the matrix is allowed to operate until all elements are limited. As learning goes on, members of the input set start to separate, so different final states emerge. When learning has ceased (i.e., all elements of the input vector saturate in seven iterations) all or almost all of the input set have separate corners.

This model has several psychologically interesting aspects. The first is its categorization behavior. Anderson *et al.* [4] pointed out that this model duplicates some of the qualitative properties of categorical perception in speech perception. Second, the model tends to work both faster and better as it learns. The most common aspects of the stimulus set are learned first. Third, the macrofeatures that the model develops are indeed satisfactory in representing the input set (see Anderson and Mozer [3]). Fourth, the model has been used to give a quantitative account of a classical effect in statistical learning theory called "probability matching." Fifth, it can be used to generate concepts and compute with conceptlike elements in cognitive applications, as we discuss next.

Brain Damage

One of the properties claimed for distributed models is that they are damage resistant. If function is spread over many elements, loss of a few will not do much harm. Wood [62] has done simulations on the neural model presented here studying the effect of selective "ablations" of matrix elements. The effects are more complex than at first might be thought. Although the statistical predictions are clear-cut, removing some elements may be harmful for particular associations, giving a mixed picture of distribution of function (sometimes) and localization (sometimes). Also, real brains have topographic representations of sensory and motor areas, and localized lesions there will often give rise to very specific deficits, no matter how distributed is the rest of the system.

We have also performed ablation studies on a brain-state-in-a-box simulation, confirming Wood's observations [1]. We used a 50-dimensional system, presented with an input set of vectors representing 26 letters, using oriented line segments to represent the letters. (Details are available in Anderson and Mozer [3].) After a few thousand learning trials, a very stable set of final categories was formed, so that all input vectors representing different letters were either in corners by themselves or with a small number of other letters. (The codings used by design contained some very difficult discriminations with highly correlated input vectors.) Initially, the connectivity matrix was 90-percent connected; that is, ten percent of the matrix elements were permanently zero. After 45 000 more learning trials, no significant changes occurred in the final corners. The matrix at 5000 learning trials was used for the ablation. Small numbers of elements were randomly set to zero, and categorization behavior of the system was observed. Physiologically, this corresponds to loss of synapses rather than neurons. The connectivity was changed in four-percent decrements to a final value of ten percent. Fig. 11 shows the average value of correlation between corners at 90 percent and corners at intermediate stages. Essentially, no change in categorization occurred until 20 percent of the matrix elements had been removed. It was possible to see an increase in the number of iterations required to reach a corner before the change in categorization.

Ablation studies in animals usually show that slow damage is much less harmful than rapid damage. The brain, like most organs, is powerfully homeostatic and will resist change. Suppose we allow learning between ablations. When the matrix was allowed to learn for 1000 trials

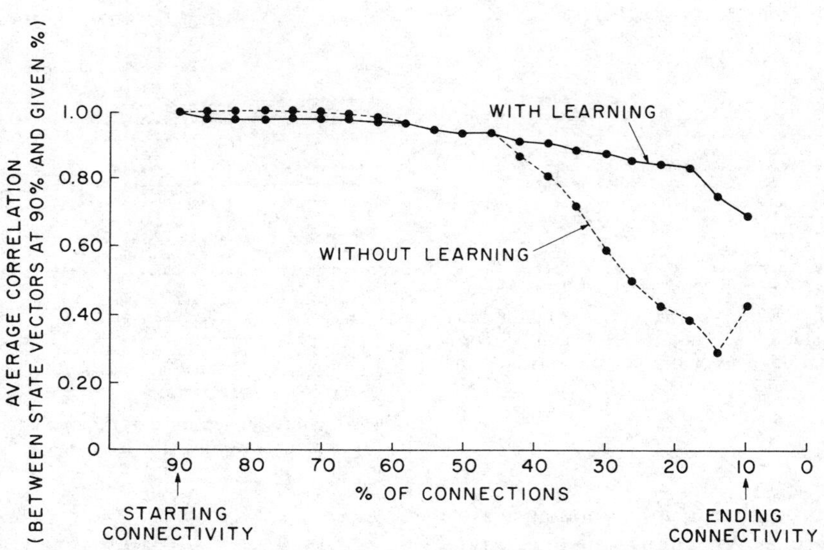

Fig. 11. Computer ablation study. Set of codings designed to represent letters was categorized by brain-state-in-a-box model with 90-percent connectivity. Connections were removed, four percent at time, and resulting categorizations were observed. With learning, system was allowed to learn for 1000 presentations of letters between each ablation. From Anderson [1], reprinted with permission.

between each four-percent ablation, we saw similar behavior in the simulation. As can be seen from Fig. 11, learning maintained the category structure of the system in the face of significantly larger amounts of diffuse damage.

IV. An Example of a Cognitive Computation

Let us give an example of a simple cognitive computation. We have discussed simple models for association, abstraction, and feature analysis, as well as a few of the biological constraints that our models must fulfill. One way to proceed is to use these models as tools to build complex structures to perform the kinds of operations that we perform. This allows us to see if our models are computationally adequate.

An important cognitive function is the following: can the models make use of partial information to generalize or infer facts not specifically presented? Humans are extremely good at this. A successful model for distributed inference using state vectors is given in [25]. Hinton's elements were somewhat more intelligent than the model neurons we used, but the distributed representation of information is similar. See also [14] for an example of a parallel system which can perform mathematical conjecture, studying many examples of numerical behavior and inferring regularities from its experience. McClelland and Rumelhart [37], [51] have described a distributed word and letter recognition simulation which uses a network of lateral and hierarchical connections between elements. Their model does an impressive job of accounting for many effects found in the psychological literature on the perception of words and letters, and its reconstructive behavior acts similarly to the model to be described

Suppose we have some information we want to represent in a small nervous system: specifically, we have several words. These words represent entities in the real world. Because of computer limitations and for ease in presentation, we will arrange our state vectors in a convenient way. We use a 50-dimensional system. Individual words are sets of 16 nonzero elements. We use our general assumption about neural coding: things that are different in the world are different in their neural codes. The coding is sufficiently rich so that different things will have orthogonal codings for their state vectors. We assume the state vectors are partitioned so that elements 1–16 contain names (Socrates, Alcibiades, Plato, Zeus, Apollo, Diana), elements 17–32 contain supernatural status (man or god), and elements 33–48 contain life span (immortal or mortal). Elements 49–50 were not used in this simulation and were initially set to zero. We assumed that all state vectors were orthogonal and values could only be $+1$ or -1, represented by $+$ and $-$ in the figures. Other elements were set to zero, with "." representing zero.

Orthogonality in this system can be achieved in two ways. Members of groups (i.e., Zeus and Socrates) use the same neurons but have orthogonal codings (in this case, Walsh functions). Members of different groups (i.e., Zeus and immortal) use different neurons entirely. This structure conforms to the psychological truth that antonyms (black–white or mortal–immortal) are actually very similar, since they make use of the same set of features in different ways, often differing from one another along a single dimension. Things dissimilar (shoes–sealing wax or cabbages–kings) share no or very few common conceptual elements. The convenient partition of the state vector is artificial. A more realistic simulation would take the active elements, mix them together arbitrarily, and add in several hundred zero elements to represent nonresponding cells. The ten different word vectors used are presented in Fig. 12.

```
                         Words -- Inference Program

Name              Species           Life span            Title

++++++++-------- ................ ................ ..  Socrates
----++++----++++ ................ ................ ..  Alcibiades
+-+-+-+-+-+-+-+- ................ ................ ..  Plato
--++--++--++--++ ................ ................ ..  Zeus
++++--------++++ ................ ................ ..  Apollo
+--++--++--++--+ ................ ................ ..  Diana

................ +-+-+-+-+-+-+-+- ................ ..  Man
................ --++--++--++--++ ................ ..  God

................ ................ +--++--++--++--+ ..  Mortal
................ ................ --------++++++++ ..  Immortal
```

Fig. 12. Fifty-dimensional state vectors learned by system for interference simulation. Plus is value of +1, minus is −1, and "." corresponds to zero. These small 16-dimensional vectors were words that matrix learned first.

```
                    Learned Patterns -- Inference Program

Name              Species           Life span            Title

++++++++-------- ................ +--++--++--++--+ ..  Socrates mortal
----++++----++++ ................ +--++--++--++--+ ..  Alcibiades mortal
+-+-+-+-+-+-+-+- ................ +--++--++--++--+ ..  Plato mortal

++++++++-------- +-+-+-+-+-+-+-+- ................ ..  Socrates man
----++++----++++ +-+-+-+-+-+-+-+- ................ ..  Alcibiades man
+-+-+-+-+-+-+-+- +-+-+-+-+-+-+-+- ................ ..  Plato man

--++--++--++--++ ................ --------++++++++ ..  Zeus immortal
++++--------++++ ................ --------++++++++ ..  Apollo immortal
+--++--++--++--+ ................ --------++++++++ ..  Diana immortal

--++--++--++--++ --++--++--++--++ ................ ..  Zeus god
++++--------++++ --++--++--++--++ ................ ..  Apollo god
+--++--++--++--+ --++--++--++--++ ................ ..  Diana god

................ +-+-+-+-+-+-+-+- +--++--++--++--+ ..  Man mortal
................ --++--++--++--++ --------++++++++ ..  God immortal
```

Fig. 13. Fifty-dimensional state vectors representing associations between pairs of words. After learning words, system next learned pairs of words.

```
               Response to Learned Patterns -- Inference Program

Name              Species           Life span            Title

-+++++++----+--- +-+-+-+-+-+-+-+- +--++--++--++--+ --  Socrates mortal
----++++----++++ +-+-+-+-+-+-+-+- +--++--++--++--+ --  Alcibiades mortal
+-+-+-+-+-+-+-+- +-+-+-+-+-+-+-+- +--++--++--++--+ --  Plato mortal

-+++++++----+--- +-+-+-+-+-+-+-+- +--++--++--++--+ --  Socrates man
----++++----++++ +-+-+-+-+-+-+-+- +--++--++--++--+ --  Alcibiades man
+-+-+-+-+-+-+-+- +-+-+-+-+-+-+-+- +--++--++--++--+ --  Plato man

---+---+--++--++ --++--++--++--++ --------++++++++ --  Zeus immortal
++++---+----+++- --++--++--++--++ --------++++++++ --  Apollo immortal
+--++--++--++--+ --++--++--++--++ --------++++++++ --  Diana immortal

---+---+--++--++ --++--++--++--++ --------++++++++ --  Zeus god
++++---+----+++- --++--++--++--++ --------++++++++ --  Apollo god
+--++--++--++--+ --++--++--++--++ --------++++++++ --  Diana god

+-+-+++----+--++ +-+-+-+-+-+-+-+- +--++--++--++--+ --  Man mortal
---+---+--++--++ --++--++--++--++ --------++++++++ --  God immortal
```

Fig. 14. Fifty-dimensional state vectors corresponding to final states of system after learning. Limits of box were set at 1.5, so plus now corresponds to 1.5, and minus to −1.5. Note that system has filled in missing parts of input state vectors (Fig. 13) in way consistent with what it has learned.

Teaching the Matrix

We wish our system to be able to infer missing bits of information when appropriate. We will use the brain-state-in-a-box model to do the learning. The essence of this model is that it is an automatic classification algorithm, that generates an output state vector from an input one, driven by the synaptic connectivity matrix. It is a categorizer with only a discrete number of final states and thus can perfectly reconstruct missing vector information in appropriate situations. Again, we emphasize the importance of this behavior to the nervous system: the nervous system is not trying to analyze anything, it is trying to generate appropriate behavior. It is action oriented, as Arbib has said, and its output is a suitable set of neuron discharges.

We use a partially connected matrix (from 50 to 75 percent in this simulation). Zeros appear along the main diagonal, for aesthetic reasons. Feedback of a neuron on itself exists in the nervous system but is almost always "special" in some way, often serving an inhibitory gain control or gating function. Renshaw cells which feedback on and gate by inhibition spinal motor neurons provides one example. A small amount of Gaussian noise is present, for realism.

First the system is taught the words. The developing matrix was presented the words randomly for 500 learning trials. Second, since we wish to test ability to regenerate missing information, we will teach the matrix pairs of words. We present "Socrates mortal," "Socrates man," "Zeus immortal," and "Zeus god," for example, randomly for 1000 trials. The complete set of assertions learned is give in Fig. 13.

The entire teaching process given here takes about 5 min of CPU time on a VAX 11/780. A number of parameters exist, but exact values are not critical. After a few false starts getting the parameters in the right range, the matrix learned satisfactorily three times in a row using different initial conditions. The critical variable was to ensure that there was sufficient synaptic flexibility to learn the new information being presented. This was achieved most directly by learning the words with 50-percent connectivity and then learning the pairs of words with 75-percent connectivity, ensuring 25 percent uninstructed synapses.

Operation of the System

Having learned that Socrates is a man and that men are mortal, we would like to generate the triple, "Socrates is a man and mortal." This would be a satisfactory output from the program. Given a new person, say, Herb, who is also a man, if we present "Herb is a man," we would like to retrieve at the output "Herb is a man and mortal." The matrix we have generated will do this. Fig. 14 shows responses to the pairs of words the system originally learned.

The system supplies the missing information in all the cases the system learned. The system was never actually presented with a triple, but with pairs of words. In every pair containing a name, the missing information is filled in correctly. For names, the output pattern is not exactly the same as the input for the name but may have changed in one or another sign; the pattern of signs for the second and third word locations were identical to those actually learned in the case presented here, but this is not always the case. If the correct triples are presented, the final states are exactly those presented here as the final states for incomplete information. It would be possible to force the system to a desired final state using a correction procedure as described earlier if this was felt to be necessary.

Two pairs do not contain a name: "man mortal" and "god immortal." In the first case, the final state contains nonsense in the name location (a pattern which does not correspond to any name the system saw). In the second case, the final state reads "Zeus god immortal." If we present only the pattern "god," we obtain this triple. Zeus has become the prototypical god, whereas the prototypical man was not one of those actually learned. Further analysis seemed unpropitious.

If we present a new example of a man, say Herb, with a state vector orthogonal to those learned, then the final state corresponds to "Herb man mortal," but the name location contains several unsaturated elements, corresponding to long reaction time (time to reach a corner) and what might be interpreted as uncertainty. Vector Frank, not orthogonal to the other names, is transmuted in the memory process to be close to Plato. Odin, also not orthogonal, ends near to Zeus, suggesting Odin and Zeus are different names for the same thing. Statements the system saw or which conform to the information presented reach corners rapidly. If we deliberately present a state vector containing an error, the system can respond in several ways. Fig. 15 give examples of system responses to different test vectors which contain partial or erroneous information.

If we present "Socrates immortal," then the final state contains "god immortal" but a nonsense pattern containing an unsaturated element in the name location. If we present "Plato god immortal," then the system ends up containing "god immortal," but the name location contains nonsense with three unsaturated elements. If we present "Zeus man immortal," then we get nonsense in both the name and "man" location. "Zeus man mortal" generates several errors in the name location.

Conclusion

We have produced a system which can generate missing information. This could easily be considered to be inference, under one interpretation, since presentation of partial information generated a consistent whole. It is also similar to what is called "property inheritance," another interpretation. This is because partial information automatically brings in and presents associated information.

Relations to Formal Logic

The reason this particular set of names was used was obviously that it conforms in structure to the most famous of the classic syllogisms: "Socrates is a man, men are mortal, therefore Socrates is mortal." Clearly, our system is not doing formal logic. It is not clear that humans do formal logic, either. Logic is extremely difficult for most humans, and we need machines, diagrams, and extensive use of memory to work with formal logic. Human reasoning and logic is highly memory-oriented, using analogy, probabalistic inference, and a very effective but nonlogical set of strategies to infer information about a real, not an abstract, world. Our model has more similarities to human logic than formal logic.

```
                 Test Stimuli -- Inference Program

Name             Species          Life span           Title

Learned Patterns - Mortals:

-+++++++----+--- +-+-+-+-+-+-+-+- +--++--++--++--+ --  Socrates
----++++----++++ +-+-+-+-+-+-+-+- +--++--++--++--+ --  Alcibiades
+-+-+-+-+-+-+-+- +-+-+-+-+-+-+-+- +--++--++--++--+ --  Plato

New mortals:

--.+++++--..---+ +-+-+-+-+-+-+-+- +--++--++--++--+ --  Herb
-..+++++--.-.--+ +-+-+-+-+-+-+-+- +--++--++--++--+ --  Herb man
-..+++++--.-.--+ +-+-+-+-+-+-+-+- +--++--++--++--+ --  Herb mortal
+-+-+-+-+-+-+-+- +-+-+-+-+-+-+-+- +--++--++--++--+ --  Frank man


Learned patterns - Gods:

---+---+--++--++ --++--++--++--++ --------++++++++ --  Zeus
++++---+----+++- --++--++--++--++ --------++++++++ --  Apollo
+--++--++--++--+ --++--++--++--++ --------++++++++ --  Diana

New god:

--.+---+--++--++ --++--++--++--++ --------++++++++ --  Odin immortal

Learned patterns:

+-+-+++----+-++ +-+-+-+-+-+-+-+- +--++--++--++--+ --  Man
---+---+--++--++ --++--++--++--++ --------++++++++ --  God
+-+-+++----+-++ +-+-+-+-+-+-+-+- +--++--++--++--+ --  Mortal
---+---+--++--++ --++--++--++--++ --------++++++++ --  Immortal

Deliberate errors:

+-+---++-++--++ +-+-+-+-+-+-+-++ --------++++++++ --  Man immortal
+.+++-.++---+--. --++--++--++--+- +--++--++--++--+ --  God mortal

-+-+++-+---.++-- --++--++--++--++ --------++++++++ --  Socrates immortal
-+-+++-+---.++-- --++--++--++--++ --------++++++++ --  Socrates god

+--..---+++.+- --++--++--++--++ --------++++++++ --  Plato god immortal
+---+-+-+-+-+-+- +-+-+-+-+-+-+-+. --------++++++++ --  Plato man immortal

--++---+--++--++ +-+-+-+-+-+-+-++ --------++++++++ --  Zeus man immortal
--+-.-++.-+---++ +-+-+-+-+-+-+-+- +--++--++--++--+ --  Zeus man mortal
```

Fig. 15. Fifty-dimensional state vectors used to test stimuli after learning. These special, partial, or erroneous stimuli were used to check different aspects of resulting inference system (see text). Limits of box were set at 1.5 as in Fig. 14. "." now means that element did not reach limit in 50 interations.

V. Summary

We have used vectorlike quantities as elementary entities in all these models. We have showed that these entities can be used to perform operations reminscent of simplified version of a few psychological abilities of humans. Using state vectors in this way may not be the most effective or efficient way to do the computation. The resulting systems have serious trouble with logic and accuracy and have problems with unpredictable errors. However, in return, they provide properties like abstraction, concepts, and possibly inference that looks somewhat like ours. Use of systems like these is a constraint forced on us, I feel, by nervous system organization. Perhaps the virtues of the approach for certain kinds of computations make their drawbacks worthwhile.

Acknowledgment

Some of this work has appeared in more detail elsewhere. My collaborators Jack Silverstein, Stephen Ritz, Randall Jones, Andrew Knapp, and Michael Mozer have had a major part in the development of these ideas. I would like to acknowledge my debt to Geoffrey Hinton who suggested to me that it was indeed feasible to do computations with parallel systems. I would also like to express special thanks to Teuvo Kohonen and his collaborators whose pioneering work in the field of parallel, associative models has benefited us all. At Brown I have learned a great deal from discussions with Stuart Geman, Barry Davis, Gregory Murphy, and Richard Heath. A summer at U.S.C.D. allowed me to talk with Geoffrey Hinton. Donald Norman, David Rumelhart, and Jay McClelland and suggested a host of new problems to think about. Leon Cooper and the Center for Neural Science have provided immense help over the past few years. Computer simulations described here were performed on the VAX 11/780 of the Center for Cognitive Science, Richard Millward, Director.

References

[1] J. A. Anderson, "Neural models and a little about language," in *Biological Bases of Language*, D. Caplan, A. Smith, and A. Roche-Lecour, Eds. Cambridge, MA: MIT Press (to appear).

[2] ____, "Neural models with cognitive implications," in *Basic Processes in Reading*, D. LaBerge and S. J. Samuels, Eds. Hillsdale, NJ: Erlbaum, 1977.

[3] J. A. Anderson and M. Mozer, "Categorization and selective neurons," in *Parallel Models of Associative Memory*, G. Hinton and J. A. Anderson, Eds. Hillsdale, NJ: Erlbaum, 1981.

[4] J. A. Anderson, J. W. Silverstein, S. A. Ritz, and R. S. Jones, "Distinctive features, categorical perception, and probability learning: Some applications of a neural model," *Psychol. Rev.*, vol. 84, pp. 413–451, 1977.

[5] J. A. Anderson and J. W. Silverstein, "Reply to Grossberg," *Psychol. Rev.*, vol. 85, pp. 597–603, 1978.

[6] M. A. Arbib, *The Metaphorical Brain*. New York: Wiley, 1972.

[7] R. Sorabji, tr., *Aristotle on Memory*. Providence, RI: Brown Univ. Press, 1972.

[8] H. B. Barlow, "Single units and sensation," *Perception*, vol. 1, pp. 371–394, 1972.

[9] E. L. Bienenstock, L. N. Cooper, and P. W. Monro, "A theory for the development of neuron selectivity: Orientation selectivity and binocular interactions in visual cortex," *J. Neurosci.*, vol. 2, pp. 32–48, 1982.

[10] S. E. Brodie, B. W. Knight, and F. Ratliff, "The responses of the Limulus retina to moving stimuli: Prediction by Fourier synthesis," *J. General Physiol.*, vol. 72, pp. 129–166, 1978.

[11] ____, "The spatio-temporal transfer function of the Limulus lateral eye," *J. Gen. Physiol.*, vol. 72, pp. 167–202, 1978.

[12] M. Colonnier, "The electron-microscopic analysis of the neuronal organization of the cerebral cortex," in *The Organization of the Cerebral Cortex*, F. O. Schmitt, F. G. Worden, G. Adelman, and S. G. Dennis, Eds. Cambridge, MA: MIT Press, 1981.

[13] L. N. Cooper, "Distributed memory in the central nervous system: Possible test of assumptions in visual cortex," in *The Organization of the Cerebral Cortex*, F. O. Schmitt, F. G. Worden, G. Adelman, and S. G. Dennis, Eds. Cambridge, MA: MIT Press, 1981.

[14] B. Davis, "A neurobiological approach to machine intelligence," Ph.D. thesis, Div. of Appl. Math., Brown Univ., Providence, RI, June 1982.

[15] R. O. Duda and P. E. Hart, *Pattern Classification and Scene Analysis*. New York: Wiley, 1973.

[16] Editors of *Scientific American*, *The Brain*. San Francisco, CA: Freeman, 1979.

[17] J. M. Eich, "A composite holographic associative recall model," *Psychol. Rev.*, vol. 89, pp. 627–661, 1982.

[18] J. A. Feldman and D. H. Ballard, "Connectionist models and their properties," *Cognitive Sci.*, vol. 6, pp. 205–254, 1982.

[19] S. Geman, "Application of stochastic averaging to learning systems," *Brain Theory Newsletter*, vol. 3, pp. 69–71, 1978.

[20] S. Geman, "The law of large numbers in neural modelling," *SIAM-AMS Proc.*, vol. 13, pp. 91–105, 1981.

[21] S. Grossberg, "How does the brain build a cognitive code?," *Psychol. Rev.*, vol. 87, pp. 1–51, 1980.

[22] D. O. Hebb, *The Organization of Behavior*. New York: Wiley, 1949.

[23] R. A. Heath, "A model for signal detection based on an adaptive filter," *Biol. Cybern.*, in press.

[24] G. E. Hinton, "Relaxation and its role in vision," Ph.D. dissertation, Univ. of Edinburgh, 1976.

[25] ____, "Implementing semantic networks in parallel hardware," in *Parallel Models of Associative Memory*, G. E. Hinton and J. A. Anderson, Ed. Hillsdale, NJ: Erlbaum, 1981.

[26] G. Hinton and J. A. Anderson, Eds., *Parallel Models of Associative Memory*. Hillsdale, NJ: Erlbaum, 1981.

[27] W. James, *Psychology (Briefer Course)*. New York: Collier, 1962 (originally published 1890).

[28] E. Kandel, "Small systems of neurons," in *The Brain*, Editors of *Scientific American*, Eds. San Francisco, CA: Freeman, 1979.

[29] A. Knapp and J. A. Anderson, "A signal averaging model for concept formation," *J. Exp. Psychol., Learning, Memory, and Cognition*, submitted.

[30] T. Kohonen, *Associative Memory: A System Theoretic Approach*. Berlin, Germany: Springer-Verlag, 1977.

[31] P. Liepa, "Models of content addressable distributed associative memory (CADAM)," unpublished manuscript, Univ. of Toronto, Toronto, ON, Canada, 1977.

[32] A. R. Luria, *The Mind of a Mnemonist*. New York: Basic Books, 1968.

[33] E. Mach, "Ernst Mach," in *Dictionary of Scientific Biography*, vol. VIII, C. C. Gillespie, Ed. New York: Scribners, 1973.

[34] D. Marr, "A theory of cerebellar cortex," *J. Physiol.*, vol. 202, pp. 437–470 1969.

[35] ____, "A theory for cerebral neocortex," *Proc. Roy. Soc.*, Ser. B, vol. 176, pp. 161–234, 1970.

[36] ____, *Vision*. San Francisco, CA: Freeman, 1982.

[37] J. L. McClelland, and D. E. Rumelhart, "An interactive activation model of context effects in letter perception: Part 1. An account of basic findings," *Psychol. Rev.*, vol. 88, pp. 375–497, 1981.

[38] W. S. McCulloch and W. Pitts, "A logical calculus of the ideas immanent in nervous activity," *Bull. Math. Biophys.*, vol. 5, pp. 115–133, 1943.

[39] M. Minsky, "K-lines: A theory of memory," *Cognitive Sci.*, vol. 4, pp. 117–133, 1980.

[40] M. Minsky and S. Papert, *Perceptrons*. Cambridge, MA: MIT Press, 1969.

[41] B. B. Murdock, Jr., "A theory for the storage and retrieval of item and associative information," *Psychol. Rev.*, pp. 609–626, 1982.

[42] N. J. Nilsson, *Learning Machines*. New York: McGraw-Hill, 1965.

[43] A. Pellionisz and R. Llinas, "Brain modelling by tensor network theory and computer simulation. The Cerebellum: Distributed processor for predictive coordination," *Neurosci.*, vol. 4, pp. 323–348, 1979.

[44] W. Pitts and W. S. McCulloch, "How we know universals: The perception of auditory and visual forms," *Bull. Math. Biophys.*, vol. 9, pp. 127–147, 1947.

[45] M. I. Posner and S. W. Keele, "On the genesis of abstract ideas," *J. Exp. Psychol.*, vol. 77, pp. 353–363, 1968.

[46] ____, "Retention of abstract ideas," *J. Exp. Psychol.*, vol. 83, pp. 304–308, 1970.

[47] F. Ratliff, "Form and function: Linear and nonlinear analyses of neural networks in the visual system," in *Neural Mechanisms in Behavior*, D. McFadden, Ed. New York: Springer, 1980.

[48] A. Rosenfeld, "Iterative methods in image analysis," *Pattern Recognition*, vol. 10, pp. 181–187, 1978.

[49] E. Rosch, "Principles of categorization," in *Cognition and Categorization*, E. Rosch and B. B. Lloyd, Eds. Hillsdale, NJ: Erlbaum, 1978.

[50] E. Rosch and B. B. Lloyd, Eds., *Cognition and Categorization*. Hillsdale, NJ: Erlbaum, 1978.

[51] D. E. Rumelhart and J. L. McClelland, "An interactive activation model of context effects in letter perception: Part 2. The contextual enhancement effect and some tests and extensions of the model," *Psychol. Rev.*, vol. 89, pp. 60–94, 1982.

[52] F. O. Schmitt, F. G. Worden, G. Adelman, and S. G. Dennis, *The Organization of the Cerebral Cortex*. Cambridge, MA: MIT Press, 1981.

[53] T. J. Sejnowski, "Skeleton filters in the brain," in *Parallel Models of*

Associative Memory, G. E. Hinton and J. A. Anderson, Eds. Hillsdale, NJ: Erlbaum, 1981.

[54] G. Shepherd, *The Synaptic Organization of the Brain*, 2nd ed. New York: Oxford Univ. Press, 1979.

[55] _____, *Neurobiology*. New York: Oxford Univ. Press, 1983.

[56] E. E. Smith and D. L. Medin, *Categories and Concepts*. Cambridge, MA: Harvard Univ. Press, 1981.

[57] R. S. Sutton and A. G. Barto, "Toward a modern theory of adaptive networks: expectation and prediction," *Psychol. Rev.*, vol. 88, pp. 135–170, 1981.

[58] J. Szentagothai, "Specificity versus (quasi) randomness in cortical connectivity," in *Architectonics of the Cerebral Cortex*, M. A. B. Brazier and H. Petsche, Eds. New York: Raven Press, 1978.

[59] J. Szentagothai and M. Arbib, "Conceptual models of neural organization," *Neurosci. Res. Program Bull.*, vol. 12, pp. 307–510, 1974.

[60] R. J. Tusa, L. A. Palmer, and A. C. Rosenquist, "The retinotopic organization of area 17 (Striate Cortex) in the cat," *J. Comp. Neurol.*, vol. 177, pp. 213–235, 1978.

[61] C. Wood, "Variations on a theme by Lashley: Lesion experiments on the neural models of Anderson, Silverstein, Ritz, and Jones," *Psychol. Rev.*, vol. 85, 582–591, 1978.

[62] _____, "Implications of simulated lesion experiments for the interpretation of lesions in real nervous systems," in *Neural Models of Language Processes*, M. A. Arbib, D. Caplan, and J. C. Marshall, Eds. New York: Academic, 1983.

[63] T. Y. Young and T. W. Calvert, *Classification, Estimation, and Pattern Recognition*. New York: American Elsevier, 1974.

An Introduction to Computing with Neural Nets

Reprinted from IEEE ASSP Magazine, April 1987, pp. 4-22.

Richard P. Lippmann

Abstract

Artificial neural net models have been studied for many years in the hope of achieving human-like performance in the fields of speech and image recognition. These models are composed of many nonlinear computational elements operating in parallel and arranged in patterns reminiscent of biological neural nets. Computational elements or nodes are connected via weights that are typically adapted during use to improve performance. There has been a recent resurgence in the field of artificial neural nets caused by new net topologies and algorithms, analog VLSI implementation techniques, and the belief that massive parallelism is essential for high performance speech and image recognition. This paper provides an introduction to the field of artificial neural nets by reviewing six important neural net models that can be used for pattern classification. These nets are highly parallel building blocks that illustrate neural- net components and design principles and can be used to construct more complex systems. In addition to describing these nets, a major emphasis is placed on exploring how some existing classification and clustering algorithms can be performed using simple neuron-like components. Single-layer nets can implement algorithms required by Gaussian maximum-likelihood classifiers and optimum minimum-error classifiers for binary patterns corrupted by noise. More generally, the decision regions required by any classification algorithm can be generated in a straightforward manner by three-layer feed-forward nets.

INTRODUCTION

Artificial neural net models or simply "neural nets" go by many names such as connectionist models, parallel distributed processing models, and neuromorphic systems. Whatever the name, all these models attempt to achieve good performance via dense interconnection of simple computational elements. In this respect, artificial neural net structure is based on our present understanding of biological nervous systems. Neural net models have greatest potential in areas such as speech and image recognition where many hypotheses are pursued in parallel, high computation rates are required, and the current best systems are far from equaling human performance. Instead of performing a program of instructions sequentially as in a von Neumann computer, neural net models explore many competing hypotheses simultaneously using massively parallel nets composed of many computational elements connected by links with variable weights.

Computational elements or nodes used in neural net models are nonlinear, are typically analog, and may be slow compared to modern digital circuitry. The simplest node sums N weighted inputs and passes the result through a nonlinearity as shown in Fig. 1. The node is characterized by an internal threshold or offset θ and by the type of nonlinearity. Figure 1 illustrates three common types of nonlinearities; hard limiters, threshold logic elements, and sigmoidal nonlinearities. More complex nodes may include temporal integration or other types of time dependencies and more complex mathematical operations than summation.

Neural net models are specified by the net topology, node characteristics, and training or learning rules. These rules specify an initial set of weights and indicate how weights should be adapted during use to improve performance. Both design procedures and training rules are the topic of much current research.

The potential benefits of neural nets extend beyond the high computation rates provided by massive parallelism. Neural nets typically provide a greater degree of robustness or fault tolerance than von Neumann sequential computers because there are many more processing nodes, each with primarily local connections. Damage to a few nodes or links thus need not impair overall performance significantly. Most neural net algorithms also adapt connection weights in time to improve performance based on current results. Adaptation or learning is a major focus of neural net research. The ability to adapt and continue learning is essential in areas such as speech recognition where training data is limited and new talkers, new words, new dialects, new phrases, and new environments are continuously encountered. Adaptation also provides a degree of robustness by compensating for minor variabilities in characteristics of processing elements. Traditional statistical techniques are not adaptive but typically process all training data simultaneously before being used with new data. Neural net classifiers are also non-parametric and make weaker assumptions concerning the shapes of underlying distributions than traditional statistical classifiers. They may thus prove to be more robust when distributions are generated by nonlinear processes and are strongly non-Gaussian. Designing artificial neural nets to solve problems and studying real biological nets may also change the way we think about problems and lead to new insights and algorithmic improvements.

Work on artificial neural net models has a long history. Development of detailed mathematical models began more than 40 years ago with the work of McCulloch and Pitts [30], Hebb [17], Rosenblatt [39], Widrow [47] and others [38]. More recent work by Hopfield [18, 19, 20], Rumelhart and McClelland [40], Sejnowski [43], Feldman [9], Grossberg [15], and others has led to a new resurgence of the field. This new interest is due to the development of new net topologies and algorithms [18, 19, 20, 41, 9], new analog VLSI implementation techniques [31], and some intriguing demonstrations [43, 20] as well as by a growing fascination with the functioning of the human brain. Recent interest is also driven by the realization that human-like performance in the areas of speech and image recognition will require enormous amounts of processing. Neural nets provide one technique for obtaining the required processing capacity using large numbers of simple processing elements operating in parallel.

This paper provides an introduction to the field of neural nets by reviewing six important neural net models that can be used for pattern classification. These massively parallel nets are important building blocks which can be used to construct more complex systems. The main purpose of this review is to describe the purpose and design of each net in detail, to relate each net to existing pattern classification and clustering algorithms that are normally implemented on sequential von Neumann computers, and to illustrate design principles used to obtain parallelism using neural-like processing elements.

Neural net and traditional classifiers

Block diagrams of traditional and neural net classifiers are presented in Fig. 2. Both types of classifiers determine which of M classes is most representative of an unknown static input pattern containing N input elements. In a speech recognizer the inputs might be the output envelope values from a filter bank spectral analyzer sampled at one time instant and the classes might represent different vowels. In an image classifier the inputs might be the gray scale level of each pixel for a picture and the classes might represent different objects.

The traditional classifier in the top of Fig. 2 contains two stages. The first computes matching scores for each class and the second selects the class with the maximum score. Inputs to the first stage are symbols representing values of the N input elements. These symbols are entered sequentially and decoded from the external symbolic form into an internal representation useful for performing arithmetic and symbolic operations. An algorithm computes a matching score for each of the M classes which indicates how closely the input matches the exemplar pattern for each class. This exemplar pattern is that pattern which is most representative of each class. In many situations a probabilistic model is used to model the generation of input patterns from exemplars and the matching score represents the likelihood or probability that the input pattern was generated from each of the M possible exemplars. In those cases, strong assumptions are typically made concerning underlying distributions of the input elements. Parameters of distributions can then be estimated using a training data as shown in Fig. 2. Multivariate Gaussian distributions are often used leading to relatively simple algorithms for computing matching scores [7]. Matching scores are coded into symbolic representations and passed sequentially to the second stage of

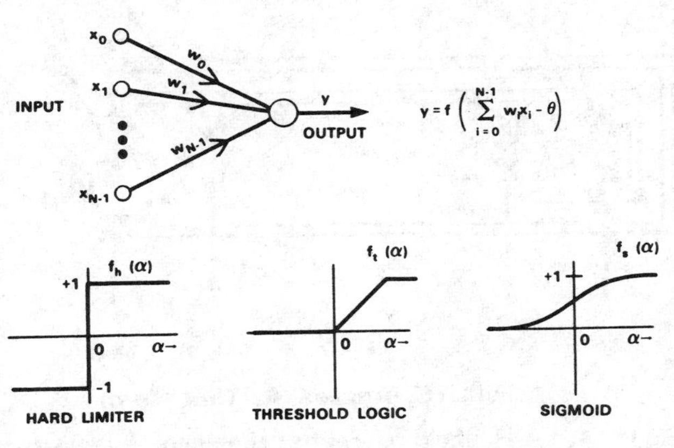

Figure 1. Computational element or node which forms a weighted sum of N inputs and passes the result through a nonlinearity. Three representative nonlinearities are shown.

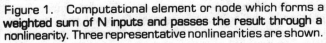

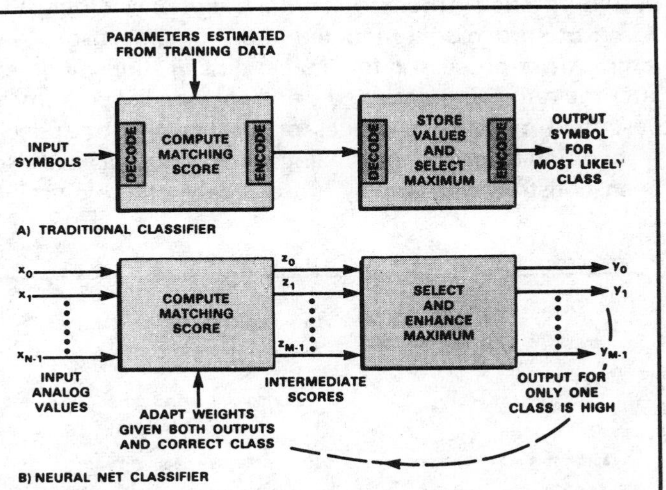

Figure 2. Block diagrams of traditional (A) and neural net (B) classifiers. Inputs and outputs of the traditional classifier are passed serially and internal computations are performed sequentially. In addition, parameters are typically estimated from training data and then held constant. Inputs and outputs to the neural net classifier are in parallel and internal computations are performed in parallel. Internal parameters or weights are typically adapted or trained during use using the output values and labels specifying the correct class.

the classifier. Here they are decoded and the class with the maximum score is selected. A symbol representing that class is then sent out to complete the classification task.

An adaptive neural net classifier is shown at the bottom of Fig. 2. Here input values are fed in parallel to the first stage via N input connections. Each connection carries an analog value which may take on two levels for binary inputs or may vary over a large range for continuous valued inputs. The first stage computes matching scores and outputs these scores in parallel to the next stage over M analog output lines. Here the maximum of these values is selected and enhanced. The second stage has one output for each of the M classes. After classification is complete, only that output corresponding to the most likely class will be on strongly or "high"; other outputs will be "low". Note that in this design, outputs exist for every class and that this multiplicity of outputs must be preserved in further processing stages as long as the classes are considered distinct. In the simplest classification system these output lines might go directly to lights with labels that specify class identities. In more complicated cases they may go to further stages of processing where inputs from other modalities or temporal dependencies are taken into consideration. If the correct class is provided, then this information and the classifier outputs can be fed back to the first stage of the classifier to adapt weights using a learning algorithm as shown in Fig. 2. Adaptation will make a correct response more likely for succeeding input patterns that are similar to the current pattern.

The parallel inputs required by neural net classifiers suggest that real-time hardware implementations should include special purpose pre-processors. One strategy for designing such processors is to build physiologically-based pre-processors modeled after human sensory systems. A pre-processor for image classification modeled after the retina and designed using analog VLSI circuitry is described in [31]. Pre-processor filter banks for speech recognition that are crude analogs of the cochlea have also been constructed [34, 29]. More recent physiologically-based pre-processor algorithms for speech recognition attempt to provide information similar to that available on the auditory nerve [11, 44, 27, 5]. Many of these algorithms include filter bank spectral analysis, automatic gain control, and processing which uses timing or synchrony information in addition to information from smoothed filter output envelopes.

Classifiers in Fig. 2 can perform three different tasks. First, as described above, they can identify which class best represents an input pattern, where it is assumed that inputs have been corrupted by noise or some other process. This is a classical decision theory problem. Second, the classifiers can be used as a content-addressable or associative memory, where the class exemplar is desired and the input pattern is used to determine which exemplar to produce. A content-addressable memory is useful when only part of an input pattern is available and the complete pattern is required, as in bibliographic retrieval of journal references from partial information. This normally requires the addition of a third stage in Fig. 2 to regenerate the exemplar for the most likely class. An additional stage is unnecessary for some neural nets such as the Hopfield net which are designed specifically as content-addressable memories. A third task these classifiers can perform is to vector quantize [28] or cluster [16, 7] the N inputs into M clusters. Vector quantizers are used in image and speech transmission systems to reduce the number of bits necessary to transmit analog data. In speech and image recognition applications they are used to compress the amount of data that must be processed without losing important information. In either application the number of clusters can be pre-specified or may be allowed to grow up to a limit determined by the number ber of nodes available in the first stage.

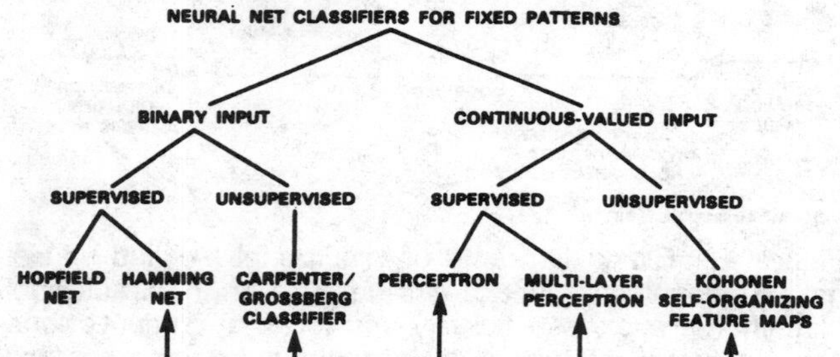

Figure 3. A taxonomy of six neural nets that can be used as classifiers. Classical algorithms which are most similar to the neural net models are listed along the bottom.

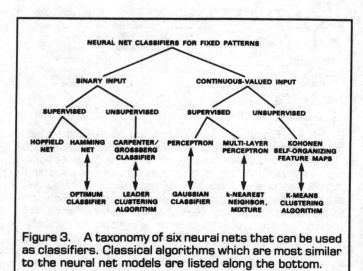

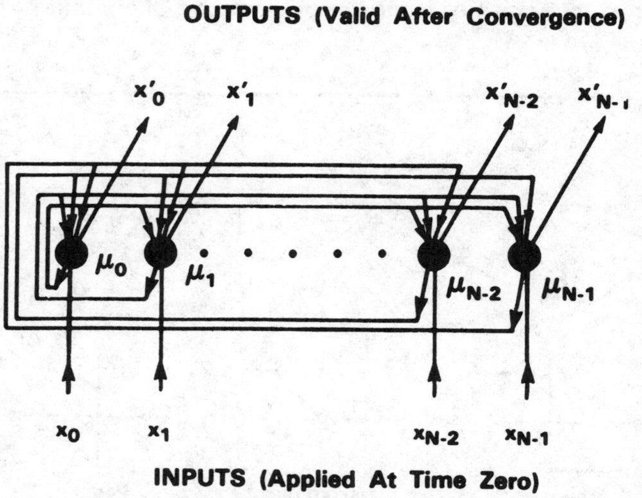

Figure 4. A Hopfield neural net that can be used as a content-addressable memory. An unknown binary input pattern is applied at time zero and the net then iterates until convergence when node outputs remain unchanged. The output is that pattern produced by node outputs after convergence.

A TAXONOMY OF NEURAL NETS

A taxonomy of six important neural nets that can be used for classification of static patterns is presented in Fig. 3. This taxonomy is first divided between nets with binary and continuous valued inputs. Below this, nets are divided between those trained with and without supervision. Nets trained with supervision such as the Hopfield net [18] and perceptrons [39] are used as associative memories or as classifiers. These nets are provided with side information or labels that specify the correct class for new input patterns during training. Most traditional statistical classifiers, such as Gaussian classifiers [7], are trained with supervision using labeled training data. Nets trained without supervision, such as the Kohonen's feature-map forming nets [22], are used as vector quantizers or to form clusters. No information concerning the correct class is provided to these nets during training. The classical K-means [7] and leader [16] clustering algorithms are trained without supervision. A further difference between nets, not indicated in Fig. 3, is whether adaptive training is supported. Although all the nets shown can be trained adaptively, the Hopfield net and the Hamming net are generally used with fixed weights.

The algorithms listed at the bottom of Fig. 3 are those classical algorithms which are most similar to or perform the same function as the corresponding neural net. In some cases a net implements a classical algorithm exactly. For example, the Hamming net [25] is a neural net implementation of the optimum classifier for binary patterns corrupted by random noise [10]. It can also be shown that the perceptron structure performs those calculations required by a Gaussian classifier [7] when weights and thresholds are selected appropriately. In other cases the neural net algorithms are different from the classical algorithms. For example, perceptrons trained with the perceptron convergence procedure [39] behave differently than Gaussian classifiers. Also, Kohonen's net [22] does not perform the iterative K-means training algorithm. Instead, each new pattern is presented only once and weights are modified after each presentation. The Kohonen net does, however, form a pre-specified number of clusters as in the K-means algorithm, where the K refers to the number of clusters formed.

THE HOPFIELD NET

The Hopfield net and two other nets in Fig. 3 are normally used with binary inputs. These nets are most appropriate when exact binary representations are possible as with black and white images where input elements are pixel values, or with ASCII text where input values could represent bits in the 8-bit ASCII representation of each character. These nets are less appropriate when input values are actually continuous, because a fundamental representation problem must be addressed to convert the analog quantities to binary values.

Hopfield rekindled interest in neural nets by his extensive work on different versions of the Hopfield net [18, 19, 20]. This net can be used as an associative memory or to solve optimization problems. One version of the original net [18] which can be used as a content addressable memory is described in this paper. This net, shown in Fig. 4, has N nodes containing hard limiting nonlinearities and binary inputs and outputs taking on the values +1 and −1. The output of each node is fed back to all other nodes via weights denoted t_{ij}. The operation of this net is described in Box 1. First, weights are set using the given recipe from exemplar patterns for all classes. Then an unknown pattern is imposed on the net at time zero by forcing the output of the net to match the unknown pattern. Following this initialization, the net iterates in discrete time steps using the given formula. The net is considered to have converged when outputs no longer change on successive iterations. The pattern specified by the node outputs after convergence is the net output.

Hopfield [18] and others [4] have proven that this net converges when the weights are symmetric ($t_{ij} = t_{ji}$) and

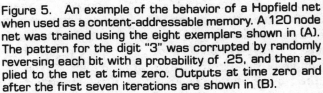

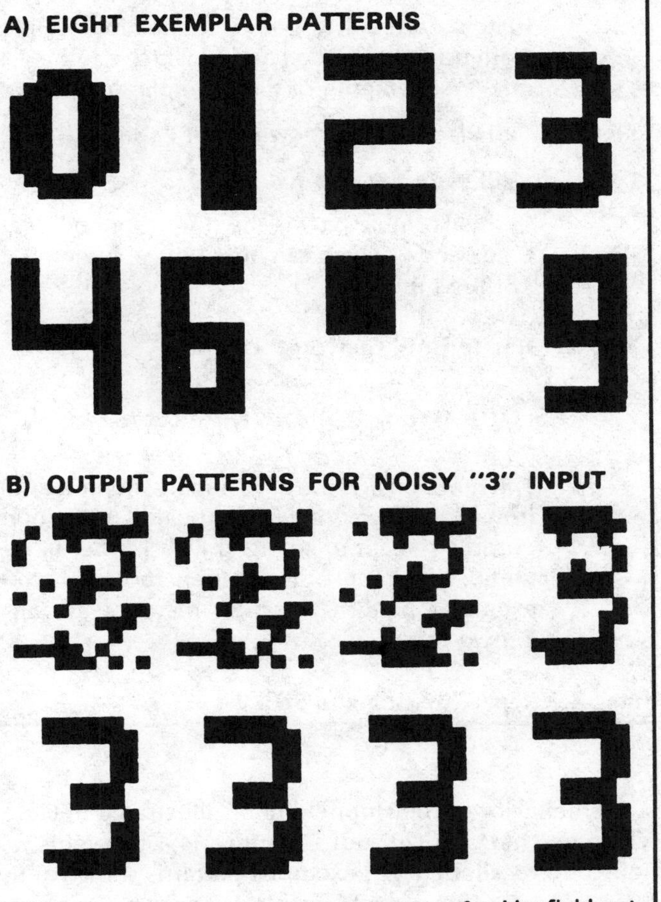

Figure 5. An example of the behavior of a Hopfield net when used as a content-addressable memory. A 120 node net was trained using the eight exemplars shown in (A). The pattern for the digit "3" was corrupted by randomly reversing each bit with a probability of .25, and then applied to the net at time zero. Outputs at time zero and after the first seven iterations are shown in (B).

node outputs are updated asynchronously using the equations in Box 1. Hopfield [19] also demonstrated that the net converges when graded nonlinearities similar to the sigmoid nonlinearity in Fig. 1 are used. When the Hopfield net is used as an associative memory, the net output after convergence is used directly as the complete restored memory. When the Hopfield net is used as a classifier, the output after convergence must be compared to the M exemplars to determine if it matches an exemplar exactly. If it does, the output is that class whose exemplar matched the output pattern. If it does not then a "no match" result occurs.

Box 1. Hopfield Net Algorithm

Step 1. Assign Connection Weights

$$t_{ij} = \begin{cases} \sum_{s=0}^{M-1} x_i^s x_j^s, & i \neq j \\ 0, & i = j,\ 0 \leq i, j \leq M\text{-}1 \end{cases}$$

In this Formula t_{ij} is the connection weight from node i to node j and x_i^s which can be +1 or −1 is element i of the exemplar for class s.

Step 2. Initialize with Unknown Input Pattern

$$\mu_i(0) = x_i, \qquad 0 \leq i \leq N-1$$

In this Formula $\mu_i(t)$ is the output of node i at time t and x_i which can be +1 or −1 is element i of the input pattern.

Step 3. Iterate Until Convergence

$$\mu_j(t+1) = f_h\left[\sum_{i=0}^{N-1} t_{ij}\,\mu_i(t)\right], \quad 0 \leq j \leq M\text{-}1$$

The function f_h is the hard limiting nonlinearity from Fig. 1. The process is repeated until node outputs remain unchanged with further iterations. The node outputs then represent the exemplar pattern that best matches the unknown input.

Step 4. Repeat by Going to Step 2

The behavior of the Hopfield net is illustrated in Fig. 5. A Hopfield net with 120 nodes and thus 14,400 weights was trained to recall the eight exemplar patterns shown at the top of Fig. 5. These digit-like black and white patterns contain 120 pixels each and were hand crafted to provide good performance. Input elements to the net take on the value +1 for black pixels and −1 for white pixels. In the example presented, the pattern for the digit "3" was corrupted by randomly reversing each bit independently from +1 to −1 and vice versa with a probability of 0.25. This pattern was then applied to the net at time zero. Patterns produced at the output of the net on iterations zero to seven are presented at the bottom of Fig. 5. The corrupted input pattern is present unaltered at iteration zero. As the net iterates the output becomes more and more like the correct exemplar pattern until at iteration six the net has converged to the pattern for the digit three.

The Hopfield net has two major limitations when used as a content addressable memory. First, the number of patterns that can be stored and accurately recalled is severely limited. If too many patterns are stored, the net may converge to a novel spurious pattern different from all exemplar patterns. Such a spurious pattern will produce a "no match" output when the net is used as a classifier. Hopfield [18] showed that this occurs infrequently when exemplar patterns are generated randomly and the number of classes (M) is less than .15 times the number of input elements or nodes in the net (N). The number of classes is thus typically kept well below .15N. For example, a Hopfield net for only 10 classes might require more than 70 nodes and more than roughly 5,000 connection weights. A second limitation of the Hopfield net is that an exemplar pattern will be unstable if it shares many bits in common with another exemplar pattern. Here an exemplar is considered unstable if it is applied at time zero and the net converges to some other exemplar. This problem can be eliminated and performance can be improved by a number of orthogonalization procedures [14, 46].

THE HAMMING NET

The Hopfield net is often tested on problems where inputs are generated by selecting an exemplar and reversing bit values randomly and independently with a given probability [18, 12, 46]. This is a classic problem in communications theory that occurs when binary fixed-length signals are sent through a memoryless binary symmetric channel. The optimum minimum error classifier in this case calculates the Hamming distance to the exemplar for each class and selects that class with the minimum Hamming distance [10]. The Hamming distance is the number of bits in the input which do not match the corresponding exemplar bits. A net which will be called a Hamming net implements this algorithm using neural net components and is shown in Fig. 6.

The operation of the Hamming net is described in Box 2. Weights and thresholds are first set in the lower subnet such that the matching scores generated by the outputs of the middle nodes of Fig. 6 are equal to N minus the Hamming distances to the exemplar patterns. These matching scores will range from 0 to the number of elements in the input (N) and are highest for those nodes corresponding to classes with exemplars that best match the input. Thresholds and weights in the MAXNET subnet are fixed. All thresholds are set to zero and weights from each node to itself are 1. Weights between nodes are inhibitory with a value of $-\epsilon$ where $\epsilon < 1/M$.

After weights and thresholds have been set, a binary pattern with N elements is presented at the bottom of the Hamming net. It must be presented long enough to allow the matching score outputs of the lower subnet to settle and initialize the output values of the MAXNET. The input is then removed and the MAXNET iterates until the output of only one node is positive. Classification is then complete and the selected class is that corresponding to the node with a positive output.

The behavior of the Hamming net is illustrated in Fig. 7.

Box 2. Hamming Net Algorithm

Step 1. Assign Connection Weights and Offsets

In the lower subnet:

$$w_{ij} = \frac{x_i^j}{2}, \qquad \theta_j = \frac{N}{2},$$

$$0 \le i \le N-1, \qquad 0 \le j \le M-1$$

In the upper subnet:

$$t_{kl} = \begin{cases} 1, & k = l \\ -\varepsilon, & k \ne l, \quad \varepsilon < \frac{1}{M}, \end{cases}$$

$$0 \le k,l \le M-1$$

In these equations w_{ij} is the connection weight from input i to node j in the lower subnet and θ is the threshold in that node. The connection weight from node k to node l in the upper subnet is t_{kl} and all thresholds in this subnet are zero. x_i^j is element i of exemplar j as in Box 1.

Step 2. Initialize with Unknown Input Pattern

$$\mu_j(0) = f_t\left(\sum_{i=0}^{N-1} w_{ij}x_i - \theta_j\right)$$

$$0 \le j \le M-1$$

In this equation $\mu_j(t)$ is the output of node j in the upper subnet at time t, x_i is element i of the input as in Box 1, and f_t is the threshold logic nonlinearity from Fig. 1. Here and below it is assumed that the maximum input to this nonlinearity never causes the output to saturate.

Step 3. Iterate Until Convergence

$$\mu_j(t+1) = f_t\left(\mu_j(t) - \varepsilon\sum_{k \ne j} \mu_k(t)\right)$$

$$0 \le j,k \le M-1$$

This process is repeated until convergence after which the output of only one node remains positive.

Step 4. Repeat by Going to Step 2

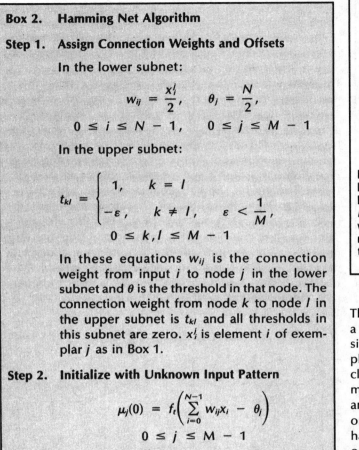

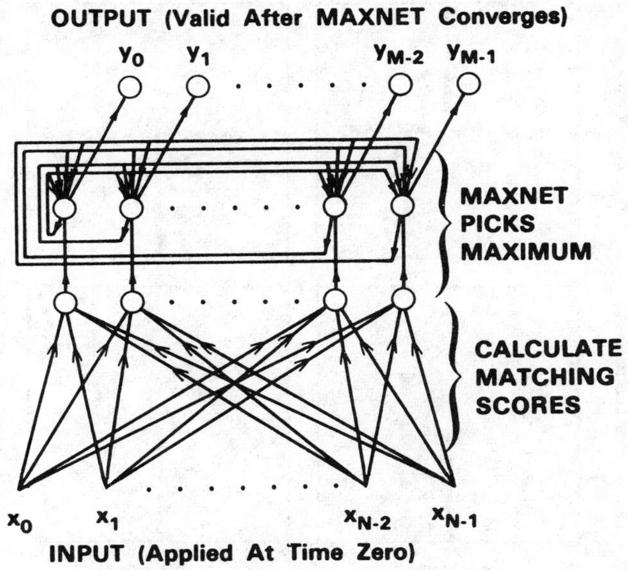

Figure 6. A feed-forward Hamming net maximum likelihood classifier for binary inputs corrupted by noise. The lower subnet calculates N minus the Hamming distance to M exemplar patterns. The upper net selects that node with the maximum output. All nodes use threshold-logic nonlinearities where it is assumed that the outputs of these nonlinearities never saturate.

The four plots in this figure show the outputs of nodes in a MAXNET with 100 nodes on iterations 0, 3, 6, and 9. These simulations were obtained using randomly selected exemplar patterns with 1000 elements each. The exemplar for class 50 was presented at time zero and then removed. The matching score at time zero is maximum (1000) for node 50 and has a random value near 500 for other nodes. After only 3 iterations, the outputs of all nodes except node 50 have been greatly reduced and after 9 iterations only the output for node 50 is non-zero. Simulations with different probabilities of reversing bits on input patterns and with different numbers of classes and elements in the input patterns have demonstrated that the MAXNET typically converges in less than 10 iterations in this application [25]. In addition, it can be proven that the MAXNET will always converge and find the node with the maximum value when $\varepsilon < 1/M$ [25].

The Hamming net has a number of obvious advantages over the Hopfield net. It implements the optimum minimum error classifier when bit errors are random and independent, and thus the performance of the Hopfield net must either be worse than or equivalent to that of the Hamming net in such situations. Comparisons between the two nets on problems such as character recognition, recognition of random patterns, and bibliographic retrieval have demonstrated this difference in performance [25]. The Hamming net also requires many fewer connections than the Hopfield net. For example, with 100 inputs and 10 classes the Hamming net requires only 1,100 connections while the Hopfield net requires almost 10,000. Furthermore, the difference in number of connections required increases as the number of inputs increases, because the number of connections in the Hopfield net grows as the square of the number of inputs while the number of connections in the Hamming net grows linearly. The Hamming net can also be modified to be a minimum error classifier when errors are generated by reversing input elements from +1 to −1 and from −1 to +1 asymmetrically with different probabilities [25] and when the values of specific input elements are unknown [2]. Finally, the Hamming net does not suffer from spurious output patterns which can produce a "no-match" result.

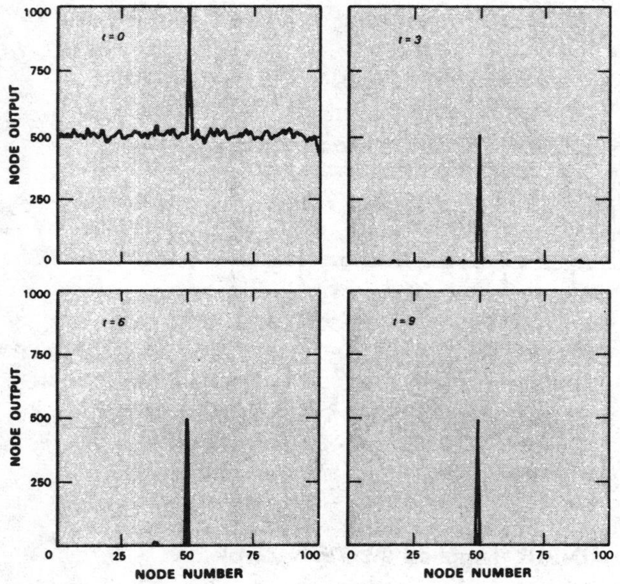

Figure 7. Node outputs for a Hamming net with 1,000 binary inputs and 100 output nodes or classes. Output values of all 100 nodes are presented at time zero and after 3, 6, and 9 iterations. The input was the exemplar pattern corresponding to output node 50.

SELECTING OR ENHANCING THE MAXIMUM INPUT

The need to select or enhance the input with a maximum value occurs frequently in classification problems. Several different neural nets can perform this operation. The MAXNET described above uses heavy lateral inhibition similar to that used in other net designs where a maximum was desired [20, 22, 9]. These designs create a "winner-take-all" type of net whose design mimics the heavy use of lateral inhibition evident in the biological neural nets of the human brain [21]. Other techniques to pick a maximum are also possible [25]. One is illustrated in Fig. 8. This figure shows a comparator subnet which is described in [29]. It uses threshold logic nodes to pick the maximum of two inputs and then feeds this maximum value forward. This net is useful when the maximum value must be passed unaltered to the output. Comparator subnets can be layered into roughly $\log_2(M)$ layers to pick the maximum of M inputs. A net that uses these subnets to pick the maximum of 8 inputs is presented in Fig. 9.

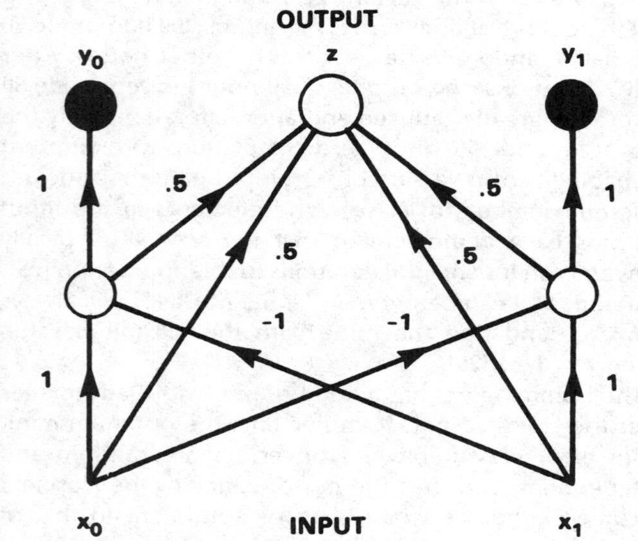

Figure 8. A comparator subnet that selects the maximum of two analog inputs. The output labeled z is the maximum value and the outputs labeled y_0 and y_1 indicate which input was maximum. Internal thresholds on threshold logic nodes (open circles) and hard limiting nodes (filled circles) are zero. Weights are as shown.

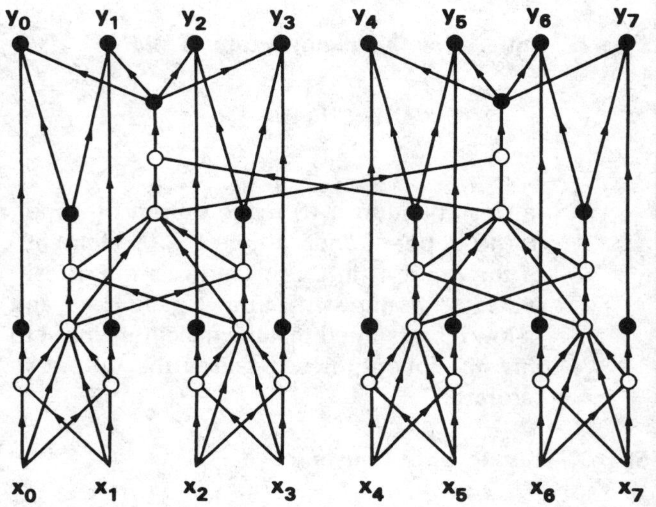

Figure 9. A feed-forward net that determines which of eight inputs is maximum using a binary tree and comparator subnets from Fig. 8. After an input vector is applied, only that output corresponding to the maximum input element will be high. Internal thresholds on threshold-logic nodes (open circles) and on hard limiting nodes (filled circles) are zero except for the output nodes. Thresholds in the output nodes are 2.5. Weights for the comparator subnets are as in Fig. 8 and all other weights are 1.

In some situations a maximum is not required and matching scores must instead be compared to a threshold. This can be done using an array of hard-limiting nodes with internal thresholds set to the desired threshold values. Outputs of these nodes will be −1 unless the inputs exceed the threshold values. Alternatively, thresholds could be set adaptively using a common inhibitory input fed to all nodes. This threshold could be ramped up or down until the output of only one node was positive.

THE CARPENTER/GROSSBERG CLASSIFIER

Carpenter and Grossberg [3], in the development of their Adaptive Resonance Theory have designed a net which forms clusters and is trained without supervision. This net implements a clustering algorithm that is very similar to the simple sequential leader clustering algorithm described in [16]. The leader algorithm selects the first input as the exemplar for the first cluster. The next input is compared to the first cluster exemplar. It "follows the leader" and is clustered with the first if the distance to the first is less than a threshold. Otherwise it is the exemplar for a new cluster. This process is repeated for all following inputs. The number of clusters thus grows with time and depends on both the threshold and the distance metric used to compare inputs to cluster exemplars.

The major components of a Carpenter/Grossberg classification net with three inputs and two output nodes is presented in Fig. 10. The structure of this net is similar to that of the Hamming net. Matching scores are computed using feed-forward connections and the maximum value is enhanced using lateral inhibition among the output nodes. This net differs from the Hamming net in that feedback connections are provided from the output nodes to the input nodes. Mechanisms are also provided to turn off that output node with a maximum value, and to compare exemplars to the input for the threshold test required by the leader algorithm. This net is completely described using nonlinear differential equations, includes extensive feedback, and has been shown to be stable [3]. In typical operation, the differential equations can be shown to implement the clustering algorithm presented in Box 3.

Box 3. Carpenter/Grossberg Net Algorithm

Step 1. Initialization

$$t_{ij}(0) = 1$$

$$b_{ij}(0) = \frac{1}{1 + N}$$

$$0 \leq i \leq N - 1,$$

$$0 \leq j \leq M - 1$$

$$\text{Set } \rho, \qquad 0 \leq \rho \leq 1$$

In these equations $b_{ij}(t)$ is the bottom up and $t_{ij}(t)$ is the top down connection weight between input node i and output node j at time t. These weights define the exemplar specified by output node j. The fraction ρ is the vigilance threshold which indicates how close an input must be to a stored exemplar to match.

Step 2. Apply New Input

Step 3. Compute Matching Scores

$$\mu_j = \sum_{i=0}^{N-1} b_{ij}(t)x_i \qquad 0 \leq j \leq M - 1$$

In this equation μ_j is the output of output node j and x_i is element i of the input which can be 0 or 1.

Step 4. Select Best Matching Exemplar

$$\mu_j^* = \max_j \{\mu_j\}$$

This is performed using extensive lateral inhibition as in the maxnet.

Step 5. Vigilance Test

$$\|X\| = \sum_{i=0}^{N-1} x_i$$

$$\|T \cdot X\| = \sum_{i=0}^{N-1} t_{ij^*}x_i$$

$$\text{is } \frac{\|T \cdot X\|}{\|X\|} > \rho \text{ ?}$$

NO — GO TO STEP 6

YES — GO TO STEP 7

Step 6. Disable Best Matching Exemplar

The output of the best matching node selected in Step 4 is temporarily set to zero and no longer takes part in the maximization of Step 4. Then go to Step 3.

Step 7. Adapt Best Matching Exemplar

$$t_{ij^*}(t + 1) = t_{ij^*}(t)x_i$$

$$b_{ij^*}(t + 1) = \frac{t_{ij}{}^*(t)x_i}{.5 + \sum_{i=0}^{N-1} t_{ij^*}(t)x_i}$$

Step 8. Repeat by Going to Step 2

(First enable any nodes disabled in Step 6)

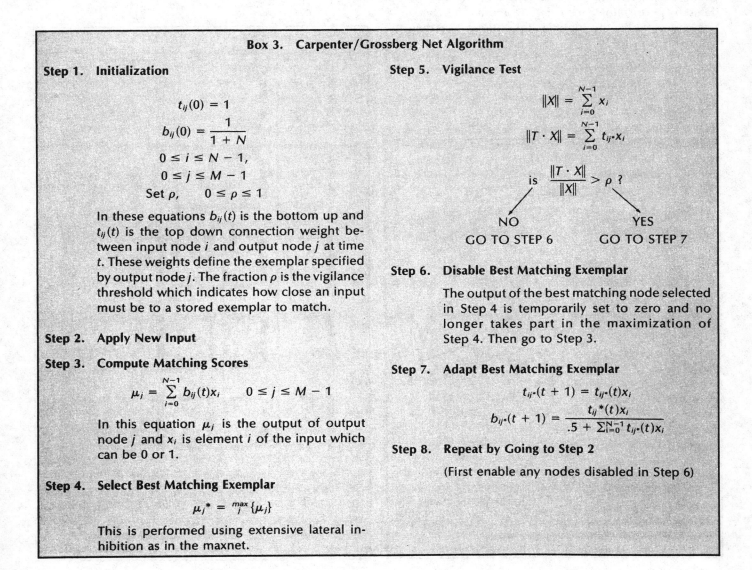

The algorithm presented in Box 3 assumes that "fast learning" is used as in the simulations presented in [3] and thus that elements of both inputs and stored exemplars take on only the values 0 and 1. The net is initialized by effectively setting all exemplars represented by connection weights to zero. In addition, a matching threshold called *vigilance* which ranges between 0.0 and 1.0 must be set. This threshold determines how close a new input pattern must be to a stored exemplar to be considered similar. A value near one requires a close match and smaller values accept a poorer match. New inputs are presented sequentially at the bottom of the net as in the Hamming net. After presentation, the input is compared to all stored exemplars in parallel as in the Hamming net to produce matching scores. The exemplar with the highest matching score is selected using lateral inhibition. It is then compared to the input by computing the ratio of the dot product of the input and the best matching exemplar (number of 1 bits in common) divided by the number of 1 bits in the input. If this ratio is greater than the vigilance threshold, then the input is considered to be similar to the best matching exemplar and that exemplar is updated by performing a logical AND operation between its bits and those in the input. If the ratio is less than the vigilance threshold, then the input is considered to be different from all exemplars and it is added as a new exemplar. Each additional new exemplar requires one node and 2N connections to compute matching scores.

The behavior of the Carpenter/Grossberg net is illustrated in Fig. 11. Here it is assumed that patterns to be recognized are the three patterns of the letters *"C"*, *"E"*, and *"F"* shown in the left side of this figure. These patterns have 64 pixels each that take on the value 1 when black and 0 when white. Results are presented when the vigilance threshold was set to 0.9. This forces separate exemplar patterns to be created for each letter.

The left side of Fig. 11 shows the input to the net on successive trials. The right side presents exemplar patterns formed after each pattern had been applied. In this example "C" was presented first followed by "E" followed by "F", etc. After the net is initialized and a "C" is applied, internal connection weights are altered to form an internal exemplar that is identical to the "C". After an "E" is then applied, a new "E" exemplar is added. Behavior is similar for a new "F" leading to three stored exemplars. If the vigilance threshold had been slightly lower, only two exemplars would have been present after the "F"; one for "F" and one for both "C" and "E" that would have been identical to "C" pattern. Now, when a noisy "F" is applied

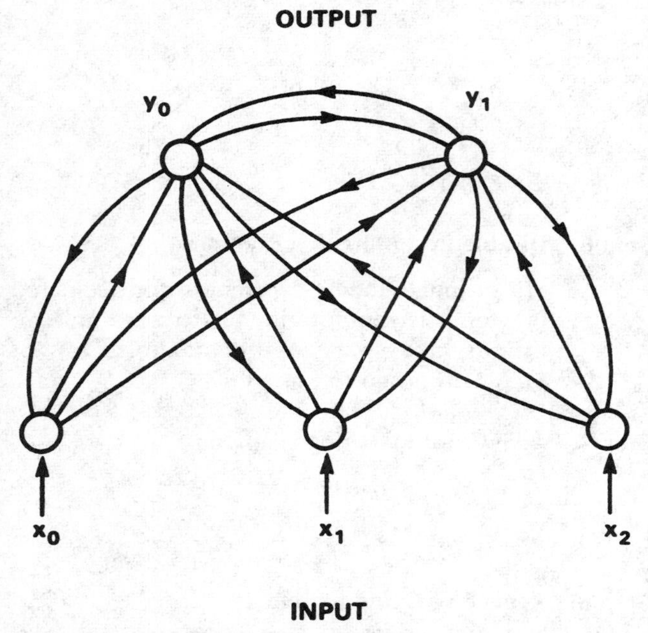

Figure 10. The major components of the Carpenter Grossberg Classification net. A binary input is presented at the bottom and when classification is complete only one output is high. Not shown are additional components required to perform the vigilance test and to disable the output node with the largest output.

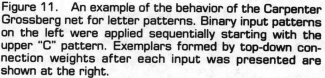

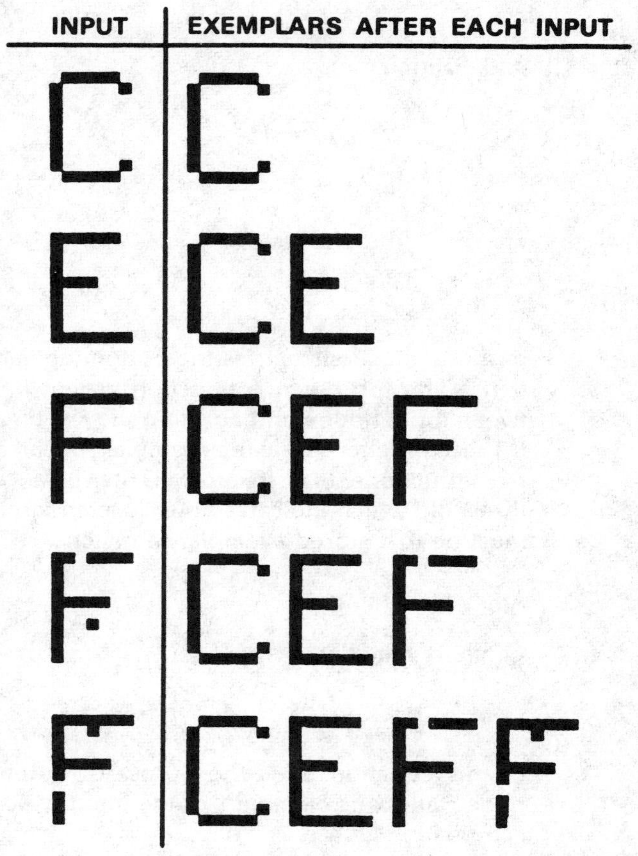

Figure 11. An example of the behavior of the Carpenter Grossberg net for letter patterns. Binary input patterns on the left were applied sequentially starting with the upper "C" pattern. Exemplars formed by top-down connection weights after each input was presented are shown at the right.

with a missing black pixel in the upper edge it is accepted as being similar to the "F" exemplar and degrades this exemplar due to the AND operation performed during updating. When another noisy "F" is applied again with only one black pixel missing, it is considered different from existing exemplars and a new noisy "F" exemplar is added. This will occur for further noisy "F" inputs leading to a growth of noisy "F" exemplars.

These results illustrate that the Carpenter/Grossberg algorithm can perform well with perfect input patterns but that even a small amount of noise can cause problems. With no noise, the vigilance threshold can be set such that the two patterns which are most similar are considered different. In noise, however, this level may be too high and the number of stored exemplars can rapidly grow until all available nodes are used up. Modifications are necessary to enhance the performance of this algorithm in noise. These could include adapting weights more slowly and changing the vigilance threshold during training and testing as suggested in [3].

SINGLE LAYER PERCEPTRON

The single layer perceptron [39] is the first of three nets from the taxonomy in Fig. 3 that can be used with both continuous valued and binary inputs. This simple net generated much interest when initially developed because of its ability to learn to recognize simple patterns. A perceptron that decides whether an input belongs to one of two classes (denoted A or B) is shown in the top of Fig. 12. The single node computes a weighted sum of the input elements, subtracts a threshold (θ) and passes the result through a hard limiting nonlinearity such that the output y is either $+1$ or -1. The decision rule is to respond class A if the output is $+1$ and class B if the output is -1. A useful technique for analyzing the behavior of nets such as the perceptron is to plot a map of the decision regions created in the multidimensional space spanned by the input variables. These decision regions specify which input values result in a class A and which result in a class B response. The perceptron forms two decision regions separated by a hyperplane. These regions are shown in the right side of Fig. 12 when there are only two inputs and the hyperplane is a line. In this case inputs above the boundary line lead to class A responses and inputs below the line lead to class B responses. As can be seen, the equation of the boundary line depends on the connection weights and the threshold.

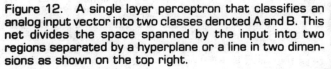

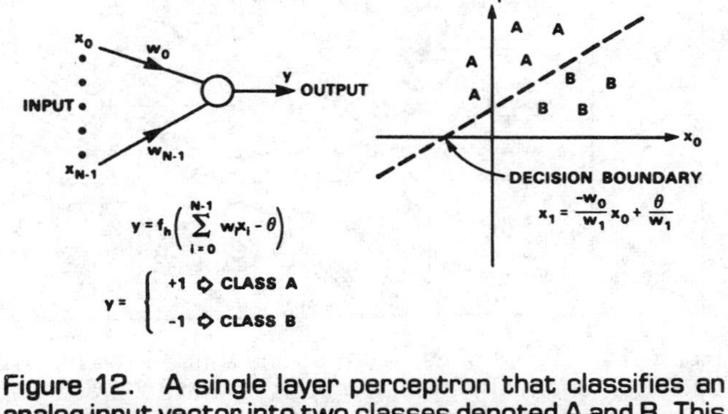

Figure 12. A single layer perceptron that classifies an analog input vector into two classes denoted A and B. This net divides the space spanned by the input into two regions separated by a hyperplane or a line in two dimensions as shown on the top right.

Connection weights and the threshold in a perceptron can be fixed or adapted using a number of different algorithms. The original perceptron convergence procedure for adjusting weights was developed by Rosenblatt [39]. It is described in Box 4. First connection weights and the threshold value are initialized to small random non-zero values. Then a new input with N continuous valued elements is applied to the input and the output is computed as in Fig. 12. Connection weights are adapted only when an error occurs using the formula in step 4 of Box 4. This formula includes a gain term (η) that ranges from 0.0 to 1.0 and controls the adaptation rate. This gain term must be adjusted to satisfy the conflicting requirements of fast adaptation for real changes in the input distributions and averaging of past inputs to provide stable weight estimates.

Box 4. The Perceptron Convergence Procedure

Step 1. Initialize Weights and Threshold

Set $w_i(0)$ $(0 \leq i \leq N - 1)$ and θ to small random values. Here $w_i(t)$ is the weight from input i at time t and θ is the threshold in the output node.

Step 2. Present New Input and Desired Output

Present new continuous valued input $x_0, x_1 \ldots x_{N-1}$ along with the desired output $d(t)$.

Step 3. Calculate Actual Output

$$y(t) = f_h\left(\sum_{i=0}^{N-1} w_i(t)x_i(t) - \theta\right)$$

Step 4. Adapt Weights

$$w_i(t + 1) = w_i(t) + \eta[d(t) - y(t)]x_i(t),$$
$$0 \leq i \leq N - 1$$

$$d(t) = \begin{cases} +1 \text{ if input from class A} \\ -1 \text{ if input from class B} \end{cases}$$

In these equations η is a positive gain fraction less than 1 and $d(t)$ is the desired correct output for the current input. Note that weights are unchanged if the correct decision is made by the net.

Step 5. Repeat by Going to Step 2

An example of the use of the perceptron convergence procedure is presented in Fig. 13. Samples from class A in this figure are represented by circles and samples from class B are represented by crosses. Samples from classes A and B were presented alternately until 80 inputs had been presented. The four lines show the four decision boundaries after weights had been adjusted following errors on trials 0, 2, 4, and 80. In this example the classes were well separated after only four trials and the gain term was .01.

Rosenblatt [39] proved that if the inputs presented from the two classes are separable (that is they fall on opposite sides of some hyperplane), then the perceptron convergence procedure converges and positions the decision hyperplane between those two classes. Such a hyperplane is illustrated in the upper right of Fig. 12. This decision boundary separates all samples from the A and B classes. One problem with the perceptron convergence procedure is that decision boundaries may oscillate continuously when inputs are not separable and distributions overlap. A modification to the perceptron convergence procedure can form the least mean square (LMS) solution in this case. This solution minimizes the mean square error between the desired output of a perceptron-like net and the actual output. The algorithm that forms the LMS solution is called the Widrow-Hoff or LMS algorithm [47,48,7].

The LMS algorithm is identical to the perceptron convergence procedure described in Box 4 except the hard limiting nonlinearity is made linear or replaced by a threshold-logic nonlinearity. Weights are thus corrected on every trial by an amount that depends on the difference between the desired and the actual input. A classifier that uses the LMS training algorithm could use desired outputs of 1 for class A and 0 for class B. During operation the input would then be assigned to class A only if the output was above 0.5.

The decision regions formed by perceptrons are similar to those formed by maximum likelihood Gaussian classifiers which assume inputs are uncorrelated and distributions for different classes differ only in mean values. This type of Gaussian classifier and the associated weighted Euclidean or straight Euclidean distance metric is often used in speech recognizers when there is limited training data and inputs have been orthogonalized by a suitable transformation [36]. Box 5 demonstrates how the weights and threshold in a perceptron can be selected such that the perceptron structure computes the difference between log likelihoods required by such a Gaussian classifier [7]. Perceptron-like structures can also be used to perform the linear computations required by a Karhunen Loeve transformation [36]. These computations can be used to transform a set of $N + K$ correlated Gaussian inputs into a reduced set of N uncorrelated inputs which can be used with the above Gaussian classifier.

It is straightforward to generalize the derivation of Box 5 to demonstrate how a Gaussian classifier for M classes can be constructed from M perceptron-like structures followed by a net that picks the maximum. The required net is identical in structure to the Hamming Net of Fig. 6. In this case, however, inputs are analog and the weights and node thresholds are calculated from terms II and III in likelihood equations similar to those for L_A in Box 5. It is likewise straightforward to generalize the Widrow-Hoff

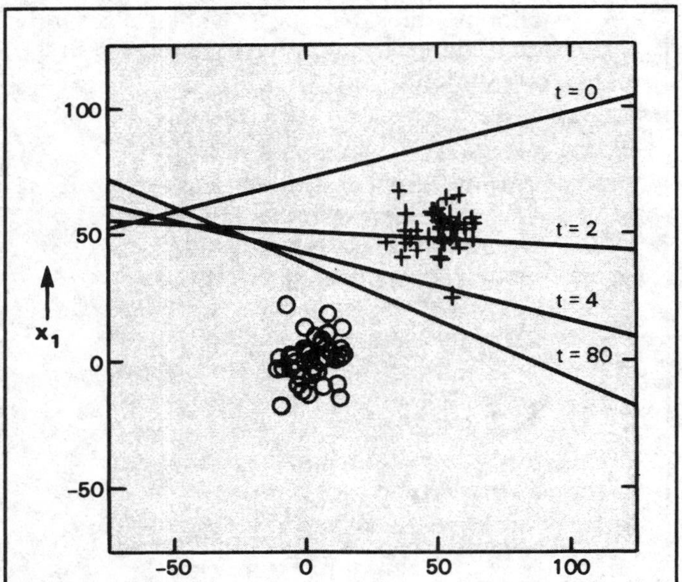

Figure 13. An example of the decision boundaries formed by the perceptron convergence procedure with two classes. Samples from class A are represented by circles and samples from class B by crosses. Lines represent decision boundaries after trials where errors occurred and weights were adapted.

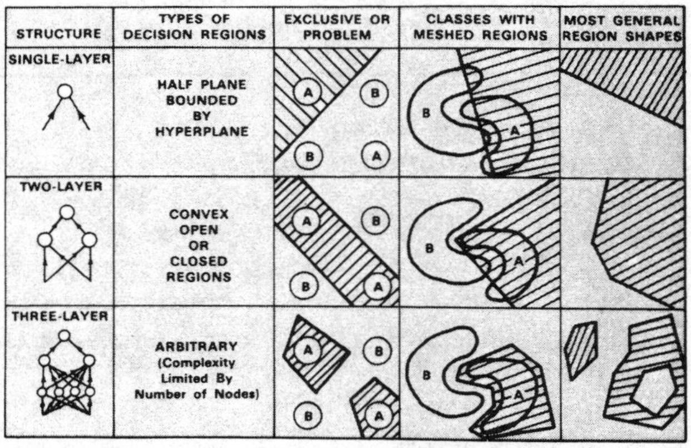

Figure 14. Types of decision regions that can be formed by single- and multi-layer perceptrons with one and two layers of hidden units and two inputs. Shading denotes decision regions for class A. Smooth closed contours bound input distributions for classes A and B. Nodes in all nets use hard limiting nonlinearities.

variant of the perceptron convergence procedure to apply for M classes. This requires a structure identical to the Hamming Net and a classification rule that selects the class corresponding to the node with the maximum output. During adaptation the desired output values can be set to 1 for the correct class and 0 for all others.

Box 5. A Gaussian Classifier Implemented Using the Perceptron Structure

If m_{Ai} and σ_{Ai}^2 are the mean and variance of input x_i when the input is from class A and M_{Bi} and σ_{Bi}^2 are the mean and variance of input x_i for class B and $\sigma_i^2 = \sigma_{Ai}^2 = \sigma_{Bi}^2$, then the likelihood values required by a maximum likelihood classifier are monotonically related to

$$L_A = -\sum_{i=0}^{N-1} \frac{(x_i - M_{Ai})^2}{\sigma_i^2}$$
$$= -\sum \frac{x_i^2}{\sigma_i^2} + 2\sum \frac{M_{Ai}x_i}{\sigma_i^2} - \sum \frac{M_{Ai}^2}{\sigma_i^2}$$

and

$$L_B = -\sum_{i=0}^{N-1} \frac{(x_i - M_{Bi})^2}{\sigma_i^2}$$
$$= -\underset{\uparrow \atop \text{Term I}}{\sum \frac{x_i^2}{\sigma_i^2}} + \underset{\uparrow \atop \text{Term II}}{2\sum \frac{M_{Bi}x_i}{\sigma_i^2}} - \underset{\uparrow \atop \text{Term III}}{\sum \frac{M_{Bi}^2}{\sigma_i^2}}.$$

A maximum likelihood classifier must calculate L_A and L_B and select the class with the highest likelihood. Since Term I in these equations is identical for L_A and L_B, it can be dropped. Term II is a product of the input times weights and can be calculated by a perception and Term III is a constant which can be obtained from the threshold in a perceptron node. A Gaussian classifier for two classes can thus be formed by using the perceptron of Fig. 12 to calculate $L_A - L_B$ by setting

$$w_i = \frac{2(M_{Ai} - M_{Bi})}{\sigma_i{}^2},$$

and

$$\theta = \sum_{i=0}^{N-1} \frac{M_{Ai}^2 - M_{Bi}^2}{\sigma_i^2}.$$

The perceptron structure can be used to implement either a Gaussian maximum likelihood classifier or classifiers which use the perceptron training algorithm or one of its variants. The choice depends on the application. The perceptron training algorithm makes no assumptions concerning the shape of underlying distributions but focuses on errors that occur where distributions overlap. It may thus be more robust than classical techniques and work well when inputs are generated by nonlinear processes and are heavily skewed and non-Gaussian. The Gaussian classifier makes strong assumptions concerning underlying distributions and is more appropriate when distributions are known and match the Gaussian assumption. The adaptation algorithm defined by the perceptron convergence procedure is simple to implement and doesn't require storing any more information than is present in the weights and the threshold. The Gaussian classifier can be made adaptive [24], but extra information must be stored and the computations required are more complex.

Neither the perceptron convergence procedure nor the Gaussian classifier is appropriate when classes cannot be separated by a hyperplane. Two such situations are presented in the upper section of Fig. 14. The smooth closed contours labeled A and B in this figure are the input distributions for the two classes when there are two continuous valued inputs to the different nets. The shaded areas are the decision regions created by a single-layer perceptron and other feed-forward nets. Distributions for the two classes for the exclusive OR problem are disjoint and cannot be separated by a single straight line. This problem was used to illustrate the weakness of the perceptron by Minsky and Papert [32]. If the lower left B cluster is taken to be at the origin of this two dimensional space then the output of the classifier must be "high" only if one but not both of the inputs is "high". One possible decision region for class A which a perceptron might create is illustrated by the shaded region in the first row of Fig. 14. Input distributions for the second problem shown in this figure are meshed and also can not be separated by a single straight line. Situations similar to these may occur when parameters such as formant frequencies are used for speech recognition.

MULTI-LAYER PERCEPTRON

Multi-layer perceptrons are feed-forward nets with one or more layers of nodes between the input and output nodes. These additional layers contain hidden units or nodes that are not directly connected to both the input and output nodes. A three-layer perceptron with two layers of hidden units is shown in Fig. 15. Multi-layer perceptrons overcome many of the limitations of single-layer perceptrons, but were generally not used in the past because effective training algorithms were not available. This has recently changed with the development of new training algorithms [40]. Although it cannot be proven that these algorithms converge as with single layer perceptrons, they have been shown to be successful for many problems of interest [40].

The capabilities of multi-layer perceptrons stem from the nonlinearities used within nodes. If nodes were linear elements, then a single-layer net with appropriately chosen weights could exactly duplicate those calculations performed by any multi-layer net. The capabilities of perceptrons with one, two, and three layers that use hard-limiting nonlinearities are illustrated in Fig. 14. The second column in this figure indicates the types of decision regions that can be formed with different nets. The next two columns present examples of decision regions which could be formed for the exclusive OR problem and a problem with meshed regions. The rightmost column gives examples of the most general decision regions that can be formed.

As noted above, a single-layer perceptron forms half-plane decision regions. A two-layer perceptron can form any, possibly unbounded, convex region in the space spanned by the inputs. Such regions include convex polygons sometimes called convex hulls, and the unbounded convex regions shown in the middle row of Fig. 14. Here the term convex means that any line joining points on the border of a region goes only through points within that region. Convex regions are formed from intersections of the half-plane regions formed by each node in the first layer of the multi-layer perceptron. Each node in the first layer behaves like a single-layer perceptron and has a "high" output only for points on one side of the hyperplane formed by its weights and offset. If weights to an output node from N_1 first-layer nodes are all 1.0, and the threshold in the output node is $N_1 - \varepsilon$ where $0 < \varepsilon < 1$, then the output node will be "high" only if the outputs of all first-layer nodes are "high". This corresponds to performing a logical AND operation in the output node and results in a final decision region that is the intersection of all the half-plane regions formed in the first layer. Intersections of such half planes form convex regions as described above. These convex regions have at the most as many sides as there are nodes in the first layer.

This analysis provides some insight into the problem of selecting the number of nodes to use in a two-layer perceptron. The number of nodes must be large enough to form a decision region that is as complex as is required by a given problem. It must not, however, be so large that the many weights required can not be reliably estimated from the available training data. For example, two nodes are sufficient to solve the exclusive OR problem as shown in the second row of Fig. 14. No number of nodes, however, can separate the meshed class regions in Fig. 14 with a two-layer perceptron.

A three-layer perceptron can form arbitrarily complex decision regions and can separate the meshed classes as shown in the bottom of Fig. 14. It can form regions as complex as those formed using mixture distributions and nearest-neighbor classifiers [7]. This can be proven by construction. The proof depends on partitioning the desired decision region into small hypercubes (squares when there are two inputs). Each hypercube requires $2N$ nodes in the first layer (four nodes when there are two inputs), one for each side of the hypercube, and one node in the second layer that takes the logical AND of the outputs from the first-layer nodes. The outputs of second-layer nodes will be "high" only for inputs within each hypercube. Hypercubes are assigned to the proper decision regions by connecting the output of each second-layer node only to the output node corresponding to the decision region that node's hypercube is in and performing a logical OR operation in each output node. A logical OR operation will be performed if these connection weights from the second hidden layer to the output layer are one and thresholds in the output nodes are 0.5. This construction procedure can be generalized to use arbitrarily shaped convex regions instead of small hypercubes and is capable of generating the disconnected and non-convex regions shown at the bottom of Fig. 14.

The above analysis demonstrates that no more than three layers are required in perceptron-like feed-forward nets because a three-layer net can generate arbitrarily complex decision regions. It also provides some insight into the problem of selecting the number of nodes to use in three-layer perceptrons. The number of nodes in the second layer must be greater than one when decision regions are disconnected or meshed and cannot be formed from one convex area. The number of second layer nodes required in the worst case is equal to the number of disconnected regions in input distributions. The number of nodes in the first layer must typically be sufficient to provide three or more edges for each convex area generated by every second-layer node. There should thus typically be more than three times as many nodes in the second as in the first layer.

The above discussion centered primarily on multi-layer perceptrons with one output when hard limiting nonlinearities are used. Similar behavior is exhibited by multi-layer perceptrons with multiple output nodes when sigmoidal nonlinearities are used and the decision rule is to select the class corresponding to the output node with the largest output. The behavior of these nets is more complex because decision regions are typically bounded by smooth curves instead of by straight line segments and analysis is thus more difficult. These nets, however, can be trained with the new back-propagation training algorithm [40].

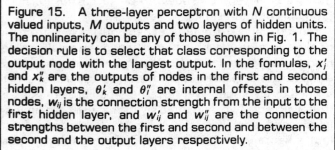

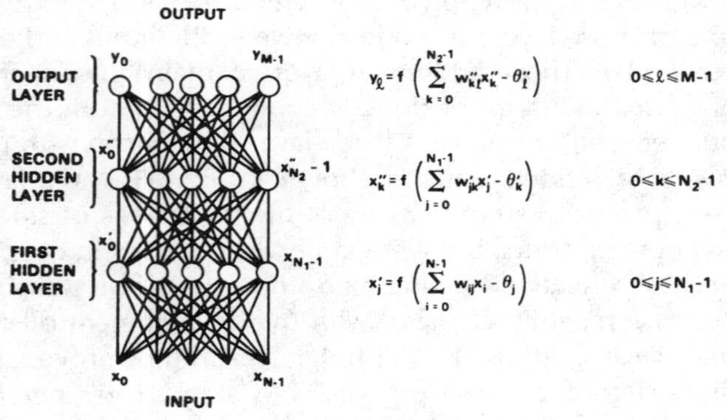

Figure 15. A three-layer perceptron with N continuous valued inputs, M outputs and two layers of hidden units. The nonlinearity can be any of those shown in Fig. 1. The decision rule is to select that class corresponding to the output node with the largest output. In the formulas, x'_j and x''_k are the outputs of nodes in the first and second hidden layers, θ'_k and θ''_l are internal offsets in those nodes, w_{ij} is the connection strength from the input to the first hidden layer, and w'_{ij} and w''_{ij} are the connection strengths between the first and second and between the second and the output layers respectively.

$$y_l = f\left(\sum_{k=0}^{N_2-1} w''_{kl} x''_k - \theta''_l\right) \quad 0 \leq l \leq M-1$$

$$x''_k = f\left(\sum_{j=0}^{N_1-1} w'_{jk} x'_j - \theta'_k\right) \quad 0 \leq k \leq N_2-1$$

$$x'_j = f\left(\sum_{i=0}^{N-1} w_{ij} x_i - \theta_j\right) \quad 0 \leq j \leq N_1-1$$

The back-propagation algorithm described in Box 6 is a generalization of the LMS algorithm. It uses a gradient search technique to minimize a cost function equal to the mean square difference between the desired and the actual net outputs. The desired output of all nodes is typically "low" (0 or <0.1) unless that node corresponds to the class the current input is from in which case it is "high" (1.0 or >0.9). The net is trained by initially selecting small random weights and internal thresholds and then presenting all training data repeatedly. Weights are adjusted after every trial using side information specifying the correct class until weights converge and the cost function is reduced to an acceptable value. An essential component of the algorithm is the iterative method described in Box 6 that propagates error terms required to adapt weights back from nodes in the output layer to nodes in lower layers.

An example of the behavior of the back propagation algorithm is presented in Fig. 16. This figure shows decision regions formed by a two-layer perceptron with two inputs, eight nodes in the hidden layer, and two output nodes corresponding to two classes. Sigmoid nonlinearities were used as in Box 6, the gain term η was 0.3, the momentum term α was 0.7, random samples from classes A and B were presented on alternate trials, and the desired outputs were either 1 or 0. Samples from class A were distributed uniformly over a circle of radius 1 centered at the origin. Samples from class B were distributed uniformly outside this circle up to a radius of 5. The initial decision region is a slightly curved hyperplane. This gradually changes to a circular region that encloses the circular distribution of class A after 200 trails (100 samples from each class). This decision region is near that optimal region that would be produced by a Maximum Likelihood classifier.

The back propagation algorithm has been tested with a number of deterministic problems such as the exclusive OR problem [40], on problems related to speech synthesis

Box 6. The Back-Propagation Training Algorithm

The back-propagation training algorithm is an iterative gradient algorithm designed to minimize the mean square error between the actual output of a multilayer feed-forward perceptron and the desired output. It requires continuous differentiable non-linearities. The following assumes a sigmoid logistic nonlinearity is used where the function $f(\alpha)$ in Fig. 1 is

$$f(\alpha) = \frac{1}{1 + e^{-(\alpha-\theta)}}$$

Step 1. Initialize Weights and Offsets

Set all weights and node offsets to small random values.

Step 2. Present Input and Desired Outputs

Present a continuous valued input vector $x_0, x_1, \ldots x_{N-1}$ and specify the desired outputs $d_0, d_1, \ldots d_{M-1}$. If the net is used as a classifier then all desired outputs are typically set to zero except for that corresponding to the class the input is from. That desired output is 1. The input could be new on each trial or samples from a training set could be presented cyclically until weights stabilize.

Step 3. Calculate Actual Outputs

Use the sigmoid nonlinearity from above and formulas as in Fig. 15 to calculate outputs $y_0, y_1 \ldots y_{M-1}$.

Step 4. Adapt Weights

Use a recursive algorithm starting at the output nodes and working back to the first hidden layer. Adjust weights by

$$w_{ij}(t+1) = w_{ij}(t) + \eta\delta_j x_i'$$

In this equation $w_{ij}(t)$ is the weight from hidden node i or from an input to node j at time t, x_i' is either the output of node i or is an input, η is a gain term, and δ_j is an error term for node j. If node j is an output node, then

$$\delta_j = y_j(1 - y_j)(d_j - y_j),$$

where d_j is the desired output of node j and y_j is the actual output.

If node j is an internal hidden node, then

$$\delta_j = x_j'(1 - x_j')\sum_k \delta_k w_{jk},$$

where k is over all nodes in the layers above node j. Internal node thresholds are adapted in a similar manner by assuming they are connection weights on links from auxiliary constant-valued inputs. Convergence is sometimes faster if a momentum term is added and weight changes are smoothed by

$$w_{ij}(t+1) = w_{ij}(t) + \eta\delta_j x_i' + \alpha(w_{ij}(t) - w_{ij}(t-1)),$$

where $0 < \alpha < 1$.

Step 5. Repeat by Going to Step 2

and recognition [43, 37, 8] and on problems related to visual pattern recognition [40]. It has been found to perform well in most cases and to find good solutions to the problems posed. A demonstration of the power of this algorithm was provided by Sejnowski [43]. He trained a two-layer perceptron with 120 hidden units and more than 20,000 weights to form letter to phoneme transcription rules. The input to this net was a binary code indicating those letters in a sliding window seven letters long that was moved over a written transcription of spoken text. The desired output was a binary code indicating the phonemic transcription of the letter at the center of the window. After 50 times through a dialog containing 1024 words, the transcription error rate was only 5%. This increased to 22% for a continuation of that dialog that was not used during training.

The generally good performance found for the back propagation algorithm is somewhat surprising considering that it is a gradient search technique that may find a local minimum in the LMS cost function instead of the desired global minimum. Suggestions to improve performance and reduce the occurrence of local minima include allowing extra hidden units, lowering the gain term used to adapt weights, and making many training runs starting with different sets of random weights. When used with classification problems, the number of nodes could be set using considerations described above. The problem of local minima in this case corresponds to clustering two or more disjoint class regions into one. This can be minimized by using multiple starts with different random weights and a low gain to adapt weights. One difficulty noted with the backward-propagation algorithm is that in many cases the number of presentations of training data required for convergence has been large (more than 100 passes through all the training data). Although a number of more complex adaptation algorithms have been proposed to speed convergence [35] it seems unlikely that the complex decision regions formed by multi-layer perceptrons can be generated in few trials when class regions are disconnected.

An interesting theorem that sheds some light on the capabilities of multi-layer perceptrons was proven by Kolmogorov and is described in [26]. This theorem states that any continuous function of N variables can be computed using only linear summations and nonlinear but continuously increasing functions of only one variable. It effectively states that a three layer perceptron with $N(2N + 1)$ nodes using continuously increasing nonlinearities can compute any continuous function of N variables. A three-layer perceptron could thus be used to create any continuous likelihood function required in a classifier. Unfortunately, the theorem does not indicate how weights or nonlinearities in the net should be selected or how sensitive the output function is to variations in the weights and internal functions.

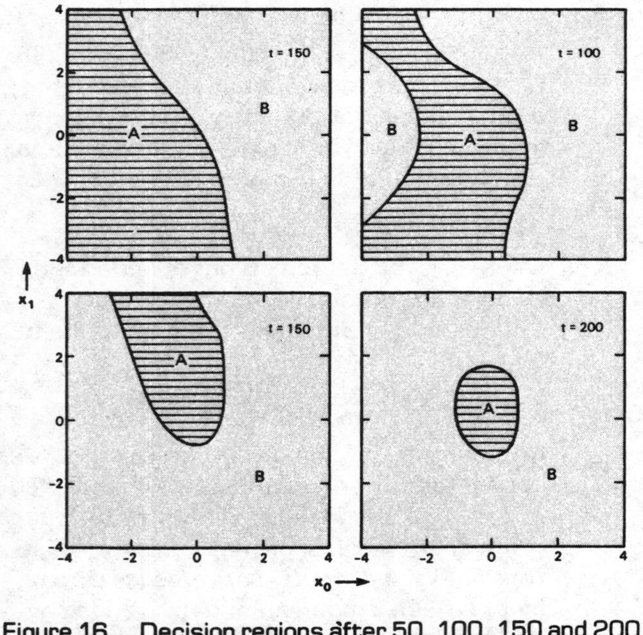

Figure 16. Decision regions after 50, 100, 150 and 200 trials generated by a two layer perceptron using the back-propagation training algorithm. Inputs from classes A and B were presented on alternate trials. Samples from class A were distributed uniformly over a circle of radius 1 centered at the origin. Samples from class B were distributed uniformly outside the circle. The shaded area denotes the decision region for class A.

KOHONEN'S SELF ORGANIZING FEATURE MAPS

One important organizing principle of sensory pathways in the brain is that the placement of neurons is orderly and often reflects some physical characteristic of the external stimulus being sensed [21]. For example, at each level of the auditory pathway, nerve cells and fibers are arranged anatomically in relation to the frequency which elicits the greatest response in each neuron. This tono-

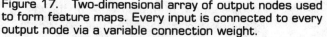

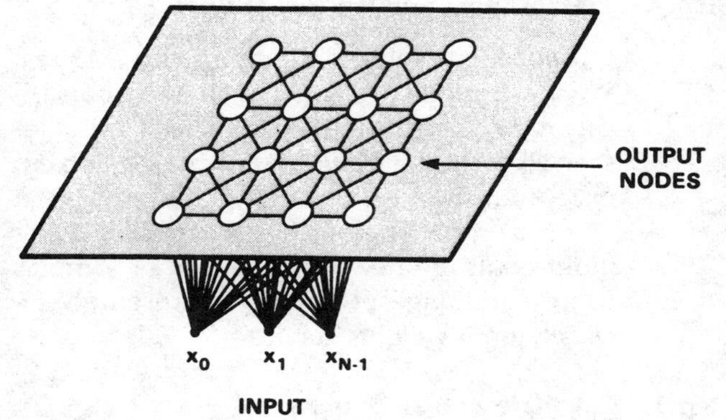

Figure 17. Two-dimensional array of output nodes used to form feature maps. Every input is connected to every output node via a variable connection weight.

topic organization in the auditory pathway extends up to the auditory cortex [33, 21]. Although much of the low-level organization is genetically pre-determined, it is likely that some of the organization at higher levels is created during learning by algorithms which promote self-organization. Kohonen [22] presents one such algorithm which produces what he calls self-organizing feature maps similar to those that occur in the brain.

Kohonen's algorithm creates a vector quantizer by adjusting weights from common input nodes to M output nodes arranged in a two dimensional grid as shown in Fig. 17. Output nodes are extensively interconnected with many local connections. Continuous-valued input vectors are presented sequentially in time without specifying the desired output. After enough input vectors have been presented, weights will specify cluster or vector centers that sample the input space such that the point density function of the vector centers tends to approximate the probability density function of the input vectors [22]. In addition, the weights will be organized such that topologically close nodes are sensitive to inputs that are physically similar. Output nodes will thus be ordered in a natural manner. This may be important in complex systems with many layers of processing because it can reduce lengths of inter-layer connections.

The algorithm that forms feature maps requires a neighborhood to be defined around each node as shown in Fig. 18. This neighborhood slowly decreases in size with time as shown. Kohonen's algorithm is described in Box 7. Weights between input and output nodes are initially set to small random values and an input is presented. The distance between the input and all nodes is computed as shown. If the weight vectors are normalized to have constant length (the sum of the squared weights from all inputs to each output are identical) then the node with the minimum Euclidean distance can be found by using the net of Fig. 17 to form the dot product of the input and the weights. The selection required in step 4 then turns into a problem of finding the node with a maximum value. This node can be selected using extensive lateral inhibition as in the MAXNET in the top of Fig. 6. Once this node is selected, weights to it and to other nodes in its neighborhood are modified to make these nodes more responsive to the current input. This process is repeated for further inputs. Weights eventually converge and are fixed after the gain term in step 5 is reduced to zero.

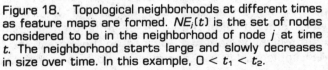

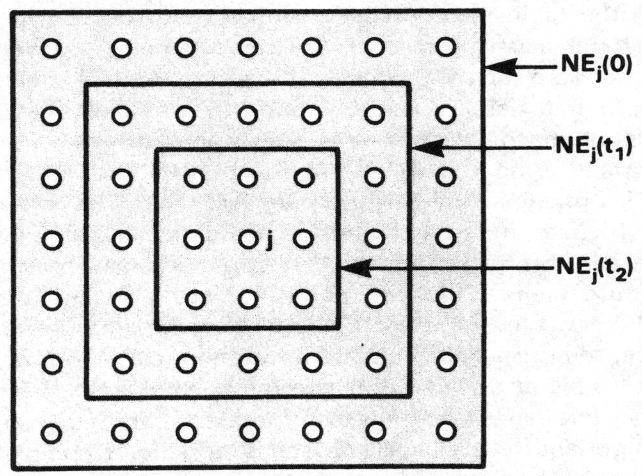

Figure 18. Topological neighborhoods at different times as feature maps are formed. $NE_j(t)$ is the set of nodes considered to be in the neighborhood of node j at time t. The neighborhood starts large and slowly decreases in size over time. In this example, $0 < t_1 < t_2$.

Box 7. An Algorithm to Produce Self-Organizing Feature Maps

Step 1. Initialize Weights

Initialize weights from N inputs to the M output nodes shown in Fig. 17 to small random values. Set the initial radius of the neighborhood shown in Fig. 18.

Step 2. Present New Input

Step 3. Compute Distance to All Nodes

Compute distances d_j between the input and each output node j using

$$d_j = \sum_{i=0}^{N-1} (x_i(t) - w_{ij}(t))^2$$

where $x_i(t)$ is the input to node i at time t and $w_{ij}(t)$ is the weight from input node i to output node j at time t.

Step 4. Select Output Node with Minimum Distance

Select node j^* as that output node with minimum d_j.

Step 5. Update Weights to Node j^* and Neighbors

Weights are updated for node j^* and all nodes in the neighborhood defined by $NE_{j^*}(t)$ as shown in Fig. 18. New weights are

$$w_{ij}(t+1) = w_{ij}(t) + \eta(t)(x_i(t) - w_{ij}(t))$$

For $j \in NE_{j^*}(t) \qquad 0 \leq i \leq N-1$

The term $\eta(t)$ is a gain term $(0 < \eta(t) < 1)$ that decreases in time.

Step 6. Repeat by Going to Step 2

An example of the behavior of this algorithm is presented in Fig. 19. The weights for 100 output nodes are plotted in these six subplots when there are two random independent inputs uniformly distributed over the region enclosed by the boxed areas. Line intersections in these plots specify weights for one output node. Weights from

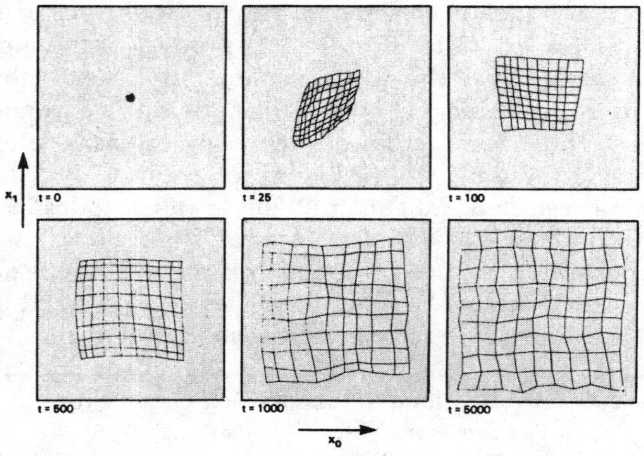

Figure 19. Weights to 100 output nodes from two input nodes as a feature map is being formed. The horizontal axis represents the value of the weight from input x_0 and the vertical axis represents the value of the weight from input x_1. Line intersections specify the two weights for each node. Lines connect weights for nodes that are nearest neighbors. An orderly grid indicates that topologically close nodes code inputs that are physically similar. Inputs were random, independent, and uniformly distributed over the area shown.

input x_0 are specified by the position along the horizontal axis and weights from input x_1 are specified by the position along the vertical axis. Lines connect weight values for nodes that are topological nearest neighbors. Weights start at time zero clustered at the center of the plot. Weights then gradually expand in an orderly way until their point density approximates the uniform distribution of the input samples. In this example, the gain term in step 5 of Box 7 was a Gaussian function of the distance to the node selected in step 4 with a width that decreased in time.

Kohonen [22] presents many other examples and proofs related to this algorithm. He also demonstrates how the algorithm can be used in a speech recognizer as a vector quantizer [23]. Unlike the Carpenter/Grossberg classifier, this algorithm can perform relatively well in noise because the number of classes is fixed, weights adapt slowly, and adaptation stops after training. This algorithm is thus a viable sequential vector quantizer when the number of clusters desired can be specified before use and the amount of training data is large relative to the number of clusters desired. It is similar to the K-means clustering algorithm in this respect. Results, however, may depend on the presentation order of input data for small amounts of training data.

INTRODUCTORY REFERENCES TO NEURAL NET LITERATURE

More detailed information concerning the six algorithms described above and other neural net algorithms can be found in [3, 7, 15, 18, 19, 20, 22, 25, 32, 39, 40]. Descriptions of many other algorithms including the Boltzmann machine and background historical information can be found in a recent book on parallel distributed processing edited by Rumelhart and McClelland [41]. Feldman [9] presents a good introduction to the connectionist philosophy that complements this book. Papers describing recent research efforts are available in the proceedings of the 1986 Conference on Neural Networks for Computing held in Snowbird, Utah [6]. Descriptions of how the Hopfield net can be used to solve a number of different optimization problems including the traveling salesman problem are presented in [20, 45]. A discussion of how content-addressable memories can be implemented using optical techniques is available in [1] and an introduction to the field of neurobiology is available in [21] and other basic texts.

In addition to the above papers and books, there are a number of neural net conferences being held in 1987. These include the "1987 Snowbird Meeting on Neural Networks for Computing" in Snowbird, Utah, April 1–5, the "IEEE First Annual International Conference on Neural Networks" in San Diego, California, June 21–24, and the "IEEE Conference on Neural Information Processing Systems—Natural and Synthetic" in Boulder, Colorado, November 8–12. This last conference is cosponsored by the IEEE Acoustics, Speech, and Signal Processing Society.

CONCLUDING REMARKS

The above review provides an introduction to an interesting field that is immature and rapidly changing. The six nets described are common components in many more complex systems that are under development. Although there have been no practical applications of neural nets yet, preliminary results such as those of Sejnowski [43] have demonstrated the potential of the newer learning algorithms. The greatest potential of neural nets remains in the high-speed processing that could be provided through massively parallel VLSI implementations. Several groups are currently exploring different VLSI implementation strategies [31, 13, 42]. Demonstrations that existing algorithms for speech and image recognition can be performed using neural nets support the potential applicability of any neural-net VLSI hardware that is developed.

The current research effort in neural nets has attracted researchers trained in engineering, physics, mathematics, neuroscience, biology, computer sciences and psychology. Current research is aimed at analyzing learning and self-organization algorithms used in multi-layer nets, at developing design principles and techniques to solve dynamic range and sensitivity problems which become important for large analog systems, at building complete systems for image and speech and recognition and obtaining experience with these systems, and at determining which current algorithms can be implemented using neuron-like components. Advances in these areas and in VLSI implementation techniques could lead to practical real-time neural-net systems.

ACKNOWLEDGMENTS

I have constantly benefited from discussions with Ben Gold and Joe Tierney. I would also like to thank Don Johnson for his encouragement, Bill Huang for his simulation studies, and Carolyn for her patience.

REFERENCES

[1] Y. S. Abu-Mostafa and D. Pslatis, "Optical Neural Computers," *Scientific American*, 256, 88–95, March 1987.

[2] E. B. Baum, J. Moody, and F. Wilczek, "Internal Representations for Associative Memory," NSF-ITP-86-138 Institute for Theoretical Physics, University of California, Santa Barbara, California, 1986.

[3] G. A. Carpenter, and S. Grossberg, "Neural Dynamics of Category Learning and Recognition: Attention, Memory Consolidation, and Amnesia," in J. Davis, R. Newburgh, and E. Wegman (Eds.) *Brain Structure, Learning, and Memory,* AAAS Symposium Series, 1986.

[4] M. A. Cohen, and S. Grossberg, "Absolute Stability of Global Pattern Formation and Parallel Memory Storage by Competitive Neural Networks," *IEEE Trans. Syst. Man Cybern.* SMC-13, 815–826, 1983.

[5] B. Delgutte, "Speech Coding in the Auditory Nerve: II. Processing Schemes for Vowel-Like Sounds," *J. Acoust. Soc. Am.* 75, 879–886, 1984.

[6] J. S. Denker, *AIP Conference Proceedings 151, Neural Networks for Computing, Snowbird Utah, AIP,* 1986.

[7] R. O. Duda and P. E. Hart, *Pattern Classification and Scene Analysis,* John Wiley & Sons, New York (1973).

[8] J. L. Elman and D. Zipser, "Learning the Hidden Structure of Speech," Institute for Cognitive Science, University of California at San Diego, *ICS Report 8701,* Feb. 1987.

[9] J. A. Feldman and D. H. Ballard, "Connectionist Models and Their Properties," *Cognitive Science, Vol. 6,* 205–254, 1982.

[10] R. G. Gallager, *Information Theory and Reliable Communication,* John Wiley & Sons, New York (1968).

[11] O. Ghitza, "Robustness Against Noise: The Role of Timing-Synchrony Measurement," in *Proceedings International Conference on Acoustics Speech and Signal Processing,* ICASSP-87, Dallas, Texas, April 1987.

[12] B. Gold, "Hopfield Model Applied to Vowel and Consonant Discrimination," *MIT Lincoln Laboratory Technical Report, TR-747, AD-A169742,* June 1986.

[13] H. P. Graf, L. D. Jackel, R. E. Howard, B. Straughn, J. S. Denker, W. Hubbard, D. M. Tennant, and D. Schwartz, "VLSI Implementation of a Neural Network Memory With Several Hundreds of Neurons," in J. S. Denker (Ed.) *AIP Conference Proceedings 151, Neural Networks for Computing, Snowbird Utah, AIP,* 1986.

[14] P. M. Grant and J. P. Sage, "A Comparison of Neural Network and Matched Filter Processing for Detecting Lines in Images," in J. S. Denker (Ed.) *AIP Conference Proceedings 151, Neural Networks for Computing, Snowbird Utah, AIP,* 1986.

[15] S. Grossberg, *The Adaptive Brain I: Cognition, Learning, Reinforcement, and Rhythm,* and *The Adaptive Brain II: Vision, Speech, Language, and Motor Control,* Elsevier/North-Holland, Amsterdam (1986).

[16] J. A. Hartigan, *Clustering Algorithms,* John Wiley & Sons, New York (1975).

[17] D. O. Hebb, *The Organization of Behavior,* John Wiley & Sons, New York (1949).

[18] J. J. Hopfield, "Neural Networks and Physical Systems with Emergent Collective Computational Abilities," *Proc. Natl. Acad. Sci.* USA, Vol. 79, 2554–2558, April 1982.

[19] J. J. Hopfield, "Neurons with Graded Response Have Collective Computational Properties Like Those of Two-State Neurons," *Proc. Natl. Acad. Sci.* USA, Vol. 81, 3088–3092, May 1984.

[20] J. J. Hopfield, and D. W. Tank, "Computing with Neural Circuits: A Model," *Science,* Vol. 233, 625–633, August 1986.

[21] E. R. Kandel and J. H. Schwartz, *Principles of Neural Science,* Elsevier, New York (1985).

[22] T. Kohonen, *Self-Organization and Associative Memory,* Springer-Verlag, Berlin (1984).

[23] T. Kohonen, K. Masisara and T. Saramaki, "Phonotopic Maps—Insightful Representation of Phonological Features for Speech Representation," *Proceedings IEEE 7th Inter. Conf. on Pattern Recognition,* Montreal, Canada, 1984.

[24] F. L. Lewis, *Optimal Estimation,* John Wiley & Sons, New York (1986).

[25] R. P. Lippmann, B. Gold, and M. L. Malpass, "A Comparison of Hamming and Hopfield Neural Nets for Pattern Classification," *MIT Lincoln Laboratory Technical Report, TR-769,* to be published.

[26] G. G. Lorentz, "The 13th Problem of Hilbert," in F. E. Browder (Ed.), *Mathematical Developments Arising from Hilbert Problems,* American Mathematical Society, Providence, R.I. (1976).

[27] R. F. Lyon and E. P. Loeb, "Isolated Digit Recognition Experiments with a Cochlear Model," in *Proceedings International Conference on Acoustics Speech and Signal Processing, ICASSP-87,* Dallas, Texas, April 1987.

[28] J. Makhoul, S. Roucos, and H. Gish, "Vector Quantization in Speech Coding," *IEEE Proceedings, 73,* 1551–1588, Nov. 1985.

[29] T. Martin, *Acoustic Recognition of a Limited Vocabulary in Continuous Speech,* Ph.D. Thesis, Dept. Electrical Engineering Univ. Pennsylvania, 1970.

[30] W. S. McCulloch, and W. Pitts, "A Logical Calculus of the Ideas Imminent in Nervous Activity," *Bulletin of Mathematical Biophysics,* 5, 115–133, 1943.

[31] C. A. Mead, *Analog VLSI and Neural Systems,* Course Notes, Computer Science Dept., California Institute of Technology, 1986.

[32] M. Minsky, and S. Papert, *Perceptrons: An Intro-*

duction to Computational Geometry, MIT Press (1969).

[33] A. R. Moller, *Auditory Physiology,* Academic Press, New York (1983).

[34] P. Mueller, and J. Lazzaro, "A Machine for Neural Computation of Acoustical Patterns with Application to Real-Time Speech Recognition," in J. S. Denker (Ed.) *AIP Conference Proceedings 151, Neural Networks for Computing, Snowbird Utah, AIP,* 1986.

[35] D. B. Parker, "A Comparison of Algorithms for Neuron-Like Cells," in J. S. Denker (Ed.) *AIP Conference Proceedings 151, Neural Networks for Computing, Snowbird Utah, AIP,* 1986.

[36] T. Parsons, *Voice and Speech Processing,* McGraw-Hill, New York (1986).

[37] S. M. Peeling, R. K. Moore, and M. J. Tomlinson, "The Multi-Layer Perceptron as a Tool for Speech Pattern Processing Research," in *Proc. IoA Autumn Conf. on Speech and Hearing,* 1986.

[38] T. E. Posch, "Models of the Generation and Processing of Signals by Nerve Cells: A Categorically Indexed Abridged Bibliography," *USCEE Report 290,* August 1968.

[39] R. Rosenblatt, *Principles of Neurodynamics,* New York, Spartan Books (1959).

[40] D. E. Rumelhart, G. E. Hinton, and R. J. Williams, "Learning Internal Representations by Error Propagation" in D. E. Rumelhart & J. L. McClelland (Eds.), *Parallel Distributed Processing: Explorations in the Microstructure of Cognition. Vol. 1: Foundations.* MIT Press (1986).

[41] D. E. Rumelhart, and J. L. McClelland, *Parallel Distributed Processing: Explorations in the Microstructure of Cognition,* MIT Press (1986).

[42] J. P. Sage, K. Thompson, and R. S. Withers, "An Artificial Neural Network Integrated Circuit Based on MNOS/CD Principles," in J. S. Denker (Ed.) *AIP Conference Proceedings 151, Neural Networks for Computing, Snowbird Utah, AIP,* 1986.

[43] T. Sejnowski and C. R. Rosenberg, "NETtalk: A Parallel Network That Learns to Read Aloud," *Johns Hopkins Univ. Technical Report JHU/EECS-86/01,* 1986.

[44] S. Seneff, "A Computational Model for the Peripheral Auditory System: Application to Speech Recognition Research," in *Proceedings International Conference on Acoustics Speech and Signal Processing, ICASSP-86,* 4, 37.8.1-37.8.4, 1986.

[45] D. W. Tank and J. J. Hopfield, "Simple 'Neural' Optimization Networks: An A/D Converter, Signal Decision Circuit, and a Linear Programming Circuit," *IEEE Trans. Circuits Systems CAS-33,* 533–541, 1986.

[46] D. J. Wallace, "Memory and Learning in a Class of Neural Models," in B. Bunk and K. H. Mutter (Eds.) *Proceedings of the Workshop on Lattice Gauge Theory, Wuppertal, 1985,* Plenum (1986).

[47] B. Widrow, and M. E. Hoff, "Adaptive Switching Circuits," *1960 IRE WESCON Conv. Record, Part 4,* 96–104, August 1960.

[48] B. Widrow and S. D. Stearns, *Adaptive Signal Processing,* Prentice-Hall, New Jersey (1985).

Richard P. Lippmann (M'85) was born in Mineola, NY, in 1948. He received the B.S. degree in electrical engineering from the Polytechnic Inst. of Brooklyn in 1970 and the S.M. and Ph.D. degrees in electrical engineering from the Massachusetts Institute of Technology, in 1973 and 1978 respectively. His S.M. thesis dealt with the psychoacoustics of intensity perception and his Ph.D. thesis with signal processing for the hearing impaired.

From 1978 to 1981 he was the Director of Communication Engineering Laboratory at the Boys Town Institute for Communication Disorders in Children, in Omaha, NE. He worked on speech recognition, speech training aids for deaf children, sound alerting aids for the deaf, and signal processing for hearing aids. In 1981 he joined the MIT Lincoln Laboratory in Lexington, MA. He has worked on speech recognition, on speech I/O systems, and on routing and system control of circuit-switched networks. His current interests include speech recognition, neural net algorithms, statistics, and human physiology, memory, and learning.

Reprinted from IEEE Transactions on Systems, Man, and Cybernetics 2(5), November 1972, pp. 643-657.

Characteristics of Random Nets of Analog Neuron-Like Elements

SHUN-ICHI AMARI, MEMBER, IEEE

***Abstract*—The dynamic behavior of randomly connected analog neuron-like elements that process pulse-frequency modulated signals is investigated from the macroscopic point of view. By extracting two statistical parameters, the macroscopic state equations are derived in terms of these parameters under some hypotheses on the stochastics of microscopic states. It is shown that a random net of statistically symmetric structure is monostable or bistable, and the stability criteria are explicitly given. Random nets consisting of many different classes of elements are also analyzed. Special attention is paid to nets of randomly connected excitatory and inhibitory elements. It is shown that a stable oscillation exists in such a net—in contrast with the fact that no stable oscillations exist in a net of statistically symmetric structure even if negative as well as positive synaptic weights are permitted at a time. The results are checked by computer-simulated experiments.**

Manuscript received April 4, 1971. This work was supported by the Matsunaga Science Foundation.

The author is with the Department of Mathematical Engineering and Instrumentation Physics, University of Tokyo, Tokyo, Japan.

I. Introduction

IT IS BELIEVED that the brain, consisting of an enormous number of neurons, has a stable structure in the sense that the failure of a certain fraction of neurons seldom destroys its function. For this reason, the macroscopic viewpoint is well thought of as an approach to understanding the information-processing manner of neural networks. Networks of randomly connected neuron-like elements have been used by many investigators (e.g., [1]–[6]) for the purpose of clarifying the macroscopic characteristics of neural networks.

In a series of investigations ([7]–[15], etc.), random nets of symmetrical structure were studied by adopting the total activity level that designates the percentage of exciting elements, as a quantity representing the macroscopic state of a net. (Additional large-scale nonuniform random nets are also studied as systems composed of random nets [14], [15].) The main concern of the preceding investigations is the dynamics of the activity level, and it has been shown in various ways that random nets are monostable, bistable, or oscillatory according to the statistical properties of connection weights and threshold values of the component elements. It is pointed out by Rozonoer [9], in analogy with the chaos hypothesis of statistical mechanics, that some stochastic hypotheses are indispensable for the theoretical treatment of random nets. A theoretical analysis has been given by Amari [14] for random nets of simple threshold elements or McCulloch–Pitts formal neurons by extracting two parameters that depend on the statistics of connection weights and thresholds. It has been shown that these parameters are sufficient to determine the network characteristics, and the stability criteria for random nets have explicitly been given in terms of these parameters.

It is difficult, however, to apply the theoretical methods adopted in these investigations to those nets whose elements have a refractory period of more than one. If the refractory period plays an important role, a theory should take it into account. It is convenient for the treatment of a refractory period to introduce a more macroscopic standpoint from which the input and output signals are considered to be analog quantities represented by pulse frequencies and time is treated as a continuous parameter. The property of the refractory period to prevent the output pulse frequency from increasing indefinitely appears in the macroscopic model as the nonlinear saturation character of the output function of an element. Hence, by studying random nets of analog neuron-like elements, the refractory period effect is fully taken into account. Symmetric random nets consisting of analog elements have already been discussed by Averbukh [16] under a restricting condition.

The present paper aims at the theoretical study of characteristics of random nets of analog neuron-like elements consisting of not only one homogeneous class but of many different classes of elements. The macroscopic state equations that describe the dynamic behavior of the activity level will be obtained for random nets of symmetrical structure under a stochastic hypothesis on the microscopic states. In deriving the equations two statistical parameters are extracted that are sufficient to determine the network characteristics. The stability criteria of nets are explicitly given in terms of these parameters, and it is proved that random nets are monostable or bistable according to their statistical properties. The validity of the equations is confirmed by comparing the theoretical results with computer-simulated experiments.

The macroscopic state equations will also be obtained for random nets consisting of several different classes of elements. Random nets consisting of two kinds of elements, the excitatory and inhibitory, are of special interest and are studied in detail. It will be shown that these nets are not only monostable, bistable, or tristable, but also oscillatory according to their statistical properties. It is noteworthy that stable oscillations exist in random nets consisting of excitatory and inhibitory elements, whereas no stable oscillations exist in a random net consisting of one homogeneous class of elements. It may be speculated that the brain wave is produced by the interaction of such oscillators having various periods.

II. Random Nets of Analog Neuron-Like Elements

A. Analog Neuron-Like Elements

Let us consider a neuron-like element that has n inputs and one output. The state of an element is represented by a scalar u_0, called the potential, which may be compared to the time-average of the membrane potential of a neuron. The dynamic behavior of the potential is described by a differential equation as follows. Potential u_0 increases in proportion to the weighted sum $(1/n) \sum w_i x_i$ of the input variables x_i, $i = 1,2,\cdots,n$, where w_i is called the (synaptic) weight of the ith input, and it decays with time constant τ. By choosing an appropriate time scale, τ can be put equal to one without loss of generality. Hence the potential is subject to

$$\frac{du_0(t)}{dt} = \frac{1}{n} \sum w_i x_i(t) - u_0(t) \tag{1}$$

where $x_i(t)$ is the value of the ith input at time t. Since $x_i(t)$ represents an input pulse rate at time t, the effect of temporal summation of inputs is summarized in the equation as well as the spatial summation.

The output $x(t)$ of an element is determined by the potential $u_0(t)$. It is written in terms of a monotonically increasing function $\phi(u_0)$, called an output function, as

$$x = \phi(u_0 - h) \tag{2}$$

where h is a quantity called the threshold value. The output x is also an analog quantity representing the output pulse rate.

B. Microscopic Consideration on Output Function

The character of an output function is closely related to the refractory period. The relation is briefly considered here (see also [16]). Microscopically observed, the output of an element is a series of pulses whose time rate is understood as the macroscopic output x. In order to explain the mechanism of pulse emission, one more (microscopic) state quantity, the inner threshold, is needed, together with the potential. A pulse is emitted whenever the potential u_0 exceeds the inner threshold. After a pulse emission, the inner threshold grows and remains infinitely large for an interval called the absolute refractory period, and then it gradually decreases. Let $h(\tau)$ be the inner threshold at τ after a pulse emission. Then $h(\tau) = \infty$, for $0 < \tau \leq \tau_a$, and $h(\tau)$ is continuous and monotonically decreasing for $\tau > \tau_a$, where τ_a is the absolute refractory period. Obviously, an element cannot fire (i.e., cannot emit a pulse) during the absolute refractory period.

Microscopically speaking, the potential rapidly decays after the time when a pulse is emitted. However, it will soon recover and maintain the former level, provided the input pulses continue to arrive at constant rates. When the recovering time constant is small, this rapid fluctuation of u_0 can be disregarded, and u_0 is treated as a macroscopic quantity obtained by smoothing it. The change of u_0 is therefore considered to be sufficiently slow compared with that of the inner threshold.

Assume that the potential maintains a level u_0 for a period. Then the element continues to emit pulses at every such τ satisfying $h(\tau) = u_0$, i.e., $\tau = h^{-1}(u_0)$, where h^{-1} is the inverse function of $h(\tau)$.[1] Therefore, the output pulse rate is given by $1/\tau = 1/h^{-1}(u_0)$. Since the absolute refractory period is τ_a, the maximum rate is limited to $1/\tau_a$. It is convenient to normalize the output in such a manner that the maximum output is equal to 1. The normalized output x is determined by

$$x = \frac{\tau_a}{\tau} = \frac{\tau_a}{h^{-1}(u_0)}. \tag{3}$$

Let h be the inner threshold at $\tau = 2\tau_a$,

$$h = h(2\tau_a)$$

which really agrees with the (macroscopic) threshold of an element. Obviously, when $u_0 = h$, $x = \frac{1}{2}$ holds, and the output pulse rate is exactly one-half of the maximum. By setting

$$\tau_a h^{-1}(u_0) = \phi(u_0 - h) \tag{4}$$

the output x is written as

$$x = \phi(u_0 - h).$$

The output function $\phi(u)$ is thus derived from the function $h(\tau)$ representing the refractory characteristics. The output function $\phi(u)$ is a monotonically increasing continuous function satisfying

$$\phi(-\infty) = 0 \qquad \phi(0) = \tfrac{1}{2} \qquad \phi(\infty) = 1.$$

In the following, instead of u_0, the new potential

$$u = u_0 - h \tag{5}$$

measured from the threshold h will be used for simplicity's sake. Equations (1) and (2) are then replaced by

$$\frac{du}{dt} = \frac{1}{n}\sum w_i x_i - u - h \tag{1'}$$

$$x = \phi(u). \tag{2'}$$

C. Random Nets of Neuron-Like Elements

A neuron-like element is specified by n weights w_i, $i = 1,2,\cdots,n$, a threshold h, and an output function $\phi(u)$. Consider a net consisting of n elements. Let u_i, h_i, and x_i be, respectively, the potential, the threshold, and the output of the ith element. Moreover, let $w_{i1},w_{i2},\cdots,w_{in}$ be the weights of the ith element. Assume that these n elements are interconnected in such a manner that the output x_i of the ith element is fed back to all the elements as the ith input. In this case, the weight w_{ij} represents the transmission efficiency of a signal from the jth element to the ith element. The weight may be zero or negative. When it is zero, no connection exists from the jth element to the ith element. The behavior of the net is described by the following set of equations:

$$\frac{du_i(t)}{dt} = \frac{1}{n}\sum_j w_{ij}x_j(t) - h_i - u_i(t) \tag{6}$$

$$x_i(t) = \phi(u_i(t)). \tag{7}$$

In order to study the macroscopic characteristics of large-scale nets, the concept of random nets will be theoretically introduced. When weights w_{ij} and thresholds h_i are random variables, a net is called random.[2] When all the weights w_{ij} are independent random variables subject to one and the same probability distribution, and when all the thresholds h_i are also independent random variables subject to another probability distribution, a random net is called symmetric. A symmetric random net can be considered as a net composed of one homogeneous class of random elements. The characteristics of symmetric random nets will be studied first. Nonsymmetrical nets or nets composed of several different classes of random elements will be analyzed in Sections V and VI.

The macroscopic characteristics that we intend to clarify are those that depend only on the statistical properties of a random net and hold for almost all sample nets. As the statistical parameters of a net, the expectation $\overline{w}$ and the variance $\sigma_w{}^2$ of weights w_{ij}, as well as the expectation $\overline{h}$ and the variance $\sigma_h{}^2$ of thresholds h_i, are chosen. In terms of these parameters the equations governing the macroscopic state of a random net will be derived provided the number of constituent elements is sufficiently large.

III. Macroscopic State Equations

A. Macroscopic State

The microscopic state of a random net has been described by the potentials $u_i(t)$ of the component elements. It is difficult, however, to solve the equations governing the $u_i(t)$. Moreover, what is interesting is, in many cases, not the microscopic behavior of each element, but the macroscopic behavior of a net as a whole. Therefore, by introducing variables representing the macroscopic state of a net, the macroscopic equations can be set up. For a symmetric random net, the macroscopic variables are given by symmetric functions of the microscopic variables $u_i(t)$. As such variables, the following two quantities will be chosen:

$$U = \frac{1}{n}\sum u_i \tag{8}$$

$$V = \frac{1}{n}\sum (u_i - U)^2. \tag{9}$$

These are the mean and variance, respectively, of the potentials over all the constituent elements.

Corresponding to the microscopic outputs $x_i(t)$, the two quantities

$$X = \frac{1}{n}\sum x_i \tag{10}$$

[1] When there is no τ satisfying $h(\tau) = u$, put $h^{-1}(u) = \infty$.

[2] An actual net is a sample of a random net. Weights w_{ij} and thresholds h_i of an actual net are regarded as samples of the corresponding random variables.

and

$$Y = \frac{1}{n} \sum x_i^2 \tag{11}$$

will also be used as representing the macroscopic output of a net. Obviously, X denotes the mean of the rates of pulses produced in a net.

B. Stochastic Hypothesis on Microscopic State

By integrating (6),

$$u_i(t) = \int_0^t \left\{ \frac{1}{n} \sum w_{ij} x_j(\tau) - h_i \right\} e^{\tau - t} \, d\tau + u_{i0} e^{-t}$$

is derived, where u_{i0} is the initial value of $u_i(t)$. For sufficiently large t, the term e^{-t} can be neglected. Therefore, by setting

$$\tilde{x}_j(t) = \int_0^t x_j(\tau) e^{\tau - t} \, d\tau \tag{12}$$

where $\tilde{x}_j(t)$ is the weighted mean of the past values of $x_j(t)$,

$$u_i(t) = \frac{1}{n} \sum_j w_{ij} \tilde{x}_j(t) - h_i \tag{13}$$

is derived.

Since the $n^2 + n$ parameters w_{ij} and h_i are random variables, the $u_i(t)$ are also random variables depending on them. Since the variables w_{ij} and h_i have, respectively, the same distribution functions, the $u_i(t)$ have also a common distribution function provided the initial values u_{i0} are also random variables having a common distribution function. If $\tilde{x}_i(t)$ is independent of parameters w_{jk} and h_j, $u_i(t)$ is a linear combination of the independent random variables w_{ij} and h_i, as is shown by (13). Therefore, if h_i has a normal distribution, it is expected that the distribution of $u_i(t)$ is nearly normal. However, $\tilde{x}_j(t)$ is determined by $u_j(t - \tau)$, $0 < \tau < t$, so that it is also a random variable depending on all the parameters w_{ik} and h_i. Therefore, $u_i(t)$ is not a simple linear combination of w_{ij} and h_i, and its distribution is very complicated.

It should be noted, however, that though $\tilde{x}_j(t)$ directly depends on w_{jk} and h_j, it depends on all the other w_{ik} and h_i, $i \neq j$ in a very indirect, complicated, and chaotic manner. Therefore, if n is sufficiently large, all the chaotic dependency being averaged out, the stochastic property of the sum $(1/n) \sum_j w_{ij} \tilde{x}_j(t)$ is expected to resemble that of a mere linear combination of w_{ij}.

Taking account of the preceding situations, we postulate the following hypothesis on the probability distribution of the microscopic state, provided n is sufficiently large. This hypothesis connects the macroscopic state variables U and V with the macroscopic output variables X and Y. It may be regarded as a version of Rozonoer's chaos hypothesis [9].

Hypothesis 1: All $u_i(t)$ are stochastically independent and have a common normal distribution.

By the use of this hypothesis, every macroscopic quantity can be calculated from the macroscopic state of a net. Let $f(u)$ be an arbitrary function, and let F be the mean of $f(u_i)$ over all the component elements

$$F = \frac{1}{n} \sum_i f(u_i). \tag{14}$$

Since the u_i are random variables, the macroscopic quantity F is also a random variable. Since all $f(u_i)$ have the same distribution function, the expectation $\bar{F}$ of F is calculated by

$$\bar{F} = \int_{-\infty}^{\infty} \frac{1}{\sqrt{2\pi \bar{V}}} f(u) \exp\left\{ -\frac{(u - \bar{U})^2}{2\bar{V}} \right\} du$$

where $\bar{U}$ and $\bar{V}$ denote the expectation and variance, respectively, of an arbitrary u_i. Moreover, the law of large numbers guarantees that almost all samples of F are distributed sufficiently near to the expectation $\bar{F}$ as n becomes large. In other words, for an arbitrary positive ε the probability $\Pr\{|F - \bar{F}| > \varepsilon\}$ can be made as small as desired by choosing a sufficiently large n.

Since the variance of F is proportional to $1/n$, F may be written as

$$F = \bar{F} + O\left(\frac{1}{\sqrt{n}}\right)$$

where $O(1/\sqrt{n})$ denotes the small fluctuational term of order $1/\sqrt{n}$. When the fluctuational term is disregarded, F may be identified with $\bar{F}$, that is, a macroscopic quantity F can be regarded as a nonrandom quantity $\bar{F}$ to within a small fluctuational term of order $1/\sqrt{n}$. Since the state variables U and V themselves are macroscopic quantities of this kind, they may be regarded as nonrandom quantities except for fluctuating terms of order $1/\sqrt{n}$. These considerations are summarized in the following theorem.

Theorem 1: When n is sufficiently large for almost all samples of a random net, a macroscopic quantity F can be calculated from the macroscopic state variables U and V by

$$F = \int_{-\infty}^{\infty} \frac{1}{\sqrt{2\pi V}} f(u) \exp\left\{ -\frac{(u - U)^2}{2V} \right\} du \tag{15}$$

except for a small fluctuational term of order $1/\sqrt{n}$.

Hypothesis 1 is used only to derive Theorem 1. Therefore, if Hypothesis 1 is considered to be too severe, it may be replaced by Theorem 1. Applying Theorem 1 to the macroscopic outputs X and Y, the following corollary is obtained.

Corollary: The macroscopic outputs are connected with the macroscopic state by

$$X(U,V) = \int_{-\infty}^{\infty} \frac{1}{\sqrt{2\pi V}} \phi(u) \exp\left\{ -\frac{(u - U)^2}{2V} \right\} du \tag{16a}$$

$$Y(U,V) = \int_{-\infty}^{\infty} \frac{1}{\sqrt{2\pi V}} \phi^2(u) \exp\left\{ -\frac{(u - U)^2}{2V} \right\} du. \tag{16b}$$

When σ_w^2/n does not tend to 0 for large n,[3] one more hypothesis is needed in order to derive the macroscopic state equations.

Hypothesis 2: For large n and t, $(1/n) \sum x_i(t) \tilde{x}_i(t)$ can be approximated by Y.

[3] Such cases are treated in Appendix II.

This hypothesis may be supported by the fact pointed out in [11] that, in a discrete random net, almost all outputs $x_i(t)$ converge to 1 or 0 as t goes to infinity. This suggests that for large t

$$\tilde{x}_i(t) = x_i(t)$$

holds. When σ_w^2/n tends to 0, Hypothesis 2 is unnecessary and can be removed.

C. Macroscopic State Equations

When c_i, $i = 1,2,\cdots,n$, are n independent random variables having a common distribution function, their arithmetic mean $(1/n) \sum c_i$ coincides with the expectation $\bar{c}$ of c except for a fluctuational term of order $1/\sqrt{n}$. When the term of order $1/\sqrt{n}$ may be neglected, the mean $\sum c_i/n$ can be replaced by expectation $\bar{c}$. The macroscopic state equations are derived with the help of such replacement procedures.

Theorem 2: The macroscopic state equations are given by

$$\frac{dU}{dt} = \bar{w}X - U - \bar{h} \tag{17}$$

$$\frac{dV}{dt} = 2\left(\frac{\sigma_w^2}{n} Y + \sigma_h^2 - V\right) \tag{18}$$

where X and Y are functions of U and V.

Proof: By summing all the equations of (6) with respect to i,

$$\frac{dU}{dt} = \frac{1}{n}\sum_i \left(\frac{1}{n}\sum_j w_{ij}x_j - h_i - u_i\right)$$

$$= \frac{1}{n}\sum_j \left(\frac{1}{n}\sum_i w_{ij}\right) x_j - \frac{1}{n}\sum h_i - U$$

follows. The replacement of $\sum_i w_{ij}/n$ and $\sum h_i/n$ by $\bar{w}$ and $\bar{h}$, respectively, yields

$$\frac{dU}{dt} = \bar{w}\frac{1}{n}\sum x_i - \bar{h} - U.$$

The former equation of the theorem is derived by virtue of (10). By differentiating (9),

$$\frac{dV}{dt} \doteq \frac{2}{n}\sum (u_i - U)(\dot{u}_i - \dot{U}) \tag{19}$$

is obtained, wnere the dot denotes the time derivative, e.g.,

$$\dot{u} = \frac{du}{dt}.$$

By the use of similar but fairly complicated procedures of reduction, which are given in Appendix I, the latter equation is proved.

For further studies on the dynamic behavior of random nets, the output function $\phi(u)$ should be specified. In what follows the output function is assumed to be of the form

$$\phi(u) = \Phi\left(\frac{u}{a}\right) \tag{20}$$

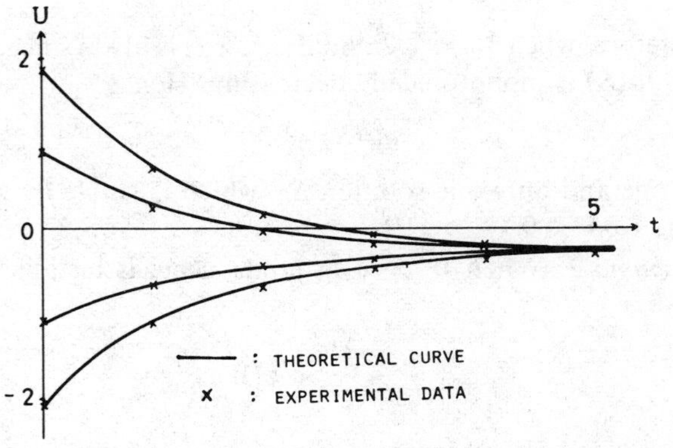

Fig. 1. Behavior of macroscopic state; $n = 100$, $\bar{w} = 1.0$, $\bar{h} = 0.7$, $\sigma_w^2 = 10.0$, $\sigma_h^2 = 1.0$, $a = 1.0$.

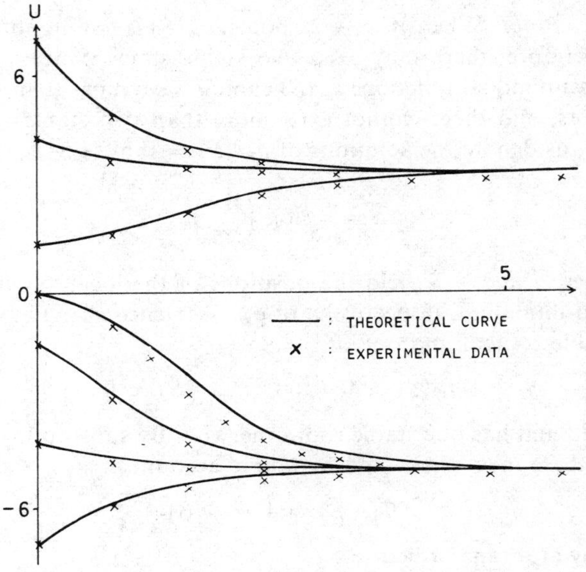

Fig. 2. Behavior of macroscopic state; $n = 100$, $\bar{w} = 8.5$, $\bar{h} = 5.0$, $\sigma_w^2 = 10.0$, $\sigma_h^2 = 1.0$, $a = 1.0$.

where $\Phi(u)$ is the integral of the normal distribution function

$$\Phi(u) = \frac{1}{\sqrt{2\pi}}\int_{-\infty}^{u} \exp\left\{-\frac{s^2}{2}\right\} ds$$

and a is a constant called the linearity factor. As is well known, $\Phi(u)$ is a monotonically increasing function, satisfying $0 < \Phi(u) < 1$, $\Phi(0) = \frac{1}{2}$. When a is large, the linearity between x and u holds within a considerably wide range of u, whereas when a becomes small, $\phi(u)$ approaches the step function, and the nonlinear character is emphasized.

When the output function is given by (20), integral calculations yield

$$X(U,V) = \int \frac{1}{\sqrt{2\pi V}} \Phi\left(\frac{u}{a}\right) \exp\left\{-\frac{(u-U)^2}{2V}\right\} du$$

$$= \Phi\left(\frac{U}{\sqrt{a^2 + V}}\right). \tag{21}$$

Therefore, when $W < \sqrt{2\pi}$ holds, $g_W'(S)$ is always negative, and $g_W(S)$ is monotonically decreasing. Hence

$$g_W(S) = 0$$

has one and only one solution S_0, which is stable by virtue of $g_W'(S_0) < 0$.

Lemma 2: When $W > \sqrt{2\pi}$ holds, a net is bistable if H satisfies

$$\left|\frac{H}{W} - \frac{1}{2}\right| < f(W) \tag{30}$$

and monostable otherwise, where

$$f(x) = \Phi\left(\sqrt{\log\left(\frac{x^2}{2\pi}\right)}\right) - \frac{1}{x}\sqrt{\log\left(\frac{x^2}{2\pi}\right)} - \frac{1}{2}. \tag{31}$$

Proof: When $W > \sqrt{2\pi}$ holds, $g_W(S)$ is not monotonic. Therefore, there may exist two stable states. Since $g_W'(S)$ is a unimodal function, $g_W(S)$ cannot have more than three roots, and there cannot exist more than two stable roots. Let us denote the solutions of $g_W'(S) = 0$ by $\pm\tilde{S}$:

$$\tilde{S} = \sqrt{\log\left(\frac{W^2}{2\pi}\right)}. \tag{32}$$

Then $\tilde{S}$ and $-\tilde{S}$ yield the positions of the local maximum and minimum, respectively, of $g_W(S)$. Hence $g_W(S)$ has two stable roots if and only if

$$g_W(\tilde{S}) > 0 \quad \text{and} \quad g_W(-\tilde{S}) < 0$$

hold and has one stable root otherwise. By substituting (32) in these inequalities and by taking account of

$$\Phi(-\tilde{S}) = 1 - \Phi(\tilde{S})$$

they are transformed to

$$\frac{H}{W} < \Phi(\tilde{S}) - \frac{\tilde{S}}{W} = f(W) + \tfrac{1}{2}$$

$$\frac{H}{W} > 1 - \left\{\Phi(\tilde{S}) + \frac{\tilde{S}}{W}\right\} = -\{f(W) + \tfrac{1}{2}\}.$$

By combining the preceding two inequalities, the lemma is proved.

From the foregoing two lemmas, the following theorem is derived as one of the main results of the present paper.

Theorem 4: Symmetric random nets are categorized into the following two classes according to their normalized connection weights W:

1) monostable net: $W \leq \sqrt{2\pi}$;
2) monostable–bistable net: $W > \sqrt{2\pi}$.

A net of the first class is monostable irrespective of H, whereas the stability of a net of the second class depends on H. A net of the second class is bistable when H satisfies

$$\left|\frac{H}{W} - \frac{1}{2}\right| < f(W)$$

and monostable otherwise.

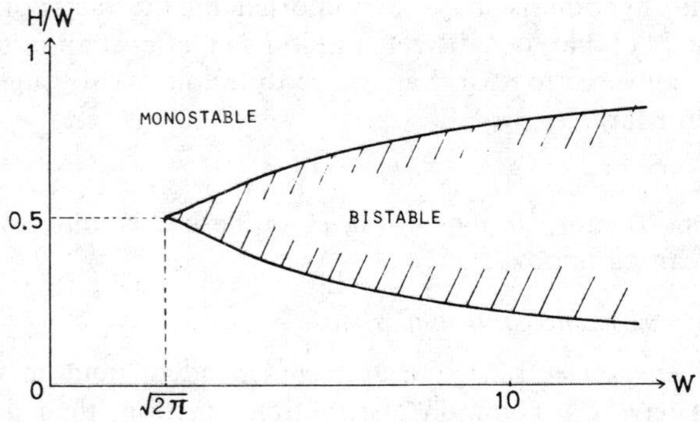

Fig. 3. Stability of random nets.

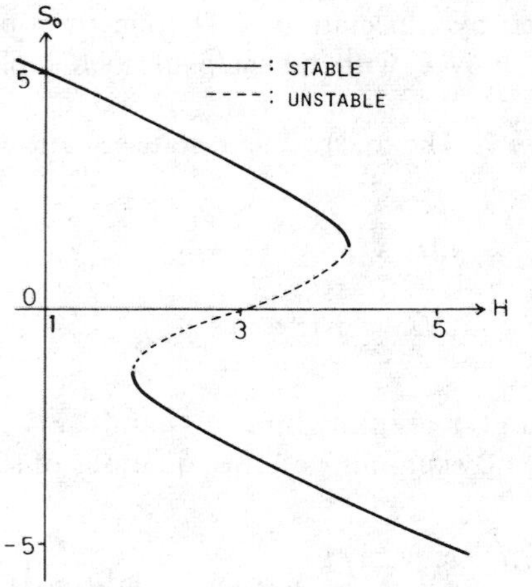

Fig. 4. Equilibrium states versus H; $W = 6.0$.

The stability of symmetrical random nets is thus clarified. The stability criteria of random nets are graphically shown in Fig. 3. The stable state S_0 changes with H. Moreover, in a monostable–bistable net, the stability itself changes with H. The importance of this feature is understood from the fact that H can be controlled by the outputs of other nets connected thereto (see [14]). Such a feature cannot be obtained by a linear model of a random net. In Fig. 4 an example of the relation between the stable states S_0 and H is shown for a net of the second class.

It is interesting to note that random nets of the analog type have a similar structure to that of the discrete type studied in [14] except that a trivial stable oscillation of period 2 exists for a discrete random net of $W < -\sqrt{\pi/2}$.

V. Random Nets Consisting of Different Classes of Elements

The random nets thus far considered are composed of one homogeneous class of random elements in the sense that every component element of a net has the same stochastic structure. Random nets consisting of many classes of elements will now be studied. Consider a random net consisting of m classes of elements. Let $u_i^{\alpha}(t)$ be the potential of the ith element belonging to the αth class, $\alpha = 1,2,\cdots,m$, $i = 1,2,\cdots,n_\alpha$, where n_α is the number of

D. Results of Computer-Simulated Experiments

Since the macroscopic state equations are derived under assumptions that are difficult to prove theoretically, they should be checked by experiments. A series of computer-simulated experiments were carried out by HITAC 5020E in the Computation Center at the University of Tokyo. In the experiments, the number of elements ranges from 5 to 100. Parameters w_{ij} and h_i and initial values u_{i0} are produced from the normal-random-number generator. As has been stated, the mean values $\sum\sum w_{ij}/n^2$ and $\sum h_i/n$ coincide with the prescribed parameters $\bar{w}$ and $\bar{h}$ only to within fluctuational terms of $O(1/n)$ and $O(1/\sqrt{n})$, respectively. When n is not large, the effect of fluctuation is not negligible. In order to avoid the preceding shortcoming, the mean values $\sum\sum w_{ij}/n^2$ and $\sum h_i/n$ are adopted as the macroscopic parameters $\bar{w}$ and $\bar{h}$, respectively, instead of as the theoretical expectations of w_{ij} and h_i.

Figs. 1 and 2 show typical examples of the experiments, where the behavior of U, starting from various initial values, is plotted. The experimental data agree sufficiently well with the theoretical curves derived from the macroscopic state equations. The macroscopic equations hold fairly well even when n is small. Even when n is 10 the experimental data were in qualitative agreement for many cases.

IV. Stability of Random Nets

A. Simplified State Equation

When the probability distribution of w_{ij} is independent of n, σ_w^2/n converges to 0 as n becomes large. In this case the term σ_w^2/n can be neglected if n is sufficiently large. The stability of random nets is studied in this section under this assumption. The case in which σ_w^2/n is not negligible will be treated in Appendix II.[4]

If the term σ_w^2/n vanishes, (18) simplifies to

$$\frac{dV}{dt} = 2(\sigma_h^2 - V)$$

the solution of which is given by

$$V(t) = \sigma_h^2(1 - e^{-2t}) + V_0 e^{-2t} \tag{22}$$

where V_0 is the initial value of $V(t)$. Since $V(t)$ rapidly converges to σ_h^2 independently of the value of $U(t)$, by disregarding $V(t)$, macroscopic potential U only may be treated as the macroscopic state variable.

So far as the behavior of a net for large t is concerned, the limit value σ_h^2 may be substituted for V. In this case, by virtue of (21), the macroscopic state equation reduces to

$$\frac{dU}{dt} = \bar{w}\Phi\left(\frac{U}{\sigma}\right) - \bar{h} - U \tag{23}$$

where

$$\sigma = \sqrt{a^2 + \sigma_h^2}. \tag{24}$$

By dividing both sides of (23) by σ,

$$\frac{dS}{dt} = W\Phi(S) - H - S \tag{25}$$

is derived, where

$$W = \frac{\bar{w}}{\sigma} \tag{26}$$

$$H = \frac{\bar{h}}{\sigma} \tag{27}$$

$$S = \frac{U}{\sigma}. \tag{28}$$

Equation (25) is called the simplified state equation, and the new state variable S is called the normalized potential of a net. The macroscopic parameters W and H will be called the normalized connection weight and normalized threshold, respectively. The stability of a random net is sufficiently revealed by the simplified state equation. Therefore, the following theorem is obtained.

Theorem 3: The stability of a random net is determined by two parameters W and H.

It should be noted that the linearity factor a plays the same role as that of σ_h.

B. Stability Theorem

The stability of random nets is investigated by using the simplified state equation. A net is called monostable when it has one and only one stable equilibrium state to which every macroscopic state converges. A net is called bistable when it has exactly two stable equilibrium states to either of which every state converges. The stability criteria will explicitly be given in terms of W and H.

As is well known, equilibrium states are given by the solutions of

$$g_W(S) = 0$$

where $g_W(S)$ is the right side of (25):

$$g_W(S) = W\Phi(S) - H - S. \tag{29}$$

An equilibrium state S_0 is stable when

$$g_W'(S_0) < 0$$

and unstable when

$$g_W'(S) > 0.$$[5]

Lemma 1: When $W < \sqrt{2\pi}$ holds, a net is monostable.

Proof: The function $g_W(S)$ is continuous and satisfies

$$g_W(-\infty) = \infty \qquad g_W(\infty) = -\infty.$$

Its derivative is given by

$$g_W'(S) = \frac{W}{\sqrt{2\pi}} \exp\left\{-\frac{S^2}{2}\right\} - 1.$$

[4] When the number of inputs to an element is limited to less than a constant independently of n, σ_w^2/n does not vanish, even if n becomes large. See Appendix II.

[5] When $g_W'(S_0) = 0$ holds, a higher order derivative of $g_W(S)$ needs to be tested. Such a critical case will be omitted from the present consideration.

elements of the αth class. Let x_i^α and h_i^α be the output and the threshold of this element, respectively. Obviously, $x_i^\alpha(t)$ is determined by $u_i^\alpha(t)$ as

$$x_i^\alpha = \Phi\left(\frac{u_i^\alpha}{a_\alpha}\right) \tag{33}$$

where a_α is the linearity factor of an element of the αth class.

Let us denote by $w_{ij}^{\alpha\beta}$ the weight attached to the input that stems from the jth element of the βth class and enters into the ith element of the αth class. Then the behaviors of all the elements are described by the following microscopic state equations:

$$\frac{du_i^\alpha(t)}{dt} = \sum_{\beta=1}^{m} \frac{1}{n_\beta} \sum_{j=1}^{n_\beta} w_{ij}^{\alpha\beta} x_j^\beta(t) - h_i^\alpha - u_i^\alpha(t). \tag{34}$$

Assume that all of $w_{ij}^{\alpha\beta}$ and h_i^α are independent random variables and that all the $w_{ij}^{\alpha\beta}$ (α and β fixed) have a common probability distribution specified by indices α and β. Assume, also, that all h_i^α (α fixed) have a common distribution specified by α. Let the average and variance of $w_{ij}^{\alpha\beta}$ be denoted by $\bar{w}_{\alpha\beta}$ and $\sigma^2_{w\alpha\beta}$, respectively. Obviously, $\bar{w}_{\alpha\beta}$ represents the average connection weight from an element of the βth class to an element of the αth class. Let $\bar{h}_\alpha$ and $\sigma_{h\alpha}{}^2$ be the average and variance, respectively, of h_i^α.

The following two groups of quantities

$$U_\alpha = \frac{1}{n_\alpha} \sum_i u_i^\alpha \tag{35}$$

$$V_\alpha = \frac{1}{n_\alpha} \sum_i (u_i^\alpha - U_\alpha)^2 \tag{36}$$

are introduced as the macroscopic state variables, and

$$X_\alpha = \frac{1}{n_\alpha} \sum_i x_i^\alpha \tag{37}$$

$$Y_\alpha = \frac{1}{n_\alpha} \sum_i (x_i^\alpha)^2 \tag{38}$$

are introduced as the macroscopic outputs. In terms of these quantities, the following set of macroscopic state equations are derived in a manner quite similar to that used in Section III provided Hypotheses 1 and 2 hold for every class of elements.

Theorem 5: The macroscopic state equations for a random net of many classes of elements are given by

$$\frac{dU_\alpha}{dt} = \sum_\beta \bar{w}_{\alpha\beta} X_\beta - \bar{h}_\alpha - U_\alpha \tag{39}$$

$$\frac{dV_\alpha}{dt} = 2\left(\sum_\beta \frac{\sigma^2_{w\alpha\beta}}{n_\beta} Y_\beta + \sigma_{h\alpha}{}^2 - V_\alpha\right) \tag{40}$$

$$X_\alpha = \Phi\left(\frac{U_\alpha}{\sqrt{a_\alpha{}^2 + V}}\right) \tag{41}$$

$$Y_\alpha = \int \{\Phi(u)\}^2 \frac{1}{\sqrt{2\pi V_\alpha}} \exp\left\{-\frac{(u - U_\alpha)^2}{2V_\alpha}\right\} du. \tag{42}$$

In the case where $\sigma^2_{w\alpha\beta}/n$ can be neglected, (40) is easily solved to give

$$V_\alpha = \sigma_{h\alpha}{}^2$$

for large t. Put

$$\sigma_\alpha{}^2 = a_\alpha{}^2 + \sigma_{h\alpha}{}^2 \tag{43}$$

$$W_{\alpha\beta} = \frac{\bar{w}_{\alpha\beta}}{\sigma_\alpha} \tag{44}$$

$$H_\alpha = \frac{\bar{h}_\alpha}{\sigma_\alpha}. \tag{45}$$

Then, in terms of the normalized state variables

$$S_\alpha = \frac{U_\alpha}{\sigma_\alpha} \tag{46}$$

the simplified state equations are derived by substituting $\sigma_{h\alpha}{}^2$ for V_α.

Theorem 6: The simplified state equation for a random net of many classes of elements is given by

$$\frac{dS_\alpha}{dt} = \sum_\beta W_{\alpha\beta}\Phi(S_\beta) - H_\alpha - S_\alpha. \tag{47}$$

If the apparent threshold of the αth class is defined by

$$\tilde{H}_\alpha = H_\alpha - \sum_{\beta\neq\alpha} W_{\alpha\beta}\Phi(S_\beta) = H_\alpha - \sum_{\beta\neq\alpha} W_{\alpha\beta}X_\beta$$

the equation governing the normalized state S_α is written as

$$\frac{dS_\alpha}{dt} = W_{\alpha\alpha}\Phi(S_\alpha) - \tilde{H}_\alpha - S_\alpha$$

where $\tilde{H}_\alpha$ depends on the $S_\beta(\beta \neq \alpha)$. In the preceding formulation, it is shown that the activity of one type of elements affects the activity of another type by changing the apparent threshold of the latter. In other words, the normalized threshold H_α of one type of elements can be controlled by the outputs of other types of elements as has been pointed out in [14] in the case of discrete RATEN systems.

VI. Random Nets Consisting of Excitatory and Inhibitory Elements

A. Three Types of Nets

Random nets consisting of excitatory and inhibitory classes of elements are studied in this section. These nets are especially interesting because of the physiological fact that the neuron nets consist of excitatory and inhibitory elements. An excitatory element is characterized by the fact that the output stemming from it never enters into another element with a negative weight, and an inhibitory element is, on the contrary, characterized by the fact that its output never enters into another element with a positive weight. Let excitatory and inhibitory elements constitute the first and second classes, respectively. Then W_{11} and W_{21} are positive, and W_{12} and W_{22} are negative. For the sake of

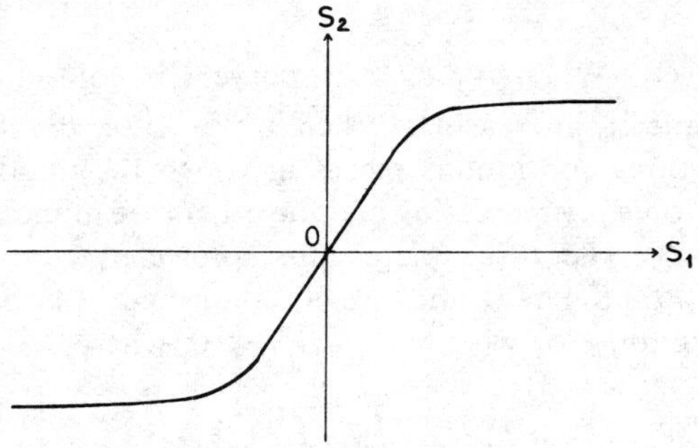

Fig. 5. Equilibrium curve II.

convenience put

$$W_1 = W_{11} > 0 \qquad W_2 = -W_{22} > 0$$

$$K_{12} = -W_{12} > 0 \qquad K_{21} = W_{21} > 0.$$

Then, the simplified macroscopic equations are written, in this case, as

$$\frac{dS_1}{dt} = f_1(S_1,S_2) = W_1\Phi(S_1) - K_{12}\Phi(S_2) - H_1 - S_1 \tag{48}$$

$$\frac{dS_2}{dt} = f_2(S_1,S_2) = K_{21}\Phi(S_1) - W_2\Phi(S_2) - H_2 - S_2. \tag{49}$$

It is not so easy to study the stability of the preceding equations in general. For the sake of simplicity, we restrict ourselves to cases where the relations

$$H_1 = \tfrac{1}{2}(W_1 - K_{12}) \tag{50}$$

$$H_2 = \tfrac{1}{2}(-W_2 + K_{21}) \tag{51}$$

hold. In these cases

$$f_1(0,0) = f_2(0,0) = 0$$

is satisfied, so that the origin $S_1 = S_2 = 0$ is always an equilibrium state. Even though the foregoing special cases only are analyzed, some interesting characteristics that random nets consisting of excitatory and inhibitory elements possess are sufficiently revealed. One of the most interesting characteristics is the existence of stable oscillations that never appear in a net consisting of one homogeneous class of elements.

An equilibrium state is given by a pair (S_1,S_2) of solutions of the simultaneous equations

$$f_1(S_1,S_2) = 0 \tag{52}$$

$$f_2(S_1,S_2) = 0 \tag{53}$$

When the points satisfying (52) are plotted on the S_1–S_2 plane, where S_1 is the abscissa and S_2 is the ordinate, a curve, called curve I, is obtained. Similarly, the points satisfying (53) constitute a curve called curve II. These two curves will be called the equilibrium curves, and their intersections denote the equilibrium states.

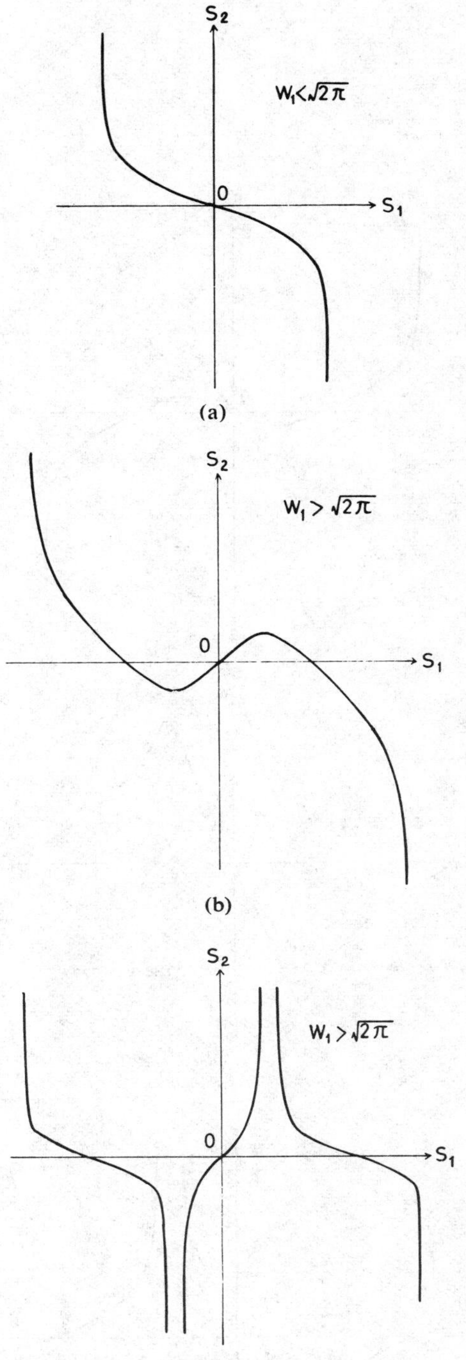

Fig. 6. Equilibrium curve I.

The features of the equilibrium curves are summarized in the following lemmas (see also Figs. 5 and 6), whose proofs are given in Appendix III.

Lemma 3: Curve II is continuous, monotonically increasing, symmetric with respect to the origin, and bounded.

Lemma 4: Curve I is symmetric with respect to the origin and is defined within a finite interval of S_1, diverging to ∞ and $-\infty$ when S_1 tends to the lower and upper bounds,

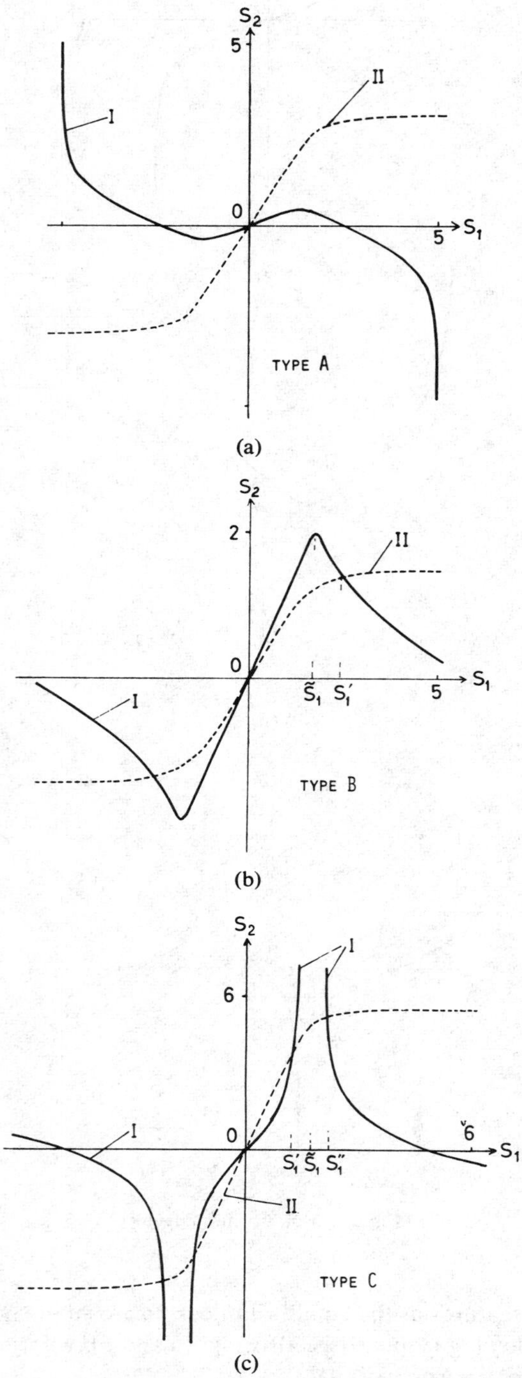

Fig. 7. Three types of random nets. (a) $W_1 = 5$, $K_{12} = -5$, $W_2 = -4$, $K_{21} = 10$. (b) $W_1 = 12$, $W_2 = -4$, $K_{12} = -8$, $K_{21} = 6$. (c) $W_1 = 10$, $W_2 = -4$, $K_{12} = -5$, $K_{21} = 15$.

respectively. When $W_1 \le \sqrt{2\pi}$, curve I is continuous and monotonically increasing. When $W_1 > \sqrt{2\pi}$, curve I consists of three continuous pieces in which the middle piece is monotonically increasing and the others are monotonically decreasing. The three pieces are connected continuously when $g_{W_1}(-\tilde{S}_1) > 0$ and are disconnected, all the pieces diverging to $\pm\infty$, when $g_{W_1}(-\tilde{S}_1) \le 0$, where

$$\tilde{S}_1 = \sqrt{\log\left(\frac{W_1{}^2}{2\pi}\right)}.$$

By virtue of the preceding lemmas, it is shown that three types of nets, A, B, and C, are obtained according to the figures of the equilibrium curves. When the curves intersect at the origin only (Fig. 7(a)), a net is called type A. When the curves intersect at three points (Fig. 7(b)), a net is called type B. When the curves intersect at five points, a net is called type C (Fig. 7(c)).[6]

Let $d_{\mathrm{I}0}$ and $d_{\mathrm{II}0}$ be the tangents of curves I and II, respectively, at the origin. They are explicitly given by

$$d_{\mathrm{I}0} = \frac{-\partial f_1(0,0)/\partial S_1}{\partial f_1(0,0)/\partial S_2} = \frac{W_1 - \sqrt{2\pi}}{K_{12}}$$

$$d_{\mathrm{II}0} = \frac{-\partial f_2(0,0)/\partial S_1}{\partial f_2(0,0)/\partial S_2} = \frac{K_{21}}{W_2 + \sqrt{2\pi}}$$

where $\Phi'(0) = 1/\sqrt{2\pi}$ is taken into account. A net of type B is distinguished from the others by the relation $d_{\mathrm{I}0} > d_{\mathrm{II}0}$ which is expressed in terms of the macroscopic parameters as

$$K_{12}K_{21} < (W_1 - \sqrt{2\pi})(W_2 + \sqrt{2\pi}). \qquad (54)$$

The following criteria for classification of nets are easily derived.

Classification Criteria: For a type B net, (54) holds, and for a type A or type C net, the contrary of (54) holds. In the latter case, when curve I consists of three split pieces (i.e., $g_W(-\tilde{S}_1) \le 0$ holds), a net is type C. Roughly speaking, a type A net is distinguished from a type C according to whether the local maximum of curve I (which is attained at $S_1 = \tilde{S}_1$) lies below curve II or not.

B. Stability Lemmas

As is well known from the theory of differential equations, the stability of an equilibrium state (S_1, S_2) can be examined by the matrix

$$J = \begin{bmatrix} \dfrac{\partial f_1}{\partial S_1} & \dfrac{\partial f_1}{\partial S_2} \\ \dfrac{\partial f_2}{\partial S_1} & \dfrac{\partial f_2}{\partial S_2} \end{bmatrix}$$

evaluated at that point. An equilibrium state is stable when two conditions, CI and CII, hold[7] and unstable when at least one of the conditions does not hold:

CI: the determinant of J is positive;
CII: the trace of J is negative.

By differentiating $f_1(S_1,S_2)$ and $f_2(S_1,S_2)$, the matrix J can be explicitly calculated:

$$J = \frac{1}{\sqrt{2\pi}}$$

$$\begin{bmatrix} W_1 \exp\left\{-\dfrac{S_1{}^2}{2}\right\} - \sqrt{2\pi} & -K_{12}\exp\left\{-\dfrac{S_2{}^2}{2}\right\} \\ K_{21}\exp\left\{-\dfrac{S_1{}^2}{2}\right\} & -W_2\exp\left\{-\dfrac{S_2{}^2}{2}\right\} - \sqrt{2\pi} \end{bmatrix} \tag{55}$$

Since $\partial f_1/\partial S_2$ and $\partial f_2/\partial S_2$ are negative, CI is written as

$$\frac{-\partial f_1/\partial S_1}{\partial f_1/\partial S_2} < \frac{-\partial f_2/\partial S_1}{\partial f_2/\partial S_2}$$

which is equivalent to

$$d_{\mathrm{I}} < d_{\mathrm{II}}$$

where d_{I} and d_{II} are the tangents of curves I and II, respectively, at the equilibrium point. Therefore, the following lemma is obtained.

Lemma 5: An equilibrium state is stable when both of

CI: $d_{\mathrm{I}} < d_{\mathrm{II}}$,

CII: $W_1 \exp\left\{-\dfrac{S_1{}^2}{2}\right\} - W_2 \exp\left\{-\dfrac{S_2{}^2}{2}\right\} < 2\sqrt{2\pi}$

hold, and is unstable, when at least one of the conditions does not hold.

When condition CI is applied to the origin, the condition

$$d_{\mathrm{I}0} < d_{\mathrm{II}0}$$

is obtained, which is in contradiction to (54). When condition CII is applied to the origin, it reduces to

$$\mathrm{CII}_0\colon\ W_1 - W_2 < 2\sqrt{2\pi}.$$

It is difficult to obtain the general criteria for the existence or nonexistence of a limit cycle. One simple criterion is given by the following lemma.

Lemma 6: When $W_1 \leq 2\sqrt{2\pi}$ holds, no limit cycles exist.

Proof: As is well known, when $\partial f_1/\partial S_1 + \partial f_2/\partial S_2$ has a constant sign in region D of the S_1–S_2 plane, no limit cycles exist in D (Bendixson's theorem). When $W_1 \leq 2\sqrt{2\pi}$,

$$\sqrt{2\pi}\left(\frac{\partial f_1}{\partial S_1} + \frac{\partial f_2}{\partial S_2}\right) = W_1 \exp\left\{-\frac{S_1{}^2}{2}\right\} - W_2 \exp\left\{-\frac{S_2{}^2}{2}\right\} - 2\sqrt{2\pi} < 0$$

always holds, so that no limit cycles exist for such a net.

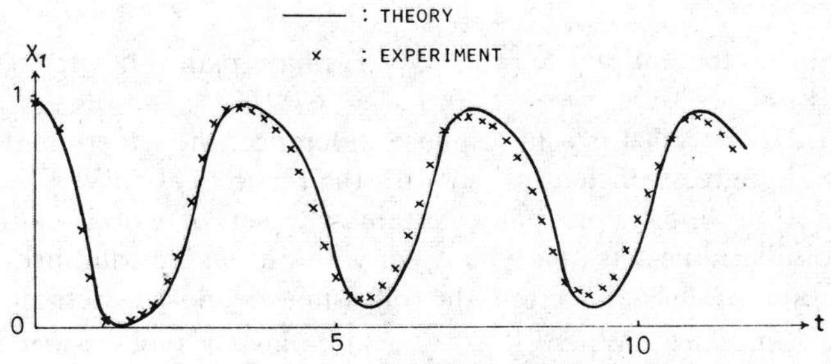

Fig. 8. Waveform of oscillation of type A net.

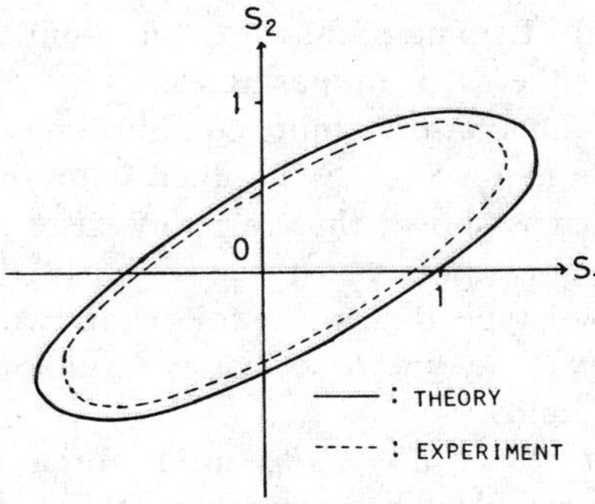

Fig. 9. Stable limit cycle of type A net.

C. *Stability Theorems*

The stability of the three types of net is studied with the help of the preceding lemmas.

Theorem 7: A random net of type A has a stable oscillation but no stable equilibrium states when the contrary of CII_0

$$\overline{\mathrm{CII}_0}\colon\ W_1 - W_2 > 2\sqrt{2\pi}$$

holds and has one and only one stable state at the origin when CII_0 holds.

Proof: The origin is the only equilibrium state of a type A net for which $d_{\mathrm{II}0} > d_{\mathrm{I}0}$ is always satisfied. Therefore, CI always holds, and hence the origin is stable when CII_0 is satisfied. On the contrary, when $\overline{\mathrm{CII}_0}$ is satisfied, the origin is unstable, and no stable states exist. Since $\Phi(S)$ is a bounded function, for sufficiently large $E = S_1{}^2 + S_2{}^2$,

$$\frac{dE}{dt} < 0$$

holds. Therefore, there are no solutions that tend to infinity. Hence by the Poincare–Bendixson theorem, at least a limit cycle representing a stable oscillation exists.

It is interesting that a stable oscillation exists in a net composed of excitatory and inhibitory kinds of elements, whereas no such oscillations exist in a random net composed of one homogeneous class of elements even if both positive and negative synaptic weights are included in it at a time.

Computer simulations were also carried out for various types of nets consisting of 100 excitatory and 100 inhibitory elements with satisfactory results. Fig. 8 shows an example of the waveform of X_1 for an astable type A net, and Fig. 9

shows the limit cycle in the S_1–S_2 phase plane ($W_1 = 10.0$, $W_2 = -4.0$, $K_{12} = -12.0$, $K_{21} = 6.0$, $H_1 = -1.06$, $H_2 = 1.07$). Except for a little phase difference, the experimental data agree sufficiently well with the theoretical curve.

It is not theoretically certain whether or not a stable oscillation exists in a type A net with one stable equilibrium state. In this connection, the following corollary is obtained.

Corollary: When $W_1 \leq 2\sqrt{2\pi}$ holds, a type A net is monostable.

Proof: When $W_1 \leq 2\sqrt{2\pi}$, CII_0 is automatically satisfied, and the net has the equilibrium state at the origin only. By virtue of Lemma 6, there exist no limit cycles in the net. Therefore, the net is monostable.

A type B net has two more equilibrium states, denoted by (S_1', S_2') and $(-S_1', -S_2')$, other than the origin. From Fig. 7(b), it is shown that in many cases $S_1' \geq \tilde{S}_1$ holds, where $\tilde{S}_1$ corresponds to the position of the maximum of curve I. For type B nets, the following two theorems hold.

Theorem 8: A type B net has two stable states, provided $S_1' \geq \tilde{S}_1$ holds.

Proof: Since $d_{10} > d_{\mathrm{II}0}$ holds for a type B net, the origin is unstable. There exist two other equilibrium states, which we denote by (S_1', S_2') and $(-S_1', -S_2')$. Obviously CI holds for these states (see Fig. 7(b)). Since $\tilde{S}_1$ is defined by

$$W_1 \exp\left\{-\frac{\tilde{S}_1^2}{2}\right\} = \sqrt{2\pi}$$

$S_1' \geq \tilde{S}_1$ guarantees

$$W_1 \exp\left\{-\frac{S_1'^2}{2}\right\} \leq \sqrt{2\pi}.$$

Therefore, CII holds by a sufficient margin, and the states are stable. (From this, we conjecture that a type B net always has two stable states.)

Theorem 9: A type B net has two stable states when CII_0 holds.

Proof: For a type B net, inequality (54)

$$K_{12}K_{21} < (W_1 - \sqrt{2\pi})(W_2 + \sqrt{2\pi})$$

holds. Moreover, for (S_1', S_2'), $d_1 < d_{\mathrm{II}}$ or

$$K_{12}K_{21} \exp\left\{-\frac{S_1'^2 + S_2'^2}{2}\right\} > \left\{W_1 \exp\left(-\frac{S_1'^2}{2}\right) - \sqrt{2\pi}\right\} \cdot \left\{W_2 \exp\left(-\frac{S_2'^2}{2}\right) + \sqrt{2\pi}\right\}$$

holds. By combining the preceding two inequalities,

$$(W_1 - \sqrt{2\pi})(W_2 + \sqrt{2\pi}) > \exp\left\{\frac{S_1'^2 + S_2'^2}{2}\right\} \left\{W_1 \exp\left(-\frac{S_1'^2}{2}\right) - \sqrt{2\pi}\right\} \cdot \left\{W_2 \exp\left(-\frac{S_2'^2}{2}\right) + \sqrt{2\pi}\right\}$$

or

$$(W_1 - W_2 - \sqrt{2\pi}) > \exp\left(\frac{S_1'^2 + S_2'^2}{2}\right) \cdot \left\{W_1 \exp\left(-\frac{S_1'^2}{2}\right) - W_2 \exp\left(-\frac{S_2'^2}{2}\right) - \sqrt{2\pi}\right\}$$

holds. We need only to prove CII,

$$T = W_1 \exp\left(-\frac{S_2'^2}{2}\right) - W_2 \exp\left(-\frac{S_2'^2}{2}\right) - 2\sqrt{2\pi} < 0$$

for $(\pm S_1', \pm S_2')$. By the use of (56),

$$T + \sqrt{2\pi} < \exp\left(-\frac{S_1'^2 + S_2'^2}{2}\right)(W_1 - W_2 - \sqrt{2\pi}) < W_1 - W_2 - \sqrt{2\pi}$$

is proved. Therefore, $T < 0$ holds when CII_0 is satisfied. Thus the proof is completed.

From this theorem, the following corollary is obtained.

Corollary: When $W_1 < 2\sqrt{2\pi}$, a type B net is bistable.

A type C net has five equilibrium states. Let them be $(-S_1'', -S_2'')$, $(-S_1', -S_2')$, $(0,0)$, (S_1', S_2'), (S_1'', S_2''), where $0 < S_1' < S_1''$ (see Fig. 7(c)). We see that $S_1'' \geq \tilde{S}_1$ holds for many cases.

Theorem 10: A type C net has two stable states when $\overline{\mathrm{CII}_0}$ holds and three stable states when CII_0 holds provided $S_1'' \geq \tilde{S}_1$ holds.

Proof: As can easily be seen from Fig. 7(c), $d_1 > d_{\mathrm{II}}$ holds for $\pm(S_1', S_2')$. Therefore, these two states are unstable. On the contrary, for $\pm(S_1'', S_2'')$, CI holds. Moreover, CII also holds for them, as is shown in the proof of Theorem 8. Therefore, these states are stable. For the origin, CI automatically holds. Hence, when $\overline{\mathrm{CII}_0}$ holds, it is stable, and when CII_0 holds, it is unstable. The theorem is thus proved.

VII. Conclusions

From the macroscopic point of view, a neuron is considered to be an analog information-processing element that processes pulse-frequency modulated signals. The macroscopic behavior of random nets of analog neuron-like elements are investigated, and the results are compared with those composed of discrete threshold elements or McCulloch–Pitts formal neurons. The statistical parameters, which are sufficient to determine the macroscopic behavior of a random net, are extracted, and the macroscopic state equations are derived in terms of these parameters. The simplified state equations are also derived. The behavior of random nets is studied with the help of these equations.

A random net consisting of one homogeneous class of elements has been proved to be monostable or bistable according to its statistical parameters even when both positive and negative synaptic weights are included in the elements. It is proved, on the other hand, that a random net consisting of excitatory and inhibitory classes of elements can be not only monostable, bistable, or tristable but also astable with a stable oscillation. This shows a characteristic feature that is related to the physiological fact that neuron nets are composed of two types, the excitatory and inhibitory elements. The stability criteria are explicitly given in terms of the statistical parameters, and the results are also checked by computer-simulated experiments.

The most interesting feature of random nets seems to be that the stability changes with the average threshold H or $\bar{h}$, which can be controlled by other networks. In this connection, it is worth noting that random analog type nets have similar structures to those of digital type without any refractory period that were studied in [14]. This fact seems to show that the nonlinear character of the output function is essential for the preceding characteristics of random nets, and the existence of the refractory period is responsible for them only through the nonlinear character of the output function that it gives rise to.

Appendix I
Derivation of (18)

Let cov $(\boldsymbol{a},\boldsymbol{b})$ be a bilinear function of two n-dimensional vectors, $\boldsymbol{a} = (a_1,a_2,\cdots,a_n)$ and $\boldsymbol{b} = (b_1,b_2,\cdots,b_n)$, defined by

$$\operatorname{cov}(\boldsymbol{a},\boldsymbol{b}) = \frac{1}{n}\sum_i (a_i - \bar{a})(b_i - \bar{b}) \tag{56}$$

where

$$\bar{a} = \frac{1}{n}\sum a_i, \qquad \bar{b} = \frac{1}{n}\sum b_i. \tag{57}$$

Obviously

$$\operatorname{cov}(\boldsymbol{a},\boldsymbol{b}) = \operatorname{cov}(\boldsymbol{b},\boldsymbol{a})$$

$$\operatorname{cov}(\alpha\boldsymbol{a} + \beta\boldsymbol{b}, \boldsymbol{c}) = \alpha \operatorname{cov}(\boldsymbol{a},\boldsymbol{c}) + \beta \operatorname{cov}(\boldsymbol{b},\boldsymbol{c})$$

hold for arbitrary scalars α, β and arbitrary vectors $\boldsymbol{a}$, $\boldsymbol{b}$, and $\boldsymbol{c}$.

By the use of covariance, (19) is rewritten as

$$\frac{dV}{dt} = 2 \operatorname{cov}(\boldsymbol{u},\dot{\boldsymbol{u}}) \tag{58}$$

where $\boldsymbol{u} = (u_i)$, $\dot{\boldsymbol{u}} = (\dot{u}_i)$. By substituting

$$\dot{\boldsymbol{u}} = \frac{1}{n}\sum_j \boldsymbol{w}_j x_j - \boldsymbol{h} - \boldsymbol{u}$$

where

$$\boldsymbol{w}_j = (w_{1j},w_{2j},\cdots,w_{nj})$$

$$\boldsymbol{h} = (h_1,h_2,\cdots,h_n)$$

(58) is transformed into

$$\frac{dV}{dt} = \frac{2}{n}\sum x_j \operatorname{cov}(\boldsymbol{u},\boldsymbol{w}_j) - 2\operatorname{cov}(\boldsymbol{u},\boldsymbol{h}) - 2\operatorname{cov}(\boldsymbol{u},\boldsymbol{u}). \tag{59}$$

As can easily be shown,

$$\operatorname{cov}(\boldsymbol{u},\boldsymbol{u}) = V$$

$$\operatorname{cov}(\boldsymbol{h},\boldsymbol{h}) = \sigma_h^2$$

$$\operatorname{cov}(\boldsymbol{w}_j,\boldsymbol{h}) = 0$$

$$\operatorname{cov}(\boldsymbol{w}_j,\boldsymbol{w}_j) = \sigma_w^2$$

$$\operatorname{cov}(\boldsymbol{w}_i,\boldsymbol{w}_j) = 0, \qquad i \neq j$$

hold to within the terms $O(1/\sqrt{n})$. Moreover, by substituting (13),

$$\operatorname{cov}(\boldsymbol{u},\boldsymbol{w}_j) = \frac{1}{n}\sum_i \tilde{x}_i \operatorname{cov}(\boldsymbol{w}_i,\boldsymbol{w}_j) - \operatorname{cov}(\boldsymbol{h},\boldsymbol{w}_j)$$

$$= \frac{1}{n}\tilde{x}_j\sigma_w^2$$

and

$$\operatorname{cov}(\boldsymbol{u},\boldsymbol{h}) = \frac{1}{n}\sum_i \tilde{x}_i \operatorname{cov}(\boldsymbol{w}_i,\boldsymbol{h}) - \operatorname{cov}(\boldsymbol{h},\boldsymbol{h})$$

$$= -\sigma_h^2$$

are proved. Therefore, by substituting these in (59),

$$\frac{dV}{dt} = \frac{2}{n^2}\sum x_j\tilde{x}_j\sigma_w^2 + 2\sigma_h^2 - 2V$$

is obtained. By virtue of Hypothesis 2, $\sum x_j\tilde{x}_j/n$ can be replaced by Y, so that (18) is obtained.

Appendix II
Stability of Random Nets with Nonvanishing σ_w^2/n

When the distribution of w_{ij} is fixed independently of n, the number of the inputs, which have nonzero weights, to an element increases in proportion to n. Therefore, as n increases infinitely, the input number increases infinitely. Instead of such a net, one can consider another kind of random net in which the number of inputs to an element is nearly fixed to a constant, say m, independently of n. In such a net, the proportionality factor $1/n$ in the weighted sum $1/n \sum_j w_{ij}x_j$ is unnecessary because only m terms are nonzero in the preceding expression, even if n increases. Therefore, if such a formulation is used, w_{ij} need be considered as a quantity increasing in proportion to n.

Consider, as an example, a random net in which w_{ij}/n is 1 with probability m/n and is 0 with probability $1 - m/n$. In such a net each component element is randomly connected to about m elements regardless of n, and the synaptic weight w_{ij}/n is equal to 1 whenever the jth element is connected to the ith element. As can easily be shown, the expectation $\bar{w}$ and the variance σ_w^2 are given by

$$\bar{w} = m$$

$$\sigma_w^2 = nm - m^2$$

respectively, so that

$$\frac{\sigma_w^2}{n} \doteqdot m$$

does not vanish even if n becomes large.

In such a model, the simplified state equation is not applicable so that it is difficult to give stability criteria explicitly in terms of the macroscopic parameters. In this appendix some stability criteria will briefly be discussed for such a net.

Since

$$0 \le Y \le 1$$

always holds, as can easily be understood from (18), V satisfies

$$\sigma_h^2 \le V \le \sigma_h^2 + \frac{\sigma_w^2}{n}$$

for sufficiently large t. The equilibrium states are given by the solutions of

$$p(U,V) = \bar{w}X - \bar{h} - U = 0 \tag{60}$$

$$q(U,V) = 2\left(\frac{\sigma_w^2}{n} Y + \sigma_h^2 - V\right) = 0. \tag{61}$$

When V is replaced by σ_h^2, the former equation is equivalent to

$$g_W(S) = 0$$

whose stability has been investigated in Section IV. A similar discussion holds in this case. When

$$\frac{\bar{w}}{\sqrt{a^2 + V}} < \sqrt{2\pi}$$

or

$$V > \frac{\bar{w}^2}{2\pi} - a^2$$

there exists one and only one U satisfying (60) for a given V, and the root is stable if V is kept constant. When

$$V < \frac{\bar{w}^2}{2\pi} - a^2$$

holds, there exist three roots satisfying (60) for a given V when and only when

$$\left|\frac{\bar{h}}{\bar{w}} - \frac{1}{2}\right| < f\left(\frac{\bar{w}}{\sqrt{a^2 + V}}\right)$$

and two of the roots are stable if V is kept constant.

Taking into account the monotonic character of the function $f(x)$ as well as the relation $q(U,V) = 0$, it is suggested that the following conditions are sufficient to determine the stability.

Lemma 7: In the case of

$$\frac{\bar{w}}{\sqrt{a^2 + \sigma_h^2}} < \sqrt{2\pi}$$

a net is monostable irrespective of the value of $\bar{h}$. In the case of

$$\frac{\bar{w}}{\sqrt{a^2 + \sigma_h^2 + \sigma_w^2/n}} > \sqrt{2\pi}$$

a net is bistable if

$$\left|\frac{\bar{h}}{\bar{w}} - \frac{1}{2}\right| < f\left(\frac{\bar{w}}{\sqrt{a^2 + \sigma_h^2 + \sigma_w^2/n}}\right)$$

holds and is monostable if

$$\left|\frac{\bar{h}}{\bar{w}} - \frac{1}{2}\right| > f\left(\frac{\bar{w}}{\sqrt{a^2 + \sigma_h^2}}\right)$$

holds.

Appendix III

Proof of Lemmas 3 and 4

The symmetry of both curves is first shown. Put

$$\Psi(S) = 2\Phi(S) - 1.$$

Then, (52) and (53) are rewritten as

$$W_1\Psi(S_1) - K_{12}\Psi(S_2) - S_1 = 0 \tag{62}$$

$$K_{21}\Psi(S_1) - W_2\Psi(S_2) - S_2 = 0 \tag{63}$$

respectively, where (50) and (51) are taken into account. Since both $\Psi(S)$ and S are odd functions, if (S_1,S_2) satisfies (62) or (63), $(-S_1,-S_2)$ also satisfies (62) or (63). Therefore, the equilibrium curves are symmetrical with respect to the origin.

The properties of curve II in Lemma 3 are next proved. Equation (53) is rewritten by the use of the function $g_W(S)$ as

$$\Phi(S_1) = -\frac{1}{K_{21}} g_{-W_2}(S_2) \tag{64}$$

where

$$g_{-W_2}(S_2) = -W_2\Phi(S_2) - H_2 - S_2.$$

Since $\Phi(S_1)$ is monotonically increasing and $g_{-W_2}(S_2)$ is monotonically decreasing, (64) denotes the monotonically increasing relation between S_1 and S_2. Moreover, $\Phi(S_1)$ is bounded

$$0 < \Phi(S_1) < 1.$$

Since $g_{-W_2}(S_2)$ is not a bounded function, curve II is bounded even when S_1 tends to infinity.

The properties of curve I are proved last. Equation (52) is rewritten as

$$\Phi(S_2) = \frac{1}{K_{12}} g_{W_1}(S_1). \tag{65}$$

When $W_1 \le \sqrt{2\pi}$, $g_{W_1}(S_1)$ is monotonically decreasing, and hence the curve is monotonically decreasing. When $W_1 > \sqrt{2\pi}$, as has been shown in Section IV, $g_{W_1}(S_1)$ is monotonically increasing in the interval

$$|S_1| < \tilde{S}_1$$

where

$$\tilde{S}_1 = \sqrt{\log\left(\frac{W_1^2}{2\pi}\right)}$$

and monotonically decreasing outside the interval. Since $\Phi(S_2)$ is monotonically increasing, curve I is also decomposed into three pieces in which the middle piece, i.e., the piece existing in the interval $|S_1| < \tilde{S}_1$, is monotonically increasing and the others are monotonically decreasing. Since $\Phi(S_2)$ is bounded by $0 < \Phi(S_2) < 1$, curve I is defined only for such S_1 that satisfy

$$0 < g_{W_1}(S_1) < K_{12}. \qquad (66)$$

Since $g_{W_1}(S_1)$ tends to $\mp\infty$ as S_1 tends to $\pm\infty$, curve I is defined in a finite interval of S_1 and tends to infinity as S_1 tends to the upper and lower bounds of (66). The three pieces of curve I are continuously connected if the local maximum $g_{W_1}(\tilde{S}_1)$ and the local minimum $g_{W_1}(-\tilde{S}_1)$ satisfy (66), and the curve is split into three disconnected pieces if this is not the case. In the latter case curve I is defined for three disjoint intervals of S_1, each piece increasing and decreasing without limit.

Acknowledgment

The author wishes to thank Prof. J. Nagumo and Dr. S. Yoshizawa for their discussions and comments on the manuscript. He would also like to thank Dr. Yoshizawa for suggesting the proof of Theorem 9.

References

[1] A. Rapoport, "Ignition phenomena in random nets," *Bull. Math. Biophys.*, vol. 14, pp. 35–44, Mar. 1952.

[2] N. Rochester *et al.*, "Tests on a cell assembly theory of the action of the brain, using a large digital computer," *IRE Trans. Inform. Theory*, vol. IT-2, pp. 80–93, Sept. 1956.

[3] J. von Neumann, "Probabilistic logic and the synthesis of reliable organisms from unreliable components," in *Automata Studies*, C. E. Shannon and J. McCarthy, Ed. Princeton, N.J.: Princeton Univ. Press, 1956.

[4] R. L. Beurle, "Properties of a mass of cells capable of regenerating pulses," *Trans. Roy. Soc.* (*London*), ser. B, vol. 240, pp. 55–94, Aug. 1956.

[5] F. Rosenblatt, *Principles of Neurodynamics*. Washington, D.C.: Spartan, 1961.

[6] B. G. Farley and W. A. Clark, "Activity in networks of neuron-like elements," in *Proc. 4th London Symp. on Information Theory*, C. Cherry, Ed. London: Butterworths, 1961.

[7] J. T. Allanson, "Some properties of randomly connected neural networks," in *Proc. 3rd London Symp. on Information Theory*, C. Cherry, Ed. London: Butterworths, 1956.

[8] D. R. Smith and C. H. Davidson, "Maintained activity in neural nets," *J. Ass. Comput. Mach.*, vol. 9, pp. 268–278, Apr. 1962.

[9] L. I. Rozonoer, "Random logical nets, I," *Avtomat. Telemekh.*, no. 5, pp. 137–147, May 1969.

[10] ——, "Random logical nets, II," *Avtomat. Telemekh.*, no. 6, pp. 99–109, June 1969.

[11] ——, "Random logical nets, III," *Avtomat. Telemakh.*, no. 7, pp. 127–136, July 1969.

[12] S. Amari, "Characteristics of random threshold-element networks" (in Japanese), Technical Group on Automata, Inst. Electron. Commun. Eng. Jap., Paper A69-55, Nov. 1969.

[13] P. A. Anninos *et al.*, "Dynamics of neural structures," *J. Theor. Biol.*, vol. 26, pp. 121–148, Jan. 1970.

[14] S. Amari, "Characteristics of randomly connected threshold-element networks and network systems," *Proc. IEEE*, vol. 59, pp. 35–47, Jan. 1971.

[15] E. M. Harth *et al.*, "Brain functions and neural dynamics," *J. Theor. Biol.*, vol. 26, pp. 93–120, Jan. 1970.

[16] D. Ya. Averbukh, "Random nets of analog neurons," *Avtomat. Telemekh.*, no. 10, pp. 116–123, Oct. 1969.

Reprinted from IEEE Transactions on Systems, Man, and Cybernetics 13(5), September/October 1983, pp. 815-26.

Absolute Stability of Global Pattern Formation and Parallel Memory Storage by Competitive Neural Networks

MICHAEL A. COHEN AND STEPHEN GROSSBERG

Abstract—The process whereby input patterns are transformed and stored by competitive cellular networks is considered. This process arises in such diverse subjects as the short-term storage of visual or language patterns by neural networks, pattern formation due to the firing of morphogenetic gradients in developmental biology, control of choice behavior during macromolecular evolution, and the design of stable context-sensitive parallel processors. In addition to systems capable of approaching one of perhaps infinitely many equilibrium points in response to arbitrary input patterns and initial data, one finds in these subjects a wide variety of other behaviors, notably traveling waves, standing waves, resonance, and chaos. The question of what general dynamical constraints cause global approach to equilibria rather than large amplitude waves is therefore of considerable interest. In another terminology, this is the question of whether global pattern formation occurs. A related question is whether the global pattern formation property persists when system parameters slowly change in an unpredictable fashion due to self-organization (development, learning). This is the question of absolute stability of global pattern formation. It is shown that many model systems which exhibit the absolute stability property can be written in the form

$$\frac{dx_i}{dt} = a_i(x_i)\left[b_i(x_i) - \sum_{k=1}^{n} c_{ik}d_k(x_k)\right] \tag{1}$$

$i = 1, 2, \cdots, n$, where the matrix $C = \|c_{ik}\|$ is symmetric and the system as a whole is competitive. Under these circumstances, this system defines a global Liapunov function. The absolute stability of systems with infinite but totally disconnected sets of equilibrium points can then be studied using the LaSalle invariance principle, the theory of several complex variables, and Sard's theorem. The symmetry of matrix C is important since competitive systems of the form (1) exist wherein C is arbitrarily close to a symmetric matrix but almost all trajectories persistently oscillate, as in the voting paradox. Slowing down the competitive feedback without violating symmetry, as in the systems

$$\frac{dx_i}{dt} = a_i(x_i)\left[b_i(x_i) - \sum_{k=1}^{n} c_{ik}d_k(y_k)\right]$$

$$\frac{dy_i}{dt} = e_i(x_i)[f_i(x_i) - y_i],$$

also enables sustained oscillations to occur. Our results thus show that the use of fast symmetric competitive feedback is a robust design constraint for guaranteeing absolute stability of global pattern formation.

Manuscript received August 1, 1982; revised April 4, 1983. This work was supported in part by the National Science Foundation under Grant NSF IST-80-00257 and in part by the Air Force Office of Scientific Research under Grant AFOSR 82-0148.
The authors are with the Center for Adaptive Systems, Department of Mathematics, Boston University, Boston, MA 02215.

I. Introduction: Absolute Stability of Global Pattern Formation in Self-Organizing Networks

THIS ARTICLE proves a global limit theorem for a class of n-dimensional competitive dynamical systems that can be written in the form

$$\dot{x}_i = a_i(x_i)\left[b_i(x_i) - \sum_{k=1}^{n} c_{ik}d_k(x_k)\right], \tag{1}$$

$i = 1, 2, \cdots, n$, where the coefficients $\|c_{ij}\|$ form a symmetric matrix. The systems (1) are more general in some respects but less general in other respects than the *adaptation level* competitive dynamical systems

$$\dot{x}_i = a_i(x)[b_i(x_i) - c(x)] \tag{2}$$

where $x = (x_1, x_2, \cdots, x_n)$ and $i = 1, 2, \cdots, n$, that have previously been globally analyzed (Grossberg [14], [18], [21]). To clarify the significance of the present theorem, some of the varied physical examples that can be written in the form (1) are summarized in this section. Section II indicates how these examples physically differ from related examples wherein sustained oscillations of various types can occur. Section III begins the mathematical development of the article.

System (1) includes the nonlinear neural networks

$$\dot{x}_i = -A_i x_i + (B_i - C_i x_i)[I_i + f_i(x_i)] - (D_i x_i + E_i)\left[J_i + \sum_{k=1}^{n} F_{ik} g_k(x_k)\right], \tag{3}$$

$i = 1, 2, \cdots, n$. In (3), x_i is the potential, or short-term memory activity, of the ith cell (population) v_i in the network. Term $-A_i x_i$ describes the passive decay of activity at rate $-A_i$. Term

$$(B_i - C_i x_i)[I_i + f_i(x_i)] \tag{4}$$

describes how an excitatory input I_i and an excitatory feedback signal $f_i(x_i)$ increase the activity x_i. If $C_i = 0$, then term (4) describes an additive effect of input and feedback signal on activity [10]. If $C_i > 0$, then the input and feedback signal become ineffective when $x_i = B_i C_i^{-1}$ since then $B_i - C_i x_i = 0$. In this case, term (4) describes a shunting or multiplicative effect of input and feedback signal on activity. In a shunting network, the initial value inequality $x_i(0) \leqslant B_i C_i^{-1}$ implies that $x_i(t) \leqslant B_i C_i^{-1}$ for all $t \geqslant 0$, as occurs in nerve cells which obey the membrane equation (Hodgkin [24], Katz [26], Kuffler and Nicholls [28]). Term

$$-(D_i x_i + E_i)\left[J_i + \sum_{k=1}^{n} F_{ik} g_k(x_k)\right] \tag{5}$$

in (3) describes how an inhibitory input J_i and inhibitory feedback signals $F_{ik} g_k(x_k)$ from cell v_k to v_i decrease the activity x_i of v_i. If $D_i = 0$, then (5) describes an additive effect of input and feedback signals on activity. If $D_i > 0$, then the input and feedback signals become ineffective when $x_i = -D_i^{-1} E_i$, since then $D_i x_i + E_i = 0$. In this case, (5) describes a shunting effect of input and feedback signals on activity. An initial value choice $x_i(0) \geqslant -D_i^{-1} E_i$ implies that $x_i(t) \geqslant -D_i^{-1} E_i$ for all $t \geqslant 0$. Thus in a shunting network, but not an additive network, each activity $x_i(t)$ is restricted to a finite interval for all time $t \geqslant 0$. Suitably designed shunting networks can automatically retune their sensitivity to maintain a sensitive response within these finite intervals even if their inputs fluctuate in size over a much broader dynamic range (Grossberg [12], [21]).

The networks (1) are part of a mathematical classification theory, reviewed in [21], which characterizes how prescribed changes in system parameters alter the transformation from input patterns $(I_1, I_2, \cdots, I_n, J_1, J_2, \cdots, J_n)$ into activity patterns $(x_1, x_2, \cdots, x_n)$. In addition to the study of prescribed transformations, the mathematical classification theory seeks the most general classes of networks wherein important general processing requirements are guaranteed. In the present article, we study a class of networks which transform arbitrary input patterns into activity patterns that are then stored in short-term memory until a future perturbation resets the stored pattern. This property, also called *global pattern formation*, means that given any physically admissible input pattern $(I_1, I_2, \cdots, I_n, J_1, J_2, \cdots, J_n)$ and initial activity pattern $x(0) = (x_1(0), x_2(0), \cdots, x_n(0))$, the limit $x(\infty) = \lim_{t \to \infty}(x_1(t), x_2(t), \cdots, x_n(t))$ exists. The networks (1) include examples wherein nondenumerably many equilibrium points $x(\infty)$ exist (Grossberg [12], [21]).

A related property is the *absolute stability* of global pattern formation, which means that global pattern formation occurs given *any* choice of parameters in (1). The absolute stability property is of fundamental importance when (1) is part of a self-organizing (e.g., developing, learning) system, as in [15], [19]. Then network parameters can slowly change due to self-organization in an unpredictable way. Each new parameter choice may determine a different transformation from input pattern to activity pattern. An absolute stability theorem guarantees that, whatever transformation occurs, the network's ability to store the activity pattern is left invariant by self-organization. Thus the identification of an absolutely stable class of systems constrains the mechanisms of self-organization with which a system can interact without becoming destabilized in certain input environments.

The neural networks (3) include a number of models from population biology, neurobiology, and evolutionary theory. The Volterra–Lotka equations

$$\dot{x}_i = G_i x_i\left(1 - \sum_{k=1}^{n} H_{ik} x_k\right) \tag{6}$$

of population biology are obtained when $A_i = C_i = I_i = E_i = J_i = 0$ and $f_i(w) = g_i(w) = w$ for all $i = 1, 2, \cdots, n$. The related Gilpin and Ayala system [6]

$$\dot{x}_i = G_i x_i\left[1 - \left(\frac{x_i}{K_i}\right)^{\theta_i} - \sum_{k=1}^{n} H_{ik}\left(\frac{x_k}{K_k}\right)\right] \tag{7}$$

is obtained when $A_i = C_i = I_i = E_i = J_i = 0$, $f_i(w) = 1 - w^{\theta_i} K_i^{-\theta_i}$ and $g_i(w) = w K_i^{-1}$ for all $i = 1, 2, \cdots, n$.

The Hartline–Ratliff equation [34]

$$r_i = e_i - \sum_{k=1}^{n} K_{ik} \max\left(r_k - r_{ik}^{(0)}, 0\right) \tag{8}$$

for the steady-state outputs r_i of the Limulus retina arises as the equation of equilibrium of an additive network ($C_i = D_i = 0$) if, in addition, $f_i(w) = 0$ and $g_i(w) = \max(w - L_i, 0)$ for all $i = 1, 2, \cdots, n$ (Grossberg [8], [9]).

The Eigen and Schuster equation [4]

$$\dot{x}_i = x_i\left(m_i x_i^{p-1} - q \sum_{k=1}^{n} m_k x_k^p\right) \tag{9}$$

for the evolutionary selection of macromolecular quasi-species is a special case of (3) such that $A_i = C_i = I_i = E_i = J_i = 0$, $B_i = F_{ik} = 1$, $D_i = q$, and $f_i(w) = g_i(w) = m_i x_i^p$ for all $i, k = 1, 2, \cdots, n$. Feedback interactions among excitatory and inhibitory morphogenetic substances leading to "firing," or contrast enhancement, of a morphogenetic gradient can also be modeled by shunting networks (Grossberg [13], [16], [20]).

II. Some sources of Sustained Oscillations

The tendency of the trajectories of (1) to approach equilibrium points is dependent on the symmetry of the matrix $\|c_{ij}\|$ of interaction coefficients. Examples exist wherein the coefficient matrix may be chosen as close to a symmetric matrix as one pleases, yet almost all trajectories persistently oscillate even if all the functions $a_i(x_i)$, $b_i(x_i)$, and $d_k(x_k)$ are linear functions of their arguments. The May and Leonard model [33] of the voting paradox is illustrative. This model is defined by the three-dimensional system

$$\dot{x}_1 = x_1(1 - x_1 - \alpha x_2 - \beta x_3)$$

$$\dot{x}_2 = x_2(1 - \beta x_1 - x_2 - \alpha x_3)$$

$$\dot{x}_3 = x_3(1 - \alpha x_1 - \beta x_2 - x_3). \tag{10}$$

Grossberg [17] and Schuster *et al.* [36] proved that if $\beta > 1 > \alpha$ and $\alpha + \beta > 2$, then all positive trajectories except the uniform trajectories $x_1(0) = x_2(0) = x_3(0)$ persistently oscillate as $t \to \infty$. The matrix

$$\begin{pmatrix} 1 & \alpha & \beta \\ \beta & 1 & \alpha \\ \alpha & \beta & 1 \end{pmatrix} \tag{11}$$

can be chosen arbitrarily close to a symmetric matrix by letting α and β approach one without violating the hypotheses of Grossberg's theorem.

In a neural network such as (3), the hypothesis that the coefficient matrix $\|F_{ij}\|$ is symmetric is justified when the inhibitory interaction strengths F_{ij} and F_{ji} between cell v_i and cell v_j depend on the intercellular distance. Thus the tendency of the trajectories of (1) to approach equilibrium is interpreted in physical examples as a consequence of intercellular geometry.

The tendency to approach equilibrium also depends upon the rapidity with which feedback signals are registered. In (3), for example, the excitatory and inhibitory feedback signals $f_i(x_i)$ and $F_{ik}g_k(x_k)$, respectively, both depend explicitly on the excitatory activities x_i. *In vivo* these feedback signals are often emitted by interneuronal cells that are activated by the activities x_i before they return signals to v_i. Then (3) is replaced by the more general system

$$\dot{x}_i = -A_i x_i + (B_i - C_i x_i)[I_i + f_i(w_i)] - (D_i x_i + E_i)\left[J_i + \sum_{k=1}^{n} F_{ik} g_k(y_k)\right] \tag{12}$$

$$\dot{w}_i = U_i(x_i)[W_i(x_i) - w_i] \tag{13}$$

$$\dot{y}_i = V_i(x_i)[Y_i(x_i) - y_i] \tag{14}$$

where w_i is the potential of an excitatory interneuron and y_i is the potential of an inhibitory interneuron that is activated by x_i. Large amplitude standing and traveling periodic waves have been found in continuum analogs of (12)–(14) (Ellias and Grossberg [5]). System (12)–(14) is more general than (3) because (12)–(14) reduce to a system of the form (3) when both w_i and y_i equilibrate very rapidly to fluctuations in x_i. Thus the tendency to approach equilibrium in (1) is due to both the symmetry and the speed of its feedback signals. Often as one perturbs off system (3) to a system of the form (12)–(14), one finds limiting patterns followed by standing waves followed by traveling waves [5]. In the neural network theory of short-term memory storage, both limiting patterns and standing waves are acceptable storage mechanisms; see [15], [19] for physical background. One approach to achieving these properties is to prove directly the global existence of limiting patterns for fast feedback systems such as (1), as we do in this article, and then to perturb off (1) by slowing down the feedback to characterize the parameter region wherein large amplitude standing waves are found before they bifurcate into large amplitude traveling waves.

Much more complex oscillations can also be inferred to exist in neural networks due to a mathematical relationship that exists between neural networks and models of individual nerve cells wherein complex oscillations have been proved to exist (Carpenter [1], [2]). This relationship allows the inference that traveling bursts and chaotic waveforms can be generated by suitably designed networks. To see why this is so, consider the following generalization of system (12)–(14):

$$\dot{x}_i = -A_i x_i + (B - C_i x_i)\left[I_i + \sum_{k=1}^{n} f_{ik}(w_k) z_{ik}\right] - (D_i x_i + E_i)\left[J_i + \sum_{k=1}^{n} g_{ik}(y_k)\right] \tag{15}$$

$$\dot{w}_i = U_i(x_i)[W_i(x_i) - w_i] \tag{13}$$

$$\dot{y}_i = V_i(x_i)[Y_i(x_i) - y_i] \tag{14}$$

and

$$\dot{z}_{ik} = M_{ik} - N_{ik} z_{ik} - P_{ik} f_{ik}(w_k) z_{ik}. \tag{16}$$

Equation (15) permits excitatory feedback signaling from a cell v_k to v_i via the term $f_{ik}(w_k)z_{ik}$, as well as inhibitory feedback signaling via the term $g_{ik}(y_k)$. The new terms z_{ik} *gate* the excitatory feedback signal $f_{ik}(w_k)$ before it reaches v_i. *In vivo* such a gating action often corresponds to the release of a chemical transmitter at a rate proportional to $f_{ik}(w_k)z_{ik}$. Correspondingly, term $M_{ik} - N_{ik}z_{ik}$ in (16) describes the transmitter's slow accumulation to an asymptote $M_{ik}N_{ik}^{-1}$, whereas term $P_{ik}f_{ik}(w_k)z_{ik}$ describes the removal of transmitter at a rate proportional to $f_{ik}(w_k)z_{ik}$ (Grossberg [8], [11]). Equation (16) can be rewritten, analogous to (13) and (14), in the form

$$\dot{z}_{ik} = Q_{ik}(w_k)[Z_{ik}(w_k) - z_{ik}]. \tag{17}$$

However, whereas $W_i(x_i)$ and $Y_i(x_i)$ in (13) and (14) are increasing functions of x_i,

$$Z_{ik}(w_k) = M_{ik}[N_{ik} + P_{ik}f_{ik}(w_k)]^{-1} \quad (18)$$

is a decreasing function of w_k. Often *in vivo* the excitatory interneuronal potential w_i equilibrates rapidly to x_i in (13). Then $Z_{ik}(w_k)$ may be approximated by a decreasing function of x_i. When this is true, the variables w_i, y_i, and z_{ik} play a role in the network that is formally analogous to the role played by the variables m, n, and h of the Hodgkin–Huxley equations for nerve impulse transmissions [1], [2]. By relabeling cells appropriately, letting w_i rapidly equilibrate to x_i, and making a special choice of parameters and signals, the sum $-A_i x_i + (B - C_i x_i)\sum_{k=1}^n f_{ik}(w_k) z_{ik}$ in (15) can be rewritten in the form

$$D(x_{i-1} + x_{i+1} - 2x_i) + (B - x_i)h_i(x_i)z_i. \quad (19)$$

Term $D(x_{i-1} + x_{i+1} - 2x_i)$ plays the role of the diffusion term in the Hodgkin–Huxley equations. Carpenter's results on bursts and chaotic waves therefore hold in neural networks just so long as a spatially discrete version of the Hodgkin–Huxley equations can also support these waves.

Our concern in this article is not, however, to generate complex traveling waves but rather to rule them out. To accomplish this in a robust fashion, we turn to (1) because it eliminates both the waves due to fast feedback in an asymmetric geometry and the waves due to slow feedback in a symmetric geometry.

III. A Global Liapunov Function

The adaptation level competitive systems

$$\dot{x}_i = a_i(x)(b_i(x_i) - c(x)) \quad (2)$$

were globally analyzed by associating a suitable Liapunov functional $M^+(x_t)$ to every such system. This functional, which is an integral of a maximum function

$$M^+(x_t) = \int_0^t \max_i [b_i(x_i(v)) - c(x(v))]\, dv, \quad (20)$$

permitted a concept of *jump*, or *decision*, to be associated with (2). Using this concept, the idea could be explicated that the decision schemes of adaptation level systems are globally consistent and thereby cause every trajectory to approach an equilibrium point [14], [18]. By contrast, when the same method was applied to the voting paradox system (10), it was found that the decision scheme of this system is globally inconsistent, and thus almost all trajectories persistently oscillate [17], [18]. Although every competitive system defines such a Liapunov functional and a decision scheme, this method has not yet succeeded in proving that the decision scheme of (1) is globally consistent. Such a theorem is greatly to be desired.

In its absence, we have found that the systems (1) admit a global Liapunov function which can be analyzed. A considerable amount of work has already been done on finding Liapunov functions for special cases of (1). For example, a Liapunov function which proves local asymptotic stability of isolated equilibrium points of Volterra–Lotka systems was described in a classical paper of MacArthur [32]. Global Liapunov functions for Volterra–Lotka and Gilpin–Ayala systems have been found in cases where only one equilibrium point exists (Goh and Agnew [7]). This constraint is much too strong in systems that are designed to transform and store a large variety of patterns. Our analysis includes systems which possess infinitely many equilibrium points. Liapunov functions have also been described for Volterra–Lotka systems whose off-diagonal interaction terms are relatively small (Kilmer [27], Takeuchi *et al.* [37]). We do not need this type of constraint to derive our results.

The function

$$V(x) = -\sum_{i=1}^n \int_0^{x_i} b_i(\xi_i) d_i'(\xi_i)\, d\xi_i + \frac{1}{2}\sum_{j,k=1}^n c_{jk} d_j(x_j) d_k(x_k) \quad (21)$$

is a global Liapunov function for (1) because

$$\dot{V}(x) = -\sum_{i=1}^n a_i(x_i) d_i'(x_i)\left[b_i(x_i) - \sum_{k=1}^n c_{ik} d_k(x_k)\right]^2. \quad (22)$$

Function $\dot{V}(x) \leqslant 0$ along trajectories just so long as every function $d_i(x_i)$ is monotone nondecreasing. This condition implies that (1) is competitive. In (3), where $d_i \equiv g_i$, the condition means that inhibitory feedback $g_i(x_i)$ cannot decrease as activity x_i increases. Systems (1) can, in fact, be written in the gradient form

$$\dot{x} = A(x)\nabla B(x) \quad (23)$$

if each function $d_i(x_i)$ is strictly increasing by choosing the matrix $A(x) = \|A_{ij}(x)\|$ to satisfy

$$A_{ij}(x) = \frac{a_i(x_i)\delta_{ij}}{d_i'(x_i)} \quad (24)$$

and $B(x) = -V(x)$.

The standard theorems about Liapunov functions and gradient representations imply that each trajectory converges to the largest invariant set M contained in the set E where [22]

$$\frac{d}{dt}V = 0. \quad (25)$$

Given definition (21) of $V(x)$, it is easy to see that points in E are equilibrium points if each function $d_i(x_i)$ is strictly increasing. It still remains to show in this case that each trajectory approaches a unique equilibrium point, although for all practical purposes every trajectory that approaches M becomes approximately constant in any bounded interval of sufficiently large times.

Further argument is required when each function $d_i(x_i)$ is not strictly increasing, which is the typical situation in a neural network. There each inhibitory feedback signal function $d_i(x_i)$ can possess an *inhibitory signal threshold* Γ_i^- such that $d_i(x_i) = 0$ if $x_i \leqslant \Gamma_i^-$ and $d_i'(x_i) > 0$ if $x_i > \Gamma_i^-$. Since each $d_i(x_i)$ is still monotone nondecreasing, although not strictly increasing, function $V(x)$ in (21) continued to define a Liapunov function. Consequently, every trajectory still converges to the invariant set M. However, further analysis is now required to guarantee that M consists of equilibrium points, let alone isolated equilibrium points. Even in the cases wherein no such degeneracy occurs, it has not previously been noticed that so many physically important examples can be written in the form (1) and that (1) admits a global Liapunov function.

IV. Application of the LaSalle Invariance Principle

We will study the general system

$$\dot{x}_i = a_i(x_i)\left[b_i(x_i) - \sum_{k=1}^{n} c_{ik} d_k(x_k)\right] \tag{1}$$

under hypotheses that include the shunting competitive neural networks

$$\dot{y}_i = -A_i y_i + (B_i - C_i y_i)[I_i + f_i(y_i)] - (D_i y_i + E_i)\left[J_i + \sum_{k=1}^{n} F_{ik} g_k(y_k)\right]. \tag{26}$$

In the shunting case, $C_i \neq 0 \neq D_i$. The simpler additive neural networks wherein $C_i = 0 = D_i$ are also included in our analysis but will not be explicitly discussed. In the shunting case, (26) can be rewritten without loss of generality in the form

$$\dot{y}_i = -A_i y_i + (B_i - y_i)[I_i + f_i(y_i)] - (y_i + C_i)\left[J_i + \sum_{k=1}^{n} F_{ik} g_k(y_k)\right] \tag{27}$$

by a suitable redefinition of terms.

We distinguish x_i in (1) from y_i in (27) because our hypotheses hold when

$$x_i = y_i + C_i. \tag{28}$$

Then (27) reduces to (1) via the definitions

$$a_i(x_i) = x_i, \tag{29}$$

$$b_i(x_i) = x_i^{-1}\{A_i C_i - (A_i + J_i)x_i + (B_i + C_i - x_i)[I_i + f_i(x_i - C_i)]\}, \tag{30}$$

$$c_{ik} = F_{ik}, \tag{31}$$

and

$$d_k(x_k) = g_k(x_k - C_k). \tag{32}$$

Our first task is to prove that $V(x)$ is a Liapunov function of x in the positive orthant $\mathbb{R}_n^+$. To do this, we study (1) under the following hypotheses:

a) *symmetry*: matrix $\|c_{ij}\|$ is a symmetric matrix of nonnegative constants;

b) *continuity*: function $a_i(\xi)$ is continuous for $\xi \geq 0$; function $b_i(\xi)$ is continuous for $\xi > 0$;

c) *positivity*: function $a_i(\xi) > 0$ for $\xi > 0$; function $d_i(\xi) \geq 0$ for $\xi \in (-\infty, \infty)$.

d) *smoothness and monotonicity*: function $d_i(\xi)$ is differentiable and monotone nondecreasing for $\xi \geq 0$.

To prove that $V(x)$ is a Liapunov function, we first show that positive initial data generate positive bounded trajectories of (1), henceforth called *admissible* trajectories. This can be shown if two more hypotheses are assumed. The choice of hypotheses (34)–(36) below is influenced by the fact that function b_i in (30) may become unbounded as $x_i \to 0+$.

Lemma 1 (Boundedness and Positivity):

Boundedness: For each $i = 1, 2, \cdots, n$, suppose that

$$\limsup_{\xi \to \infty} [b_i(\xi) - c_{ii} d_i(\xi)] < 0. \tag{33}$$

Positivity: For each $i = 1, 2, \cdots, n$, suppose either that

$$\lim_{\xi \to 0+} b_i(\xi) = \infty \tag{34}$$

or that

$$\lim_{\xi \to 0+} b_i(\xi) < \infty \tag{35}$$

and

$$\int_0^{\epsilon} \frac{d\xi}{a_i(\xi)} = \infty \qquad \text{for some } \epsilon > 0. \tag{36}$$

Then any positive initial data generate an admissible trajectory.

Proof: Boundedness is proved using (33) as follows. Inequality

$$b_i(x_i) - \sum_{k=1}^{n} c_{ik} d_k(x_k) \leq b_i(x_i) - c_{ii} d_i(x_i) \tag{37}$$

is true because all c_{ik} and d_k are nonnegative. Since also $a_i(x_i)$ is positive at large x_i values, (37) shows that $(d/dt)x_i < 0$ at large x_i values. Indeed, given any positive initial data, an $L_i < \infty$ exists such that $x_i(t) \leq L_i$ at sufficiently large times t, $i = 1, 2, \cdots, n$.

Condition (34) implies positivity because each term $\sum_{k=1}^{n} c_{ik} d_k(x_k)$ is bounded if all $x_k \leq L_k$, $k = 1, 2, \cdots, n$; hence term $b_i(x_i) - \sum_{k=1}^{n} c_{ik} d_k(x_k)$ becomes positive if all $x_k \leq L_k$, $k = 1, 2, \cdots, n$ as $x_i \to 0+$. Since also $a_i(x_i) > 0$ for $x_i > 0$, $(d/dt)x_i > 0$ before x_i reaches 0, hence x_i can never reach zero.

If (35) and (36) hold, then at the first time $t = T$ such that $x_i(T) = 0$,

$$-\infty = \int_{x_i(0)}^{0} \frac{d\xi}{a_i(\xi)} = \int_0^T \left[b_i(x_i(t)) - \sum_{k=1}^{n} c_{ik} d_k(x_k(t))\right] dt > -\infty. \tag{38}$$

which is a contradiction. Hence $x_i(t)$ remains positive for all $t \geq 0$.

Using the fact that positive initial data generate admissible trajectories, we can easily verify that the function

$$V(x) = -\sum_{k=1}^{n} \int_0^{x_i} b_i(\xi_i) d_i'(\xi_i)\, d\xi_i$$
$$+\frac{1}{2} \sum_{j,k=1}^{n} c_{jk} d_j(x_j) d_k(x_k) \quad (21)$$

is a Liapunov function.

Proposition 1 (Liapunov Function): The function $V(x)$ satisfies

$$\frac{d}{dt} V(x(t)) \leqslant 0 \quad (39)$$

on admissible trajectories.

Proof: By direct computation,

$$\frac{d}{dt} V(x(t)) = -\sum_{i=1}^{n} a_i(x_i(t)) d_i'(x_i(t))$$
$$\cdot \left[b_i(x_i(t)) - \sum_{k=1}^{n} c_{ik} d_k(x_k(t)) \right]^2. \quad (22)$$

Since $a_i \geqslant 0$ on admissible trajectories and $d_i' \geqslant 0$ by hypothesis, (39) follows.

In some cases where d_i admits a threshold, d_i' is only piecewise differentiable. In these cases, the trajectory derivative $(d/dt)V$ can be replaced by

$$D^+ V(x) = \liminf_{h \to 0+} \frac{1}{h}[V(x + h\dot{x}) - V(x)] \quad (40)$$

and the Riemann integral $\int_0^{x_i} b_i(\xi_i) d_i'(\xi_i)\, d\xi$ in the definition of $V(x)$ can be replaced by a Radon integral.

To apply the LaSalle invariance principle [22], [29], [30] to $V(x)$, we also need to guarantee that $V(x)$ is bounded and continuous on admissible trajectories.

Proposition 2: If the hypotheses of Lemma 1 hold, then $V(x)$ (or a simple redefinition thereof) is bounded and continuous on admissible trajectories.

Proof: If (35) holds, then the integrals

$$\int_0^{x_i} b_i(\xi_i) d_i'(\xi_i)\, d\xi_i \quad (41)$$

in (21) are bounded because admissible trajectories are bounded. The remaining terms

$$\sum_{j,k=1}^{n} c_{jk} d_j(x_j) d_k(x_k) \quad (42)$$

of (21) are bounded because the functions $d_j(x_j)$ are continuous functions of bounded variables.

If (34) holds but

$$\lim_{\xi \to 0+} |b_i(\xi) d_i'(\xi)| < \infty, \quad (43)$$

then the same argument as above is valid. If (43) does not hold, then the integral $\int_0^{x_i}$ in (21) can be replaced by an integral $\int_{\lambda_i}^{x_i}$, where λ_i is a positive constant that is chosen below. Such a choice is possible due to several facts working together. Each d_k is a nonnegative and monotone nondecreasing function of the variable x_k, where $0 \leqslant x_k \leqslant L_k$ at sufficiently large times, $k = 1, 2, \cdots, n$. Consequently, a positive finite L exists such that

$$\sum_{k=1}^{n} c_{ik} d_k(x_k) \leqslant L \quad (44)$$

on all admissible trajectories at sufficiently large times. Since (34) holds, an interval $[0, 2\lambda_i]$ exists such that

$$b_i(x_i) - \sum_{k=1}^{n} c_{ik} d_k(x_k) \geqslant L \quad (45)$$

and thus

$$\dot{x}_i \geqslant L a_i(x_i) \quad (46)$$

whenever $0 < x_i \leqslant 2\lambda_i$ on any admissible trajectory at sufficiently large times. Since function a_i is positive on any interval $[x_i(T), 2\lambda_i]$ where $x_i(T) > 0$, a_i has a positive lower bound on this interval. Thus by (46), if T is chosen so large that (44) holds for $t \geqslant T$, then $x_i(t)$ increases at least at a linear rate until it exceeds λ_i and remains larger than λ_i thereafter. Since this argument holds for any admissible trajectory, the choice of λ_i in the integral $\int_{\lambda_i}^{x_i}$ is justified.

Continuity follows by inspection of each term in (21), replacing the integral $\int_0^{x_i}$ by $\int_{\lambda_i}^{x_i}$ where necessary.

The LaSalle invariance principle therefore implies the following theorem.

Theorem 1 (Convergence of Trajectories): In any system

$$\dot{x}_i = a_i(x_i)\left[b_i(x_i) - \sum_{k=1}^{n} c_{ik} d_k(x_k) \right] \quad (1)$$

such that

a) matrix $\|c_{ij}\|$ is symmetric and all $c_{ij} \geqslant 0$;
b) function a_i is continuous for $\xi \geqslant 0$; function b_i is continuous for $\xi > 0$;
c) function $a_i > 0$ for $\xi > 0$; function $d_i \geqslant 0$ for all ξ;
d) function d_i is differentiable and monotone nondecreasing for $\xi \geqslant 0$;
e) $\limsup_{\xi \to \infty} [b_i(\xi) - c_{ii} d_i(\xi)] < 0$ (33)
for all $i = 1, 2, \cdots, n$;
f) and either

$$\lim_{\xi \to 0+} b_i(\xi) = \infty \quad (34)$$

or

$$\lim_{\xi \to 0+} b_i(\xi) < \infty \quad (35)$$

and

$$\int_0^{\epsilon} \frac{d\xi}{a_i(\xi)} = \infty \quad \text{for some } \epsilon > 0; \quad (36)$$

all admissible trajectories approach the largest invariant set M contained in the set

$$E = \left\{ y \in \mathbb{R}^n : \frac{d}{dt} V(y) = 0,\ y \geqslant 0 \right\}. \quad (47)$$

where

$$\frac{d}{dt}V = -\sum_{i=1}^{n} a_i d_i'\left[b_i - \sum_{k=1}^{n} c_{ik} d_k\right]^2. \quad (22)$$

Corollary 1: If each function d_i is strictly increasing, then the set E consists of equilibrium points of (1).

Proof: Because each function a_i and d_i' is nonnegative on admissible trajectories, each summand in (22) is nonnegative. Hence the result follows by inspection of (47) and (22).

V. Decomposition of Equilibria into Suprathreshold and Subthreshold Variables

Our strategy for analyzing M when the functions d_i can have thresholds is to decompose the variables x_i into suprathreshold and subthreshold variables, and then to show how sets of suprathreshold equilibria can be used to characterize the ω-limit set of the full system (1). To say this more precisely, we now define some concepts.

The *inhibitory threshold* of d_i is a constant $\Gamma_i^- \geqslant 0$ such that

$$\left.\begin{aligned} d_i(\xi) &= 0, && \text{if } \xi \leqslant \Gamma_i^- \\ d_i'(\xi) &> 0, && \text{if } \xi > \Gamma_i^- \end{aligned}\right\}. \quad (48)$$

The function $x_i(t)$ is *suprathreshold* at t if $x_i(t) > \Gamma_i^-$ and *subthreshold* at t if $x_i(t) \leqslant \Gamma_i^-$. At any time t, suprathreshold variables receive signals only from other suprathreshold variables.

Because only suprathreshold variables signal other suprathreshold variables, we can first restrict attention to all possible subsets of suprathreshold values that occur in the ω-limit points $\omega(\gamma)$ of each admissible trajectory γ. Using the fact that each function d_i is strictly increasing in the suprathreshold range, we will show that the suprathreshold subset corresponding to each ω-limit point defines an equilibrium point of the subsystem of (1) that is constructed by eliminating all the subthreshold variables of that ω-limit point. We will show that the set of all such subsystem suprathreshold equilibrium points is countable. We can then show that under a weak additional hypothesis, the ω-limit set of each trajectory is an equilibrium point, and that the set of equilibrium points is totally disconnected. First we make a generic statement about almost all systems (1), and then we study particular classes of neural networks (3) whose global pattern formation properties can be directly verified.

VI. Almost All Suprathreshold Equilibrium Sets Are Countable

In this section, we observe that, for almost all choices of the parameters c_{ik} in (1), Sard's theorem routinely implies that the set of suprathreshold equilibrium points is countable [23], [25]. A generic statement can also be made by varying functions a_i, b_i, and d_i within the class C^1 by combining the Sard theorem with Fubini's theorem. The Sard theorem is stated as Theorem 2 for completeness.

Let X be an open set in $\mathbb{R}^m$, P an open set in $\mathbb{R}^k$, and Z an open set in $\mathbb{R}^n$. Let $S: X \times P \to Z$ be a C^1 map. A point $z \in \mathbb{R}^n$ is said to be a *regular value* of S if rank $dS(\cdot,\cdot) = n$ whenever $S(x, p) = z$, where dS denotes the $n \times (m + k)$ Jacobian matrix of S.

Theorem 2 (Sard): Let z be a regular value of S. Then z is a regular value of $S(\cdot, p)$ for almost all $p \in P$ in the sense of Lebesque measure.

Corollary 2: Let each a_i, b_i, and d_i be in $C^1(0, \infty)$. Let P denote the matrix of parameters $\|c_{ik}\|$. Then a measure zero subset $Q \subset P$ exists such that the suprathreshold equilibria of (1) corresponding to parameters $p \in P \setminus Q$ are countable.

Proof: To consider the equilibrium points of (1), we let $z = 0$ and define the vector function $S = (S_1, S_2, \cdots, S_n)$ by

$$S_i(x) = a_i(x_i)\left[b_i(x_i) - \sum_{k=1}^{n} c_{ik} d_k(x_k)\right], \qquad i = 1, 2, \cdots, n. \quad (49)$$

Then the points for which $S = 0$ are the equilibrium points of (1).

To prove that $dS(\cdot,\cdot)$ has rank n at the suprathreshold equilibria $S = 0$, we prove the stronger statement that $dS(\cdot,\cdot)$ has rank n at all suprathreshold vectors x; that is, at all $x_i > \Gamma_i^- \geqslant 0$, $i = 1, 2, \cdots, n$. By (49)

$$\frac{\partial S_i}{\partial c_{ii}} = -a_i(x_i)d_i(x_i) \quad (50)$$

where, by the positivity of a_i when $x_i > 0$ and the inhibitory threshold condition (48), $a_i(x_i)d_i(x_i) > 0$ at any suprathreshold value of x_i. The corresponding n rows and columns of dS form a diagonal submatrix whose ith entry is given by (50). Matrix dS therefore has rank n at all suprathreshold vectors x.

The main condition of Sard's theorem is hereby satisfied by this matrix S. Thus a set Q of measure zero exists such that $dS(\cdot, p)$ has rank n for all $p \in P \setminus Q$. Now the inverse function theorem can be used at each $p \in P \setminus Q$ to show that the suprathreshold equilibrium points x of $S(x, p) = 0$ are isolated, hence countable.

VII. All ω-Limit Points Are Equilibria

Theorem 3 (Global Pattern Formation) Let all the hypotheses of Theorem 1 hold. Also suppose that no level sets of the functions b_i contain an open interval and that the subsystem suprathreshold equilibrium vectors are countable. Then each admissible trajectory converges to an equilibrium point.

Proof: Consider the ω-limit set $\omega(\gamma)$ of a given admissible trajectory γ. Since Theorem 1 holds, each component x_i of $x \in \omega(\gamma)$ satisfies either

$$a_i(x_i)\left[b_i(x_i) - \sum_{k=1}^{n} c_{ik} d_k(x_k)\right] = 0 \quad (51)$$

or

$$d_i'(x_i) = 0. \quad (52)$$

In the former case, x_i is suprathreshold; in the latter case, subthreshold.

Using this decomposition, we can show that a unique vector of subsystem suprathreshold values exists corresponding to each $\omega(\gamma)$ in the following way. The set $\omega(\gamma)$ is connected. If two or more vectors of subsystem suprathreshold values existed, an uncountable set of subsystem suprathreshold vectors would exist in $\omega(\gamma)$. This basic fact can be seen by projecting $\omega(\gamma)$ onto a coordinate where the two hypothesized vectors differ. The image of $\omega(\gamma)$ on this coordinate is a connected set. This fact, together with the definition of a suprathreshold value, implies that a nontrivial interval of suprathreshold values exists in this image. The inverse image of this interval therefore contains a nondenumerable set of subsystem suprathreshold vectors, a conclusion that contradicts the hypothesis that the set of subsystem suprathreshold vectors is countable. Hence no more than one subsystem suprathreshold vector exists in each $\omega(\gamma)$.

Using this fact, we now show that the subthreshold values of each $\omega(\gamma)$ are uniquely determined. Let $U(\gamma)$ be the indices of the unique subsystem suprathreshold vector $(x_i^* : i \in U(\gamma))$ of $\omega(\gamma)$. For every $i \notin U(\gamma)$, (1) can be rewritten as

$$\dot{x}_i = a_i(x_i)[b_i(x_i) - e_i] + \epsilon(t) \tag{53}$$

where the constant e_i satisfies

$$e_i = \sum_{k \in U(\gamma)} c_{ik} d_k(x_k^*) \tag{54}$$

and

$$\lim_{t \to \infty} \epsilon(t) = 0 \tag{55}$$

because a_i is bounded on admissible trajectories. To complete the proof, we use the fact that the level sets of b_i do not contain an open interval to conclude that each x_i, $i \notin U(\gamma)$, has a limit. Since also each x_i, $i \in U(\gamma)$, has a limit, it will follow that each $\omega(\gamma)$ is an equilibrium point.

The proof shows that the ω-limit set of the one-dimensional equation (53) is a point. Suppose not. Since (53) defines a one-dimensional system, the ω-limit set, being connected, is then a nontrivial closed interval V_i. By hypothesis, the function $b_i - e_i$ in (53) cannot vanish identically on any nontrivial subinterval of V_i. Since function $b_i - e_i$ is continuous, a subinterval $W_i \subset V_i$ and an $\epsilon > 0$ exist such that either $b_i(\xi) - e_i \geqslant \epsilon$ if $\xi \in W_i$ or $b_i(\xi) - e_i \leqslant -\epsilon$ if $\xi \in W_i$. In either case, x_i will be forced off interval W_i at all sufficiently large times by (55) and the fact that $a_i > 0$ except when $x_i = 0$. Hence no nontrivial interval W_i can be contained in the ω-limit set of (53). This ω-limit set is thus a point, and the proof is complete.

Corollary 3 (Almost Absolute Stability): Consider the class of systems (1) such that

1) hypotheses a)–f) of Theorem 1 hold;
2) each function a_i, b_i, and d_i is in $C^1(0, \infty)$;
3) none of the level sets of b_i contains an open interval.

Then for almost all choices of the parameters c_{ik}, global pattern formation occurs.

Proof: The proof follows directly from Corollary 2 and Theorem 3.

The hypotheses of Theorem 3 allow us to conclude that the set of all equilibrium points of (1) is a totally disconnected set. A *totally disconnected* set is a set whose largest connected subset is a point.

Instead of considering the solutions of $b_i(\xi) = e_i$ corresponding to the ω-limit set $\omega(\gamma)$ of individual trajectories, as we did to prove Theorem 3, in this proof we consider the set of solutions of $b_i(\xi) = e_i$ generated by arbitrary admissible trajectories.

Theorem 4 (Totally Disconnected Equilibrium Set): Suppose that each b_i is continuous, that no level set of b_i contains an open interval, and that the system suprathreshold equilibrium vectors are countable. Then the set of all equilibrium points of (1) is totally disconnected.

Proof: Each choice of subsystem suprathreshold vector defines a constant value of e_i in (54). For fixed e_i, the level set

$$\{\xi : b_i(\xi) - e_i = 0\} \tag{56}$$

is nowhere dense, since if (56) were dense on some interval, the continuity of b_i would imply that the level set (56) contains an open interval, which is impossible.

By hypothesis, only countably many choices of e_i exist for each $i = 1, 2, \cdots, n$. Since each set (56) is nowhere dense, the set of all subthreshold equilibrium solutions of (53) is a countable union of nowhere dense sets and is therefore nowhere dense by the Baire category theorem. By hypothesis, the set of all subsystem suprathreshold equilibrium solutions of (1) is countable. The set of all x_i corresponding to the subsystem suprathreshold equilibrium solutions of (1) is therefore also countable. The union P_i of the nowhere dense subthreshold set and the countable suprathreshold set is totally disconnected. The product set $X_{i=1}^n P_i$ is also totally disconnected. Since the set of all equilibria of (1) is contained in $X_{i=1}^n P_i$, it is totally disconnected.

VIII. Neural Networks with Finitely Many Suprathreshold Equilibrium Points

To remove the "almost all" from results such as Corollary 3, we consider various special cases that are of physical interest, notably the shunting competitive networks (27) with polynomial or sigmoid feedback signal functions. We write the networks (27) using the change of variables

$$x_i = y_i + C_i \tag{28}$$

to make the results comparable to previous results about (1). Then (27) can be written as

$$\dot{x}_i = S_i(x), \qquad i = 1, 2, \cdots, n \tag{57}$$

such that

$$S_i(x) = \alpha_i + (\beta_i - x_i) F_i(x_i) - x_i \left(\gamma_i + \sum_{k=1}^{n} c_{ik} G_k(x_k) \right) \tag{58}$$

where

$$\alpha_i = a_i c_i + (b_i + c_i) I_i, \tag{59}$$

$$\beta_i = b_i + c_i, \tag{60}$$

$$\gamma_i = a_i + I_i + J_i, \tag{61}$$

$$F_i(x_i) = f_i(x_i - c_i), \tag{62}$$

and

$$G_i(x_i) = g_i(x_i - c_i). \tag{63}$$

One natural approach to proving that only finitely many suprathreshold equilibrium points exist is to apply a basic theorem from the theory of several complex variables [35]. The following results illustrate rather than exhaust the applications of this theorem to our systems.

The theorem in question concerns analytic subvarieties of a connected open set Ω of $\mathbb{C}^n = \{n\text{-tuplets of complex variables}\}$. A set $V \subset \Omega$ is an *analytic subvariety* of Ω if every point $p \in \Omega$ has a neighborhood $N(p)$ such that

$$V \cap N(p) = \bigcap_{i=1}^{r} Z(h_i) \tag{64}$$

where $Z(h_i)$ is the set of zeros of the function h_i holomorphic in $N(p)$. Our applications derive from the following theorem.

Theorem 5: Every compact analytic subvariety of a connected open set Ω is a finite set of points.

A general strategy for applying Theorem 5 to neural networks can be stated as five steps.

1) Choose the signal function F_i and G_i in (62) and (63), respectively, to be real analytic on their suprathreshold intervals.

2) Extend the definitions of F_i and G_i to make them complex analytic inside a sufficiently large open disk. (It does not matter that the analytic extension of the signal function to the subthreshold interval no longer agrees with the original definition of the function.)

3) Extend S_i in (58) to be an analytic function $\Phi_i(z)$ in an open connected set $\Omega_i \subset C^n$.

4) Show that the solutions to the system of equations

$$\phi_i(z) = 0, \qquad i = 1, 2, \ldots, n \tag{65}$$

are contained in a bounded open set P whose closure is contained in $\Omega = \cap_{i=1}^{n} \Omega_i$. Since the set of zeros is closed, the set of zeros is a compact analytic subvariety of Ω, hence finite.

5) Set all imaginary parts of these zeros equal to zero to prove that finitely many suprathreshold equilibria exist.

The method is illustrated by the following three theorems.

Theorem 6 (Polynomial Signals): Let each function $F_i(\xi)$ and $G_i(\xi)$ be a polynomial in the suprathreshold domain $\xi \geq \Gamma_i^-$, and suppose that $\deg F_i > \deg G_j$ whenever $c_{ij} > 0$, $i, j = 1, 2, \cdots, n$. Then only finitely many suprathreshold equilibrium points of (1) exist.

Proof: Analytically continue the functions $S_i(x)$, $x_i \geq \Gamma_i^-$, $i = 1, 2, \cdots, n$ to be polynomial functions $\tilde{S}_i(z)$ of n complex variables z. The zeros of system $\tilde{S}_i(z) = 0$, $i = 1, 2, \cdots, n$, are thus an analytic subvariety W of $\mathbb{C}^n$. We show that W is bounded, hence compact. Then using Theorem 5 and the fact that $S_i(x) = \tilde{S}_i(z)$ when z is real and $x_i \geq \Gamma_i^-$, $i = 1, 2, \cdots, n$, it follows that at most finitely many suprathreshold equilibria of (57) exist.

Boundedness is easily proved as follows. Choose any $z = (z_1, z_2, \cdots, z_n) \in \mathbb{C}^n$. Let z_i be the component of maximal modulus in z; that is, $|z_i| \geq |z_j|$, $j \neq i$. Consider the highest degree term of $\tilde{S}_i(z)$. This term corresponds to the highest degree term of the analytic continuation of term $x_i F_i(x_i)$ in $S_i(x)$. If $|z|$ is chosen sufficiently large, the degree condition on the signal functions along with the inequalities $|z_i| \geq |z_j|$, $j \neq i$, imply that the modulus of this highest degree term exceeds the sum of moduli of all other terms in $\tilde{S}_i(z)$. Consequently, $\tilde{S}_i(z) \neq 0$ if $|z| \gg 0$. In other words, no zero exists of the full system $\tilde{S}_i(z) = 0$, $i = 1, 2, \cdots, n$, outside some bounded ball in $\mathbb{C}^n$, and the proof is complete.

Corollary 4 (Polynomial Absolute Stability): Let system (57) be given with a symmetric matrix $\|c_{ij}\|$ of nonnegative interaction coefficients and signal functions that are polynomial in their suprathreshold region such that $\deg F_i > \deg G_j$ for all $c_{ij} > 0$ and each G_j has nonnegative coefficients. Then global pattern formation is absolutely stable within this class of networks.

The proof consists in verifying that the hypotheses of Theorems 1, 3, and 6 are satisfied.

Theorem 6 demonstrates that suprathreshold polynomial signal functions for which the norm of excitatory feedback grows more quickly than the norm of inhibitory feedback lead to global pattern formation. Any smooth signal functions can be uniformly approximated within this class of polynomials, but that does not imply that (58) has countably many zeros using these signal functions. The next result considers sigmoid signal functions to illustrate how Theorem 5 can be applied to a nonpolynomial case of great physical interest (Grossberg [12], [21]). Sigmoid signal functions, unlike polynomials, approach finite asymptotes at large activity values. Absolute stability holds within a class of sigmoid functions wherein a trade-off exists between the rate of signal growth, the asymptote of signal growth, and the spatial breadth and size of inhibitory interaction strengths.

To illustrate the factors that control sigmoid signal behavior, we consider sigmoid signal functions such that if $x_i \geq \Gamma_i^-$,

$$F_i(x_i) = \frac{p_i (x_i - \Gamma_i^-)^{N_i}}{q^{N_i} + (x_i - \Gamma_i^-)^{N_i}} \tag{66}$$

and

$$G_i(x_i) = \frac{(x_i - \Gamma_i^-)^{M_i}}{r^{M_i} + (x_i - \Gamma_i^-)^{M_i}} \tag{67}$$

where M_i and N_i are positive integers, $i = 1, 2, \cdots, n$. The asymptote of G_i is set equal to one without loss of generality because G_i multiplies a coefficient c_{ij} in all its appearances in (55), and the symmetry $c_{ij} = c_{ji}$ is not needed in the following estimate.

Theorem 7 (Sigmoid Signals): Suppose that the parameters in (66) and (67) are chosen to satisfy the following three conditions

1) $\epsilon > 0$ and $\delta > 1$ exist such that

$$\max(b_i + c_i - \Gamma_i^-, q_i) < \epsilon < \delta\epsilon < r_i, \quad i = 1, 2, \cdots, n. \tag{68}$$

2) The constants

$$s_i = \sum_{k=1}^{n} c_{ik}(\delta^{M_k} - 1)^{-1} \tag{69}$$

satisfy the inequalities

$$2s_i < p_i, \qquad i = 1, 2, \cdots, n. \tag{70}$$

3) The inequality

$$(p_i - 2s_i)q_i > 2|\alpha_i - \gamma_i\Gamma_i^-| + p_i|\beta_i - \Gamma_i^-| + 2s_i\Gamma_i^- \tag{71}$$

holds, $i = 1, 2, \cdots, n$.

Then at most finitely many suprathreshold equilibrium points of (57) exist.

Remark: Inequality (68) says that the excitatory signal functions change faster-than-linearly at smaller activities than the inhibitory signal functions, and that the turning points q_i and r_i are uniformly separated across signal functions. Inequality (70) says that the excitatory feedback elicited by large activities dominates the total inhibitory feedback elicited by these activities. These two inequalities are thus analogous to the conditions on polynomial degrees in the previous theorem. The left-hand side of inequality (71) refines these constraints by requiring the faster-than-linear range of the excitatory signal function to occur at large activities if the strength of feedback inhibition is close to the strength of feedback excitation at these activities.

Proof: To simplify notation, let $w_i = x_i - \Gamma_i^-$ and define $S_i^*(w) = S_i(x)$. Now multiply $S_i^*(w)$ by the denominator of F_i to find

$$U_i(w) = (q_i^{N_i} + z_i^{N_i})S_i^*(w). \tag{72}$$

Function $U_i(w) = 0$ at some $w \in \mathbb{R}_+^n$ iff $S_i(x) = 0$ at a suprathreshold value of x, $i = 1, 2, \cdots, n$. Use inequality (68) to analytically continue $U_i(w)$ to a function $\tilde{U}_i(z)$ analytic on the polydisk $\Omega = \{z : |z_i| < \epsilon\}$. (In fact, we could define $\tilde{U}_i(z)$ analytically for $|z_i| < r_i$). Inequality (68) guarantees that all real suprathreshold zeros are included in Ω. We will show the subvariety W of zeros $\tilde{U}_i(z) = 0$, $i = 1, 2, \cdots, n$, is contained in the polydisk $\Omega' = \{z : |z_i| < q_i\}$. By (68), $q_i < \epsilon$, $i = 1, 2, \cdots, n$. Hence the subvariety W is compact, and the theorem will follow.

To complete the proof, we write $\tilde{U}_i(z)$ in the following form using the notation $R_i(z)$ for the sum of inhibitory feedback terms that analytically continue $\sum_{k=1}^{n} c_{ik}G_k(w_k + \Gamma_k^-)$:

$$\begin{aligned}\tilde{U}_i(z) = &-z_i^{N_i+1}[\gamma_i + p_i + R_i(z)] \\ &+ z_i^{N_i}[\alpha_i - \gamma_i\Gamma_i^- + p_i(\beta_i - \Gamma_i^-) - \Gamma_i^- R_i(z)] \\ &- z_i q_i^{N_i}[\gamma_i + \Gamma_i^- R_i(z)] \\ &+ q_i^{N_i}[\alpha_i - \gamma_i\Gamma_i^- - \Gamma_i^- R_i(z)].\end{aligned} \tag{73}$$

The analytic continuation $\tilde{G}_k(z_k)$ of $G_k(w_k + \Gamma_i^-)$ can be rewritten as

$$\tilde{G}_k(z_k) = \frac{1}{r_k^{M_k} z_k^{-M_k} + 1}. \tag{74}$$

Because $|z_k| \leqslant \epsilon$, (68) implies

$$|\tilde{G}_k(z_k)| \leqslant (\delta^{M_k} - 1)^{-1}. \tag{75}$$

Since (75) is true for every z_k when $z \in \Omega$, it follows for every $i = 1, 2, \cdots, n$ that

$$|R_i(z)| \leqslant s_i \qquad \text{if } z \in \Omega. \tag{76}$$

By (73) and (75), if $z \in \Omega$

$$|\tilde{U}_i(z)| \geqslant L_i(|z_i|) \tag{77}$$

where

$$\begin{aligned}L_i(\xi) = &\,\xi^{N_i+1}(\gamma_i + p_i - s_i) \\ &- \xi^{N_i}[|\alpha_i - \gamma_i\Gamma_i^-| + p_i|\beta_i - \Gamma_i^-| + \Gamma_i^- s_i] \\ &- \xi q_i^{N_i}[\gamma_i + s_i] - q_i^{N_i}[|\alpha_i - \gamma_i\Gamma_i^-| + \Gamma_i^{-1}s_i].\end{aligned} \tag{78}$$

To show that $L_i(|z_i|) > 0$ if $\epsilon > |z_i| \geqslant q_i$, we verify that $L_i(q_i) > 0$ and $(dL_i/d\xi)(\xi) \geqslant 0$ for $\epsilon > \xi \geqslant q_i$ using (71). This fact along with (76) completes the proof.

Inequality (68) requires that $q_i < r_i$. Analogous results hold even if $q_i \geqslant r_i$ when both q_i and r_i are chosen sufficiently large. We state without proof such a theorem.

Theorem 8 (Sigmoid Signals): Suppose that $\epsilon > 0$ and $\delta > 1$ exist such that

$$\max_i(b_i + c_i - \gamma_i, v_i) < \epsilon < \delta\epsilon < \min_{j,k}(q_k, r_k) \tag{79}$$

where

$$v_i = \frac{|\alpha_i - \gamma_i\Gamma_i^-| + \beta_i t_i + \Gamma_i^-(s_i + t_i)}{\gamma_i - (s_i + t_i)}, \tag{80}$$

s_i is defined as in (69),

$$t_i = (\delta^{N_i} - 1)^{-1}, \tag{81}$$

and

$$\gamma_i > s_i + t_i, \tag{82}$$

$i = 1, 2, \cdots, n$. Then there are at most finitely many suprathreshold equilibrium points of (57).

Because not all parameter choices of the sigmoid signal functions (66) and (67) have been shown to imply global pattern formation, it is inappropriate to summarize Theorems 7 and 8 as absolute stability results. Instead we summarize the constraints which have been shown to yield global pattern formation when these sigmoid signal functions are used.

Corollary 5 (Sigmoid Global Pattern Formation): Let system (57) possess a nonnegative symmetric interaction matrix $\|c_{ij}\|$, positive decay rates A_i, and suprathreshold sigmoid signal functions (66) and (67) that satisfy the constraints of Theorem 7 or 8 and the inequalities $M_i > 1$ in (67), $i = 1, 2, \cdots, n$. Then global pattern formation occurs.

Proof: The new constraint $M_i > 1$ implies that d_i is differentiable even when $x_i = \Gamma_i^-$, as is required by Theorem 1. The constraint of Theorem 3 that b_i possess no nontrivial level intervals can be violated in (30) only if

$$A_i C_i + (B_i + C_i) I_i = 0. \tag{83}$$

Since $A_i > 0$, this case can only occur if $C_i = 0 = I_i$, which implies that x_i remains between 0 and B_i. Suppose $\Gamma_i^- = 0$. Then all $x_i > 0$ are suprathreshold values, and x_i can attain only one subthreshold equilibrium value, namely zero. Suppose $\Gamma_i^- > 0$. If $x_i(T) \leqslant \Gamma_i^-$ for some $t = T$, then $x_i(t) \leqslant \Gamma_i^-$ for all $t = T$. This is true because the excitatory threshold of F_i in (66) equals the inhibitory threshold Γ_i^- of G_i in (67), no input I_i can excite x_i due to (83), and all other v_k, $k \neq i$, can only inhibit x_i. Thus for $t \geqslant T$, $\dot{x}_i \leqslant -A_i x_i$, so that x_i approaches the unique subthreshold value zero. In all cases, only one subthreshold equilibrium value of each x_i can exist, which completes the proof.

IX. Concluding Remarks

The present article notes that systems (1) that are competitive and possess symmetric interactions admit a global Liapunov function. Given this observation, it remains to characterize the set E and its relationship to the equilibrium points of (1). Despite useful partial results, this approach has not yet handled all of the physically interesting neural networks wherein absolute stability may be conjectured to occur. For example, extensive numerical analysis of neural networks of the form

$$\dot{x}_i = -A_i x_i + (B_i - C_i x_i)\left[I_i + \sum_{k=1}^{n} D_{ik} f_k(x_k)\right] - (E_i x_i + F_i)\left[J_i + \sum_{k=1}^{n} G_{ik} g_k(x_k)\right] \tag{84}$$

where both matrices $D = \|D_{ik}\|$ and $G = \|G_{ik}\|$ are symmetric suggests that an absolute stability result should exist for these networks, which generalize (3) [3], [5], [31]. In these networks, cooperative interactions $\sum_{k=1}^{n} D_{ik} f_k(x_k)$ as well as competitive interactions $\sum_{k=1}^{n} G_{ik} g_k(x_k)$ are permissible. A global Liapunov function whose equilibrium set can be effectively analyzed has not yet been discovered for the networks (84).

It remains an open question whether the Liapunov function approach, which requires a study of equilibrium points, or an alternative global approach, such as the Liapunov functional approach which sidesteps a direct study of equilibrium points [14], [18], [21], will ultimately handle all of the physically important cases.

References

[1] G. A. Carpenter, "Bursting phenomena in excitable membranes," *SIAM J. Appl. Math.*, vol. 36, pp. 334–372, 1979.

[2] ____, "Normal and abnormal signal patterns in nerve cells," in *Mathematical Psychology and Psychophysiology*, S. Grossberg, Ed. Providence, RI: Amer. Math. Soc., 1981, pp. 48–90.

[3] M. A. Cohen and S. Grossberg, "Some global properties of binocular resonances: Disparity matching, filling-in, and figure ground systhesis," in *Figural Synthesis*, T. Caelli and P. Dodwell, Eds. Hillsdale, NJ: Erlbaum Press, 1983.

[4] M. Eigen and P. Schuster, "The hypercycle: A principle of natural self-organization. B. The abstract hypercycle," *Naturwissenschaften*, vol. 65, pp. 7–41, 1978.

[5] S. A. Ellias and S. Grossberg, "Pattern formation, contrast control, and oscillations in the short term memory of shunting on-center off-surround networks," *Biol. Cybern.*, vol. 20, pp. 69–98, 1975.

[6] M. E. Gilpin and F. J. Ayala, "Global models of growth and competition," *Proc. Nat. Acad. Sci.*, vol. 70, pp. 3590–3593, 1973.

[7] B. S. Goh and T. T. Agnew, "Stability in Gilpin and Ayala's models of competition," *J. Math. Biol.*, vol. 4, pp. 275–279, 1977.

[8] S. Grossberg, "Some physiological and biochemical consequences of psychological postulates," *Proc. Nat. Acad. Sci.*, vol. 60, pp. 758–765, 1968.

[9] ____, "On learning information, lateral inhibition, and transmitters," *Math. Biosci.*, vol. 4, pp. 225–310, 1969.

[10] ____, "Neural pattern discrimination," *J. Theoret. Biol.*, vol. 27, pp. 291–337, 1970.

[11] ____, "A neural theory of punishment and avoidance. II. Quantitative theory," *Math. Biosci.*, vol. 15, pp. 39–67, 1972.

[12] ____, "Contour enhancement, short term memory, and constancies in reverberating neural networks," *Studies in Appl. Math.*, vol. 52, pp. 217–257, 1973.

[13] ____, "On the development of feature detectors in the visual cortex with applications to learning and reaction diffusion systems," *Biol. Cybern.*, vol. 21, pp. 145–159, 1976.

[14] ____, "Competition, decision, and consensus," *J. Math. Anal. Appl.*, vol. 66, pp. 470–493, 1978.

[15] ____, "A theory of human memory: Self-organization and performance of sensory-motor codes, maps, and plans," in *Progress Theoretical Biology*, vol. 5, R. Rosen and F. Snell, Eds. New York: Academic, 1978.

[16] ____, "Communication, memory, and development," in *Progress in Theoretical Biology*, vol. 5, R. Rosen and F. Snell, Eds. New York: Academic, 1978.

[17] ____, "Decisions, patterns, and oscillations in the dynamics of competitive systems with applications to Volterra-Lotka systems," *J. Theoret. Biol.*, vol. 73, pp. 101–130, 1978.

[18] ____, "Biological competition: Decision rules, pattern formation, and oscillations," *Proc. Nat. Acad. Sci.*, vol. 77, pp. 2338–2342, 1980.

[19] ____, "How does a brain build a cognitive code?" *Psychol. Rev.*, vol. 58, pp. 1–51, 1980.

[20] ____, "Intracellular mechanisms of adaptation and self-regulation in self-organizing networks: The role of chemical transducers," *Bull. Math. Biol.*, vol. 42, 1980.

[21] ____, "Adaptive resonance in development, perception, and cognition," in *Mathematical Psychology and Psychophysiology*, S. Grossberg, Ed. Providence RI: Amer. Math. Soc., 1981.

[22] J. Hale, *Ordinary Differential Equations*. New York: Wiley-Interscience, 1969.

[23] M. W. Hirsch, *Differential Topology*. New York: Springer-Verlag, 1976.

[24] A. L. Hodgkin, *The Conduction of the Nervous Impulse*. Liverpool, England: Liverpool Univ. Press, 1964.

[25] J. Kaplan and J. Yorke, "Competitive exclusion and nonequilibrium co-existence," *Amer. Naturalist*, vol. 111, pp. 1031–1036, 1977.

[26] B. Katz, *Nerve, Muscle, and Synapse*. New York: McGraw-Hill, 1966.

[27] Kilmer, W. L., "On some realistic constraints in prey-predator

mathematics," *J. Theoret. Biol.*, vol. 36, pp. 9–22, 1972.

[28] S. W. Kuffler and J. G. Nicholls, *From Neuron to Brain*. Sundenland, MA: Sinauer Assoc., 1976.

[29] J. P. LaSalle, "An invariance principle in the theory of stability," in *Differential Equations and Dynamical Systems*, J. K. Hale and J. P. LaSalle, Eds. New York: Academic, 1967.

[30] ——, "Stability theory for ordinary differential equations," *J. Differential Equations*, vol. 4, pp. 57–65, 1968.

[31] D. Levine and S. Grossberg, "On visual illusions in neural networks: Line neutralization, tilt aftereffect, and angle expansion," *J. Theoret. Biol.*, vol. 61, pp. 477–504, 1976.

[32] R. H. MacArthur, "Species packing and competitive equilibrium for many species," *Theoret. Population Biol.*, vol. 1, pp. 1–11, 1970.

[33] R. M. May and W. J. Leonard, "Nonlinear aspects of competition between three species," *SIAM J. Appl. Math.*, vol. 29, pp. 243–253, 1975.

[34] F. Ratliff, *Mach Bands: Quantitative Studies of Neural Networks in the Retina*. San Francisco, CA: Holden-Day, 1965.

[35] W. Rudin, *Function Theory on the Unit Ball of* $\mathbb{C}^n$. New York: Springer-Verlag, 1980.

[36] P. Schuster, K. Sigmund, and R. Wolff, "On ω-limits for competition between three species," *SIAM J. Appl. Math.*, vol. 37, pp. 49–54, 1979.

[37] Y. Takeuchi, N. Adachi, and H. Tokumaru, "The stability of generalized Volterra equations," *J. Math. Anal. Appl.*, vol. 62, pp. 453–473, 1978.

Reprinted from Proceedings of the National Academy of Sciences USA 81, May 1984, pp. 3088-92. Copyright © 1984 by the National Academy of Sciences USA.

Neurons with graded response have collective computational properties like those of two-state neurons

(associative memory/neural network/stability/action potentials)

J. J. Hopfield

Divisions of Chemistry and Biology, California Institute of Technology, Pasadena, CA 91125; and Bell Laboratories, Murray Hill, NJ 07974

Contributed by J. J. Hopfield, February 13, 1984

ABSTRACT **A model for a large network of "neurons" with a graded response (or sigmoid input–output relation) is studied. This deterministic system has collective properties in very close correspondence with the earlier stochastic model based on McCulloch–Pitts neurons. The content-addressable memory and other emergent collective properties of the original model also are present in the graded response model. The idea that such collective properties are used in biological systems is given added credence by the continued presence of such properties for more nearly biological "neurons." Collective analog electrical circuits of the kind described will certainly function. The collective states of the two models have a simple correspondence. The original model will continue to be useful for simulations, because its connection to graded response systems is established. Equations that include the effect of action potentials in the graded response system are also developed.**

Recent papers (1–3) have explored the ability of a system of highly interconnected "neurons" to have useful collective computational properties. These properties emerge spontaneously in a system having a large number of elementary "neurons." Content-addressable memory (CAM) is one of the simplest collective properties of such a system. The mathematical modeling has been based on "neurons" that are different both from real biological neurons and from the realistic functioning of simple electronic circuits. Some of these differences are major enough that neurobiologists and circuit engineers alike have questioned whether real neural or electrical circuits would actually exhibit the kind of behaviors found in the model system even if the "neurons" were connected in the fashion envisioned.

Two major divergences between the model and biological or physical systems stand out. Real neurons (and real physical devices such as operational amplifiers that might mimic them) have continuous input–output relations. (Action potentials are omitted until *Discussion*.) The original modeling used two-state McCulloch–Pitts (4) threshold devices having outputs of 0 or 1 only. Real neurons and real physical circuits have integrative time delays due to capacitance, and the time evolution of the state of such systems should be represented by a differential equation (perhaps with added noise). The original modeling used a stochastic algorithm involving sudden 0–1 or 1–0 changes of states of neurons at random times. This paper shows that the important properties of the original model remain intact when these two simplifications of the modeling are eliminated. Although it is uncertain whether the properties of these new continuous "neurons" are yet close enough to the essential properties of real neurons (and/or their dendritic arborization) to be directly applicable to neurobiology, a major conceptual obstacle has been eliminated. It is certain that a CAM constructed on the basic ideas of the original model (1) but built of operational amplifiers and resistors will function.

Form of the Original Model

The original model used two-state threshold "neurons" that followed a stochastic algorithm. Each model neuron i had two states, characterized by the output V_i of the neuron having the values V_i^0 or V_i^1 (which may often be taken as 0 and 1, respectively). The input of each neuron came from two sources, external inputs I_i and inputs from other neurons. The total input to neuron i is then

$$\text{Input to } i = H_i = \sum_{j \neq i} T_{ij} V_j + I_i. \quad [1]$$

The element T_{ij} can be biologically viewed as a description of the synaptic interconnection strength from neuron j to neuron i.

CAM and other useful computations in this system involve the change of state of the system with time. The motion of the state of a system of N neurons in state space describes the computation that the set of neurons is performing. A model therefore must describe how the state evolves in time, and the original model describes this in terms of a stochastic evolution. Each neuron samples its input at random times. It changes the value of its output or leaves it fixed according to a threshold rule with thresholds U_i.

$$\begin{aligned} V_i &\to V_i^0 \text{ if } \sum_{j \neq i} T_{ij} V_j + I_i < U_i \\ &\to V_i^1 \text{ if } \sum_{j \neq i} T_{ij} V_j + I_i > U_i. \end{aligned} \quad [2]$$

The interrogation of each neuron is a stochastic process, taking place at a mean rate W for each neuron. The times of interrogation of each neuron are independent of the times at which other neurons are interrogated. The algorithm is thus *asynchronous*, in contrast to the usual kind of processing done with threshold devices. This asynchrony was deliberately introduced to represent a combination of propagation delays, jitter, and noise in real neural systems. Synchronous systems might have additional collective properties (5, 6).

The original model behaves as an associative memory (or CAM) when the state space flow generated by the algorithm is characterized by a set of stable fixed points. If these stable points describe a simple flow in which nearby points in state space tend to remain close during the flow (i.e., a nonmixing flow), then initial states that are close (in Hamming distance) to a particular stable state and far from all others will tend to terminate in that nearby stable state.

The publication costs of this article were defrayed in part by page charge payment. This article must therefore be hereby marked "*advertisement*" in accordance with 18 U.S.C. §1734 solely to indicate this fact.

Abbreviations: CAM, content-addressable memory; RC, resistance–capacitance.

If the location of a particular stable point in state space is thought of as the information of a particular memory of the system, states near to that particular stable point contain partial information about that memory. From an initial state of partial information about a memory, a final stable state with all the information of the memory is found. The memory is reached not by knowing an address, but rather by supplying in the initial state some subpart of the memory. Any subpart of adequate size will do—the memory is truly addressable by *content* rather than location. A given T matrix contains many memories simultaneously, which are reconstructed individually from partial information in an initial state.

Convergent flow to stable states is the essential feature of this CAM operation. There is a simple mathematical condition which guarantees that the state space flow algorithm converges on stable states. Any symmetric T with zero diagonal elements (i.e., $T_{ij} = T_{ji}$, $T_{ii} = 0$) will produce such a flow. The proof of this property followed from the construction of an appropriate energy function that is always decreased by any state change produced by the algorithm. Consider the function

$$E = -\frac{1}{2}\sum\sum_{i \neq j} T_{ij}V_iV_j - \sum_i I_iV_i + \sum_i U_iV_i. \quad [3]$$

The change ΔE in E due to changing the state of neuron i by ΔV_i is

$$\Delta E = -\left[\sum_{j \neq i} T_{ij}V_j + I_i - U_i\right]\Delta V_i. \quad [4]$$

But according to the algorithm, ΔV_i is positive only when the bracket is positive, and similarly for the negative case. Thus any change in E under the algorithm is negative. E is bounded, so the iteration of the algorithm must lead to stable states that do not further change with time.

A Continuous, Deterministic Model

We now construct a model that is based on continuous variables and responses but retains all the significant behaviors of the original model. Let the output variable V_i for neuron i have the range $V_i^0 \leq V_i \leq V_i^1$ and be a continuous and monotone-increasing function of the instantaneous input u_i to neuron i. The typical input–output relation $g_i(u_i)$ shown in Fig. 1*a* is sigmoid with asymptotes V_i^0 and V_i^1. For neurons exhibiting action potentials, u_i could be thought of as the mean soma potential of a neuron from the total effect of its excitatory and inhibitory inputs. V_i can be viewed as the short-term average of the firing rate of the cell i. Other biological interpretations are possible—for example, nonlinear processing may be done at junctions in a dendritic arbor (7), and the model "neurons" could represent such junctions. In terms of electrical circuits, $g_i(u_i)$ represents the input–output characteristic of a nonlinear amplifier with negligible response time. It is convenient also to define the inverse output–input relation, $g_i^{-1}(V)$.

In a biological system, u_i will lag behind the instantaneous outputs V_j of the other cells because of the input capacitance C of the cell membranes, the transmembrane resistance R, and the finite impedance T_{ij}^{-1} between the output V_j and the cell body of cell i. Thus there is a resistance–capacitance (RC) charging equation that determines the rate of change of u_i.

$$C_i(du_i/dt) = \sum_j T_{ij}V_j - u_i/R_i + I_i$$
$$u_i = g_i^{-1}(V_i). \quad [5]$$

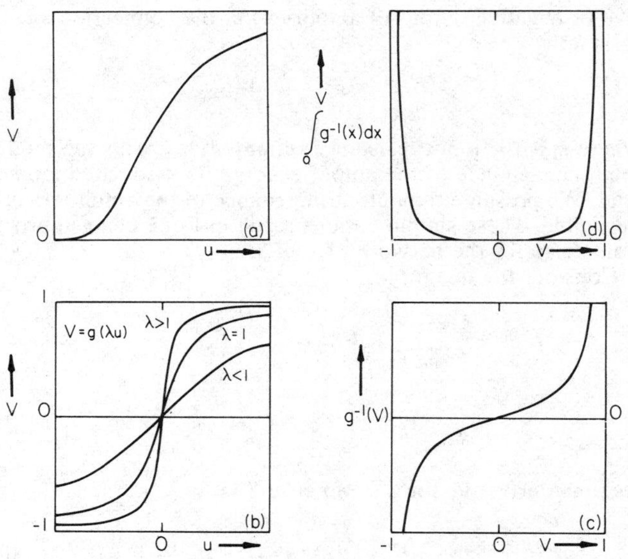

FIG. 1. (*a*) The sigmoid input–output relation for a typical neuron. All the $g(u)$ of this paper have such a form, with possible horizontal and vertical translations. (*b*) The input–output relation $g(\lambda u)$ for the "neurons" of the continuous model for three values of the gain scaling parameter λ. (*c*) The output–input relation $u = g^{-1}(V)$ for the g shown in *b*. (*d*) The contribution of g to the energy of Eq. **5** as a function of V.

$T_{ij}V_j$ represents the electrical current input to cell i due to the present potential of cell j, and T_{ij} is thus the synapse efficacy. Linear summing of inputs is assumed. T_{ij} of both signs should occur. I_i is any other (fixed) input current to neuron i.

The same set of equations represents the resistively connected network of electrical amplifiers sketched in Fig. 2. It appears more complicated than the description of the neural system because the electrical problem of providing inhibition and excitation requires an additional inverting amplifier and a negative signal wire. The magnitude of T_{ij} is $1/R_{ij}$, where R_{ij} is the resistor connecting the output of j to the input line i, while the sign of T_{ij} is determined by the choice of the posi-

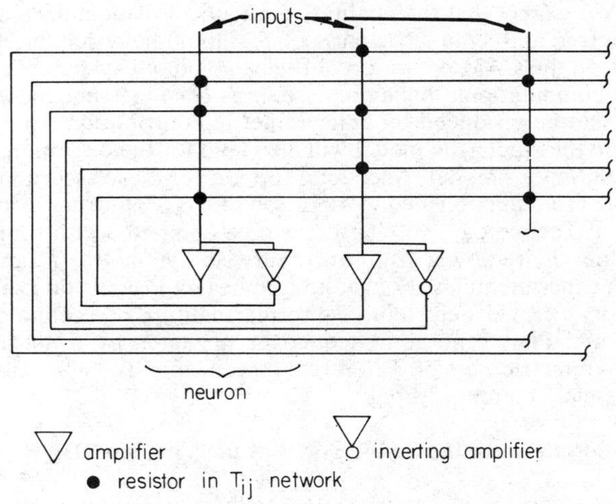

FIG. 2. An electrical circuit that corresponds to Eq. **5** when the amplifiers are fast. The input capacitance and resistances are not drawn. A particularly simple special case can have all positive T_{ij} of the same strength and no negative T_{ij} and replaces the array of negative wires with a single negative feedback amplifier sending a common output to each "neuron."

tive or negative output of amplifier j at the connection site. R_i is now

$$1/R_i = 1/\rho_i + \sum_j 1/R_{ij}, \quad [6]$$

where ρ_i is the input resistance of amplifier i. C_i is the total input capacitance of the amplifier i and its associated input lead. We presume the output impedance of the amplifiers is negligible. These simplifications result in Eq. **5** being appropriate also for the network of Fig. 2.

Consider the quantity

$$E = -\frac{1}{2}\sum_{i,j}\sum T_{ij}V_iV_j + \sum_i (1/R_i)\int_0^{V_i} g_i^{-1}(V)dV + \sum_i I_iV_i. \quad [7]$$

Its time derivative for a symmetric T is

$$dE/dt = -\sum_i dV_i/dt\left(\sum_j T_{ij}V_j - u_i/R_i + I_i\right). \quad [8]$$

The parenthesis is the right-hand side of Eq. **5**, so

$$dE/dT = -\sum C_i(dV_i/dt)(du_i/dt) = -\sum C_i g_i^{-1\prime}(V_i)(dV_i/dt)^2. \quad [9]$$

Since $g_i^{-1}(V_i)$ is a monotone increasing function and C_i is positive, each term in this sum is nonnegative. Therefore

$$dE/dt \le 0,\ dE/dt = 0 \rightarrow dV_i/dt = 0 \text{ for all } i. \quad [10]$$

Together with the boundedness of E, Eq. **10** shows that the time evolution of the system is a motion in state space that seeks out minima in E and comes to a stop at such points. E is a Liapunov function for the system.

This deterministic model has the same flow properties in its continuous space that the stochastic model does in its discrete space. It can therefore be used in CAM or any other computational task for which an energy function is essential (3). We expect that the qualitative effects of disorganized or organized anti-symmetric parts of T_{ij} should have similar effects on the CAM operation of the new and old system. The new computational behaviors (such as learning sequences) that can be produced by antisymmetric contributions to T_{ij} within the stochastic model will also hold for the deterministic continuous model. Anecdotal support for these assertions comes from unpublished work of John Platt (California Institute of Technology) solving Eq. **5** on a computer with some random T_{ij} removed from an otherwise symmetric T, and from experimental work of John Lambe (Jet Propulsion Laboratory), David Feinstein (California Institute of Technology), and Platt generating sequences of states by using an antisymmetric part of T in a real circuit of a six "neurons" (personal communications).

Relation Between the Stable States of the Two Models

For a given T, the stable states of the continuous system have a simple correspondence with the stable states of the stochastic system. We will work with a slightly simplified instance of the general equations to put a minimum of mathematics in the way of seeing the correspondence. The same basic idea carries over, with more arithmetic, to the general case.

Consider the case in which $V_i^0 < 0 < V_i^1$ for all i. Then the zero of voltage for each V_i can be chosen such that $g_i(0) = 0$ for all i. Because the values of asymptotes are totally unimportant in all that follows, we will simplify notation by taking them as ± 1 for all i. The second simplification is to treat the case in which $I_i = 0$ for all i. Finally, while the continuous case has an energy function with self-connections T_{ii}, the discrete case need not, so $T_{ii} = 0$ will be assumed for the following analysis.

This continuous system has for symmetric T the underlying energy function

$$E = -\frac{1}{2}\sum_{j\neq i}\sum T_{ij}V_iV_j + \sum 1/R_i\int_0^{V_i} g_i^{-1}(V)dV. \quad [11]$$

Where are the maxima and minima of the *first term* of Eq. **11** in the domain of the hypercube $-1 \le V_i \le 1$ for all i? In the usual case, all extrema lie at *corners* of the N-dimensional hypercube space. [In the pathological case that T is a positive or negative definite matrix, an extremum is also possible in the interior of the space. This is not the case for information storage matrices of the usual type (1).]

The discrete, stochastic algorithm searches for minimal states at the corners of the hypercube—corners that are lower than adjacent corners. Since E is a linear function of a single V_i along any cube edge, the energy minima (or maxima) of

$$E = -\frac{1}{2}\sum_{i\neq j}\sum T_{ij}V_iV_j \quad [12]$$

for the discrete space $V_i = \pm 1$ are exactly the same corners as the energy maxima and minima for the continuous case $-1 \le V_i \le 1$.

The second term in Eq. **11** alters the overall picture somewhat. To understand that alteration most easily, the gain g can be scaled, replacing

$$V_i = g_i(u_i) \text{ by } V_i = g_i(\lambda u_i)$$

and

$$u_i = g_i^{-1}(V_i) \text{ by } u_i = (1/\lambda)g_i^{-1}(V_i). \quad [13]$$

This scaling changes the steepness of the sigmoid gain curve without altering the output asymptotes, as indicated in Fig. 1*b*. $g_i(x)$ now represents a standard form in which the scale factor $\lambda = 1$ corresponds to a standard gain, $\lambda >> 1$ to a system with very high gain and step-like gain curve, and λ small corresponds to a low gain and flat sigmoid curve (Fig. 1*b*). The second term in E is now

$$+\frac{1}{\lambda}\sum_i 1/R_i\int_0^{V_i} g_i^{-1}(V)dV. \quad [14]$$

The integral is zero for $V_i = 0$ and positive otherwise, getting very large as V_i approaches ± 1 because of the slowness with which $g(V)$ approaches its asymptotes (Fig. 1*d*). However, in the high-gain limit $\lambda \rightarrow \infty$ this second term becomes negligible, and the locations of the maxima and minima of the full energy expression become the same as that of Eq. **12** or Eq. **3** in the absence of inputs and zero thresholds. *The only stable points of the very high gain, continuous, deterministic system therefore correspond to the stable points of the stochastic system.*

For large but finite λ, the second term in Eq. **11** begins to contribute. The form of $g_i(V_i)$ leads to a large positive contribution near all surfaces, edges, and corners of the hypercube while it still contributes negligibly far from the surfaces. This leads to an energy surface that still has its maxima at corners but the minima become displaced slightly toward the interior

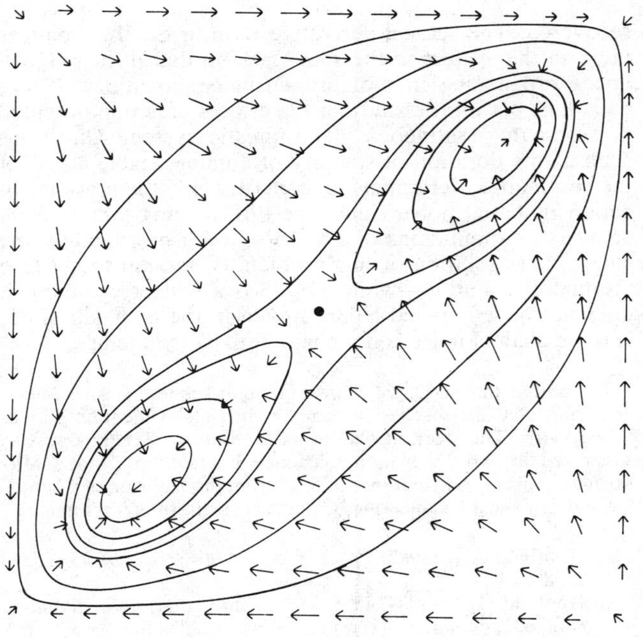

FIG. 3. An energy contour map for a two-neuron, two-stable-state system. The ordinate and abscissa are the outputs of the two neurons. Stable states are located near the lower left and upper right corners, and unstable extrema at the other two corners. The arrows show the motion of the state from Eq. **5**. This motion is not in general perpendicular to the energy contours. The system parameters are $T_{12} = T_{21} = 1$, $\lambda = 1.4$, and $g(u) = (2/\pi)\tan^{-1}(\pi\lambda u/2)$. Energy contours are 0.449, 0.156, 0.017, −0.003, −0.023, and −0.041.

of the space. As λ decreases, each minimum moves further inward. As λ is further decreased, minima disappear one at a time, when the topology of the energy surface makes a minimum and a saddle point coalesce. Ultimately, for very small λ, the second term in Eq. **11** dominates, and the only minimum is at $V_i = 0$. When the gain is large enough that there are many minima, each is associated with a well-defined minimum of the infinite gain case—as the gain is increased, each minimum will move until it reaches a particular cube corner when $\lambda \to \infty$. The same kind of mapping relation holds in general between the continuous deterministic system with sigmoid response curves and the stochastic model.

An energy contour map for a two-neuron (or two operational amplifier) system with two stable states is illustrated in Fig. 3. The two axes are the outputs of the two amplifiers. The upper left and lower right corners are stable minima for infinite gain, and the minima are displaced inward by the finite gain.

There are many general theorems about stability in networks of differential equations representing chemistry, circuits, and biology (8–12). The importance of this simple symmetric system is not merely its stability, but the fact that the correspondence with a discrete system lends it a special relation to elementary computational devices and concepts.

DISCUSSION

Real neurons and real amplifiers have graded, continuous outputs as a function of their inputs (or sigmoid input–output curves of finite steepness) rather than steplike, two-state response curves. Our original stochastic model of CAM and other collective properties of assemblies of neurons was based on two-state neurons. A continuous, deterministic neuron network of interconnected neurons with graded responses has been analyzed in the previous two sections. It functions as a CAM in precisely the same collective way as did the original stochastic model of CAM. A set of memories can be nonlocally stored in a matrix of synaptic (or resistive) interconnections in such a way that particular memories can be reconstructed from a starting state that gives partial information about one of them.

The convergence of the neuronal state of the continuous, deterministic model to its stable states (memories) is based on the existence of an energy function that directs the flow in state space. Such a function can be constructed in the continuous, deterministic model when T is symmetric, just as was the case for the original stochastic model with two-state neurons. Other interesting uses and interpretations of the behaviors of the original model based on the existence of an underlying energy function will also hold for the continuous ("graded response") model (3).

A direct correspondence between the stable states of the two models was shown. For steep response curves (high gain) there is a 1:1 correspondence between the memories of the two models. When the response is less steep (lower gain) the continuous-response model can have fewer stable states than the stochastic model with the same T matrix, but the existing stable states will still correspond to particular stable states of the stochastic model. This simple correspondence is possible because of the quadratic form of the interaction between different neurons in the energy function. More complicated energy functions, which have occasionally been used in constraint satisfaction problems (13, 14), may have in addition stable states within the interior of the domain of state space in the continuous model which have no correspondence within the discrete two-state model.

This analysis indicates that a real circuit of operational amplifiers, capacitors, and resistors should be able to operate as a CAM, reconstructing the stable states that have been designed into T. As long as T is symmetric and the amplifiers are fast compared with the characteristic RC time of the input network, the system will converge to stable states and cannot oscillate or display chaotic behavior. While the symmetry of the network is essential to the mathematics, a pragmatic view indicates that approximate symmetry will suffice, as was experimentally shown in the stochastic model. Equivalence of the gain curves and input capacitance of the amplifiers is not needed. For high-gain systems, the stable states of the real circuit will be exactly those predicted by the stochastic model.

Neuronal and electromagnetic signals have finite propagation velocities. A neural circuit that is to operate in the mode described must have propagation delays that are considerably shorter than the RC or chemical integration time of the network. The same must be true for the slowness of amplifier response in the case of the electrical circuit.

The continuous model supplements, rather than replaces, the original stochastic description. The important properties of the original model are not due to its simplifications, but come from the general structure lying behind the model. Because the original model is very efficient to simulate on a digital computer, it will often be more practical to develop ideas and simulations on that model even when use on biological neurons or analog circuits is intended. The interesting collective properties transcend the 0–1 stochastic simplifications.

Neurons often communicate through action potentials. The output of such neurons consists of a series of sharp spikes having a mean frequency (when averaged over a short time) that is described by the input–output relation of Fig. 1*a*. In addition, the delivery of transmitter at a synapse is quantized in vesicles. Thus Eq. **5** can be only an equation for the behavior of a neural network neglecting the quantal noise due to action potentials and the releases of discrete vesicles. Because the system operates by moving downhill on an energy surface, the injection of a small amount of quantal noise will not greatly change the minimum-seeking behavior.

Eq. **5** has a generalization to include action potentials. Let all neurons have the same gain curves $g(u)$, input capacitance C, input impedance R, and maximum firing rate F. Let $g(u)$ have asymptotes 0 and 1. When a neuron has an input u, it is presumed to produce action potentials $V_0\delta(t - t_{\text{firing}})$ in a stochastic fashion with a probability $Fg(u)$ of producing an action potential per unit time. This stochastic view preserves the basic idea of the input signal being transformed into a firing rate but does not allow precise timing of individual action potentials. A synapse with strength T_{ij} will deliver a quantal charge V_0T_{ij} to the input capacitance of neuron i when neuron j produces an action potential. Let $P(u_1, u_2, \ldots u_i, \ldots, u_N, t)du_1, du_2, \ldots, du_N$ be the probability that input potential 1 has the value $u_1, \ldots$ The evolution of the state of the network is described by

$$\partial P/\partial t = \sum_i (1/RC)(\partial(u_iP)/\partial u_i)$$

$$+ \sum_j Fg(u_j)[-P + P(u_1 - T_{1j}V_0/C, \ldots, u_i - T_{ij}V_0/C, \ldots)]. \quad \textbf{[15]}$$

If V_0 is small, the term in brackets can be expanded in a Taylor series, yielding

$$\partial P/\partial t = \sum_i (1/RC)(\partial(u_iP)/\partial u_i)$$

$$- \sum_j (\partial P/\partial u_i)(V_0F/C) \sum_i T_{ij}\, g(u_j)$$

$$+ V_0^2F/2C^2 \sum_{i,j,k} g(u_k)T_{ik}T_{jk}\,(\partial^2 P/\partial u_i \partial u_j). \quad \textbf{[16]}$$

In the limit as $V_0 \to 0$, $F \to \infty$ such that FV_0 = constant, the second derivative term can be omitted. This simplification has the solutions that are identical to those of the continuous, deterministic model, namely

$$P = \prod \delta(u_i - u_i(t)),$$

where $u_i(t)$ obeys Eq. **5**.

In the model, stochastic noise from the action potentials disappears in this limit and the continuous model of Eq. **5** is recovered. The second derivative term in Eq. **16** produces noise in the system in the same fashion that diffusion produces broadening in mobility–diffusion equations. These equations permit the study of the effects of action potential noise on the continuous, deterministic system. Questions such as the duration of stability of nominal stable states of the continuous, deterministic model Eq. **5** in the presence of action potential noise should be directly answerable from analysis or simulations of Eq. **15** or **16**. Unfortunately the steady-state solution of this problem is *not* equivalent to a thermal distribution—while Eq. **15** is a master equation, it does not have detailed balance even in the high-gain limit, and the quantal noise is not characterized by a temperature.

The author thanks David Feinstein, John Lambe, Carver Mead, and John Platt for discussions and permission to mention unpublished work. The work at California Institute of Technology was supported in part by National Science Foundation Grant DMR-8107494. This is contribution no. 6975 from the Division of Chemistry and Chemical Engineering, California Institute of Technology.

1. Hopfield, J. J. (1982) *Proc. Natl. Acad. Sci. USA* **79,** 2554–2558.
2. Hopfield, J. J. (1984) in *Modeling and Analysis in Biomedicine*, ed. Nicolini, C. (World Scientific Publishing, New York), in press.
3. Hinton, G. E. & Sejnowski, T. J. (1983) in *Proceedings of the IEEE Computer Science Conference on Computer Vision and Pattern Recognition* (Washington, DC), pp. 448–453.
4. McCulloch, W. A. & Pitts, W. (1943) *Bull. Math. Biophys.* **5,** 115–133.
5. Little, W. A. (1974) *Math. Biosci.* **19,** 101–120.
6. Little, W. A. & Shaw, G. L. (1978) *Math. Biosci.* **39,** 281–289.
7. Poggio, T. & Torre, V. (1981) in *Theoretical Approaches to Neurobiology*, eds. Reichardt, W. E. & Poggio, T. (MIT Press, Cambridge, MA), pp. 28–38.
8. Glansdorf, P. & Prigogine, R. (1971) in *Thermodynamic Theory of Structure, Stability, and Fluctuations* (Wiley, New York), pp. 61–67.
9. Landauer, R. (1975) *J. Stat. Phys.* **13,** 1–16.
10. Glass, L. & Kauffman, S. A. (1973) *J. Theor. Biol.* **39,** 103–129.
11. Grossberg, S. (1973) *Stud. Appl. Math.* **52,** 213–257.
12. Glass, L. (1975) *J. Chem. Phys.* **63,** 1325–1335.
13. Kirkpatrick, S., Gelatt, C. D. & Vecchi, M. P. (1983) *Science* **220,** 671–680.
14. Geman, S. & Geman, D. (1984) *IEEE Transactions Pat. Anal. Mech. Intell.*, in press.

Simple "Neural" Optimization Networks: An A/D Converter, Signal Decision Circuit, and a Linear Programming Circuit

DAVID W. TANK AND JOHN J. HOPFIELD

Abstract — **We describe how several optimization problems can be rapidly solved by highly interconnected networks of simple analog processors. Analog-to-digital (A/D) conversion was considered as a simple optimization problem, and an A/D converter of novel architecture was designed. A/D conversion is a simple example of a more general class of signal-decision problems which we show could also be solved by appropriately constructed networks. Circuits to solve these problems were designed using general principles which result from an understanding of the basic collective computational properties of a specific class of analog-processor networks. We also show that a network which solves linear programming problems can be understood from the same concepts.**

I. Introduction

WE HAVE shown in earlier work [1], [2] how highly interconnected networks of simple analog processors can collectively compute good solutions to difficult optimization problems. For example, a network was designed to provide solutions to the traveling salesman problem. This problem is of the *np*-complete class [3] and the network could provide good solutions during an elapsed time of only a few characteristic time constants of the circuit. This computation can be considered as a rapid and efficient contraction of the possible solution space. However, a globally optimal solution to the problem is not guaranteed; the networks compute locally optimal solutions. For the traveling salesman problem, even among the extremely good solutions, the topology of the optimization surface in the solution space is very rough; many good solutions are at least locally similar to the best solution, and a complicated set of local minima exist. In difficult problems of recognition and perception, where rapidly calculated good solutions may be more beneficial than slowly computed globally optimal solutions, collective computation in circuits of this design may be of practical use.

We have recently found that several less complicated optimization problems which are not of the *np*-complete class can be solved by networks of analog processors. The two circuits described in detail here are an A/D converter and a circuit for solving linear programming problems. These networks are guaranteed of obtaining globally optimal solutions since the solution spaces (in the vicinity of specific initial conditions) have no local minima. The A/D converter is actually one simple example of a *class* of problems for which appropriately constructed collective networks should rapidly provide good solutions. The general class consists of signal decomposition problems in which the goal is the calculation of the optimum fit of an integer coefficient combination of basis functions (possibly a nonorthogonal set) to an analog signal. The systematic approach we have developed to design such networks should be more broadly applicable.

Fahlman [4] has suggested a rough classification of parallel-processor architectures based upon the complexity of the messages that are passed between processing units. At the highest complexity are networks in which each processor has the power of a complete von Neumann computer, and the messages which are passed between individual processors can be complicated strings of information. The simplest parallel architectures are of the "value-passing" type. Processor-to-processor communication between local computations consists of a single binary or analog value. The collective analog networks considered here are in this class; each processor makes a simple computation or decision based upon its analysis of many analog values (information) it receives in parallel from other processors in the network. Our motivation for studying the computational properties of circuits with this organization arose from an attempt to understand how known biophysical properties and architectural organization of neural systems can provide the immense computational power characteristic of the brains of higher animals. In our theoretical modeling of neural circuits [1], [2], [5], [6], each neuron is a simple analog processor, while the rich connectivity provided in real neural circuits by the synapses formed between neurons are provided by the parallel communication lines in the value-passing analog processor networks. Hence, in addition to designs for conventional implementation with electrical components, the circuits and design principles described here add to the known repertoire of neural circuits which seem neurobiologically plausible. In general, a consideration of such circuits provides a methodology for assigning function to anatomical structure in real neural circuits.

Manuscript received August 27, 1985; revised This work was supported in part by the National Science Foundation under Grant PCM-8406049.
D. W. Tank is with the Molecular Biophysics Research Department, AT&T Bell Laboratories, Murray Hill, NJ 07974.
J. J. Hopfield is with the Division of Chemistry and Biology, California Institute of Technology, Pasadena, CA 91125.
IEEE Log Number 8607497.

II. The A/D Converter Network

We have presented in detail [1], [2], [5] the basic ideas involved in designing networks of analog processors to solve specific optimization problems. The general structure of the networks we have studied is shown in Fig. 1(b). The processing elements are modeled as amplifiers having a sigmoid monotonic input–output relation, as shown in Fig. 1(a). The function $V_j = g_j(u_j)$ which characterizes this input–output relation describes the output voltage V_j of amplifier j due to an input voltage u_j. The time constants of the amplifiers are assumed negligible. However, each amplifier has an input resistor leading to a reference ground and an input capacitor. These components partially define (see [1] and [5]) the time constants of the network and provide for integrative analog summation of input currents from other processors in the network. These input currents are provided through resistors of conductance T_{ij} connected between the output and amplifier j and the input of amplifier i. In order to provide for output currents of both signs from the same processor, each amplifier is given two outputs, a normal output, and an inverted output. The minimum and maximum outputs of the normal amplifier are taken as 0 and 1, while the inverted output has corresponding values of 0 and -1. A connection between two processors is defined by a conductance T_{ij} which connects one of the two outputs of amplifier j to the input of amplifier i. This connection is made with a resistor of value $R_{ij} = 1/|T_{ij}|$. (In Fig. 1, resistors connecting 2 wires are schematically indicated by squares.) If $T_{ij} > 0$, this resistor is connected to the normal output of amplifier j. If $T_{ij} < 0$, it is connected to the inverted output of amplifier j. The matrix T_{ij} defines the connectivity among the processors. The net input current to any processor (and hence the input voltage u_i) is the sum of the currents flowing through the set of resistors connecting its input to the outputs of the other processors. Also, as indicated in Fig. 1(b), externally supplied input currents (I_i) are also present for each processor. In the circuits discussed here, these external inputs can be constant biases which effectively shift the input–output relation along the u_i axis and/or problem-specific input currents which correspond to data in the problem.

We have shown [5] that in the case of symmetric connections ($T_{ij} = T_{ji}$), the equations of motion for this network of analog processors always lead to a convergence to *stable states*, in which the output voltages of all amplifiers remain constant. Also, when the diagonal elements (T_{ii}) are 0 and the width of the amplifier gain curve (Fig. 1(a)) is narrow —the high-gain limit—the stable states of a network comprised of N processors are the local minima of the quantity

$$E = -\frac{1}{2}\sum_{i=1}^{N}\sum_{j=1}^{N} T_{ij}V_iV_j - \sum_{i=1}^{N} V_iI_i. \qquad (1)$$

We refer to E as the computational energy of the system. By construction, the state space over which the circuit operates is the *interior* of the N-dimensional hypercube defined by $V_i = 0$ or 1. However, we have shown that in the

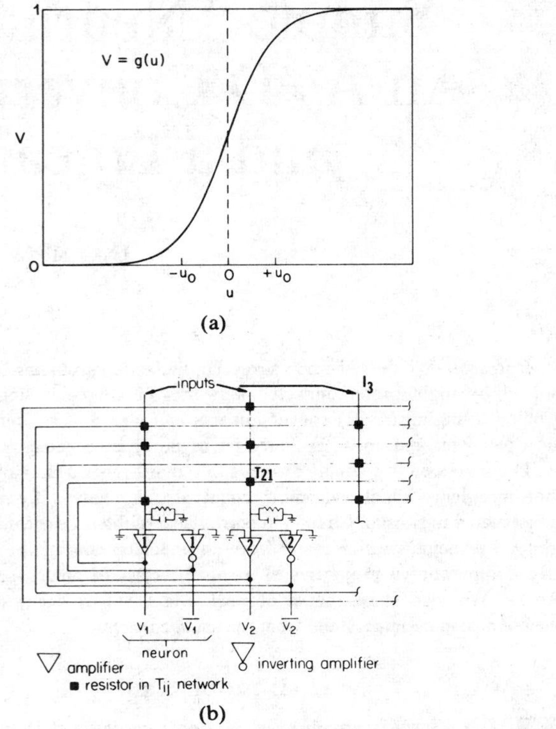

Fig. 1. (a) The input–output relation for the processors (amplifiers) in Fig. 1(b). (b) The network of analog processors. The output of any neuron can potentially be connected to the input of any other neuron. Black squares at intersections represent resistive connections (T_{ij}'s) between outputs and inputs. Connections between inverted outputs and inputs represent negative (inhibitory) connections.

high-gain limit networks with vanishing diagonal connections (T_{ii}) = 0 have minima only at *corners* of this space [5]. Under these conditions the stable states of the network correspond to those locations in the discrete space consisting of the 2^N corners of this hypercube which minimize E (1). (Somewhat less restrictive conditions will often suffice, which allow leeway for nonzero, T_{ii}. Negative T_{ii} do not necessarily cause problems.)

Networks of analog processors with this basic organization can be used to compute solutions to specific optimization problems by relating the minimization of the problems cost function to the minimization of the E function of the network. Since the energy function can be used to define the values of the connectivities (T_{ij}) and input bias currents (I_i), relating a specific problem to a specific E function provides the information for a detailed circuit diagram for the network which will compute solutions to the problem. The computation consists of providing an initial set of amplifier input voltages u_i, and then allowing the analog system to converge to a stable state which minimizes the E function. The solution to the problem is then interpreted from the final stable state using a predetermined rule.

The A/D converter we shall describe is a specific example of such an optimization network. For clarity, we will limit the present discussion to a 4-bit converter. Its wiring diagram is shown in Fig. 2. The circuit consists of 4 amplifiers (only inverting outputs are needed—see below) whose output voltages will be decoded to obtain the output

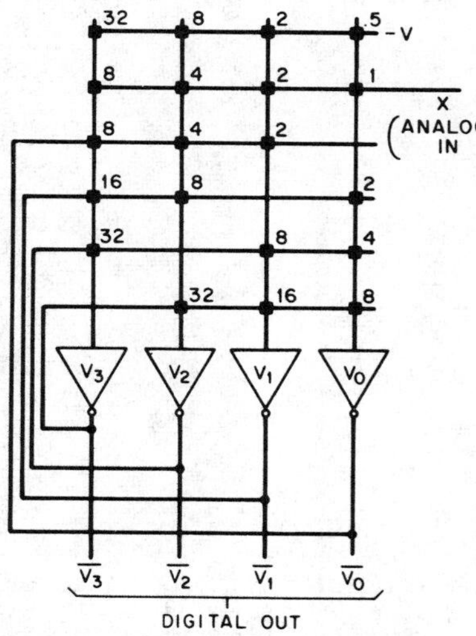

Fig. 2. The 4-bit A/D converter computational network. The analog input voltage is x, while the complement of the digital word $V_3V_2V_1V_0$ which is computed to be the binary value of x is read out as the 0 or 1 values of the amplifier output voltages.

binary word of the converter, a network of feedback resistors connecting the outputs of one amplifier to the inputs of the others, a set of resistors (top row) which feed different constant current values into the input lines of the amplifiers, and another set of resistors (second row) which inject current onto the input lines of the amplifiers which are proportional to the analog input voltage x, which is to be converted by the circuit. For the present we assume that the output voltages (V_i) of the amplifiers can range between a minimum of 0 V and a maximum of 1 V. Thus as described above for the variables in (1), the V_i range over the domain [0,1]. We further assume that the value of x in volts is the numerical value of the input which is to be converted. The converter network is operating properly when the integer value of the binary word represented by the output states of the amplifiers is numerically equal to the analog input voltage. In terms of the variables defined above, this criterion can be written as

$$\sum_{i=0}^{3} V_i 2^i \approx x. \tag{2}$$

The circuit of Fig. 2 is organized so that this expression always holds.

The strategy employed in creating this design is to consider A/D conversion as a simple example of an optimization problem. If the word $V_3V_2V_1V_0$ is to be the "best" digital representation of x, then two criteria must be fulfilled. The first is that each of the V_i have the value of 0 or 1, or at least be close enough to these values so that a separate comparator circuit can establish digital logic levels. The second criterion is that the particular set of 1's and 0's chosen is that which "best" represents the analog signal. This second criterion can be expressed, in a least-squares sense, as the choice of V_i which minimize the energy function

$$E = \frac{1}{2}\left(x - \sum_{i=0}^{3} V_i 2^i\right)^2 \tag{3}$$

because the quadratic is a minimum when the parenthesized term has a minimum absolute value. If this function is expanded and rearranged, it can be put in the form of (1) (plus a constant). There would, therefore, be a real circuit of the class shown in Fig. 1 which would compute by trying to minimize (3).

However, with this simple energy function there is no guarantee that the values of V_i will be near enough to 0 or 1 to be identified as digital logic levels. Since (3) contains diagonal elements of the T-matrix of the form $\alpha(V_i)^2$ which are nonzero, the minimal points to the E function (3) will not necessarily lie on the corners of the space, and thus represent a digital word (see [5]). Since there are many combinations of the V_i which can be linearly combined to obtain x, a minimum can be found which is not at a corner of the space.

We can eliminate this problem by adding one additional term to the E function. Its form can be chosen as

$$-\frac{1}{2}\sum_{i=0}^{3} (2^i)^2 [V_i(V_i - 1)]. \tag{4}$$

The *structure* of this term was chosen to favor digital representations. Note that this term has minimal value when, for each i, either $V_i = 1$ or $V_i = 0$. Although any set of (negative) coefficients will provide this bias towards a digital representation, the *coefficients* in (4) were chosen so as to cancel out the diagonal elements in (3). The elimination of diagonal connection strengths will generally lead to stable points only at corners of the space. The term (4) equally favors *all* corners of the space, and does not favor any particular digital answer. Thus the total energy E which contains the sum of the two terms in (3) and (4) has minimal value when the V_i are a *digital* representation close to x.

This completes the energy function for the A/D converter. It can be expanded and rearranged into the form

$$E = -\frac{1}{2}\sum_{j=0}^{3}\sum_{i \neq j=0}^{3} (-2^{i+j}) V_i V_j - \sum_{i=0}^{3} (-2^{(2i-1)} + 2^i x) V_i. \tag{5}$$

This is of the form of (1) if we identify the connection matrix elements and the input currents as

$$T_{ij} = -2^{(i+j)}$$
$$I_i = (-2^{(2i-1)} + 2^i x). \tag{6}$$

The complete circuit for this 4-bit A/D converter with components as defined above is the network shown in Fig. 2. The inverting output of each amplifier is connected to the input of the other amplifiers through a resistor of conductance 2^{i+j}. The other input currents to each amplifier are provided through resistors of conductance 2^i connected to the input voltage x and through resistors of conductance $2^{(2i-1)}$ connected to a −1-V reference potential. These numbers for the resistive connections on the feedback network and the input lines represent the appropriate *relative* conductances of the components and assume that the constant terms in the input currents are provided by connecting the input lines through resistors to a -1-V reference potential, that the minimum and maximum output voltages of the amplifiers are to be 0 and 1 V, and that the analog input voltage to be digitized is in the range $(-0.5, 15.5)$ V. When building a real circuit, the values of the resistors chosen should satisfy the relative conductances indicated in the figure and in the above equations, but their absolute values will depend upon the real voltage rails of the amplifiers, the specific input voltage range to be digitized, and reasonable values for the power dissipation. If the real output voltage range for the amplifiers is $[0, V_{BB}]$, the voltage range to be digitized is $[0, V_H]$, and the reference voltage to be used for the constant input currents is $-V_R$, then it is straightforward to show that the relative conductances (which must now only be scaled for power dissipation) for the feedback connections are

$$T_{ij} = -\frac{2^{(i+j)}}{V_{BB}}$$

while the input voltage x will be fed into the ith amplifier through a resistor of conductance $2^{(4+i)}/V_H$, and the constant current is provided through resistors of conductance $(2^{(i-1)} + (2^{(2i-1)}/V_R))$ connected to the $-V_R$ reference voltage.

The ability of the network to compute the correct digital representation of x was studied in a series of computer experiments and actual circuit construction. In the computer experiments, the dynamic behavior of the network was simulated by integration of the differential equations which describe the circuit (for details, see [1], [5]). The convergence of the network was studied as a function of the analog input x, for 160 different values contained in the interval -0.5 to 15.5 V. The digital solutions computed at a fixed value of x depend upon the initial conditions of the network. These initial conditions are defined by the input voltages (u_i) on the amplifiers at the time that the calculation is initiated. In Fig. 3 is plotted the value of the binary word $V_3V_2V_1V_0$ computed by the network as a function of the value of $(x+0.5)$ for the initial conditions $u_i = 0$. The response is the staircase function characteristic of an A/D converter. In a real circuit, separate electronics which would ground the input lines of the amplifiers before each convergence would be required to implement the initial conditions ($u_i = 0$) used in these simulations. If the input lines are not zeroed before each calculation, then the circuit exhibits hysteresis as the input voltage x is being continuously varied. For example, if x is slowly turned up through the same series of values used in the calculation of Fig. 3, but, instead of zeroing the input lines before a simulated convergence, we allow the u_i to retain the values stabilized at the end of the previous calculation, we obtain the response shown in Fig. 4. Slowly turning down the x input from its maximum value would provide a response which is the "inverse" of Fig. 4. (The value for any x, in the experiment with x descending, is equal to 15.0 minus the value for $(16.0 - x)$ in the experiment with x ascending.) Some stable states of the network are skipped under this set of initial conditions.

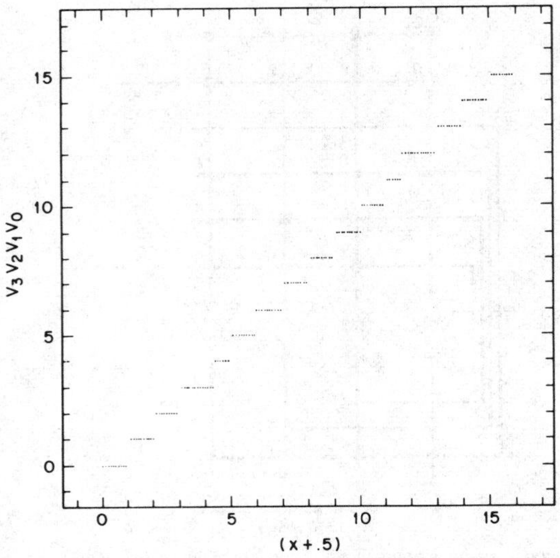

Fig. 3. The digital word computed in simulations of the circuit shown in Fig. 2 as a function of the analog input voltage x. The initial conditions for each of the calculations is $u_i = 0$, for all i.

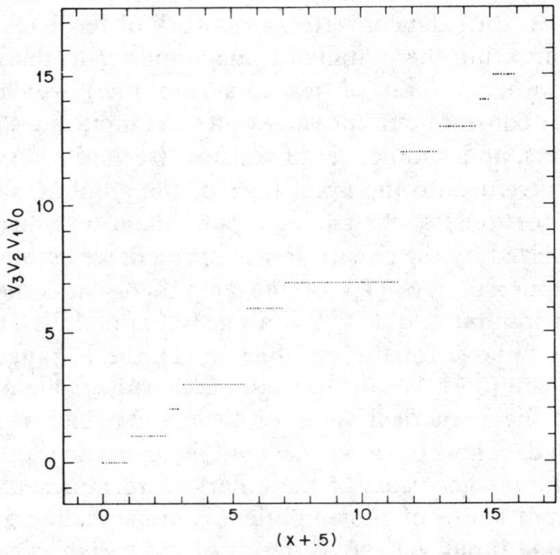

Fig. 4. The results of a calculation similar to that described in Fig. 3 except that the initial conditions were determined by the u_i which stabilized during the previous calculation. Calculations were performed with monotonically increasing values of the analog input voltage x, starting at $x = 0$ V.

One can understand this hysteresis, and its absence for the $u_i = 0$ initial conditions, by considering the topology of the energy surface for fixed x and how it changes as x is varied. In Fig. 5 is shown a *stylized* representation of the energy surface for two different x values. The energy at specific locations in state space is represented, with energy value along the vertical axis. Different corners of state space near the global minimum in E (with value $E = 0$) are indicated along the curve by the set of indices $V_3V_2V_1V_0$. As shown in Fig. 5(a), the energy function for $x = 7$ V has a deep minimum at the corner of state space which is the digital representation of 7, and has local minima at higher E values at the digital representations of 6 and 8. Al-

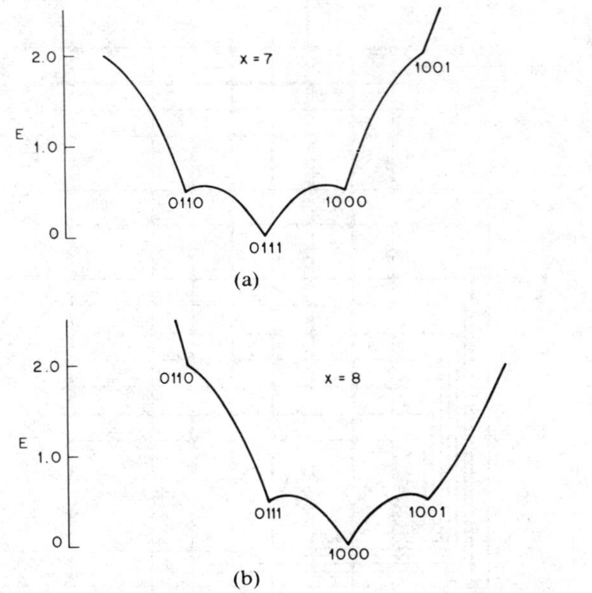

Fig. 5. A schematic drawing of the energy surface in the vicinity of the global minima for two analog input voltages.

though, as shown above (Fig. 3), the circuit dynamics can lead from a location in state space corresponding to all $u_i = 0$ to that corresponding to the deep minima, if x is changed to 8 V while the u_i are at the $x = 7$ V corner, then although the energy surface will change to that as shown in Fig. 5(b), the system will remain stuck in the now-local minima at the corner corresponding to 7. However, if the circuit is again allowed to compute from the initial conditions $u_i = 0$, but now with $x = 8$ V, the correct deep minima can be obtained. The local minima are a direct consequence of the term (4) in the E function which forces the output voltages to be digital. If this term were not present, the V_i will still represent a valid set of coefficients for the linear approximation of the sum (2) to the analog value x, but the solution will in general not be at one of the corners of the solution space.

III. The Decomposition/Decision Problem

Many problems in signal processing can be described as the attempt to detect the presence or absence of a waveform having a known stereotyped shape and amplitude in the presence of other waveforms and noise. Circuits which are similar to that described above for the A/D converter can be constructed for which the minimal energy state corresponds to a decision about this signal decomposition problem. For example, consider the problem of decomposing a time-dependent analog signal which results from the temporal linear summation of overlapping stereotype Gaussian pulses of known but differing width. A typical summed signal is shown in Fig. 6(a). In Fig. 6(b) is shown the individual pulses which when added together give the signal in Fig. 6(a). The decomposition/decision problem is to determine this particular decomposition of the signal in Fig. 6(a), given the knowledge of the individual stereotype forms. To make the problem specific, we assume that

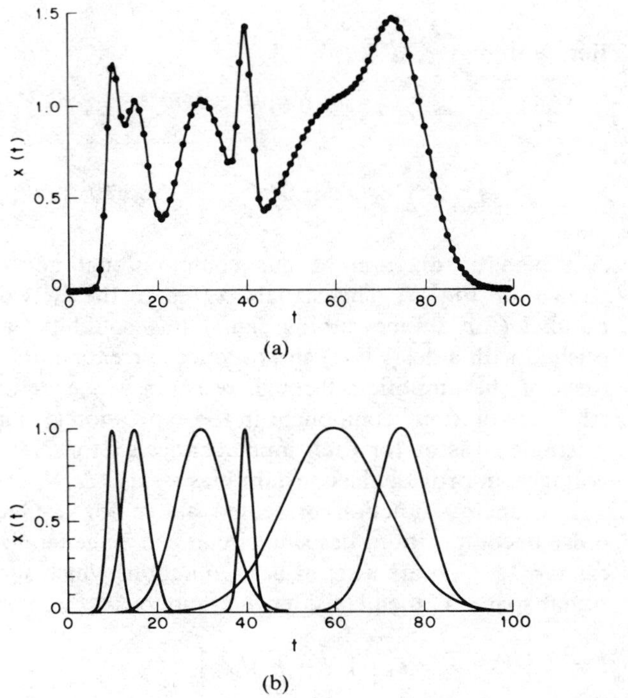

Fig. 6. (a) Analog signal comprised of a linear summation of Gaussian pulses of different width and peak location. The pulses summed in (a) are explicitly illustrated in (b).

$N \cong 100$ time points of analog data ($x(i)$; $i, \cdots, N$) have been recorded, as indicated by the filled circles in Fig. 6(a), and that the set of basis functions defining the possible "pulses" in Fig. 6(b) are the Gaussian functions of the form

$$\epsilon_{\sigma t}(i) = e^{-[(i-t)/\sigma]^2} \tag{10}$$

We will let the width parameter σ take on a finite number of possible values, while the peak position (t) of the pulse can be at any one of the N time points. Since the basis set is specified by the width and peak position parameters, the amplifiers used in the decomposition/decision network can be conveniently indexed by the double-set of indices σ, t. In describing the decomposition, each of these basis functions will have a digital coefficient ($V_{\sigma t}$) which corresponds to the output of an amplifier in the network and which represents the presence or absence of this function in the signal to be decomposed. An energy function which defines an analog computational network and which is minimum when this decomposition/decision problem is solved is

$$E = \frac{1}{2}\sum_{i=1}^{N}\left(x_i - \sum_{\sigma=\sigma_1}^{\sigma_{\max}}\sum_{t=1}^{N} V_{\sigma t}\epsilon_{\sigma t}(i)\right)^2 - \frac{1}{2}\sum_{i=1}^{N}\sum_{\sigma=\sigma_1}^{\sigma_{\max}}\sum_{t=1}^{N}(\epsilon_{\sigma t}(i))^2[V_{\sigma t}(V_{\sigma t}-1)] \tag{11}$$

with the basis functions as defined in (10). This expression is of the form (1) and, therefore, defines a set of connection strengths ($T_{\sigma t, \sigma' t'}$) and input currents ($I_{\sigma t}$) for each amplifier, with

$$T_{\sigma t,\sigma' t'} = \sum_{i=1}^{N} e^{-[[(i-t)/\sigma]^2+[(i-t')/\sigma']^2]} \tag{12}$$

$$I_{\sigma t} = \sum_{i=1}^{N} x_i e^{-[(i-t)/\sigma]^2} + \frac{1}{2}\sum_{i=1}^{N} e^{-2[(i-t)/\sigma]^2}. \tag{13}$$

A schematic diagram of this computational network is shown in Fig. 7. The signals x_i enter the network in parallel (for a time-varying signal this could be accomplished with a delay line) and produce currents in the input lines of the amplifiers through resistors which define the ith "convolution" component in the expression (13) above. A single resistor for each input connected to a reference voltage can provide the constant bias terms.

The energy function presented above for a Gaussian pulse decomposition/decision circuit can be generalized. If $\vec{\epsilon}_k$; $k = 1,\cdots,n$ are a set of basic functions which span the signal space $\vec{X}$, then consider the function

$$E = \frac{1}{2}\Big(\vec{X} - \sum_k V_k\vec{\epsilon}_k\Big)\cdot\Big(\vec{X} - \sum_k V_k\vec{\epsilon}_k\Big) - \frac{1}{2}\sum_k(\vec{\epsilon}_k\cdot\vec{\epsilon}_k)[V_k(V_k-1)]. \tag{7}$$

This function describes a network which has an energy minimum (with $E = 0$) when the "best" digital combination of basis functions are selected (with $V_i = 1$) to describe the signal. The expression (7) can be expanded and rearranged to give

$$E = \frac{1}{2}\sum_k \sum_{k'\neq k} (\vec{\epsilon}_k\cdot\vec{\epsilon}_{k'})V_kV_{k'} - \sum_k\Big[(\vec{X}\cdot\vec{\epsilon}_k) + \frac{1}{2}(\vec{\epsilon}_k\cdot\vec{\epsilon}_k)\Big]V_k + \frac{1}{2}(\vec{X}\cdot\vec{X}). \tag{8}$$

This is a function which is comprised of terms which are linear and quadratic in the V_k's. It is, therefore, of the form (1) (plus a constant), if we define

$$T_{kk'} = -(\vec{\epsilon}_k\cdot\vec{\epsilon}_{k'})$$

$$I_k = \Big[(\vec{X}\cdot\vec{\epsilon}_k) + \frac{1}{2}(\vec{\epsilon}_k\cdot\vec{\epsilon}_k)\Big]. \tag{9}$$

Hence, for the general decomposition/decision problem mapped onto the computational network in Fig. 1, the connection strengths between amplifiers correspond to the dot products of the corresponding pairs of basis functions while the input currents correspond to the convolution of the corresponding basis function with the signal and the addition of a constant bias term.

The A/D converter described earlier can be seen to be a simple example of this more general circuit. In the A/D case, the signal is one-dimensional and consists of only an analog value sampled at a single time point. The basis functions are the values 2^n; $n = 0,\cdots,(n-1)$ which are a complete set over the integers in the limited domain $[0, 2^n - 1]$. The binary word output of the circuit is comprised of the coefficients which describe a linear summation of the basis functions which is closest, in the least squares sense, to the input signal.

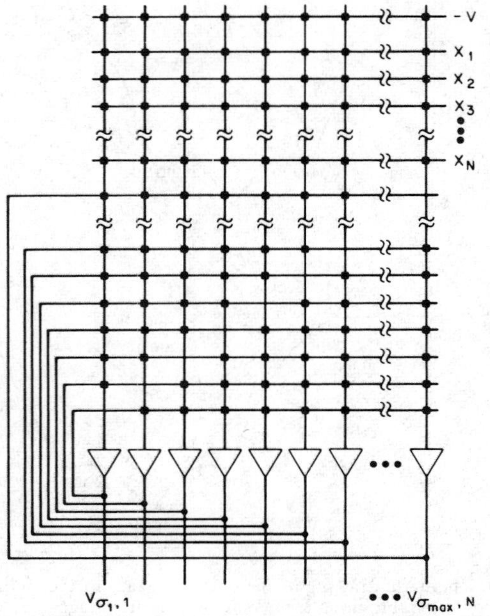

Fig. 7. The general organization of a computational network which can be used to solve a multipoint decomposition problem with nonorthogonal basis functions. The outputs of each of the amplifiers represents the presence ($V_{\sigma,t} = 1$) or absence ($V_{\sigma,t} = 0$) of a pulse of a width σ and peak location t in the signal trace.

For the A/D converter problem and the Gaussian decomposition/decision network just described, the basis functions which span the signal space are *not* orthogonal. For an orthogonal set, by definition, the connection strengths (9) would all vanish. For example, if the signal consists of N analog-sampled points of a differentiable function, and the basis functions were sines and cosines (a Fourier decomposition network), then the computational circuit would have no feedback connections since these basis functions are orthogonal. In this case, the independent computations made by each amplifier are the convolution of the signal with the particular basis function represented. This is just the familiar rule for calculating Fourier coefficients—all decisions are independent. In general, one can interpret the connections strengths in the decomposition/decision networks as the possible effect of one decision being tested (V_i) on another (V_j); these effects should be zero for orthogonal basis functions.

IV. The Linear Programming Network

The linear programming problem can be stated as the attempt to minimize a cost function

$$\pi = \vec{A}\cdot\vec{V} \tag{14}$$

where $\vec{A}$ is an N-dimensional vector of coefficients for the N variables which are the components of $\vec{V}$. This minimization is to be accomplished subject to a set of M linear constraints among the variables:

$$\vec{D}_j \cdot \vec{V} \geq B_j, \qquad j = 1, \cdots, M$$

$$\vec{D}_j = \begin{bmatrix} D_{j1} \\ D_{j2} \\ \vdots \\ D_{jN} \end{bmatrix} \tag{15}$$

where the $\vec{D}_j$, for each j, contain the N variable coefficients in a constraint equation and the B_j are the bounds. Although we know of no way to directly cast this problem into the explicit form of (1) so that a network of the form shown in Fig. 1 could be used to compute solutions to the problem, we can understand how the circuit in Fig. 8, illustrated for the specific case of two variables ($N = 2$) and four constraint equations ($M = 4$), can rapidly compute the solution to this optimization problem, by a variation of a mathematical analysis used earlier [5].

In the circuit of Fig. 8, the N outputs (V_i) of the left-hand set of amplifiers will represent the values of the variables in the linear programming problem. The components of $\vec{A}$ are proportional to input currents fed into these amplifiers. The M outputs (ψ_j) of the right-hand set of amplifiers represent constraint satisfaction. As indicated in the figure, the output (ψ_j) of the jth amplifier on the right-hand side injects current into the input lines of the V_i variable amplifiers by an amount proportional to $-D_{ji}$, the negative of the constraint coefficient for the ith variable in the jth constraint equation. Each of the M ψ_j amplifiers is fed a constant current proportional to the jth bound constant (B_j) and receives input from the ith variable amplifier by an amount proportional to D_{ji}. Like all of the amplifiers in Fig. 1, each of the V_i amplifiers in the linear programming network has an input capacitor C_i and an input resistor ρ_i in parallel, which connect the input line to ground. The input–output relations of the V_i amplifiers are linear and characterized by a linear function g_i in the relation $V_i = g(u_i)$. The ψ_i amplifiers have the nonlinear input–output relation characterized by the function

$$\psi_j = f(u_j), \qquad u_j = \vec{D}_j \cdot \vec{V} - B_j$$

where

$$f(z) = 0, \qquad z \geq 0$$
$$f(z) = -z, \qquad z < 0. \tag{16}$$

This function provides for the output of the ψ amplifiers to be a large positive value when the corresponding constraint equation it represents is being violated. (The specific form of $f(z)$ used here was chosen for convenience in building a corresponding real circuit and the stability proof only depends upon f being a function of the variable $z = \vec{D}_j \cdot \vec{V} - B_j$ (see below).) If we assume that the response time of the ψ_j is negligible compared to that of the variable amplifiers, then the circuit equation for the variable amplifiers can be written

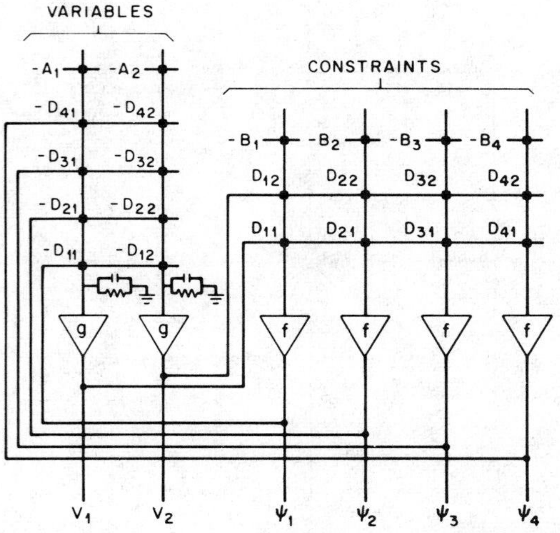

Fig. 8. The organization of a network which will solve a 2-variable 4-constant linear programming problem.

$$C_i \frac{du_i}{dt} = -A_i - \frac{u_i}{R} - \sum_j D_{ji} f(u_j)$$
$$= -A_i - \frac{u_i}{R} - \sum_j D_{ji} f(\vec{D}_j \cdot \vec{V} - B_j). \tag{17}$$

Now consider an energy function of the form

$$E = (\vec{A} \cdot \vec{V}) + \sum_j F(\vec{D}_j \cdot \vec{V} - B_j) + \sum_i \frac{1}{R} \int_0^{V_i} g^{-1}(V)\, dV$$

where

$$f(z) = \frac{dF(z)}{dz}. \tag{18}$$

Then the time derivative of E is

$$\frac{dE}{dt} = \sum_i \frac{dV_i}{dt} \left[\frac{u_i}{R} + A_i + \sum_j D_{ji} f(\vec{D}_j \cdot \vec{V} - B_j) \right]. \tag{19}$$

But, substituting for the bracketed expression from the circuit equation of motion for the V_i amplifiers (17) gives

$$\frac{dE}{dt} = -\sum_i C_i \frac{dV_i}{dt} \frac{du_i}{dt} = -\sum_i C_i g^{-1\prime}(V_i) \left(\frac{dV_i}{dt} \right)^2. \tag{20}$$

Since C_i is positive and $g^{-1}(V_i)$ is a monotone increasing function, this sum is nonnegative and

$$\frac{dE}{dt} \leq 0; \qquad \frac{dE}{dt} = 0 \rightarrow \frac{dV_i}{dt} = 0, \qquad \text{for all } i. \tag{21}$$

Thus as for the network in Fig. 1, the time evolution of the system is a motion in state space which seeks out a minima to E and stops. The network in Fig. 8 should not show any oscillation even though there are nonsymmetric connection strengths between the two sets of V_i and ψ_j amplifiers, as long as the ψ_j are sufficiently fast.

A small computational network was constructed out of conventional electronic components to solve a 2-variable

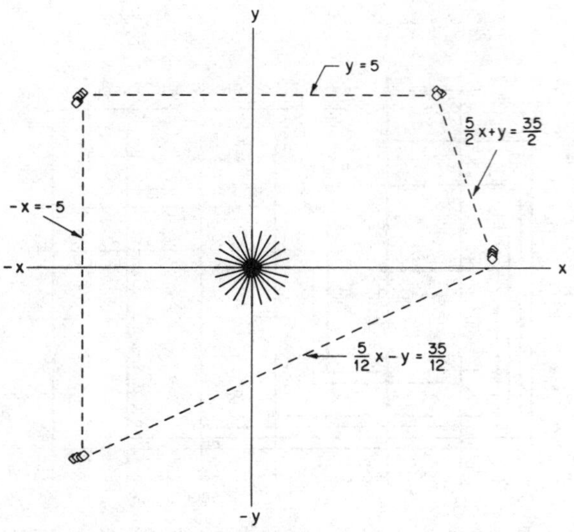

Fig. 9. A plot of the measured values of x and y for the linear programming network described in the text, as a function of the gradient of the optimization plane. The set of gradients is depicted by their projections onto the x, y plane, drawn as vectors from the origin.

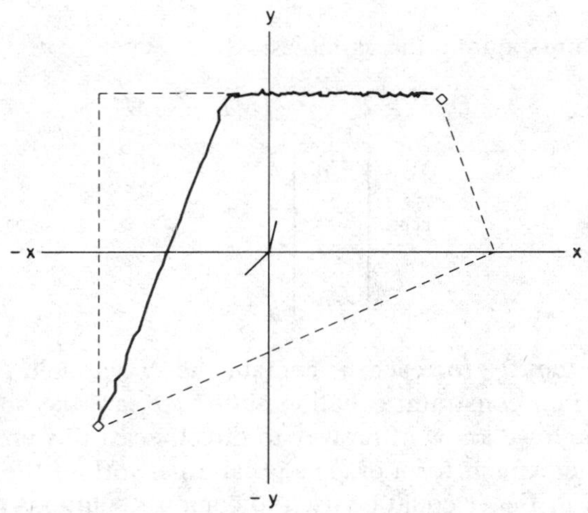

Fig. 10. The trajectory of x and y for the circuit described in the text as the gradient (indicated by the two vectors from the origin) is rapidly switched.

problem with four constraints using the network organization of Fig. 8. A simple op amp/diode active clamp circuit was used to provide the nonlinear f input–output function. The equations of constraint for the two variables (x and y) were

$$y \le 5$$
$$-x \le 5$$
$$\frac{5}{12}x - y \le \frac{35}{12}$$
$$\frac{5}{2}x + y \le \frac{35}{2}. \qquad (22)$$

These equations defined the connection strengths (D_{ji}) and the input currents (B_j) for the ψ_j amplifiers. In the xy plane characterizing the solution space, they defined the simplex shown in Fig. 9. A microcomputer-based data acquisition system was used to control the circuit and to measure the output voltages of the V_1 and V_2 amplifiers which corresponded to the x, y solutions, as a function of rapidly changing sets of input currents supplied to the input lines of these amplifiers. As indicated in Fig. 8, these input currents correspond to the coefficients A_i in the cost function which is to be minimized. For this simple 2-variable problem, the cost function can be geometrically thought of as a plane defined by the equation $z \doteq A_1x + A_2y$ hovering above the xy plane, and the direction of the gradient of that plane $A_1\hat{x} + A_2\hat{y}$ can be represented by a vector in the xy solution plane. The lowest point on the portion of this cost plane lying above the feasible solution space in the xy plane lies above the optimum simplex point. As the cost function is changed, the cost plane tilts in a new direction, the gradient projection in the xy plane rotates, and the optimum simplex point may also change. We recorded the values of x and y computed by the network for a set of cost functions. The operating points of the circuit are plotted in Fig. 9. Each diamond represents the location in the xy space at which the network stabilized at as the cost-plane gradient vector (indicated by the array of short line segments emanating from the origin) was swept in a circle. The circuit was stable at the optimum simplex points corresponding to the correct constrained choice for a given gradient direction.

In another experiment, the variable amplifiers were artificially slowed using large input capacitance and the trajectory followed by V_1 and V_2 was collected by rapid data sampling as the gradient was rapidly switched in direction. The trajectory is shown in Fig. 10. The network follows the gradient until it reaches a constraint wall which it then follows until the optimum simplex is reached. Since the solution space is always convex for linear programming problems, the network is guaranteed to find the optimum solution.

V. Conclusions

We have demonstrated how interconnected networks of simple analog processors can be used to solve decomposition/decision problems and linear programming problems. Networks for both problems were designed using conceptual tools which allow one to understand the influence of complicated feedback in highly interconnected networks of analog processors. There appears to be a large class of computation problems for which this simple concept of an "energy" function generates a complete stable circuit design without the need for a detailed dynamic analysis of stability. The function produces the required values of the many resistors from a short statement of the overall problem.

The two basic computations—digital decomposition and the linear programming network—are quite different computations in several respects. In the decomposition/decision networks discussed, the answers are digital, and this requirement that the stable states of the network lie on the corners of the solution space determines the highly nonlinear input–output relations for the variable amplifiers. Also, the equations of motion for the individual elements in the network *are of no intrinsic relevance* to the problem to be solved; they are a program which is used to compute the correct solution. In contrast, the amplifiers for the variables in the linear programming network are linear and furthermore the circuit equations of the linear programming network (17) have a more direct relationship to the problem to be solved; the constraint relationships are explicitly represented. This is similar to conventional methods of analog computation in which the processing elements are chosen to compute specific terms in a differential equation to be solved. In fact, a computational circuit similar to that in Fig. 8 has been described [7]. Here we have analytically shown the stability of this circuit design and illustrate it as a limiting case of more general networks for which the circuit equations do not necessarily relate to the problem to be solved. Another distinction is that the signal decision/deconvolution circuit makes a decision on the basis of the absolute values of its analog inputs, while the linear programming circuit decisions are based only on the relative values of the input amplitudes $\vec{A}$. This self-scaling property is often desired in signal processing and pattern recognition.

The practical usefulness of analog computational networks remains to be determined. Here, we have demonstrated, that for "simple" computational tasks and well-defined initial conditions, the networks can sometimes be guaranteed of finding the global optimum solution. The major advantage of these architectures is their potential combination of speed and computational power [1]. Interesting practical uses of such circuits for complicated problems necessitate huge numbers of connections (resistors) and amplifiers. Such circuits might be built in integrated circuit technology. Work has begun on questions of the microfabrication of extensive resistive connection matrices [8], [9]. Optical implementations of such circuits are also feasible [10].

References

[1] J. J. Hopfield and D. W. Tank, "'Neural' computation of decisions optimization problems," *Biological Cybern.*, vol. 52, pp. 141–152, 1985.

[2] J. J. Hopfield and D. W. Tank, "Collective computation with continuous variables," in *Disordered Systems and Biological Organization*, E. Bienenstock, F. Fogelman, and G. Weisbuch, Eds., Berlin, Germany: Springer-Verlag, 1985.

[3] M. R. Garey and D. S. Johnson, *Computers and Intractability*. New York: Freeman, 1979.

[4] S. E. Fahlman, "Three flavors of parallelism," in *Proc. of the Fourth National Conf. of the Canadian Society for Computational Studies of Intelligence*, Saskatoon, Sask., Canada, May 1982.

[5] J. J. Hopfield, "Neurons with graded response have collective computational properties like those of two-state neurons," *Proc. Natl. Acad. Sci. U.S.A.*, vol. 81, pp. 3088–3092, 1984.

[6] J. J. Hopfield, "Neural networks and physical systems with emergent collective computational abilities," *Proc. Natl. Acad. Sci. U.S.A.*, vol. 79, pp. 2554–2558, 1982.

[7] I. B. Pyne, "Linear programming on an electronic analogue computer," *Trans. AIEE, Part I* (*Comm. & Elect.*), vol. 75, 1956.

[8] M. Sivilotti, M. Emerling, and C. Mead, "A novel associative memory implemented using collective computation," 1985 Conf. on VLSI's, H. Fuchs, Ed., Rockville, MD: Computer Science Press, 1985, p. 329.

[9] L. D. Jackel, R. E. Howard, H. P. Graf, R. Straughn, and J. Denker, "Artificial neural networks for computing," in *Proc. of the 29th Int. Symp. on Electron, Ion, and Photon Beams*, to be published in the *J. Vac. Sci. Tech.*.

[10] D. Psaltis and N. Farhat, "Optical information processing based on an associative-memory model of neural nets with thresholding and feedback," *Opt. Lett.*, vol. 10, pp. 98–100, 1985.

David W. Tank was born in Cleveland, OH, on June 3, 1953. He received his undergraduate education from Case Western Reserve University, Cleveland, OH, and Hobart College, Geneva, NY. He received the Ph.D. degree in physics from Cornell University, Ithaca, NY in 1983.

From 1983 to 1984 he was a Post-Doctoral fellow at AT&T Bell Laboratories in Murray Hill, NJ. He has remained at Bell Laboratories, joining the Molecular Biophysics Research Department in 1984. His research interests concern the biophysics of individual nerve cells, neural representations and coding, and the computational properties of neural circuits.

John J. Hopfield received the B.A. degree from Swarthmore College in 1954 and the Ph.D. degree in physics from Cornell University, Ithaca, NY, in 1958.

His research has included work on electron transfer in photosynthesis, accuracy and proofreading in biomolecular synthesis, studies of "neural" networks in biological computation, and optical properties and impurity levels of semiconductors. He is currently Roscoe G. Dickonson Professor of Chemistry and Biology at the California Institute of Technology and a member of the Molecular Biophysics Research Department at AT&T Bell Laboratories, Murray Hill, NJ.

Information Capacity of the Hopfield Model

YASER S. ABU-MOSTAFA AND JEANNINE-MARIE ST. JACQUES

Abstract—**The information capacity of general forms of memory is formalized. The number of bits of information that can be stored in the Hopfield model of associative memory is estimated. It is found that the asymptotic information capacity of a Hopfield network of N neurons is of the order N^3 b. The number of arbitrary state vectors that can be made stable in a Hopfield network of N neurons is proved to be bounded above by N.**

I. Introduction

In contrast to the standard model for memory, where the amount of information storage is an explicit quantity, the information capacity of certain models of associative memory is a debatable issue. Associative memory is a plausible model for biological memory, where a large number of simple connected building blocks (neurons) act individually in an apparently random way, yet collectively constitute an organ that does a specific complicated task in a robust manner. Apart from this biological interpretation, the ability to carry out collective computation in a distributed system of flexible structure without global synchronization has become a recognized engineering objective.

An important step in understanding collective systems is to quantify their ability to store information and carry out computation. The Hopfield neural network [2] is a model of associative content-addressable memory with a simple flexible structure. Being a content-addressable memory, it is capable of storing information, as well as carrying out certain computational tasks such as error correction and nearest neighbor search.

In this work, we introduce a definition of information capacity that is applicable to general forms of memory. We apply this definition to the Hopfield neural network and obtain tight upper and lower bounds for the number of bits that can be stored in a network of N neurons. We then restrict the format of information storage to stable states and obtain a linear upper bound for the number of vectors that can be made stable in the model, for every N. These results are equally valid in a completely different application that has the same mathematical formulation, namely the stable states of spin glasses [5], [8].

In Section II, we introduce the Hopfield model of associative memory and explain the function of the neural network. The concept of information capacity is formalized in Section III, and the definition is applied to get a tight asymptotic estimate for the information capacity of a network of N neurons. In Section IV, the linear upper bound for the number of stable states is derived; this constitutes a measure of the useful information capacity of the model. The Appendix discusses some background material about threshold functions.

II. The Hopfield Model

Complicated electronic circuits using neuron-like architectures can be made in an attempt to produce aspects of biological memory. However, these circuits are quite complex and highly ordered. It seems highly improbable that such mechanisms would arise naturally and be used as basic building blocks for biological memory. Instead, if a large number of neurons had computationally useful collective properties, arising simply due to their number, chance would favor the use of the building block that is the simplest and the least ordered. Hopfield [2] has shown that a large number of highly stylized neurons do have collective properties. He has found that a set of asynchronously operating nonlinear neurons can store information with stability and efficiency, recall it with some error-correcting capability, and exhibit a sense of time order. Also, his model is quite robust and should work even when more neurological details are added.

A neural network consists of N pairwise connected neurons. The ith neuron can be in one of two states: $u_i = -1$ (off) or $u_i = +1$ (on). The (synaptic) connections are undirected and have strengths that are fixed real numbers. Define the state vector $\boldsymbol{u}$ to be a binary vector (± 1) whose ith component corresponds to the state of the ith neuron. Randomly and asynchronously, each neuron examines its inputs and decides whether to turn itself on or off. It does this in the following manner. Let w_{ij} be the strength (which may be negative) of the synaptic connection from neuron j to neuron i. ($w_{ij} = w_{ji}$ and $w_{ii} = 0$). Let t_i be the threshold voltage of the ith neuron. If the weighted sum over all of its inputs is greater than or equal to t_i, the ith neuron turns on and its state becomes $+1$. If the sum is less than t_i, the neuron turns off and its state becomes -1. The action of each neuron simulates a general threshold function (see the Appendix) of $N-1$ variables (the states of all the other neurons):

$$u_i = \operatorname{sgn}\left(\sum_{j=1}^{N} w_{ij} u_j - t_i \right).$$

Let W be an $N \times N$ real-valued, zero-diagonal symmetric matrix. The entries of W are the w_{ij} defined above; w_{ij}

Manuscript received August 27, 1984; revised December 19, 1984.
The authors are with the California Institute of Technology, Pasadena, CA 91125, USA.

Reprinted from IEEE Transactions on Information Theory 31(4), July 1985, pp. 461-64.

is the strength of the synaptic connection from neuron j to neuron i. Let the threshold vector $\boldsymbol{t}$ be a real-valued vector whose ith component is the threshold voltage of the ith neuron. Each choice of W and $\boldsymbol{t}$ defines a specific neural network of N neurons with specific values for the strengths of the synaptic connections and the threshold voltages of the neurons. The network starts in an initial state and runs with each neuron randomly and independently reevaluating itself. Often, the network enters a stable point in the state space in which all neurons remain in their current state after evaluating their inputs. This stable vector of states constitutes a stored word in the memory, and the basic operation of the network is to converge to a stable state if we initialize it with a nearby state vector (in the Hamming sense).

Hopfield [2] proposed a specific scheme of constructing the matrix W that makes a given set of vectors $\boldsymbol{u}^1,\cdots,\boldsymbol{u}^K$ stable states of the neural network. The scheme is based on the sum of the outer products of these vectors. We shall make no assumptions here about how the matrix W is constructed in terms of the vectors $\boldsymbol{u}^1,\cdots,\boldsymbol{u}^K$, and all the results are valid even if Hopfield's particular construction scheme is not followed.

III. Information Capacity

A Hopfield network represents a memory that stores information, and it is appropriate to ask how much information we can store in a network of N neurons. To define the information capacity C, we start with a familiar example and try to extend it.

If we have a random access memory with M address lines and one data line (an $M \times 1$ RAM, consisting of 2^M memory locations, where each location is accessed by an M-bit address and contains one bit of stored data), it is clear that we can store 2^M b of information. This is because given an *arbitrary* string of 2^M b, we can load the $M \times 1$ RAM with the string and be able to retrieve the whole string from the memory later on.

There is also another way to look at it, if we consider the string as a single object. We can store and retrieve any string (of length 2^M b) in the $M \times 1$ RAM, and there are 2^{2^M} such strings. Thus the memory can distinguish between 2^{2^M} cases. *We define the information capacity of a memory to be the logarithm of the number of cases it can distinguish between*, in this case $C = \log 2^{2^M} = 2^M$ b.

How does this definition apply to the Hopfield model? Consider a neural network with N neurons. The w_{ij} and the t_i are what distinguish one network from the other. If we had access to these values and were able to read them, the information capacity of the memory would be infinite, since a real number constitutes an infinite amount of information. However, we can only sense these values through the state transitions of the neurons. The question now becomes, how many different sets of values for w_{ij} and t_i can we distinguish between merely by observing the state transition scheme of the neurons? This corresponds to the number of distinguishable networks of N neurons. If this number is c, the capacity of the network will be $C = \log c$ b.

The key factor in estimating the number of distinguishable networks is the known estimate for the number of threshold functions (see the Appendix). The action of each neuron simulates a general threshold function of $N-1$ variables (the states of all the other neurons). There are at most $2^{(N-1)^2}$ such functions [3]. Since there are N neurons, there will be at most $(2^{(N-1)^2})^N$ distinguishable networks. The logarithm of this number is an upper bound for the information capacity C. Hence

$$C \leq \log(2^{(N-1)^2})^N = O(N^3)\,\text{b}.$$

Let us consider the lower bound now. There are at least $2^{\alpha n^2}$ threshold functions of n variables, where $\alpha \approx 0.33$ [6]. The symmetry of the matrix W makes the N threshold functions dependent, but we can take the submatrix of W consisting of the first $\lfloor N/2 \rfloor$ rows and the last $\lfloor N/2 \rfloor$ columns, and consider the partial threshold functions defined by this submatrix. Since the entries of this submatrix are independent, we have at least $\lfloor N/2 \rfloor$ functions each of $n = \lfloor N/2 \rfloor$ variables. Therefore, the number of distinguishable networks is a least $(2^{\alpha \lfloor N/2 \rfloor^2})^{\lfloor N/2 \rfloor}$. The logarithm of this number is a lower bound for the information capacity C. Hence

$$C \geq \log\left(2^{\alpha \lfloor N/2 \rfloor^2}\right)^{\lfloor N/2 \rfloor} = \Omega(N^3)\,\text{b}.$$

The conclusion is that the information capacity C of a Hopfield neural network with N neurons is exactly of the order N^3 b. This definition of information capacity is quite general, and it is interesting to investigate how it is affected by imposing certain restrictions on the format of information storage. This aspect is addressed in the next section, where the storage format is restricted to stable states.

IV. Stable States

Information in the Hopfield model is stored as stable states. A stable state $\boldsymbol{u}^s$ is a state that is a fixed point of the neural network. Each of the N neurons randomly and repeatedly looks at the weighted sum of all its inputs and then decides not to change from its previous state. To see how information is stored in the model, look at the example of pattern recognition and error correction.

A person sees a face X and wants to decide if the face is that of person A or that of person B. The visual picture of the face is processed and the description is encoded into a binary vector $\boldsymbol{u}^X$, which contains the information describing the face. $\boldsymbol{u}^X$ is then fed into the particular neural network that remembers the faces of persons A and B. That is, $\boldsymbol{u}^A$ and $\boldsymbol{u}^B$, which contain the information describing faces A and B, respectively, are stable states of this particular network. The vector $\boldsymbol{u}^X$ is fed into the network by setting the initial state of the ith neuron to the same value as the ith component of the binary vector $\boldsymbol{u}^X$.

After a period of time, the state of the network is evaluated. If $\boldsymbol{u}^X$ is close to $\boldsymbol{u}^A$, then $\boldsymbol{u}^A$ will be the network's final state. The face is then recognized as belonging to person A and similarly if $\boldsymbol{u}^X$ is close to $\boldsymbol{u}^B$. If $\boldsymbol{u}^X$ is in between $\boldsymbol{u}^A$ and $\boldsymbol{u}^B$, the system will randomly converge to one or the other of the two states. Therefore, we have a model that makes decisions and has some error-correcting capability.

It is of interest to know the number of memories that can be stored in a Hopfield network of N neurons. What is the maximum number K such that any K vectors of N binary entries can be made stable in a network of N neurons by the proper choice of W and $\boldsymbol{t}$? Since we have to come up with a network for every choice of the K vectors, and since there are $\binom{2^N}{K}$ such choices, but less than 2^{N^3} such networks, it follows that

$$\binom{2^N}{K} \leq 2^{N^3}.$$

Restricting K to be at most 2^{N-1} because of the symmetry of the choice function, we get $K = O(N^2)$. To be able to store and retrieve the order of N^2 arbitrary stable states in a Hopfield network with N neurons seems quite ambitious. Hopfield predicted experimentally that $K \approx 0.15N$ [2], and McEliece showed a statistical bound of $K \leq N/2 \log N$ [4]. However, these estimates restrict the construction of W to the sum-of-outer-products scheme [2]. We now improve on the $O(N^2)$ bound and show that the number of stable states K can be at most N, for every N, no matter how the matrix W is constructed.

Theorem: Let W denote a real-valued zero-diagonal $N \times N$ matrix, and let $\boldsymbol{t}$ denote a real-valued N vector. Suppose that $K \leq 2^{N-1}$ is an integer satisfying the following condition.

For any K-set of binary N-vectors $\boldsymbol{u}^1, \cdots, \boldsymbol{u}^K$, there is a matrix W and a vector $\boldsymbol{t}$ such that

$$\operatorname{sgn}\left(\sum_{j=1}^{N} w_{ij} u_j^k - t_i\right) = u_i^k, \qquad \text{for } k = 1, \cdots, K$$

$$\text{and } i = 1, \cdots, N,$$

then $K \leq N$.

Proof: Suppose that K satisfies this property. We construct K vector $\boldsymbol{u}^1, \boldsymbol{u}^2, \cdots, \boldsymbol{u}^K$ as follows. The first entries in these vectors, namely $u_1^1, u_1^2, \cdots, u_1^K$, are binary variables $x^1, x^2, \cdots, x^K$ to be fixed later. The remaining $N-1$ entries in each vector are fixed ± 1's such that no two vectors have exactly the same entries (always possible since $K \leq 2^{N-1}$). We apply the condition of the theorem for $i = 1$. For any choice of $x^1, \cdots, x^K$, there must be real numbers $w_{12}, w_{13}, \cdots, w_{1N}, t_1$ such that

$$\operatorname{sgn}\left(\sum_{j=2}^{N} w_{1j} u_j^k - t_1\right) = x^k$$

for $k = 1, \cdots, K$, since $w_{11} = 0$ (zero-diagonal). Therefore, for each of the 2^K choices for the values of $x^1, \cdots, x^K$, we must find a different threshold function of $N-1$ variables with K points in the domain. Let B_{N-1}^K be the number of the threshold functions of $N-1$ variables with K points in the domain. We must have

$$B_{N-1}^K \geq 2^K. \tag{1}$$

Cameron [1] and Winder [9] (see the Appendix), give the following upper bound to B_{N-1}^K:

$$B_{N-1}^K \leq 2 \sum_{i=0}^{N-1} \binom{K-1}{i}.$$

If $K > N$, then

$$B_{N-1}^K \leq 2 \sum_{i=0}^{N-1} \binom{K-1}{i} < 2 \sum_{i=0}^{K-1} \binom{K-1}{i}$$

$$= 2 \times 2^{K-1} = 2^K.$$

So if $K > N$, then $B_{N-1}^K < 2^k$, which contradicts condition (1). Therefore K must be at most N and the proof is complete.

The theorem is a formalization of the fact that a Hopfield neural network cannot have more than N arbitrary stable states. Notice that the matrix W was not required to be symmetric, and this covers the generalization of the Hopfield model where the synaptic connections become directed (allowing $w_{ij} \neq w_{ji}$). Also, there is no restriction on the method of constructing W and $\boldsymbol{t}$ in terms of $\boldsymbol{u}^1, \cdots, \boldsymbol{u}^K$. McEliece and Posner [5] predicted that a zero-diagonal symmetric matrix has an exponential number of stable states on the average. The above theorem predicts at most a linear number of arbitrary stable states for a zero-diagonal matrix. The two results imply that the average number of parasitic stable states is exponential in N.

V. Conclusion

The information capacity of general forms of memory was formalized and applied to the Hopfield model of associative memory. Exact asymptotic estimates for the number of bits that can be stored in a neural network of N neurons were derived. A linear upper bound for the number of arbitrary stable states that can be stored in a neural network of N neurons was proved. This bound is reasonably close to the experimentally achievable capacity and to the statistically predicted capacity.

Appendix
Enumeration of Threshold Functions

A switching function $f(x_1, \cdots, x_n)$ of n binary variables $x_1, \cdots, x_n$ is defined by assigning either 0 or 1 to each of the 2^n points $(x_1, \cdots, x_n)$ in $\{0,1\}^N$. We are using a binary $(-1, +1)$ convention, which is strictly equivalent to the $(0,1)$ convention. A switching function $f(x_1, \cdots, x_n)$ of n variables is linearly separable if there exists a hyperplane π in the n-dimensional space, which strictly separates the "on" set $f^{-1}(1)$ from the "off" set $f^{-1}(-1)$. In other words, $f^{-1}(1)$ lies on one side of π, and $f^{-1}(-1)$ lies on the other, and $\pi \cap \{-1, +1\}^N$ is empty. Linearly separable switching functions are also called threshold functions [3]. A threshold function simulates a neuron examining its inputs and making its decision as to its next state. Cameron [1] and Winder [9] give the following upper bound on the number of threshold functions of n variables defined on m points B_n^m:

$$B_n^m \leq 2 \sum_{i=0}^{n} \binom{m-1}{i}.$$

They arrive at their upper bound in the following manner. Define an $(n+1)$-dimensional space in which the coordinate axes correspond to the weights and to the threshold voltage. Consider a particular state $\boldsymbol{u}$. Plot $\boldsymbol{u}$ as a hyperplane in $n+1$ space, the set of all values of w_j and t such that

$$\sum_{j=1}^{n} w_j u_j - t = 0.$$

Note that the hyperplane passes through the origin and that it divides the space into two regions. Weights and threshold voltages from one of the regions make $\sum_{j=1}^{n} w_j u_j - t > 0$ and correspond to the threshold function on $\boldsymbol{u}$ being equal to 1. Weights and voltages from the other region make $\sum_{j=1}^{n} w_j u_j - t < 0$ and correspond to the threshold function on $\boldsymbol{u}$ being equal to -1. Each of the m points gives a similar hyperplane.

Thus we have m hyperplanes passing through the origin in $n+1$ space and partitioning the space into a number of regions. Each region corresponds to a threshold function. All points in any one of these regions correspond to values of w_j and t that produce the same threshold function. Two points in different regions correspond to two different functions as at least one $\boldsymbol{u}$ out of the m $\boldsymbol{u}$'s is mapped to $+1$ by one function and mapped to -1 by the other. Therefore B_n^m is less than or equal to the maximum number of regions (call the number C_{n+1}^m) made by m hyperplanes passing through the origin in $n+1$ space. Assume $m-1$ hyperplanes have made C_{n+1}^{m-1} regions in $n+1$ space. We add the mth hyperplane to make as many more regions as possible. The mth plane can intersect the other $m-1$ hyperplanes in at most $m-1$ hyperlines. The $m-1$ hyperlines can at most partition the mth plane into C_n^{m-1} hyperplane regions, since this is the same problem in n space. Since each region in the mth plane has been divided into a boundary between two regions in $n+1$ space, we have added C_n^{m-1} regions to the other C_{n+1}^{m-1} regions given by $m-1$ planes.

Therefore

$$C_{n+1}^m = C_n^{m-1} + C_{n+1}^{m-1}.$$

The solution of this recurrence relation is $C_{n+1}^m = 2\sum_{i=0}^{n} \binom{m-1}{i}$, which is an upper bound for B_n^m. If $m = 2^n$, i.e., the threshold function is defined for every binary n-vector, then we have an upper bound for the number of fully defined threshold functions of n variables (for $n \geq 4$):

$$B_n^{2^n} \leq 2 \sum_{i=0}^{n} \binom{2^n - 1}{i} \leq 2(n+1) \times \binom{2^n - 1}{n}$$

$$\leq 2(n+1) \frac{2^{n^2}}{n!} \leq 2^{n^2}.$$

References

[1] S. H. Cameron, "An estimate of the complexity requisite in a universal decision network," Bionics Symposium, Wright Airforce Dev. Div. (WADD) Rep. 60-600, pp. 197–212, 1960.

[2] J. J. Hopfield, "Neural networks and physical systems with emergent collective computational abilities," in *Proc. Nat. Academy Sci., USA*, vol. 79, 1982, pp. 2554–2558.

[3] P. M. Lewis and C. L. Coates, *Threshold Logic*. New York: Wiley, 1967.

[4] R. J. McEliece, private correspondence, 1984.

[5] R. J. McEliece and E. C. Posner, "The number of stable points of an infinite-range spin glass," unpublished manuscript, 1984.

[6] S. Muroga, "Generation of self-dual threshold functions and lower bounds of the number of threshold functions and a maximum weight," in *Proc. AIEE Symp. Switching Circuit Theory and Logical Design*, 1962, pp. 170–184.

[7] C. E. Shannon, "A mathematical theory of communication," *Bell Syst. Tech. J.*, vol. 27, pp. 379–423, 1948.

[8] F. Tanaka and S. E. Edwards, "Analytic theory of the ground state properties of a spin glass: I. Ising spin glass," *J. Phys. F: Metal Phys.*, vol. 10, pp. 2769–2778, 1980.

[9] R. O. Winder, "Threshold logic," Ph.D. dissertation, Princeton Univ., Princeton, NJ, 1962.

[10] ——, "Bounds on threshold gate realizability," *IRE Trans. Electron. Comput.*, vol. EC-12, pp. 561–564, 1963.

The Capacity of the Hopfield Associative Memory

ROBERT J. McELIECE, FELLOW, IEEE, EDWARD C. POSNER, FELLOW, IEEE, EUGENE R. RODEMICH, AND SANTOSH S. VENKATESH, STUDENT MEMBER, IEEE

***Abstract*—Techniques from coding theory are applied to study rigorously the capacity of the Hopfield associative memory. Such a memory stores n-tuple of ± 1's. The components change depending on a hard-limited version of linear functions of all other components. With symmetric connections between components, a stable state is ultimately reached. By building up the connection matrix as a sum-of-outer products of m fundamental memories, one hopes to be able to recover a certain one of the m memories by using an initial n-tuple probe vector less than a Hamming distance $n/2$ away from the fundamental memory. If m fundamental memories are chosen at random, the maximum asympotic value of m in order that most of the m original memories are exactly recoverable is $n/(2\log n)$. With the added restriction that every one of the m fundamental memories be recoverable exactly, m can be no more than $n/(4\log n)$ asymptotically as n approaches infinity. Extensions are also considered, in particular to capacity under quantization of the outer-product connection matrix. This quantized memory capacity problem is closely related to the capacity of the quantized Gaussian channel.**

I. Introduction to Neural Networks

In a very influential recent article, Hopfield [1] introduced a powerful new kind of associative or content-addressable memory based on his studies of collective computation in neural networks. For a review of earlier work, see [2] and [3]. Hopfield has demonstrated empirically that the associative memory as a network is very attractive for many applications, but as yet a good theoretical understanding of its behavior has not been found. We have discovered techniques for rigorously analyzing "Hopfield memories," which we introduce in this paper. The techniques used are quite reminiscent of coding theory, especially random coding and sphere hardening. Before we relate the theory of Hopfield memories to information and coding theory, however, let us explain the tie with neurobiology, which is quite direct. There are many other potential applications as well.

Manuscript received February 3, 1986; revised October 28, 1986. This work was supported in part by the National Aeronautics and Space Administration through the Jet Propulsion Laboratory of the California Institute of Technology and in part by the Defense Advanced Research Projects Agency. This work was partially presented at IS/T 85, Brighton, England, June 1985.

R. J. McEliece is with the Department of Electrical Engineering, California Institute of Technology, Pasadena, CA 91125.

E. C. Posner and E. R. Rodemich are with the Jet Propulsion Laboratory and the Department of Electrical Engineering, California Institute of Technology, Pasadena, CA 91125.

S. S. Venkatesh was with the California Institute of Technology, Pasadena, CA. He is now with the University of Pennsylvania, Philadelphia, PA.

IEEE Log Number 8612815.

Neuroanatomical models of brain functioning have proved fertile ground in the development of efficient systems of associative memory. Neural network models based upon mathematical idealizations of biological memory typically consist of a densely interconnected dynamical cellular cluster [4]. The processing nodes in such a structure are the *neurons*, and the neuronal interconnections are through the medium of linear *synaptic conduits*. Describing the instantaneous state of a neural network to be the collective states of each of the individual neurons (firing or nonfiring) in the system then leads to a characterization of the dynamics of the system as a motion in time through the state space of the system. In this form, then, the mathematical abstraction of neural function leads to a consideration of a finite state automaton with specified state transition rules. Other dynamical systems much akin to neural networks in this regard include the Ising spin glass models (cf. [5], for instance), and cellular automata (cf. [6]).

We consider an associative structure based upon such a neural net. The model neurons we consider are simple bistable elements each being capable of assuming two values: -1 (off) and $+1$ (on). The *state* of each neuron then represents one bit of information, and the state of the *system* as a whole is described by a binary n-tuple if there are n neurons in the system. We assume that the neural net is (possibly) densely interconnected, with neuron i transmitting information to neuron j through a linear synaptic connection T_{ij}. The neural interconnection weights T_{ij} are throughout considered to be *fixed*; i.e., learning of associations has already taken place, and no further synaptic modifications are made in the neurobiological interpretation. The connection matrix is also assumed to be symmetric with zero diagonal in almost all this paper.

The schema of Fig. 1 illustrates a typical example of the structure that we envisage for our associative memory thought of as a neural network. A five-neuron densely interconnected neural network is shown. The circles represent neurons, and the directed lines represent the direction of interneural information flow through the corresponding synaptic weight T_{ij}. The instantaneous state of the system depicted is $(x_1, x_2, x_3, x_4, x_5) = (1, -1, 1, -1, -1)$. Thus $\boldsymbol{x}$ is called the *state vector*. The T_{ij} need not be symmetric at this point but are symmetric for all the rigorous results of this paper.

Reprinted from IEEE Tansactions on Information Theory 33(4), July 1987, pp. 461-82. Copyright © 1987 by The Institute of Electrical and Electronics Engineers, Inc.

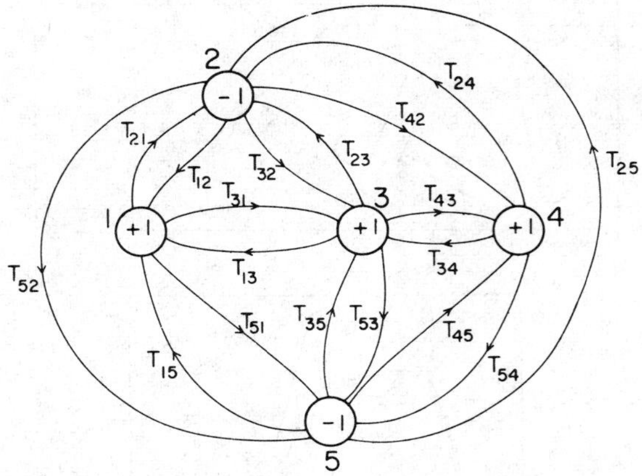

Fig. 1. Five-neuron densely interconnected neural network.

Logical computation in the network takes place at each neural site by means of a simple threshold decision rule, as shown in Fig. 2. Each neuron evaluates the weighted sum of the binary states of all the neurons in the system; the new state of the neuron is -1 if the sum is negative, and $+1$ if the sum (equals or) exceeds zero. (In this and what follows we almost always assume a threshold of zero.) Specifically, if $\boldsymbol{x} = (x_1, x_2, \cdots, x_n)$ is the present state of the system (with $x_j = \pm 1$ being the state of the jth neuron), the new state x_i' of the ith neuron is determined by the rule

$$x_i' = \operatorname{sgn}\left\{ \sum_{j=1}^{n} T_{ij} x_j \right\} = \begin{cases} +1, & \text{if } \Sigma T_{ij} x_j \geq 0 \\ -1, & \text{if } \Sigma T_{ij} x_j < 0 \end{cases}. \quad (1.1)$$

Fig. 3 shows the conceptual process of getting from an initial vector $\boldsymbol{x}$ (with all components known or guessed) to a memory. The length n is 8 in the figure. The initial state vector $\boldsymbol{x}$ is called a *probe*, for it is used to probe the memory.

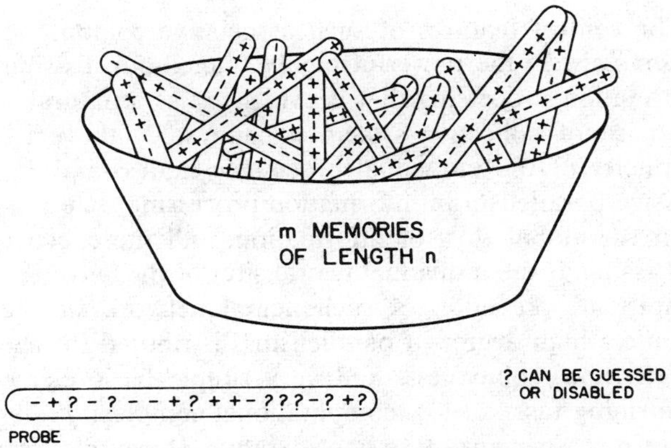

Fig. 3. Associative memory basket.

In this paper, we will discuss two modes of changing $\boldsymbol{x} \to \boldsymbol{x}'$. In *synchronous* operation, each of the n neurons *simultaneously* evaluates and updates its state according to rule (1.1). In *asynchronous* operation, the components of the current state vector $\boldsymbol{x}$ are updated one at a time according to (1.1), to produce a new state vector. The one component i chosen to be updated is selected from among the n indices i with equal probability $1/n$, independently of which components were updated previously and of what the values of the probe vector were before and after update.

In this neural network model, the linear synaptic weights provide global communication of information, while the nonlinear logical operations essential to computation take place at the neurons. Thus, in spite of the simplicity of the highly stylized neural network structure that we utilize, considerable computational power is inherent in the system. The implementation of models of learning (the Hebbian hypothesis [7]) and associative recall [7]–[13], and the solution of complex minimization problems [14], [15] using such neural networks is indicative of the computational power latent in the system.

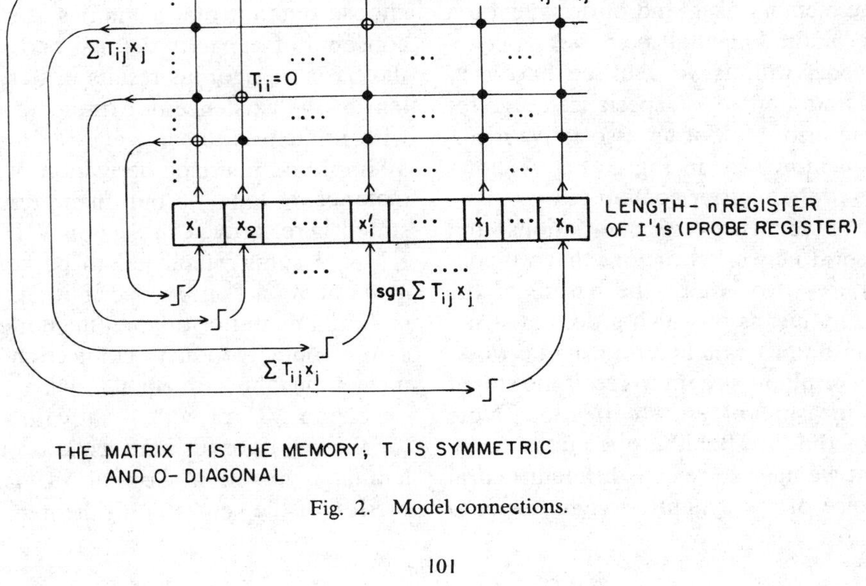

Fig. 2. Model connections.

The central features of such associative computational systems are 1) the powerful highly fanned-out distributed information processing that is evidenced as a natural consequence of collective system dynamics; 2) the extreme simplicity of the individual processing nodes; and 3) the massive parallelism in information processing that accrues from the global flow of information, and the concurrent processing at the individual neural sites of the network. To recapitulate, keynotes of such neural network structures include a high degree of parallelism, distributed storage of information, robustness, and very simple basic elements performing tasks of low computational complexity.

We now specialize to a consideration of neural associative nets. We define memory in a natural fashion for these systems. We typically require that vectors x that are memories in the state space of the neural network be fixed points of the system. Specifically, if the binary n-vector is a memory, then for each neuron $i = 1, \cdots, n$,

$$x_i = \operatorname{sgn}\left\{ \sum_{j=1}^{n} T_{ij} x_j \right\}. \tag{1.2}$$

(We shall later see that this is independent of whether we have the asynchronous or synchronous models.) However, in the structure of association, it is a desideratum that the stored memories are also *attractors*, i.e., they exercise a region of influence around them so that states which are sufficiently similar to the memory are mapped to the memory by repeated iterates of the system operator.

In essence, then, we shall require that if the probe, i.e., the initial state of the neural network, is "close" to a memory, then the system dynamics will proceed in a direction so that the numerical network settles in stable state centered at the memory, or (not considered much in this paper) at least close to it. Here we use the Hamming distance as the natural similarity measure between two states in the binary n-space under consideration. It turns out that anything less than $n/2$ away will work in many situations.

With this interpretation, our memory corrects all (or most of) the errors in the initial probe vector. We can thus think of the associative memory as a kind of decoder for a code consisting of the m fundamental memories as codewords. However, the codes will, as we shall see, have very low rates and hence find limited or specialized use for channel coding. We can also think of an associative memory as a basket of m memories, as in Fig. 3. Fig. 4 shows the time history of the probe register contents.

The incorporation of sequences of associations and memory within the neural network structure that we consider now naturally raises two issues: the nature of the memory encoding rule by means of which a desired structure of associations can be programmed into the network, and the capacity of the resultant system to recall the stored memories with some measure of error correction. Note that with the nature of the thresholding operations fixed, the only flexibility that we have to realize different neural networks is in the choice of the synaptic weights or connections T_{ij}. The memory encoding rule is, in essence then, an algorithm for the appropriate choice of weights T_{ij}.

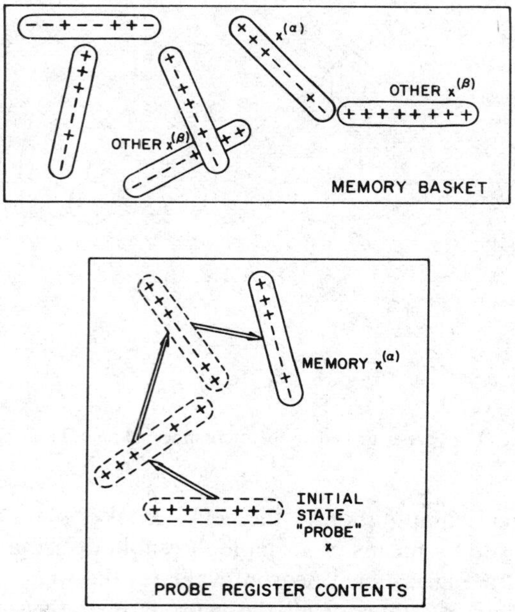

Fig. 4. Schematic representation of state space of eight-neuron neural network.

We now give a road map to the rest of the paper. Section II discusses the sum-of-outer products connection-matrix construction basic to all the results of the paper and the construction upon which current implementation plans are based. Section III gives a brief survey of other possible connection matrices that may produce higher capacity but seem much harder to build. Section IV gives a concrete example where $m = 3$ memories of length $n = 5$ are stored but with imperfect recall properties.

Next, Section V discusses various kinds of memory stability. The radius of attraction around fixed points is introduced. Some possible modes of convergence to a fixed point are described. The classical energy minimization argument that shows that we always arrive at a fixed point in the asynchronous model is presented. In Section VI, we introduce the concept of asymptotic capacity when we choose fundamental memories at random. There are three concepts of capacity defined here, only two of which are the basis of rigorous results in this paper. Next, the problem of the existence of extraneous memories is mentioned with references to some existing results. We also give here a simplified heuristic derivation of a particular important instance of one of our main results. A key conjecture stated here, proved in Section VIII, is that the number of $\Sigma T_{ij} x_j^{(\alpha)}$ sums which fail to be correct (with appropriate m, n) obeys a Poisson distribution. Here $x^{(\alpha)}$ is one of the m fundamental or original memories used to construct the sum-of-outer products connection matrix T_{ij}. "Correct" means that the sum equals $x_i^{(\alpha)}$.

Section VII provides motivating material and lemmas for the key rigorous hard lemmas of Section VIII. One key lemma reviewed in Section VII is the "large deviation" version of the central limit theorem. Another is a quantitative form of truncated inclusion and exclusion needed to prove the Poisson distribution conjecture mentioned above.

Section VIII contains two long hard lemmas, the first of which translates the large-deviation lemma of Section VII into our context. The second lemma derives an asymptotic independence result for row sum failures, needed to prove the Poisson result. The Big Theorem of Section IX then has a short proof, given all the lemmas of Sections VII and VIII. The theorem derives the capacity (corresponding to a coding theorem and its converse) when we want what amounts to immediate (one-step) convergence in the synchronous model, starting from any probe vector no more than ρn away from a fundamental memory, $0 \leq \rho < 1/2$. Two possible capacity definitions result in capacities differing by a factor of two. The larger capacity is obtained when we are allowed to fail to converge for a small fraction (approaching 0 as the memory length n approaches ∞) of the m fundamental memories.

Section X uses our prior lemmas to extend the capacity results of Section IX, to the case we are currently interested in for building memories. This is where we do not demand direct convergence, only eventual convergence. We suggest that the factor $(1-2\rho)^2$ can be removed, where we probe with a vector with ρn errors. This is not yet fully rigorous. The capacities then are (asymptotically in n) $n/(2\log n)$ or $n/(4\log n)$ depending as above on whether we allow a finite number of exceptional memories or not. The radius of attraction is any ρn, $\rho < 1/2$, but how large n must be depends on how close ρ is to $1/2$. Section X also discusses some possible implementation variations, including quantizing the T_{ij}. This turns out to reduce capacity by the same amount as quantizing detector outputs in the infinite-bandwidth Gaussian channel.

Section XI summarizes all of what we have done and discusses open problems. The most important one is the case where we allow a fraction ϵn of the n components to be wrong after the stable point is reached. It is conjectured (nearly proven) that the capacity is then asymptotic to cn where c is a constant behaving like $1/(2\log \epsilon^{-1})$ as ϵ approaches 0. This behavior is consistent with our $n/(2 \log n)$ result. We conclude Section XI and the paper with an explanation of why it may be very hard to derive a rigorous asymptotic expression for the expected number of fixed points, extraneous or otherwise.

II. Outer Product Construction

In this paper we deal almost exclusively with the memory encoding rule specified by Hopfield in [1], and formulate a rigorous answer to the simple question: What is the capacity of the Hopfield neural network structure for information storage? We will make the intuitive notion of capacity more precise later. We now turn to the Hopfield encoding rule.

Let $\boldsymbol{x} = \{\boldsymbol{x}^{(1)}, \boldsymbol{x}^{(2)}, \cdots, \boldsymbol{x}^{(m)}\}$ be an m-set of n-dimensional binary (± 1) column vectors, which are to be stored. We shall call these m vectors the (*fundamental*) *memories*. How large m can be is the subject of this paper. For each memory $\boldsymbol{x}^{(\alpha)}$ we form the $n \times n$ matrix (superscript T denotes transpose to a row vector)

$$T_\alpha = \boldsymbol{x}^{(\alpha)}(\boldsymbol{x}^{(\alpha)})^T - I_n$$

where I_n denotes the $n \times n$ identity matrix. (For some of our results, we can subtract gI_n, $0 \leq g \leq 1$.) Thus T_α is just the outer product of $\boldsymbol{x}^{(\alpha)}$ with itself, except that 0's are placed on the diagonal. Now the *Hopfield connection matrix* for the set of m memories $\{\boldsymbol{x}^{(1)}, \cdots, \boldsymbol{x}^{(m)}\}$ is defined as

$$T = \sum_{\alpha=1}^{m} T_\alpha$$

$$T = \sum_{\alpha=1}^{m} (\boldsymbol{x}^{(\alpha)})\big((\boldsymbol{x}^{(\alpha)})^T - I_n\big). \tag{2.1}$$

This is the sum-of-outer products. We assume that once T has been calculated, all other information about the $\boldsymbol{x}^{(\alpha)}$ will be "forgotten." This is an important point to note when we have to add another memory to the list of things to be remembered, that is, when we have to *learn*.

Information *retrieval* works as follows. We are given an n dimensional ± 1 vector $\boldsymbol{x} = (x_1, x_2, \cdots, x_n)$ (called as before the *probe*), and wish to find the stored memory $\boldsymbol{x}^{(\alpha)}$ which is closest to $\boldsymbol{x}$ in Hamming distance, using only the connection matrix T and neural network iteration as above. Hopfield's asynchronous algorithm for doing this is to update the components of $\boldsymbol{x}$ randomly and independently one at a time using the rule (1.1); i.e., replace the ith component of $\boldsymbol{x}$ (i is random) with the sign (± 1) of the ith component of the vector $T\boldsymbol{x}$. For any symmetric connection matrix T, such as the one here, Hopfield showed (see Section V) that in asynchronous operation, this process is convergent. This means that starting with *any* probe vector $\boldsymbol{x}$, one will always reach a *fixed vector*, i.e., a vector $\boldsymbol{y} = (y_1, y_2, \cdots, y_n)$ such that

$$\boldsymbol{y} = \operatorname{sgn}(T\boldsymbol{y}).$$

This outer product scheme has often been proposed and used in the literature [1], [2], [9], [12], [16]. In [1], Hopfield investigated the model with asynchronous dynamics and demonstrated that associative recall of chosen data was quite feasible with a measure of error correction. Nakano [9] coined the term "associatron" for the technique and demonstrated that, with synchronous dynamics, a time sequence of associations with some ability for recall and error correction could be obtained. The conditions under which long-term correlations can exist in memory have been investigated by Little [12] and Little and Shaw [16] utilizing a synchronous model.

We first make it plausible that the memories be stable (at least in a probabilistic sense). Assume that one of the memories $\boldsymbol{x}^{(\alpha)}$ is the initial state of the system. For each

$i=1,\cdots,n$, we have

$$[Tx^{(\alpha)}]_i = \sum_{j=1}^{n} T_{ij}x_j^{(\alpha)} = \sum_{\substack{j=1\\ j\neq i}}^{n}\sum_{\beta=1}^{m} x_i^{(\beta)}x_j^{(\beta)}x_j^{(\alpha)}$$
$$= (n-1)x_i^{(\alpha)} + \sum_{\beta\neq\alpha}\sum_{j\neq i} x_i^{(\beta)}x_j^{(\beta)}x_j^{(\alpha)}. \quad (2.2)$$

Now assume that the memories are random, being generated as a sequence of mn Bernoulli trials. We find that the second term of (2.2) has zero mean (actually zero *conditional* mean, given $x^{(\alpha)}$), and (conditional) variance equal to $(n-1)(m-1)$, while the first term is simply $(n-1)$ times (the sign of) $x_i^{(\alpha)}$. (The m fundamental memories $x^{(\alpha)}$ are thus approximately eigenvectors of the linear transformation T, with approximate eigenvalue n. We shall have more to say about this at the end of Section V.)

The second term in (2.2) is comprised of a sum of $(m-1)(n-1)$ independent random variables taking on values ± 1; it is hence asymptotically normal. Thus the component $x_i^{(\alpha)}$ will be stable only if the mean to standard deviation ratio given by $(n-1)^{1/2}/(m-1)^{1/2}$ is large. Thus, as long as the storage capacity of the system is not overloaded, i.e., $m \ll n$ in a way to be made precise, we expect the memories to be stable in some probabilistic sense. Section VI exploits this point of view in an argument, still nonrigorous at this point, given in some detail.

Note that the simple argument used above seems to require that $m=o(n)$. The outer product algorithm hence behaves well with regard to stability of the memories provided that the number of memories m is small enough compared to the number of components n in the memory vectors. (The $m=o(n)$ result is, however, a little unfortunate. We shall provide some relief to this in Section XI.)

III. Alternative Connection Matrix Constructions

The sum of outer products construction is the one we shall be subsequently concerned with in this paper. However, there are other possible connection matrices that one could think of that might have the m fundamental memories as fixed points. These constructions involve requiring that the fundamental memories be exactly ordinary eigenvectors of the connection matrix with positive eigenvalues. Then they will certainly be fixed points. Let the memories $x^{(\alpha)}$ be eigenvectors of T with positive eigenvalues $\lambda^{(\alpha)}$. Then

$$\operatorname{sgn}\left((Tx^{(\alpha)})i\right) = \operatorname{sgn}\left(\lambda^{(\alpha)}x_i^{(\alpha)}\right) = x_i^{(\alpha)}.$$

Thus the fundamental memories $x^{(\alpha)}$ will be fixed points.

An issue we do not consider in this paper is that of nonsymmetric connection matrices T. These of course do occur in actual neural networks. Our energy minimization argument of the next section fails for arbitrary matrices. In fact, fixed points need not even exist, and various kinds of orbital behavior can occur. However, it seems that a great deal of symmetry is not needed before behavior imitating the symmetric case occurs. All that may be necessary is a little symmetry, such as a lot of zeros at symmetric positions in the matrix. This seems to correspond to what often occurs in real neural nets, where many neurons are not connected to each other at all. We hardly discuss nonsymmetric connection matrices in this paper.

Our construction of the Hopfield model above has components changing one at a time, with no memory. We referred to this as the *asynchronous model*. One could also think of changing all the components at once, which we have called the *synchronous model*. The asynchronous model modified to provide some short-term effect of previous states may share aspects of both models. The capacity results of this paper in any case apply to both the asynchronous and synchronous models and are stated both ways. We will see one minor difficulty with the synchronous model in the next section—a fixed point need not always be reached in the synchronous model. However, (1.2) shows that a fixed point in one model is a fixed point in the other if the connection matrix is the same.

Further, we would not expect that the synchronous and asynchronous cases are very different, for we shall see that as we "home in" on the correct fundamental memory, very few components actually change anyway, synchronous or asynchronous, so it hardly matters whether we change them all at once. Also, the heuristic argument we gave providing a signal-to-Gaussian-noise ratio of approximately $\sqrt{n/m}$ is insensitive to whether we change one component at a time or all at once.

All things considered, we suspect that our capacity results do not change if a little "memory" is put into the synapses. By this we mean that a change in the ith component at time 0, say, depends, perhaps probabilistically, on some function of a generalized average of the last k values $T_{ij}x_j[-s]$, $1 \le s \le k$. Here we use $x[-s]$ to be the value of the state vector x taken s units in the past, that is, just prior to the sth previous (potential) change of a component.

There has been some other recent work on the capacity of the Hopfield associative memory. In [17], Abu-Mostafa and St. Jacques showed, using a hyperplane counting argument familiar from pattern recognition, that the capacity of a memory of length n is at most n. Here "capacity" is used in the fairly weak sense that the m memories we want to store have to be fixed points, but need not have any radius of attraction greater than zero. Any symmetric zero-diagonal connection matrix was allowed with zeros down the diagonal. An arbitrary threshold t_i (instead of zero) was allowed for the ith component, so that the memory evaluates

$$\operatorname{sgn}\left(\sum_{\substack{j=1\\ j\neq i}}^{n} T_{ij}x_j - t_i\right)$$

for $1 \le i \le n$, where x is the current state vector. Capacity m means here that *every* set of m potential fundamental memories $\{x^{(\alpha)}, 1 \le \alpha \le m\}$ that we wish to store has to have an associated symmetric zero-diagonal connection matrix $T = (T_{ij})$ and threshold vector $t = (t_i)$ such that each $x^{(\alpha)}$ is a fixed point. However, the argument of [17] would work just as well if we only required that *almost* every set of m fundamental memories be fixed with some T, t; the bound is the same and not larger in an asymptotic sense. This bound would thus cover our case of random sets of mn vectors. So ,. certainty seems an upper bound on our capacity.

That is, if we require that every single m-set of n-tuples be fixed, then the upper bound on capacity is indeed n. However, if we relax our requirements to a probabilistic bound, it turns out [18] that the correct upper bound on capacity is $2n$. Specifically, we require that the probability that a random m-set not be storable as the fixed points of some connection matrix approach 0 as n approaches infinity for the $2n$-capacity result. Finally, in Section XI, we briefly mention allowing the final stable state to have a (small) fraction ϵ of its components different from the desired fundamental memory. Whether and how much this increases the upper bound n of [17] for the outer product connection matrix it is too early to tell, but we do seem to get linear capacity with our model in this relaxed case.

Is there any way that we can attain this capacity n asymptotically? Reference [19] makes it extremely credible that we can, even with some positive radius of attraction, by the proper choice of symmetric matrix T and zero threshold vector t. (However, T will not be zero-diagonal but rather can even have *negative* diagonal elements. This negative diagonal may invalidate the argument of Section V that the memory always settles down to a stable point.) Earlier we saw that in the sum-of-outer products construction, the fundamental memories were approximately eigenvectors with eigenvalues approximately n. In [19], the matrix T is one of several natural choices which have the $m = n$ fundamental memories $x^{(\alpha)}$, assumed linearly independent, as they will be with high probability, *exactly* as their n eigenvalues.

In addition to the negative-diagonal possibility mentioned above, the constructions of [17] also have the potential difficulty that if we want to add a new memory (if we have $m < n$ already stored), we need to do a new complicated calculation involving *all* the mn components of *all* the original m memories to compute the new T. In the sum-of-outer products construction, we only need to know the previous entries themselves, which is no extra burden. In the case of the *quantized* sum-of-outer products construction discussed in Section X, we have to remember all the mn components of the $x^{(\alpha)}$ (or all the $n(n-1)/2$ sums-of-outer products *before* quantization) to compute the new T when an $(m+1)$st memory is to be added.

In spite of this additional complication, the constructions of [17] could be very important. This is because of the small capacities we have derived in this paper, which behave like $n/2\log n$ (or like $n/4 \log n$ with a slightly stronger requirement on the convergence). While we do later propose (see Section XI) that a constant asymptotic to $1/2\log(1/\epsilon)$ times n can be achieved if we allow the final stable state to have a fraction ϵ of errors, $1/2\log(1/\epsilon)$ is fairly small compared to 1 for small ϵ.

IV. Examples

The first three sections have all been rather abstract. As a simple example, suppose $n = 5$ and that we wish to store the three fundamental memories

$$x^{(1)} = (+++++)^T \qquad x^{(2)} = (+--+-)^T$$
$$x^{(3)} = (-+---)^T.$$

Then we have

$$T_1 = \begin{bmatrix} 0 & + & + & + & + \\ + & 0 & + & + & + \\ + & + & 0 & + & + \\ + & + & + & 0 & + \\ + & + & + & + & 0 \end{bmatrix}$$

$$T_2 = \begin{bmatrix} 0 & - & - & + & - \\ - & 0 & + & - & + \\ - & + & 0 & - & + \\ + & - & - & 0 & - \\ - & + & + & - & 0 \end{bmatrix}$$

$$T_3 = \begin{bmatrix} 0 & - & + & + & + \\ - & 0 & - & - & - \\ + & - & 0 & + & + \\ + & - & + & 0 & + \\ + & - & + & + & 0 \end{bmatrix},$$

and so finally

$$T = \begin{bmatrix} 0 & -1 & 1 & 3 & 1 \\ -1 & 0 & 1 & -1 & 1 \\ 1 & 1 & 0 & 1 & 3 \\ 3 & -1 & 1 & 0 & 1 \\ 1 & 1 & 3 & 1 & 0 \end{bmatrix}.$$

Now suppose we are given the probe vector $x = (+--++)^T$, at distance 1 from $x^{(2)}$. To update x, we compute Tx:

$$Tx = (+4, -3, +4, +4, -2)^T.$$

Thus if we hard-limit Tx using the rule (1.1), that is, limit all its components to ± 1, only the third and fifth components of x will change. Let us assume asynchronous operation. It we select the third component to change, the new probe will be

$$x' = (+, -, +, +, +)^T.$$

Now we compute Tx':

$$Tx' = (+6, 0, +4, +6, +4)^T.$$

Here we find (recall our convention $\operatorname{sgn}(0) = +$) that the signs of the components of Tx' are all positive. We see that we will ultimately have to change the second component of the probe to $+1$, reaching $x^{(1)}$. Now $x(1)$ is fixed:

$$Tx^{(1)} = (4, 0, 6, 4, 6)^T$$

and the sgn of all five components of $Tx^{(1)}$ is $+1$. We reach $x^{(1)}$ as a fixed point starting from x if we change the third component first. However, $x^{(1)}$ is at distance 2 from x, whereas $x^{(2)}$, the "correct" memory, is only at distance 1 from x. We have converged to an incorrect memory.

On the other hand, if we had decided to update the *fifth* component of x first, the new probe vector would have been

$$x' = (+,-,-,+,-)^T,$$

and then we would have obtained

$$Tx' = (+2,-3,-2,+2,-2)^T,$$

i.e., no changes in sign in x', so that we would have converged to the "correct" memory $(+,-,-,+,-)^T$, the memory closest to the initial probe x.

This example partially illustrates the possible problems with Hopfield's retrieval algorithm. If we begin with a probe x, the resulting fixed point a) *may not be one of the memories* or, if it is, b) *it may not be the nearest memory*. The study of the convergence behavior of Hopfield's algorithm is very complex indeed; a simpler question is, *When are the memories themselves fixed points*? This is plainly an important question, since a memory which is not a fixed point can never be exactly "recalled" by the algorithm. In our example, all three fundamental memories do happen to be fixed, since

$$Tx^{(1)} = (+4,0,+6,+4,+6)^T$$
$$\operatorname{sgn} Tx^{(1)} = (+++++)^T = x^{(1)}$$
$$Tx^{(2)} = (+2,-3,-2,+2,-2)^T$$
$$\operatorname{sgn} Tx^{(2)} = (+--+-)^T = x^{(2)}$$
$$Tx^{(3)} = (-6,0,-4,-6,-4)^T$$
$$\operatorname{sgn} Tx^{(3)} = (-+---)^T = x^{(3)}.$$

V. Stability

We want the fundamental memories to be in some sense recoverable. A weak sense for this is that they at least be fixed points under the $x \to x' = \operatorname{sgn} Tx$ mapping. Here we observe that fixed point means the same thing in the synchronous and asynchronous cases. However, this is not very useful, for merely being able to remember that everything is right when you are given everything at once could hardly be called an associative memory.

We want some error-correcting or "pull-in" capability. In this paper we generally assume a "forced choice" model in which, if some components are not known, they are guessed and are right half the time. Thus, if we know 20 percent of the n components of a memory exactly and guess the other 80 percent with error probability 1/2, this is like knowing 20 percent$+(1/2)\times 80\% = 60$ percent correctly.

One thing one could think of doing is to "clamp" any certainly known components x_i to their known ± 1 values. This means that they are not allowed to change at all; $x_i' = x_i$ at every change, regardless of $(\operatorname{sgn} Tx)_i$. However, clamping turns out not to increase capacity. What happens is that "right" components x_i would have almost never changed anyway. We discuss this in a little more detail in Section VIII. So throughout this paper, we let all components, those we may be sure about and those not, change.

We now suppose that we know at least $(1-\rho)n$ of the components when we probe the memory, so that ρn (or fewer) are wrong. (Here $0 \le \rho < 1/2$.) We do not know which ρn are wrong. We would still like the memory to settle down to the correct, i.e., closest, fundamental memory. We would then call the largest possible such ρn the *radius of attraction* as in Fig. 5. The picture is misleading, though. In Hamming space, m disjoint spheres of radius $< n/2$ cover very little of the total probability, if m is not large, and almost all the probability is concentrated near the boundary of the sphere.

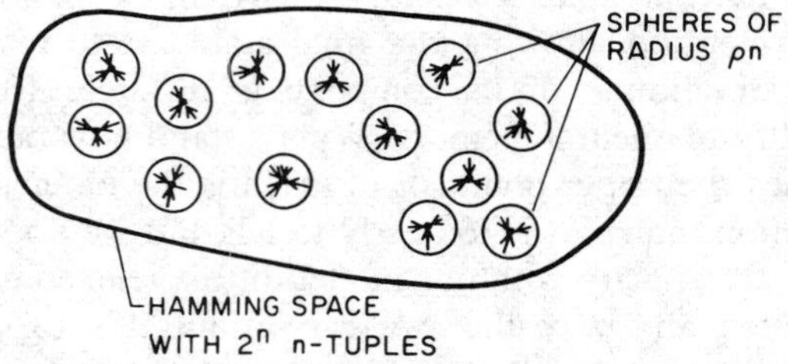

Fig. 5. Radius of attraction in Hamming space. Almost all points in almost all spheres stabilize at center of sphere, which is closest fundamental memory.

Such a property provides a true associative capability. For example, if we have convergence to the correct memory when $\rho = 0.45$, then all we need know correctly is any ten percent of the n components. We guess the other $0.9n$, and get $0.45n$ right. This, plus our $0.1n$ right to begin with, gives $0.55n$ correct, or only $0.45n$ wrong, and we get convergence to the correct memory.

There are at least three possibilities of convergence for the asynchronous case, two of which occur in this paper (see Fig. 6). First, the sphere of radius ρn may be directly or monotonically attracted to its fundamental memory center, meaning that every transition that is actually a change in a component is a change in the right direction, as in Fig. 6(a). (Alternatively, the synchronous version goes to its fundamental memory center in one step.) Second, with high enough probability but not probability 1, a random step is in the right direction, as in Fig. 6(b). After enough steps, the probe has with high probability come very close to its fundamental memory center, so that then all subsequent changes are in the right direction, i.e., we are then directly attracted. (For the synchronous case, this implies two-iteration convergence.)

The third mode of convergence, which does not occur in this paper except by allusion, does not correspond to anything obvious in the synchronous case. In this mode, components can change back and forth during their sojourn, but at least *on the average* get better, i.e., are more likely to be correct *after* a change than before. After a finite number of changes, the system settles down to a

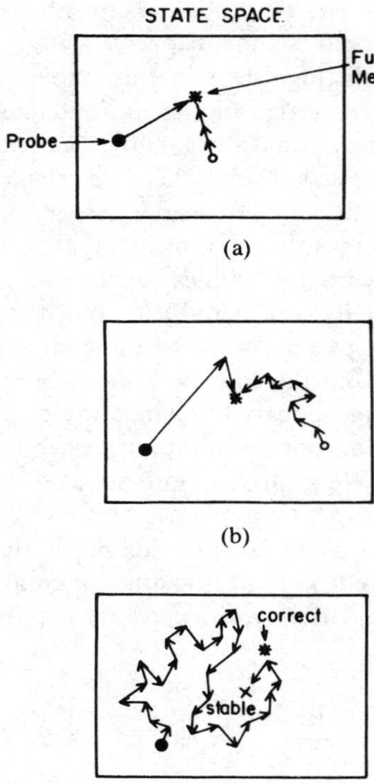

Fig. 6. Representation of various types of convergence.

fixed point, as we know it must, and this fixed point is either the correct memory or not too far from it, say within ϵn, as in Fig. 6(c).

All this presupposes that there *are* fixed points and that we wind up at one. In [1], Hopfield showed that for any symmetric connection matrix T, starting anywhere, we always reach a fixed point in the asynchronous model. He did this by observing that the "energy"

$$-\sum_i \sum_j T_{ij} x_i x_j$$

does not increase for each model-forced coordinate change, or alternatively, the inner product or correlation

$$C = T\boldsymbol{x} \cdot \boldsymbol{x} = \sum_i \sum_j T_{ij} x_i x_j$$

is nondecreasing as the state $\boldsymbol{x}$ goes through a model trajectory. Let us derive this here.

Say coordinate i_0 of the current probe vector is due for a possible change. Then

$$x'_{i_0} = \operatorname{sgn} \sum_k T_{i_0 k} x_k. \tag{5.1}$$

The correlation changes by

$$\Delta C = C' - C = \sum_{j=1}^{n} T_{i_0 j}(\Delta x_{i_0}) x_j + \sum_{i=1}^{n} T_{i i_0} x_i \cdot (\Delta x_{i_0}) + T_{i_0 i_0}(\Delta x_{i_0})^2. \tag{5.2}$$

Here $\Delta x_{i_0} = x'_{i_0} - x_{i_0}$. (Note that we are not assuming $T_{i_0 i_0} = 0$; $T_{i_0 i_0} \geq 0$, $1 \leq i_0 \leq n$, is enough.)

Continuing, we see from (5.2) and the symmetry of T that

$$\Delta C \geq 2 \Delta x_{i_0} \left(\sum_j T_{i_0 j} x_j \right) \tag{5.3}$$

since we have assumed that the diagonal elements of T are nonnegative. If $x'_{i_0} = x_{i_0}$, there is nothing to prove. If $x'_{i_0} < x_{i_0}$, then $x_{i_0} = +1$, $x'_{i_0} = -1$, and so from (5.1),

$$A = \sum_j T_{i_0 j} x_j < 0. \tag{5.4}$$

Also, in this case $\Delta x_{i_0} = -2$, and

$$\Delta C \geq (2) \cdot (-2) \cdot (A) > 0. \tag{5.5}$$

Finally, if $x'_{i_0} > x_{i_0}$ then $x_{i_0} = -1$, $x'_{i_0} = +1$, and from (5.1)

$$A = \sum_j T_{i_0 j} x_j \geq 0. \tag{5.6}$$

Here

$$\Delta x_{i_0} = +2,$$

so

$$\Delta C \geq 2 \cdot 2 \cdot A \geq 0. \tag{5.7}$$

We see that the correlation C of $\boldsymbol{x}$ with $T\boldsymbol{x}$ is nondecreasing under the asynchronous component changes forced by the Hopfield model. Since C is bounded by $\Sigma_i \Sigma_j |T_{ij}|$, a finite maximum of C is ultimately reached on each trajectory. Such an $\boldsymbol{x}$ is not necessarily a fixed point, because A can be 0 in (5.6), so that ΔC can be 0 in (5.7). However, the only changes that have $\Delta C = 0$ involve $x_{i_0} = -1$, $x'_{i_0} = +1$. After a finite number (possibly zero) of these -1 to $+1$ changes with C staying the same (of course at most n changes), no more changes are possible. We finally do reach a fixed point in the asynchronous case.

We shall now indicate why there is a region of attraction around the fundamental memories in both the asynchronous and synchronous cases. As a consequence, fixed points will exist even in the synchronous model with high enough probability to make our desired results true. The double sum in (2.2) has zero mean. With $m = o(n)$, the standard deviation is $((m-1)(n-1))^{1/2} = o(n)$. Hence, from (2.2), we see that as $n \to \infty$, the m fundamental memories $\boldsymbol{x}^{(\alpha)}$ are approximate eigenvectors of the linear transformation T, with the same m-fold degenerate approximate eigenvalue $n-1$.

In fact, with high probability the *maximum* eigenvalue of T is essentially $n-1$. For consider any vector $\boldsymbol{x}$ in the space orthogonal to the m fundamental memories. For such a vector, we then have

$$(T\boldsymbol{x})_i = \sum_{j=1}^{n} T_{ij} x_j = \sum_{\substack{j=1 \\ j \neq i}}^{n} \sum_{\alpha=1}^{m} x_i^{(\alpha)} x_j^{(\alpha)} x_j$$

$$= \sum_{\alpha=1}^{m} x_i^{(\alpha)} \left[\sum_{j \neq 1}^{n} x_j^{(\alpha)} x_j \right]$$

$$= -\sum_{\alpha=1}^{m} \left(x_i^{(\alpha)}\right)^2 x_i = -\sum_{\alpha=1}^{m} x_i. \tag{5.8}$$

This, being a sum of m random independent ± 1 random variables x_i, is of order $\sqrt{m}$ with high probability. Thus all vectors orthogonal to the m memories come close to lying in the null space of T. Since T is symmetric, its other $n-m$ eigenvectors lie in the space orthogonal to the $\boldsymbol{x}^{(\alpha)}$. Hence their eigenvalues must be nearly zero. We expect these other eigenvalues to be small compared to the maximum approximate eigenvalue $n-1$.

The above suggests that there is a domain or basin of attraction around each fundamental memory, with high probability one that contains a sphere of radius nearly $n/2$, or at least most of the sphere. That is, most probe vectors in the Hamming spheres of some positive radius about most of the fundamental memories will reach the fundamental memory at the center of the sphere as a stable or fixed point, in both the asynchronous and synchronous models, if there are not too many fundamental memories at the start. (If there are too many fundamental memories, they will not even be fixed points themselves.) The fundamental memory is reached from within the spheres, too, because wrong components merely add to the noise, not changing the qualitative behavior of the path of the state. Thus nearby memories are brought to the fundamental memory, which is a fixed point. We shall spend much of the rest of the paper making this heuristic argument as precise and rigorous as we can.

VI. Capacity Heuristics

Our capacity will be a rate of growth rather than an exact number as in traditional channel capacity in information theory. Here we choose $m = m(n)$ memories at random, where n is the number of components or the length of a memory. "At random" means -1 and $+1$ are equally likely, although imbalance may (it turns out) provide somewhat greater capacity with the sum-of-outer products construction. A preprocessor that compresses memories for a more efficient nonassociative representation would produce equal probabilities of $1/2$. We will not further study the unequal case here.

We are given fixed ρ, $0 \le \rho < 1/2$, and ask for the largest rate of growth $m(n)$ as $n \to \infty$ so that we still can recover the fundamental memory within ρn of a probe. That memory is unique with high probability if m is not too large, as the following well-known argument shows, and as also follows from the results in this paper. The probability that a given vector is within ρn of a random vector $\boldsymbol{x}^{(1)}$ is exceedingly small for $\rho < 1/2$. Since our m fundamental memories are chosen independently, the probability that the given vector is close to *two* of the $\boldsymbol{x}^{\alpha}$ is much smaller still.

We are allowed to fail with small probability, so "recover" means "with probability approaching 1 as $n \to \infty$." All our results have the property that if the rate of growth is exceeded by any fraction $1+\epsilon$ with $\epsilon > 0$, then instead of having what we want happen with probability approaching 1, it happens with probability approaching 0, just as for the word error probability in Shannon theory when we try to exceed channel capacity.

Two cases are distinguished in this paper. First, with high probability, *every* one of the m fundamental memories may be fixed, almost its entire ρn-sphere being directly attracted. Second, and this is a weaker concept, with high probability *almost every* memory is good, as above, but not necessarily *every* memory. It turns out that this weakening essentially doubles capacity.

A case not formally considered here, but which we hope to treat elsewhere, permits some of the components to be wrong at the end, but the fraction approaching zero. This still weaker concept appears to change the rate of growth of capacity from a constant times $n/\log n$ to a (small) constant times n. We shall say more about this in Section VIII.

We are going to prove later in this paper that if direct attraction is desired and *all* the fundamental memories must be recallable correctly, the capacity is (all logs natural)

$$\frac{(1-2\rho)^2}{4} n/\log n.$$

If we can have a small fraction of exceptional fundamental memories the capacity is, as we said above, doubled. If we are allowed the second type of convergence, where we can make a few wrong moves but still get close enough to the fundamental memory so that we *then* have direct convergence, then (for any *fixed* ρ, $0 < \rho < 1/2$) we get rid of the factor $(1-2\rho)^2$ above. (However, we do not have a rigorous proof of this extension.) This improvement is important when we want to recover long memories, being sure of only a small fraction. For then, as we saw in the last section, ρ is close to $1/2$.

We saw in the previous section that any symmetric connection matrix T leads in the asynchronous model to a stable point, an "energy" minimum or correlation maximum. With T being the sum-of-outer-products matrix, we hope that the fixed point, and one will essentially certainly be reached, is in fact that closest fundamental memory. (Of course, we hope the fundamental memories themselves are fixed.) The above capacity results determine when we can expect this good situation with high probability. In any case, these results show that, in the case of direct convergence, the ρn-spheres around all the fundamental memories (or around almost all, if we are in the doubled-capacity small-fraction-of-exceptional-fundamental-memories case) are almost entirely free of these extraneous fixed points. We shall have a little more to say about extraneous fixed points in Section X.

We shall now present a simplified heuristic derivation of capacity. Without loss of generality, we assume that the first memory $\boldsymbol{x}^{(1)}$ has all positive components: $\boldsymbol{x}^{(1)} = (+ + \cdots +)$. We model the $n(m-1)$ components of the remaining $(m-1)$ memories as i.i.d. ± 1 (probability $1/2$ each) random variables. We are interested in the probability that $\boldsymbol{x}^{(1)}$ is a fixed point of the retrieval algorithm, i.e., that the components of $Tx^{(1)}$ are all positive. To this end, note that (using the notation of Section II)

$$(x^{(1)})'_i = (T_1 x^{(1)})_i + \sum_{k=2}^{m} (T_k x^{(1)})_i$$
$$= s_i + z_i$$

where s_i is the "signal" and z_i is the "noise." Since $x^{(1)}$ is all $+$'s, we have

$$s_i = n - 1.$$

Our assumptions about the components of $x^{(2)}, \cdots, x^{(m)}$ imply (in the zero-diagonal case) that the noise term z_i is a sum of $(m-1)$ i.i.d. random variables, each with mean 0 and variance $n-1$. Hence if n is fixed and m is large, the normalized noise $z_i/\sqrt{(n-1)(m-1)}$ approaches a standard normal random variable. It follows then that the probability that the ith component of $(x^{(1)})'$ will be negative will be approximately

$$\Phi\left(\frac{-(n-1)}{\sqrt{(n-1)(m-1)}}\right) \approx \Phi\left(-\sqrt{\frac{n}{m}}\right) = Q\left(\sqrt{\frac{n}{m}}\right)$$

where

$$Q(z) = \frac{1}{\sqrt{2\pi}} \int_z^{\infty} e^{-t^2/2}\, dt.$$

Thus the expected number of negative components in $(x^{(1)})'$ is approximately $nQ(\sqrt{n/m})$.

So far our analysis has been fairly rigorous, but now we must defer some fairly difficult calculations and assert that with suitable restrictions, the number of negative components in $(x^{(1)})'$ is *approximately Poisson*. Given this, it follows that the probability of no negative components, i.e., the probability that $x^{(1)}$ is indeed a fixed point, is given approximately by the expression

$$\beta = \exp\left\{-nQ\left(\sqrt{\frac{n}{m}}\right)\right\}.$$

Now suppose we require that this probability be a fixed number very near 1, say $\beta = 0.999999$. Then inverting the preceding expression we get

$$Q\left(\sqrt{\frac{n}{m}}\right) = \frac{a}{n},$$

where $a = -\log \beta$. This means that

$$m = \frac{n}{\left[\Phi^{-1}\left(\frac{a}{n}\right)\right]^2}.$$

However, for small positive values of x we have $\Phi^{-1}(x) \sim \sqrt{2\log 1/x}$, and so, since a is fixed,

$$m \sim \frac{n}{2\log n}.$$

It follows then, modulo our temporarily unproved Poisson assumption, that for any value of β (the desired probability of having a given memory fixed) not equal to 0 or 1, the maximum number of memories that can be stored in a Hopfield matrix is asymptotically at most $n/(2\log n)$. If asymptotically more than this number are stored, the memories will almost surely not even be fixed points, and we will later show that if fewer than this number times $(1-2\rho)^2$ are stored, not only will they almost surely be fixed points, but also the retrieval algorithm will almost surely converge to the best memory for almost any initial probe which is at distance not more than a constant ρ (less than 1/2) times n away from a fundamental memory.

In the foregoing, we have implicitly allowed a small fraction of the m fundamental memories to be exceptional; that is, they are not fixed points. If we want all m fundamental memories to be fixed, it will turn out that we have to cut m in half asymptotically as n becomes large. Also, the probe will go directly to the fundamental memory in only one synchronous step when we cut m by $(1-2\rho)^2$, whereas before the probe was initially ρn or less away from a fundamental memory and $0 \le \rho < 1/2$.

VII. Preparation for the Formal Results

We have had a number of motivation and plausibility agreements thus far. The reader may even be willing to believe that some of our claimed results are probably true. We will make good our claims by proving some rigorous results in the next two sections. Here, we review some known preliminary lemmas needed for the delicate arguments of Section VIII, which contain essentially all the difficult rigorous mathematics. Lemma A displays a known good uniform estimate for the probability that the sum of N independent ± 1 random variables takes on a particular integer value not too far from the mean sum. The estimate is just the probability of the approximating normal over that interval of length 1 which is centered on the targetted deviation from the mean. It is a "large-deviation" theorem in that the integer need only be within $o(N^{3/4})$ of the mean if the ± 1 random variables are unbiased.

In Lemma B, Lemma A is used to get a good known uniform asymptotic expression for the cumulative distribution of a sum of N independent ± 1 random variables, valid for the same large deviations as Lemma A. The approximation is of course the usual normal distribution valid for *small* deviations. Lemma B′ is the strong form of the large-deviation central limit theorem of [20, p. 195, prob. 14]. This is precisely the version we will need, although exponent $(1/2)+\epsilon$ for any $\epsilon > 0$ would be enough, rather than the stronger $o(N^{3/4})$ result we invoke.

Lemmas A, B, and B′ are basically known results on sums of independent ± 1 random variables. Lemma C is known as Bonferroni's inequality [20, p. 110] but is also repeated here for completeness.

Lemma A: Let $x_1, \cdots, x_N$ be independent random variables with

$$x_j = \begin{cases} 1, & \Pr p \\ 0, & \Pr q = 1-p \end{cases}$$

where $0 < p < 1$, and let

$$z = \sum_{j=1}^{N} x_j.$$

As $N \to \infty$, let the integer k vary so that

$$|k - Np| < B(N) = o(N^{2/3}). \tag{7.1}$$

($o(N^{3/4})$ works if $p = q = 1/2$, the case we are mainly interested in.) Then

$$\Pr(z = k) \sim \frac{1}{\sqrt{2\pi pqN}} \int_{t = k - Np - (1/2)}^{k - Np + (1/2)} \exp\left(\frac{-t^2}{2pqN}\right) dt \tag{7.2}$$

as $N \to \infty$, uniformly for all k satisfying (7.1).

Proof: See [20, ch. VII, sec. 6].

Lemma B: Under the hypotheses of Lemma A, if the real number u varies as $N \to \infty$ so that

$$|u - Np| < B(N) = o(N^{2/3}),$$

or $o(N^{3/4})$ if $p = q = 1/2$, then

$$\Pr(z \geq u) \sim \frac{1}{\sqrt{2\pi Npq}} \int_{t = u - Np}^{\infty} \exp\left(-\frac{t^2}{2pqN}\right) dt. \tag{7.3}$$

Proof: See [20, ch. VII, sec. 6; prob. 14, p. 195].

Lemma B′: If ζ is the sum of N independent random variables, each ± 1 with probability 1/2, and $v = o(N^{3/4})$, then as $N \to \infty$,

$$\Pr(\zeta \geq v) \sim \frac{1}{\sqrt{2\pi}} \int_{t = v/\sqrt{N}}^{\infty} e^{-t^2/2} dt = \Phi\left(\frac{v}{\sqrt{N}}\right).$$

Proof: Lemma B applies here, with $z = (\zeta + N)/2$, $p = 1/2$, $u = (v + N)/2$. Hence

$$\Pr(\zeta \leq v) = \Pr(z \leq u) \sim \frac{1}{\sqrt{2\pi \cdot \frac{1}{4} N}} \int_{t = -\infty}^{v/2} e^{-2t^2/N} dt.$$

Replacing t by $\frac{1}{2} t\sqrt{N}$ leads to the claimed formula. This proves Lemma B′, which also appears as [20, prob. 14, p. 195].

Lemma C is, as mentioned, an instance of Bonferroni's inequality.

Lemma C: Let $A_1, \cdots, A_N$ be measurable subsets of a probability space. For $1 \leq k \leq N$, let σ_k be the sum of the probabilities of all sets formed by intersecting k of the $A_1, \cdots, A_N$:

$$\sigma_k = \sum_{j_1 < j_2 < \cdots < j_k} \Pr(A_{j_1} \cap A_{j_2} \cap \cdots \cap A_{j_k}).$$

Then for every K, $1 \leq K \leq N$,

$$\Pr(A_1 \cup A_2 \cup \cdots \cup A_N) = \sum_{k=1}^{K} (-1)^{k-1} \sigma_k + (-1)^K E_K \tag{7.4}$$

where $E_K \geq 0$.

Proof: Consider a point which lies in exactly L of the A_j, $1 \leq L \leq N$. On the left, this point is counted only once. On the right, it is counted exactly $\binom{L}{k}$ times in each σ_k with $k \leq L$, for a total contribution of

$$\sum_{k=1}^{\min(K,L)} (-1)^{k-1} \binom{L}{k} = \begin{cases} 1 - (1-1)^L = 1, & K \geq L \\ 1 - (-1)^K \binom{L-1}{K} & 1 \leq K < L. \end{cases}$$

The latter equality is proved by induction on k using

$$\binom{L-1}{K-1} + \binom{L-1}{K} = \binom{L}{K},$$

starting from $K = 1$, for which $L = 1 - (-1)(L-1)$. Hence if we define the random variable X by

$$X = \begin{cases} 0, & L \leq K \\ \binom{L-1}{K}, & L > K, \end{cases}$$

then (6.4) is true with

$$E_k = E(X) \geq 0.$$

(See also [20, p. 110].) This completes the proof of Lemma C.

VIII. Key Rigorous Lemmas

Let $x^{(l)}$, $l = 1, \cdots, m$, be a set of m vectors (fundamental memories) of n components $(x_1^{(l)}, \cdots, x_n^{(l)})$; this n is the number of neurons in the Hopfield memory. Here all the mn components $x_j^{(l)}$ are independent random variables with values ± 1, each with probability 1/2. We form as before (see (2.1)) the matrix $T = (T_{jk})$, the sum of outer products:

$$T_{jk} = \sum_{l=1}^{m} x_j^{(l)} x_k^{(l)} - g\delta_{jk} m,$$

where $g = 0$ or 1 (we even could consider $0 \leq g \leq 1$). The case $g = 1$ is the prior construction with zeros down the diagonal. The case $g = 0$, where we *do not* zero the diagonal, is included below as well. The notation is the same as in the preceding sections, but the choice of subscripts and superscripts is slightly different, due mainly to the prevalence of triple and quadruple products of the x's.

Consider the transformation $x \to x'$, where

$$x_j' = \operatorname{sgn}\left(\sum_k T_{jk} x_k\right).$$

Here we can ignore the case where we must take sgn(0) since that event is of very low probability. The m vectors $x^{(l)}$ are all fixed under this transformation if each of the mn sums

$$S_j^{(l)} = \sum_k T_{jk} x_j^{(l)} x_k^{(l)}, \qquad j = 1, \cdots, n,$$

are positive (synchronous fixed point, and, as previously observed, the same as asynchronous fixed point). We are interested in the number of these vectors which are fixed when $n \to \infty$, with $m \to \infty$ chosen appropriately as a function of n. More generally, as before for $0 < \rho < 1/2$, we are interested in the number of these vectors $\boldsymbol{x}^{(l)}$ whose Hamming sphere of radius ρn is directly attracted almost entirely to the central vector, which is then of course a fixed point. As before, this means that every component which changes at all, changes in the right direction, or, in synchronous operation, the central memory is reached in one step.

First let us consider the case $\rho = 0$. By symmetry, the probability of a row sum violation of the jth component for the lth fundamental memory $\boldsymbol{x}^{(l)}$,

$$p_1 = \Pr\left\{ S_j^{(l)} < 0 \right\},$$

is independent of the values of both j and l. Using the expression of T_{jk}, then, we have

$$S_j^{(l)} = \sum_{r=1}^{m} \sum_{k=1}^{n} x_j^{(l)} x_k^{(l)} x_j^{(r)} x_k^{(r)} - gm.$$

The product of the x's here is $+1$ if $r = l$ or $k = j$ or both. Hence

$$S_j^{(l)} = n + (1-g)m - 1 + \sum_{r \neq l} \sum_{k \neq j} x_j^{(l)} x_k^{(l)} x_j^{(r)} x_k^{(r)}.$$

Each term in the double sum contains the factor $x_k^{(r)}$, which occurs in no other term. These factors are mutually independent. Hence the $(m-1)\cdot(n-1)$ terms of the sum are independent ± 1's, each taking value (± 1) with probability $1/2$. Denoting this sum by $z_j^{(l)}$, we have

$$p_1 = \Pr\left(S_j^{(l)} < 0 \right) = \Pr\left[z_j^{(l)} < -(n + (1-g)m - 1) \right]. \tag{8.1}$$

In the general case, $0 \leq \rho < 1/2$, we proceed in much the same way. Consider spheres of radius ρn (the radius is assumed for notational convenience to be an integer in what follows) centered at an $\boldsymbol{x}^{(\alpha)}$. The center $\boldsymbol{x}^{(\alpha)}$ will of course still be fixed. The attraction condition is easily expressible. As we can see, the errors mean that the mn values $S_j^{(l)}$ are each to be decreased by $2\rho n$, because there are exactly ρn errors. Thus, denoting $(1-2\rho)n$ by n_ρ, we are interested in the probability

$$p_1 = \Pr\left(S_j^{(l)} < 0 \right) = \Pr\left[z_j^{(l)} < -(n_\rho + (1-g)m - 1) \right]. \tag{8.2}$$

If $S_j^{(l)} < 0$ with ρn errors with high probability, then indeed almost the entire sphere of radius ρn is attracted to its center $\boldsymbol{x}^{(l)}$, which is still of course fixed. For if $S_j^{(l)} \geq 0$ with ρn errors with high probability, then all the more strongly $S_j^{(l)} > 0$ with high probability if there are fewer than ρn errors.

Lemma 1 to follow applies the large-deviation lemma (B′) to the situation we are now faced with. The result is an asymptotic expression for p_1, the probability that a particular row sum is violated. This agrees with what we would get by a naive application of the central limit theorem.

Lemma 1: For $0 \leq \rho < 1/2$, as $n \to \infty$, if $m = o(n)$ and $m \geq C(n)$, where $C(n)/\sqrt{n} \to \infty$, then the probability p_1 of a component changing in the wrong direction, i.e., becoming wrong when it was right before the change, if the current state has ρn errors, is given by

$$p_1 = \Pr\left(S_j^{(l)} < 0 \right) \sim \frac{1}{\sqrt{2\pi}} \sqrt{\frac{m}{n'_\rho}} \exp\left[-\left(\frac{n'_\rho}{2m} + (1-2\rho)(1-g) \right) \right]. \tag{8.3}$$

(Here $n'_\rho = n(1-2\rho)^2$.) This p_1 is an upper bound to the probability of a component changing in the wrong direction when there are *at most* ρn errors in the current state.

Proof: We can apply Lemma B′ to the random variable $z_j^{(l)}$ in (8.2) with

$$N = (m-1)(n-1)$$
$$v = -\left[n_\rho + (1-g)m - 1 \right].$$

The hypotheses there are satisfied since $m \geq C(n)$. Hence

$$p_1 \sim Q\left(\frac{n_\rho + (1-g)m - 1}{\sqrt{(m-1)(n-1)}} \right).$$

Since

$$\frac{n_\rho + (1-g)m - 1}{\sqrt{(m-1)(n-1)}} \sim \left(\sqrt{\frac{n}{m}} \right)(1-2\rho) \to \infty$$

as $n \to \infty$, we can use the asymptotic formula for the left-hand tail probability of the Gaussian distribution

$$Q(t) \cong \frac{1}{\sqrt{2\pi}} \cdot \frac{1}{t} e^{-t^2/2}, \qquad t \to \infty,$$

and so

$$p_1 \sim \frac{1}{\sqrt{2\pi}} \sqrt{\frac{m}{n'_\rho}} \exp\left[-\frac{\left(n_\rho + (1-g)m - 1\right)^2}{2(n-1)(m-1)} \right].$$

Using $m/n \to 0$ and $m/\sqrt{n} \to \infty$, we have

$$\frac{\left(n_\rho + (1-g)m - 1\right)^2}{2(n-1)(m-1)} = \frac{n'_\rho}{2m} + (1-2\rho)(1-g) + o(1).$$

Hence (8.3) follows if there are ρn errors. If there are fewer than ρn errors, then the "signal" portion $n_\rho + (1-g)m - 1$ of (8.2) is increased and $\Pr(S_j^{(l)} < 0)$ is decreased from its value when there are ρn errors, i.e., p_1 is an upper bound to the probability of a step in the wrong direction anywhere in the sphere of radius ρn. This proves Lemma 1.

It is clear from foregoing discussions that uniformity holds in the following sense. If $m_1 \geq m$, then the p_1 corresponding to m_1 is at least as large as the p_1 corresponding to m, provided $\rho < 1/2$. (This is slightly easier to see in the $g = 1$ case.) The idea is that for $m_1 > m$, the random variable $z_j^{(l)}$ has more independent summands for m_1 than for m, hence it is more likely to be large negative. In fact, the distribution of the number of row sum violations for m_1 lies below that for m—more violations are likely.

The next lemma concerns the joint distribution of q sums,

$$S_{j_h}^{(l_h)}, \qquad h=1,2,\cdots,q.$$

There is a bipartite graph of q edges associated with this collection of sums. The vertices of the first type correspond to the values of j_h. The vertices of the second type correspond to the values of l_h. The edges are the connections from j_h to l_h, if the sum $S_{j_h}^{(l_h)}$ occurs.

The basic fact which makes this graph important is the following. If (and only if) this graph has no closed loops, then for any fixed k, r outside the range of the vertex sets (i.e., $k \neq j_1, j_2, \cdots, j_q$; $r \neq l_1, l_2, \cdots, l_q$), the q products $y_h = x_{j_h}^{(r)} x_k^{(l_h)}$ are independent. This is true because the y_h can be reordered so that each uses a vertex which has not occurred earlier and hence involves a new x. See Fig. 7, which shows the construction. Starting from the top left vertex, decompose the graph into connected chains from left to right to left to right, and continue in this way. After the first vertex on the left is done, drop to the next lower vertex which still has an edge from it not previously included, and continue. After this decomposition, incorporate edges in the order they were generated. A new vertex is used each time because there is only one edge connecting a given vertex to another given vertex. Otherwise, loops would be created by adding an edge whose left and right vertices are already included.

We can now state and prove Lemma 2.

Lemma 2: Under the hypotheses of Lemma 1, if $C(n) = n^{\sigma}$, where $3/4 < \sigma < 1$, then for a state at Hamming distance ρn from a fundamental memory $\boldsymbol{x}^{(l)}$ the following asymptotic expression holds for any fixed q, provided the associated graph has no loops:

$$\Pr\left(S_{j_1}^{(l_1)}, \cdots, S_{j_q}^{(l_q)} < 0\right) \sim p_1^q. \tag{8.4}$$

If the Hamming distance is *at most* ρn, p_1^q is an asymptotic upper bound on the probability in (8.4) at a random point within the Hamming sphere of radius ρn about $\boldsymbol{x}^{(l)}$, if the associated graph has no loops.

Proof: This probability is unchanged if the subscripts $j_1, \cdots, j_q$ are subjected to any permutation of $1, 2, \cdots, n$, or the superscripts $l_1, \cdots, l_q$ are subjected to any permutation of $1, 2, \cdots, m$. Hence, to simplify the notation, we assume that these $2q$ numbers are all $\leq q$.

For $j, l \leq q$,

$$\begin{aligned} S_{j_h}^{(l_h)} &= n_\rho + (1-g)m - 1 + \sum_{k \neq j_h} \sum_{r \neq l_h} x_{j_h}^{(l_h)} x_k^{(l_h)} x_{j_h}^{(r)} x_k^{(r)} \\ &= n_\rho + (1-g)m - 1 + \sum_1^{(h)} + \sum_2^{(h)} \end{aligned} \tag{8.5}$$

where $\Sigma_2^{(h)}$ is the sum of the terms with both k and $r > q$,

$$\sum_2^{(h)} = \sum_{k>q} \sum_{r>q} x_{j_h}^{(l_h)} x_k^{(l_h)} x_{j_h}^{(r)} x_k^{(r)}$$

and $\Sigma_1^{(h)}$ contains the other terms with $r \neq l, k \neq j$.

$\Sigma_1^{(h)}$ contains $(q-1)(n+m-q-1)$ terms. As noted earlier, these terms are independent. We apply Lemma B′

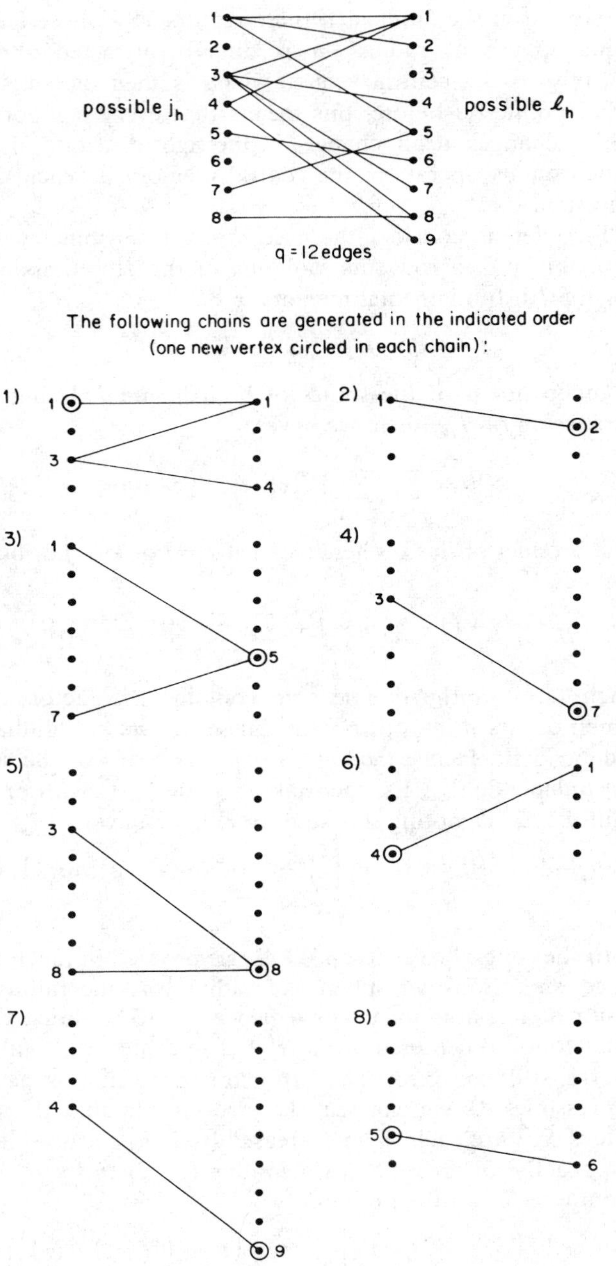
possible j_h
possible ℓ_h
q = 12 edges
The following chains are generated in the indicated order
(one new vertex circled in each chain):

Fig. 7. Bipartite graph of j_h and l_h with fixed (k, r).

to $\pm\Sigma_1^{(h)}$ with $N = (q-1)(n+m-q-1)$, $v = -n^{(1/2)+\epsilon}$, where $0 < \epsilon < 1/8$. By the asymptotic formula for the error function,

$$\begin{aligned} \Pr\left(\left|\sum_1^{(h)}\right| \geq n^{(1/2)+\epsilon}\right) &\sim 2\Phi\left(\frac{-n^{(1/2)+\epsilon}}{\sqrt{(q-1)(n+m-q-1)}}\right) \\ &= O\left(e^{-C_1 n^{2\epsilon}}\right) \end{aligned} \tag{8.6}$$

where C_1 is a positive constant.

We now consider the sums $\Sigma_2^{(h)}$ for $S_{j_h}^{(l_h)}, h = 1, \cdots, q$. For each $k > q$, $r > q$, the factor

$$v_k = x_{j_h}^{(l_h)} x_k^{(l_h)} x_{j_h}^{(r)}$$

runs through the components of a q-vector v as h varies. There are 2^q possible vectors of this type $\{v_h^{(d)}\}$, $d = 1,\cdots,2^q$. For each d let M_d be the set of pairs (k,r) (with $k,r>q$) for which $v=v^{(d)}$. The M_d are disjoint and so partition the set of pairs (k,r). We have

$$S_{j_h}^{(l_h)} = n_p + (1-g)m - 1 + \sum_1^{(h)} + \sum_{d=1}^{2^q} v_h^{(d)} \sum_{(k,r)\in M_d} x_k^{(r)}. \tag{8.7}$$

Let $\lambda_d = |M_d|$. Then λ_d can be written as the sum of the $(n-q)(m-q)$ random variables

$$\gamma_{d,k}^{(r)} = \begin{cases} 1, & (k,r)\in M_d \\ 0, & (k,r)\notin M_d, \end{cases}$$

for $k,r>q$. The occurrence of the factors $x_{j_h}^{(l_h)}$ in the components of v guarantees that these q components are independent. Hence $\gamma_{d,k}^{(r)}=1$ with probability 2^{-q}, and

$$\bar\lambda = E(\lambda_d) = \sum_{k,r>q} E(\gamma_{d,k}^{(r)})$$

$$= 2^{-q}(n-q)(m-q). \tag{8.8}$$

To estimate the probability of large deviations from this average value, we need to break up the double sum over k and r into sums of independent random variables. Since the graph associated with (j_h, l_h), $h=1,\cdots,q$ has been assumed to have no loops, for any fixed $k,r>q$ the factors $x_k^{(l_h)}x_{j_h}^{(r)}$, $h=1,\cdots,q$ are independent. Hence if we run through a set of values of (k,r) in which all the k's are distinct and all the r's are distinct, then all the components of all the corresponding v-vectors are independent, and the random variables $\gamma_{d,k}^{(r)}$ are independent.

To get a set of values with k and r distinct in a subsum of λ_d, we can take, for example,

$$\lambda_d = \sum_{k=q+1}^{n} \lambda_{d,k}$$

with

$$\lambda_{d,k} = \sum_{r=q+1}^{m} \gamma_{d,k^*}^{(r)}.$$

Here k^* (which depends on k and r) is the unique number in the range $q<k^*\le n$ with

$$k^* \equiv k + r(\operatorname{mod}(n-q)).$$

There are then $n-q$ mutually independent $\lambda_{d,k}$ in the sum defining λ_d. This is enough, as we now show.

Apply Lemma B to $\lambda_{d,k}$; here the $N^{2/3}$-form of the lemma is necessary. Estimating both tails of the distribution separately and adding, we get

$$\Pr\left\{|\lambda_{d,k} - 2^{-q}(m-q)| > n^\epsilon\sqrt{m}\right\} = O(e^{-C_2 n^{2\epsilon}})$$

where C_2 is a positive constant. Here all we need is $0<\epsilon<\sigma/6$, which is true for $\epsilon<1/8$. This is because by Lemma B, we really need $n^\epsilon\sqrt{m} = B(N)$ to be $o(m^{2/3})$ (where m is N). We have $n<m^{1/\sigma}$, $\sqrt{m}<m^{(\epsilon/\sigma)+(1/2)}$, with $(\epsilon/\sigma)+(1/2)<2/3$ if $\epsilon/\sigma<1/6$. We reach the fairly weak but still adequate conclusion that

$$\Pr\left\{|\lambda_d - \bar\lambda| > n^{1+\epsilon}\sqrt{m}\right\} = O(ne^{-C_2 n^{2\epsilon}}) \tag{8.9}$$

since this inequality cannot be true unless at least one of the preceding $(n-q)$ inequalities is true. The extra factor n in the O function does not hurt the bound; it merely means that later we shall have to take a slightly smaller C_2, which we will still call C_2.

Let

$$z_d = \sum_{(k,r)\in M_d} x_k^{(r)}.$$

Because the M_d are disjoint while the $x_k^{(r)}$ are independent, the z_d are independent. We have

$$S_{j_h}^{(l_h)} = n_p + (1-g)m - 1 + \sum_1^{(h)} + \sum_{d=1}^{2^q} v_h^{(d)} z_d.$$

Suppose that none of the inequalities of (8.9) occur. Then $\lambda_d \sim mn/2^q$. Also, the $x_k^{(r)}$ defining z_d are conditionally independent, given that all the (k,r) entering the sum for z_d are in M_d. Hence we can use Lemma B′, even though the number of summands N there was deterministic, not random. The result is

$$\Pr\left(|z_d| > n^\epsilon\sqrt{mn}\right) + O(e^{-C_3 n^{2\epsilon}}) \tag{8.10}$$

where C_3 is a positive constant.

Let S be the set in the probability space consisting of the choice of m random independent fundamental memories $\boldsymbol{x}^{(l)}$ on which the following $2^{q+1}+q$ inequalities hold:

$$|\lambda_d - \bar\lambda| \le n^{1+\epsilon}\sqrt{m}, \qquad d=1,\cdots,2^q$$

$$|z_d| \le n^\epsilon\sqrt{mn}, \qquad d=1,\cdots,2^q,$$

$$\left|\sum_1^{(h)}\right| \le n^{(1/2)+\epsilon}, \qquad h=1,\cdots,q. \tag{8.11}$$

By (8.6), (8.9), and (8.10), letting $\bar S$ denote the complement of S in the probability space,

$$\Pr(\bar S) = O(e^{-C_4 n^{2\epsilon}})$$

for any positive C_4 less than $\min(C_1, C_2, C_3)$.

Consider

$$S_{j_h}^{(l_h)}/\sqrt{\bar\lambda} = \frac{n_p + (1-g)m - 1 + \sum_1^{(h)}}{\sqrt{\bar\lambda}} + \sum_{d=1}^{2^q} v_h^{(d)}\frac{z_d}{\sqrt{\lambda_d}} + \sum_{d=1}^{2^q} v_h^{(d)} z_d\left(\frac{-1}{\sqrt{\lambda_d}} + \frac{1}{\sqrt{\bar\lambda}}\right).$$

In S, the last sum is bounded by

$$\sum_{d=1}^{2^q} |z_d| \frac{|\lambda_d - \bar\lambda|}{\sqrt{\lambda_d\bar\lambda}\left(\sqrt{\lambda_d}+\sqrt{\bar\lambda}\right)} = O\left(\frac{n^{2\epsilon}}{\sqrt{m}}\right).$$

This follows from (8.11) and (8.8). Note that $n^{2\epsilon}/\sqrt{m} = o(1)$ as $n\to\infty$, because $2\epsilon<1/4$ while $m>n^{3/4}$.

For the term $\Sigma_1^{(h)}$, we have

$$\frac{|\Sigma_1^{(h)}|}{\sqrt{\lambda}} = O\left(\frac{n^{(1/2)+\epsilon}}{\sqrt{mn}}\right) = O\left(\frac{n^{\epsilon}}{\sqrt{m}}\right) = o\left(\frac{n^{2\epsilon}}{\sqrt{m}}\right)$$

in S, and this can be absorbed into $O(n^{2\epsilon}/\sqrt{m})$. Hence in S we have

$$S_{j_h}^{(l_h)}/\sqrt{\lambda} = \frac{n_p + (1-g)m - 1}{\sqrt{\lambda}} + \sum_{d=1}^{2^q} v_h^{(d)} \frac{z_d}{\sqrt{\lambda_d}} + O\left(\frac{n^{2\epsilon}}{\sqrt{m}}\right).$$

We now define

$$f_1(b) = \Pr\left\{S;\ \sum_{d=1}^{2^q} v_h^{(d)} \frac{z_d}{\sqrt{\lambda_d}} < -\frac{n_p + (1-g)m - 1}{\sqrt{\lambda}} + b,\quad h = 1, \cdots, q\right\},$$

the probability that we are in S and that the q indicated inequalities hold as well. Then the preceding equation, plus the fact that $\Pr(\bar{S}) = O(e^{-C_4 n^{2\epsilon}})$, gives

$$f_1(-An^{2\epsilon}/\sqrt{m}) + O(e^{-C_4 n^{2\epsilon}}) < \Pr\left(S_{j_1}^{(l_1)}, \cdots, S_{j_q}^{(l_q)} < 0\right) < f_1(An^{2\epsilon}/\sqrt{m}) + O(e^{-C_4 n^{2\epsilon}}) \quad (8.12)$$

where A is some positive constant.

Let Λ be the set of values of $(\lambda_1, \cdots, \lambda_{2^q})$ that occur in S. Then

$$f_1(b) = \sum_{(\lambda_1, \cdots, \lambda_{2^q}) \in \Lambda} \Pr(\lambda_1, \cdots, \lambda_{2^q}) f_2(b; \lambda_1, \cdots, \lambda_{2^q}) \quad (8.13)$$

where $f_2(b; \lambda_1, \cdots, \lambda_{2^q})$ is the conditional probability

$$f_2(b; \lambda_1, \cdots, \lambda_{2^q}) = \Pr\left\{S,\ \sum_{d=1}^{2^q} v_h^{(d)} \frac{z_d}{\sqrt{\lambda_d}} < -\frac{n_p + (1-g)m - 1}{\sqrt{\lambda}} + b,\ h = 1, \cdots, q \mid \lambda_1, \cdots, \lambda_{2^q}\right\}. \quad (8.14)$$

Here b is the $An^{2\epsilon}/\sqrt{m}$ of (8.12). Note that we are given the sizes λ_d of the 2^q sets M_d, $1 \le d \le 2^q$, of the partition, rather than being given the partitions themselves. This is acceptable because our estimates of the probabilities will just depend on these sizes. We will use (8.13) to bound the $f_1(\pm b)$ terms in (8.12).

In S, Lemma A applies to each of the independent sums z_d. (Here we need to reason much as in the derivation of (8.10) that the random number of terms in the sum of z gives the same bound as if the number of summands were truly deterministic.) The probability of (8.14) is a sum of probabilities over the set of lattice points of allowable values of z_d in the region $D(b)$ in 2^q-dimensional space. Here "allowable" means that the integer value of z_d can arise as a sum of ± 1 values $x_k^{(r)}$ for $(k, r) \in M_d$, i.e., the parity is right, the same as that of M_d. The region $D(b)$ is defined by the $2^q + q$ inequalities

$$\sum_{d=1}^{2^q} v_h^{(d)} \frac{z_d}{\sqrt{\lambda_d}} < -\frac{n_p + (1-g)m - 1}{\sqrt{\lambda}} + b, \quad h = 1, \cdots, q; \quad (8.15)$$

$$|z_d| \le n^{\epsilon}\sqrt{mn}, \qquad d = 1, \cdots, 2^q. \quad (8.16)$$

The z_d are as we have seen (conditionally) independent, so each individual 2^q-tuple probability is the product of 2^q probabilities, one for each z_d. These factors can be replaced by integrals by Lemma A. Combining the integrals, we get a 2^q-dimensional integral over a box. These boxes fit together to form a region $\Delta(b)$ which differs from $D(b)$ only by the addition or deletion of points near the boundary. We get

$$f_2(b; \lambda_1, \cdots, \lambda_{2^q}) \sim F_2(b; \lambda_1, \cdots, \lambda_{2^q}) \quad (8.17)$$

where

$$F_2(b; \lambda_1, \cdots, \lambda_{2^q}) = \int_{\Delta(b)} \int \cdots \int \prod_{d=1}^{2^q} \frac{1}{\sqrt{2\pi\lambda_d}} e^{-(t_d^2/2\lambda_d)}\, dt_d. \quad (8.18)$$

Since each z_d varies by a range of length 2 over a box, the sums in (8.15) vary by $O(1/\sqrt{mn})$ over a box. Hence for a suitable constant C_5 (depending only on q),

$$D\left(b - \frac{C_5}{\sqrt{mn}}\right) - E_1 \subset \Delta(b) \subset D\left(b + \frac{C_5}{\sqrt{mn}}\right) + E_2$$

where the sets E_1, E_2 contain only points within distance 2 of at least one of the hyperplanes bounding the region defined by (8.16). By Lemma B′,

$$\Pr((z_1, \cdots, z_{2^q}) \in E_i | \lambda_1, \cdots, \lambda_{2^q}) = O(e^{-C_6 n^{2\epsilon}}), \quad i = 1, 2. \quad (8.19)$$

Hence if we define

$$F_3(b; \lambda_1, \cdots, \lambda_{2^q}) = \int_{D(b)} \int \cdots \int \prod_{d=1}^{2^q} \frac{1}{\sqrt{2\pi\lambda_d}} e^{-(t_d^2/2\lambda_d)}\, dt_d, \quad (8.20)$$

then

$$F_3\left(b - \frac{C_5}{\sqrt{mn}}; \lambda_1, \cdots, \lambda_{2^q}\right) + O(e^{-C_6 n^{2\epsilon}}) < F_2(b; \lambda_1, \cdots, \lambda_{2^q}) < F_3\left(b + \frac{C_5}{\sqrt{mn}}; \lambda_1, \cdots, \lambda_{2^q}\right) + O(e^{-C_6 n^{2\epsilon}}). \quad (8.21)$$

Let $\xi_1, \cdots, \xi_{2^q}$ be independent Gaussian random variables with mean zero and variance

$$E(\xi_d^2) = \lambda_d.$$

Then $F_3(b; \lambda_1, \cdots, \lambda_{2^q})$ is the probability that $(\xi_1, \cdots, \xi_{2^q})$ lies in $D(b)$. Each of the inequalities (8.16) is violated by ξ_d with probability $O(e^{-C_6 n^{2\epsilon}})$, i.e., $|\xi| > n^{\epsilon}\sqrt{mn}$ only with probability $O(e^{-C_6 n^{2\epsilon}})$. Hence if we define the region

$D_0(b)$ by the inequalities

$$\eta_h = \sum_{d=1}^{2^q} v_h^{(d)} \frac{\xi_d}{\sqrt{\lambda_d}} < -\frac{n_\rho + (1-g)m - 1}{\sqrt{\lambda}} + b, \qquad h = 1, \cdots, q, \quad (8.22)$$

then

$$\begin{aligned} F_3(b; \lambda_1, \cdots, \lambda_{2^q}) &= \Pr\left[(\xi_1, \cdots, \xi_{2^q}) \in D_0(b)\right] + O(e^{-C_6 n^{2\epsilon}}) \\ &= \Pr\left\{\eta_h < -\frac{n_\rho + (1-g)m - 1}{\sqrt{\lambda}} + b, h = 1, \cdots, q\right\} \\ &\quad + O(e^{-C_6 n^{2\epsilon}}). \end{aligned} \quad (8.23)$$

The q random variables η_h are normal with means zero and covariances

$$E(\eta_h \eta_{h'}) = \sum_{d=1}^{2^q} v_h^{(d)} v_{h'}^{(d)} = 2^q \delta_{hh'}.$$

Hence they are independent and identically distributed, and

$$\begin{aligned} &\Pr\left\{\eta_h < -\frac{n_\rho(1-g)m - 1}{\sqrt{\lambda}} + b, h = 1, \cdots, q\right\} \\ &= \left(\Phi\left[2^{-q/2}\left(-\frac{n_\rho + (1-g)m - 1}{\sqrt{\lambda}} + b\right)\right]\right)^q. \end{aligned} \quad (8.24)$$

To find the probability of (8.4), we can now proceed as follows. By (8.12), (8.13), (8.17), (8.21), and (8.23), we need to evaluate (8.24) for $b = O(n^{2\epsilon}/\sqrt{m})$. Then we have

$$\begin{aligned} x &= 2^{-q/2}\left(-\frac{n_\rho + (1-g)m - 1}{\sqrt{\lambda}} + b\right) \\ &= -2^{-q/2}\frac{n_\rho + (1-g)m - 1}{\sqrt{2^{-q}(m-q)(n-q)}} + O(n^{2\epsilon}/\sqrt{m}) \\ &= -\frac{n_\rho + (1-g)m - 1}{\sqrt{(n-q)(m-q)}} + O(n^{2\epsilon}/\sqrt{m}) \sim -\sqrt{\frac{n'_\rho}{m}} \end{aligned}$$

since $n^{2\epsilon}/\sqrt{m} = o(1)$. Also, by squaring, we see that

$$\begin{aligned} x^2 &= \frac{[n_\rho + (1-g)m - 1]^2}{(n-q)(m-q)} + O\left(\frac{n^{2\epsilon+(1/2)}}{m}\right) \\ &= \frac{n'_\rho}{m} + 2(1-2\rho)(1-g) \\ &\quad + O\left(\frac{m}{n} + \frac{n}{m^2} + \frac{n^{2\epsilon+(1/2)}}{m}\right). \end{aligned}$$

Since $\epsilon < 1/8$, while $\sigma > 3/4$ with $m \geq n^\sigma$, we see that $n^{2\epsilon+(1/2)}/m \to 0$ as $n \to \infty$. Also, $m > n^{3/4}$ so $n/m^2 = o(1)$ as well; we also had $m = o(n)$ so that $m/n = o(1)$. The result is

$$x^2 = \frac{n'_\rho}{m} + 2(1-2\rho)(1-g) + o(1).$$

It follows that

$$\Phi(x) \sim \frac{1}{\sqrt{2\pi}}\sqrt{\frac{m}{n'_\rho}}\, e^{-(n'_\rho/2m)-(1-2\rho)(1-g)} \sim p_1.$$

This is very much what we wanted to show.

Retracing the above relations, we get from (8.13)

$$\begin{aligned} f_1(b) &\sim \sum_{(\lambda_1, \cdots, \lambda_{2^q}) \in \Lambda} \Pr(\lambda_1, \cdots, \lambda_{2^q}) \cdot p_1^q + O(e^{-C_6 n^{2\epsilon}}) \\ &= p_1^q + O(e^{-C_6 n^{2\epsilon}} + e^{-C_4 n^{2\epsilon}}). \end{aligned}$$

Then from (8.12),

$$\Pr\left\{S_{j_1}^{(l_1)}, \cdots, S_{j_q}^{(l_q)} < 0\right\} \sim p_1^q + O(e^{-C_6 n^{2\epsilon}} + e^{-C_4 n^{2\epsilon}}). \quad (8.25)$$

Now by (8.3), i.e., Lemma 1, we have

$$\begin{aligned} p_1^q &\sim \text{const.}\left(\frac{m}{n}\right)^{q/2} e^{-(q/2)(n_\rho/m)} \\ &> \text{const.}\left(\frac{m}{n}\right)^{q/2} e^{-(q(1-\rho)/2)n^{1-\sigma}}. \end{aligned}$$

If $2\epsilon > 1 - \sigma$, the term p_1^q in (8.25) is dominant and the lemma follows. This is true if we pick $\epsilon > (1-\sigma)/2$. Here $3/4 < \sigma < 1$, so $(1-\sigma)/2$ is less than the previous upper bound $1/8$ on ϵ. This proves Lemma 2 when there are ρn errors. The upper bound in Lemma 1 takes care of the last part, when these are $\leq \rho n$ errors. Lemma 2 is completely proved.

Lemma 2 coupled with estimates to be derived in the Big Theorem in the next section proves that the number of row sum violations is asymptotically Poisson as $n \to \infty$. That is, for $k \geq 0$ fixed, the probability of exactly k row sum violations is asymptotic as $n \to \infty$ to $t^k e^{-t}/k!$, where $t = np_1$ is the expected number of row sum violations, held essentially constant in the Theorem by proper choice of m as a function of n.

IX. The Big Theorem

We now encapsulate the lemmas of the previous section in the Big Theorem.

Theorem: As $n \to \infty$, $t > 0$ fixed, $0 \leq \rho < 1/2$ fixed. 1) If

$$m = (1-2\rho)^2 \frac{n}{2\log n}\left[1 + \frac{\frac{1}{2}\log\log n + (1-2\rho)(1-g) + \log(t\sqrt{4\pi})}{\log n} + o\left(\frac{1}{\log n}\right)\right], \quad (9.1)$$

then the expected number of fundamental memories $x^{(\alpha)}$, whose Hamming sphere of radius ρn with the memory at the center is almost entirely directly attracted to the fixed center $x^{(\alpha)}$, is asymptotically me^{-t}. 2) If

$$m = (1-2\rho)^2 \frac{n}{4\log n}\left[1 + \frac{\frac{3}{2}\log\log n + (1-2\rho)(1-g) - 2\log(1-2\rho) + \log(8t\sqrt{2\pi})}{2\log n} + o\left(\frac{1}{\log n}\right)\right], \quad (9.2)$$

then the probability that almost all vectors within the Hamming spheres of radius ρn around all the m fundamental memories $\boldsymbol{x}^{(\alpha)}$ are directly attracted to their fixed centers is asymptotically e^{-t}.

Proof: 1) Let there be ρn errors in a state. We apply Lemma C to the n events $A_j = \{S_j^{(1)} < 0\}$, $j = 1, \cdots, n$. The hypotheses of Lemma 2 are trivially satisfied (the graph is a tree here and has no loops). Thus

$$\Pr(A_{j_1} \cap A_{j_2} \cap \cdots \cap A_{j_k}) \sim p_1^k.$$

Since σ_k contains $\binom{n}{k}$ terms,

$$\sigma_k \sim \binom{n}{k} p_1^k \sim \frac{1}{k!}(np_1)^k. \tag{9.3}$$

Using (9.1) and (8.3),

$$np_1 \sim \frac{1}{\sqrt{2\pi}} \frac{n}{\sqrt{2\log n}} \times \exp\{-\log n + \tfrac{1}{2}\log\log n + \log(t\sqrt{4\pi}) + o(1)\},$$

$$np_1 \sim t.$$

Hence, taking K even in Lemma C,

$$\sum_{k=1}^{K} (-1)^{k-1}\frac{t^k}{k!} \le \Pr(A_1 \cup A_2 \cup \cdots \cup A_n) \le \sum_{k=1}^{K-1} (-1)^{k-1}\frac{t^k}{k!}.$$

For large K, these sums are both arbitrarily close to $1 - e^{-t}$. Hence

$$\Pr(A_1 \cup A_2 \cup \cdots \cup A_n) \sim 1 - e^{-t}.$$

This is the probability that a random element on the boundary of or within the Hamming sphere of radius ρn around $\boldsymbol{x}^{(1)}$ is not directly attracted to $\boldsymbol{x}^{(1)}$. It is also the probability that $\boldsymbol{x}^{(1)}$ is not fixed. The expected number of vectors $\boldsymbol{x}^{(\alpha)}$ that are not fixed is by symmetry m times the probability that $\boldsymbol{x}^{(1)}$ is such a vector. Thus the expected number of these bad $\boldsymbol{x}^{(\alpha)}$ is me^{-t}. Except for these, a random vector in the Hamming sphere about $\boldsymbol{x}^{(\alpha)}$ is attracted to $\boldsymbol{x}^{(\alpha)}$ with probability $1 - e^{-t}$. Since t can be made to approach 0, this proves case 1).

2) The complement of the probability wanted here is

$$\Pr(A_1 \cup A_2 \cup \cdots \cup A_N),$$

with $N = nm$, and the A_k the events $S_j^{(l)} < 0$. In applying Lemma C, σ_k has $\binom{N}{k}$ terms. Most of these are asymptotically p_1^k by Lemma 2. We need to estimate the number and size of the exceptional terms corresponding to graphs with loops.

Let the number $G_k = \binom{N}{k}$ of k-tuples of sums $S_j^{(l)}$ be decomposed into

$$G_k = \sum_{s \ge 0} G_k(s)$$

where $G_k(0)$ is the number of terms whose graphs have no loops, and the $G_k(s)$, $s \ge 1$, count the graphs with loops, in a way to be described.

For each graph $\mathcal{G}$ with one or more loops, we suppose the edges (j_h, l_h) have a definite ordering, and associate a loop number s as follows. First, let (j_1', l_1') be the last edge of $\mathcal{G}$ which is in a loop. For $s_1 \ge 1$, let $\mathcal{G}_{s_1}$ be the graph obtained from $\mathcal{G}$ by eliminating (j_r', l_r'), $1 \le r \le s_1$. If this graph has no loops, put $s = s_1$ and stop. Otherwise, (j_{s_1}', l_{s_1}') is the last edge in $\mathcal{G}_{s_1}$ which lies in a loop. Continue so that s is at last defined. $G_k(s)$ is then the number of k-tuples with loop number s.

Now we estimate $G_k(s)$ from above by the number of ways to pick k edges to form a graph with loop number s. Each edge can in general be picked in $\le N = mn$ ways. However, if the rth edge closes a loop, then j_r and l_r have values which have been used earlier, so this edge can be picked in at most $(r-1)^2 < k^2$ ways. The last loop edge (j_s', l_s') has subscript j_s' which is used by a preceding edge whose superscript l_s' is used by another preceding edge. This edge can be picked in fewer than km ways. Similarly, l_s' is the superscript of a preceding edge, which can be picked in fewer than kn ways. Finally, the set of $s+2$ "distinguished" edges can be picked from the set of k edges in at most $\binom{k}{s+2}$ ways. (These $s+2$ distinguished edges are the s loop-closing edges plus the two preceding edges, one for j_s' and one for l_s'.) Hence for $k > 0$ and $s \ge 1$ we have

$$G_k(s) < \binom{k}{s+2} km \cdot kn \cdot (k^2)^s \cdot N^{k-s-2} < C(k) \cdot N^{k-s-1}.$$

Here $C(k)$ is a constant depending only on k, not on s. We then have

$$\sum_{s=1}^{k} G_k(s) = O(N^{k-2}).$$

Decompose σ_k into

$$\sigma_k = \sum_{s \ge 0} \sigma_k(s),$$

where $\sigma_k(s)$ is the sum of the terms with loop number s. First, we have

$$\sigma_k(0) \sim \left[\binom{N}{k} - O(N^{k-2})\right] p_1^k$$

by Lemma 2, hence

$$\sigma_k(0) \sim \frac{1}{k!}(Np_1)^k.$$

From (9.2),

$$Np_1 \sim t,$$

$$\sigma_k(0) \sim \frac{t^k}{k!}. \tag{9.4}$$

For $s \ge 1$, a graph with loop number s has associated with it a graph of $k - s$ edges which has no loops. Lemma 2 applies to the probability associated with this reduced graph, and furnishes an upper bound for the term in $\sigma_k(s)$. Hence

$$\sigma_k(s) \lesssim C(k) N^{k-s-1} p_1^{k-s} = O(N^{-1}).$$

Combining this with (9.4), we get

$$\sigma_k \sim \frac{t^k}{k!}.$$

From here, the proof proceeds as in case 1). This proves case 2), and completes the proof of the theorem.

Thus, if we fix t at ϵ, small, and use $e^{-\epsilon} \sim 1-\epsilon$, we see the following.

1) The expected number of fundamental memories $1-\epsilon$, the Hamming sphere of which is directly attracted to its fixed center, is asymptotically at least $m(1-\epsilon)$ if

$$m = \frac{(1-2\rho)^2 n}{2\log n}\left(1 + \frac{\frac{1}{2}\log\log n}{\log n} + O_\epsilon\left(\frac{1}{\log n}\right)\right)$$

(thus $m = [(1-2\rho)^2/2](n/\log n)$ works). That is, with the above m, the expected fraction ϵ of the memories do not have $1-\epsilon$ of their Hamming sphere of radius ρn directly attracted. Thus, with high probability, all but fraction ϵ actually do have $1-\epsilon$ of their Hamming sphere of radius ρn directly attracted.

2) The probability that there is even one of the m fundamental memories $1-\epsilon$ the Hamming sphere of radius ρn of which is not directly attracted is asymptotically at most ϵ, if

$$m = \frac{(1-2\rho)^2}{4}\frac{n}{\log n}\left(1 + \frac{\frac{3}{4}\log\log n}{\log n} + O_\epsilon\left(\frac{1}{\log n}\right)\right)$$

(thus $m = ((1-2\rho)^2/4)(n/\log n)$ works).

The converse is also true.

1) If $m \geq (1-2\rho)^2[n/(2\log n)](1+\eta)$ with $\eta > 0$, then the expected number of fundamental memories $1-\eta$ the entire Hamming sphere of radius ρn of which is directly attracted is $o(m)$. (In fact, very few of the elements of the spheres are directly attracted, as we shall see below.)

Proof: The expected number of almost directly attracted spheres is (asymptotically) me^{-t} for any fixed t in (9.1). We can get m memories with such almost directly attracted spheres where

$$m = (1-2\rho)^2 \frac{n}{2\log n}(1+\eta)$$

from (9.1) with $t = n^\eta$. The number of almost directly attracted Hamming spheres for large n is less than $me^{-n^\eta} = o(m)$. For any m' larger than the above m, the $o(m')$, actually $o(m)$, condition follows from the uniformity comments just after the proof of Lemma 1. The converse follows for case 1).

2) If $m \geq (1-2\rho)^2[n/(4\log n)](1+\eta)$ with $\eta > 0$, then the probability that almost all the Hamming spheres of radius ρn are directly attracted to their fundamental memories at the center can be made as small as we like by choosing n large depending on η.

Proof: The same as for case 1), with a t of $n^{2\eta}$ working in (9.2). The converse follows for case 2).

Thus we see that for direct attraction of almost all of the Hamming spheres of radius ρn, $[(1-2\rho)^2/2](n/\log n)$, resp. $[(1-2\rho)^2/4](n/\log n)$, are the right answers to the expected number, resp. probability, question. Trying to have asymptotically more fundamental memories causes the expectation, resp. probability, to go to 0, from originally being nearly 1.

However, we can say more for $\rho > 0$. If we try to get more then the m allowed by a factor of $1+\eta$, any $\eta > 0$, we find the following.

1) For almost every vector in the sphere of radius ρn around almost every fundamental memory, direct attraction fails.

This is because almost all vectors in the sphere of radius ρn are at distance from the center $\geq \rho n(1-\eta)$, η small, the "shell." We have also seen that almost all direct attraction fails with high probability for such a vector if η is chosen small because of the decrease in "signal" from n to $n_\rho = n(1-2\rho)$. Referring to (8.2), we see that direct attraction fails for almost all state vectors in the shell. Now there are dependencies between one vector in the shell and another, due to the $x_j^{(l)} x_k^{(l)} x_j^{(r)} x_k^{(r)}$ terms. However, we can certainly say that the *expected fraction* of the vectors in the sphere of radius ρn which fail is near 1 for almost all the fundamental memories. So the probability that almost all the vectors in the radius-ρn sphere fail for almost all the fundamental memories must also be near 1.

2) The provable analogy to the strengthened converse in 1) above is this. If we try for too many fundamental memories, then with high probability almost every error pattern of weight $\leq \rho n$ corresponds to a vector, within distance ρn of some fundamental memory, which fails to be directly attracted. This is, however, of less interest than the strengthened converse of 1).

X. Extension for Nondirect Convergence

So far we have only considered direct convergence. What if we allow an occasional wrong change? We can then try to get rid of the annoying $(1-2\rho)^2$ factors, as follows.

Choose a fixed small $\rho' > 0$. Let $m = (1-2\rho')^2 [n/2(\text{or } 4)\log n]$, so that spheres of radius $\rho' n$ are almost directly attracted. Let ρ close to 1/2 be fixed. By Lemma 1, the probability p_1 that a change is in the wrong direction is

$$p_1 \sim C\frac{1-2\rho'}{1-2\rho}\frac{1}{\sqrt{\log n}} n^{-(1-2\rho)^2/(1-2\rho')^2} \to 0 \text{ as } n \to \infty.$$

In the synchronous case, it seems clear what happens. After one iteration, only about np_1 components are wrong, with high probability. Since p_1 can be made smaller than ρ' by choosing n large, one more iteration plus our Big Theorem on almost direct attraction should get us to the required fundamental memory. Thus at most two synchronous iterations should suffice. We now let $\rho' \to 0$, ρ fixed. This makes it plausible that the $(1-2\rho)^2$ term can be dropped for any fixed $\rho < 1/2$. (Of course, n becomes large as $\rho \to 1/2$.)

In the asynchronous case, the removal of $(1-2\rho)^2$ seems still true. Here, however, we must worry about temporarily wandering out of the ρn-sphere, where the p_1 asymptotic formula might not be valid. However, we can back off from ρ by a protective fixed fraction, say η, small but $> p_1$. This means we start no more than $\rho(1-\eta)$ away from a fundamental memory and with high probability always stay in the ρn-sphere in which the p_1 estimate holds. The rest should follow as before.

The result is that for any $0 < \rho < 1/2$ and $\epsilon > 0$, if

$$m = (1-\epsilon)\frac{n}{2\log n}$$

then we expect that almost all of the ρn-sphere around almost all the m fundamental memories are ultimately attracted to the correct fundamental memory. If

$$m = (1-\epsilon)\frac{n}{4\log n}$$

then with high probability almost all of the ρn-sphere around all the fundamental memories are attracted.

However, if we try to let

$$m = (1+\epsilon)\frac{n}{2\log n},$$

then a vanishingly small fraction of the fundamental memories themselves are even fixed points. If we try to let

$$m = (1+\epsilon)\frac{n}{4\log n},$$

then with probability near 1 there is at least one fundamental memory not fixed.

Thus it is indeed appropriate to say that the capacity of a Hopfield neural associative memory of n neurons with sum-of-outer product interconnections is $m = n/(2\log n)$ if we are willing to give up being able to remember a small fraction of the m memories, and $m = n/(4\log n)$ if all memories must be remembered. This is for any radius of attraction ρn, $0 \le \rho < 1/2$, ρ fixed. We can get an arbitrarily close ratio to these m and cannot beat them by any positive fraction.

We now consider the possibility of having "don't cares." Suppose we have an initial probe in which we know a fraction β of the memories, and know that we do not reliably know the other $1-\beta$. This is the "content addressability" alluded to in Section I—from a small fraction of the n components, we want to recover the whole memory. Previously, we have been guessing the rest and getting half right by luck, so that we wind up with

$$\beta n + \frac{(1-\beta)n}{2} = \frac{(1+\beta)n}{2}$$

right. Except for the original βn, we do not exactly know where the correct ones are.

We might be tempted to "clamp" the βn we know, not letting them change. However, from what we have seen, clamping does not really help. This is because most components wind up right after their first change anyway. Another idea might be to disable the $(1-\beta)n$ components we do not know, at least until they get assigned values in the asynchronous case or for one iteration in the synchronous case. That is, we would just use the components we are sure about to compute the component of x that is to change or be given a definite ± 1 value for the first time. We would thus use 0 for a component we are not sure of in computing Tx, where x is the probe vector. (We can as well clamp the correct βn or not, as we choose, in the following discussion.) Does this help the asymptotic capacity of the Hopfield associative memory?

The answer is "No" if we are interested in indirect convergence. This is because we have strong evidence that the $n/2\log n$ capacity works no matter how close we are to having half our components wrong in our initial probe. It is just that n has to be larger and larger for the asymptotic result to take over as we get closer and closer to half wrong. We may, and presumably will, get more actual capacity for usefully small values of n by disabling the components we do not know, but the asymptotic capacity does not change for fixed β by doing this. Of course, to provide this disabling capability (or a clamping capability) is a device fabrication complexity we may wish to avoid.

If we are only interested in direct convergence (but we are not), the conclusion changes dramatically. The fraction ρ of components we have wrong in our initial probe is, as we have seen,

$$\rho = \left(\frac{1-\beta}{2}\right),$$

so that $1-2\rho = \beta$. Here then the capacity is (the $n/(4\log n)$ case with no exceptional memories being similar)

$$(1-2\rho)^2\frac{n}{2\log n} = \frac{\beta n}{2\log n}$$

if we do not disable the components we have merely guessed. What if we do disable?

A little thought shows that the "signal" term for *any* of the n components drops to βn from n, while the noise power (variance) drops to βnm, where there are m fundamental memories. Thus the signal-to-noise (power) ratio becomes

$$(\mathrm{S/N})_{\text{disabled}} \doteq (\beta n)^2/\beta mn = \beta\frac{n}{m}.$$

We have seen that in the original analysis where choice was forced the signal-to-noise ratio was

$$(\mathrm{S/N})_{\text{forced choice}} \doteq (1-2\rho)^2\frac{n^2}{nm} = \beta^2\frac{n}{m}.$$

The signal-to-noise ratio goes up by the large factor of $1/\beta$ if we disable the previously guessed components. Thus the direct-convergence capacity will go up by a factor of $1/\beta$.

to $\beta[n/(2\log n)]$. For example, if $\beta = 0.05$, so that we know five percent of the n components to begin with, the forced-choice direct-convergence capacity is only five percent of the direct-convergence capacity when we disable the guessed components.

We may, however, be interested in indirect rather than direct convergence in any memory we actually build. Also, the asymptotic capacity does not drop by forced choice although convergence may be speeded up. We have stated that providing a disabling capability may make fabrication more difficult. For these three reasons it is probably not necessary or desirable to disable the components we do not know. Merely assign random values such as the ones left over from the last time the memory was used. If, however, we *have* to give components values to begin with, which may in itself be a hardware complication, we may as well allow 0 values to be given by providing a switch-out capability.

However, there *is* a great hardware simplification whose effect on capacity we ought to study. It involves just allowing T_{ij} that are ± 1 (0 or ± 1 would be just as easy, and better). For then we only need connect input i to input j or not, with or without a sign-reversing switch. Thus, in the ± 1 case (hard limiting), we would use

$$T_{ij} = \operatorname{sgn}\left(\sum_{\alpha=1}^{m} x_i^{(\alpha)} x_j^{(\alpha)} \right).$$

(This T_{ij}, however, does not have the incremental property; to add an $(m+1)$st memory, we need to know the sum *inside* the sgn, not merely the value ± 1 of sgn.) More generally, any (symmetric, for simplicity) nonlinearity instead of sgn could be studied, although the most important nonlinearity for fabricators is probably the 0, ± 1 one. For this, we also need to set quantization thresholds.

It turns out that the loss in memory capacity is by the same factor as is the channel capacity loss with nonlinearities on each symbol detection in the additive white Gaussian channel. The optimum thresholds are the same, too. For example, for (symmetric) hard limiting, the memory capacity drops with all definitions by the well-known factor of $2/\pi$. For symmetric three-level (0, ± 1), the memory capacity decreases by only a factor of $0.810 = 0.92$ dB [21, prob. 4.16, p. 103] if we choose the optimum symmetric null-zone thresholds of about $\pm 0.61\sqrt{m}$ where there are m memories [22, pp. 401–402]. Thus about $\Phi(0.61) - \Phi(-0.61) = 2\Phi(0.61) - 1 \doteq 0.458 = 46$ percent of the T_{ij} are 0. We only lose 19 percent of capacity by this optimum three-level quantization.

We conclude that using a three-level symmetric connection matrix is a good candidate for implementation if we can dispense with the incremental property in building up the T_{ij}. (We might store the actual $\sum_{\alpha=1}^{m} x_i^{(\alpha)} x_j^{(\alpha)}$ off line in some data base.) When needing to store an additional memory $\boldsymbol{x}^{(m+1)}$, we would compute whether we should change the T_{ij} or not. We would then somehow change the few that needed changing or burn another memory chip.

However, a rigorous proof of the foregoing results on nonlinearities requires a larger set of ideas than those introduced in Section VII. The finite symmetric quantizer turns out to be not too much harder to handle than what we have done rigorously in this paper. The general symmetric nonlinearity seems much harder to handle, going beyond Section VII's large-deviation lemmas, but fortunately this general nonlinearity does not seem to be important practically. This work is still continuing.

XI. Summary and Prospectus

We have seen that the (asymptotic) capacity m of a Hopfield associative memory of length n when it is to be presented with a number m of random independent ± 1 probability $1/2$ fundamental memories to store and when probing with a probe n-tuple at most ρn away from a fundamental memory $(0 \le \rho < 1/2)$ is

1) $$\frac{(1-2\rho)^2}{2} \frac{n}{\log n}$$

if with high probability the unique fundamental memory is to be recovered by direct convergence to the fundamental memory, except for a vanishingly small fraction of the fundamental memories;

2) $$\frac{(1-2\rho)^2}{4} \frac{n}{\log n}$$

if, in the above scenario, *no* fundamental memory can be exceptional;

3) $$\frac{n}{2\log n}$$

if $0 \le \rho < 1/2$, ρ given, where some wrong moves are permitted (although two steps suffice), and we can have as above a small fraction of exceptional fundamental memories;

4) $$\frac{n}{4\log n}$$

if as above some wrong moves are permitted (although two synchronous moves suffice) but no fundamental memory can be exceptional. [3) and 4) were not rigorously proven.]

In all of the above, we are required (with high probability) to arrive at the exact fundamental memory as the stable point with no components in error, in either the synchronous or asynchronous model. (The capacities are the same in either model.)

We already mentioned in Section III for the asynchronous model that if the final stable n-tuple arrived at can have a fraction ϵ of its components in error (as above, a few fundamental memories can be exceptional), then the capacity is instead linear in n, like cn (much as in [1]), where, for small ϵ, c is asymptotic to $1/(2\log \epsilon^{-1})$. For $\epsilon = 10^{-4}$, a more exact answer gives $c = 0.0723$. Thus, with $0.0723n$ fundamental memories, a stable state is reached with only 10^{-4} of the components wrong, if n is large enough depending on ρ, $0 \le \rho < 1/2$ (here the probe has ρn wrong components out of n to begin with). This work will be reported elsewhere [23]. Rigorous proofs turn out to be harder here, and at this time, the result is not fully rigorous. A surprising result (Fig. 8) is that the stable point is essentially on the boundary of the radius-ϵn sphere even if we start *inside* the sphere, even at its center, the true memory. That is, errors are introduced if we probe with the true memory, but not too many errors.

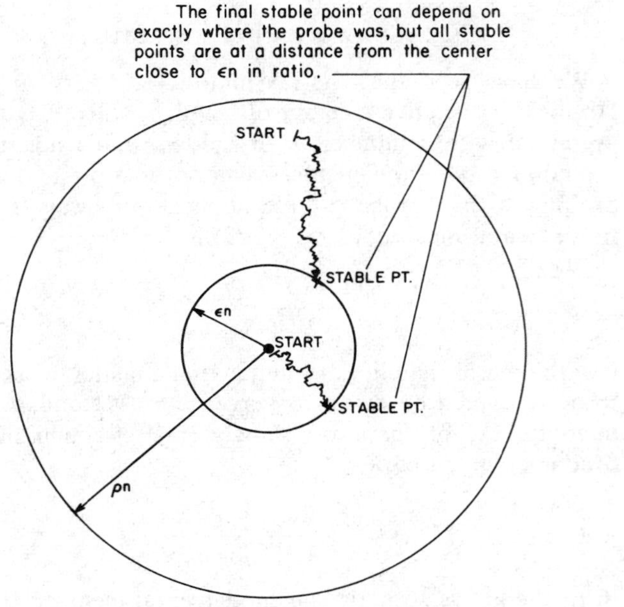
The final stable point can depend on exactly where the probe was, but all stable points are at a distance from the center close to ϵn in ratio.
START
STABLE PT.
ϵn
START
STABLE PT.
ρn

Fig. 8. Stable points on boundary starting inside or outside.

Note that the $n/(2\log\epsilon^{-1})$ result is consistent with our prior $n/(2\log n)$ result. For, if ϵ were not constant but equal to $1/n$, we might naively expect an average of $(1/n)\cdot n = 1$ error in the final stable state, according to the theory we have just described. If ϵ is still smaller, say $\epsilon = 1/(n\log n)$, then we expect $(1/(n\log n))\cdot n = 1/\log n$, very few errors, so the probability that the stable state we reach is correct will be high. This is our original criterion for a good memory. If we put $\epsilon = 1/(n\log n)$ into our $n/(2\log\epsilon^{-1})$ capacity, we get a capacity of $n/[2(\log n + \log\log n)] \sim n/(2\log n)$, our previous result.

We have mentioned extraneous fixed points earlier, that is, the fixed points that are not fundamental memories. Indeed, in the above linear-capacity result the only fixed points that matter are actually extraneous ones on or near the boundaries of the radius-ϵn spheres around the fundamental memories; very few of the original m memories will themselves be exactly fixed.

The appearance of extraneous fixed points is not all understood. One thing that is rigorously known is the expected number of fixed points as a function of n if the symmetric connection matrix T with zeros down the diagonal has as entries (in say the upper half-matrix) $n(n-1)/2$ independent identically distributed zero-mean Gaussian random variables as in a spin glass [24, p. 445], [25]. The rigorous result is that the expected number of fixed points F_n is asymptotic to the following:

$$F_n \sim (1.0505)2^{0.2874n}. \qquad (11.1)$$

We actually have the case of the sum-of-outer products connection matrix T based on m fundamental memories which are m independent Bernoulli probability-1/2 random n-tuples. The T_{ij} are approximately Gaussian and pairwise independent. Nevertheless, this seems not to be enough to carry over the above asymptotic result rigorously to our case, even if m is a constant times n rather than a constant times $n/\log n$. The difficulty is that we really need to consider an ever growing number of the T_{ij} at once.

In fact, we expect that an exact carryover may not be quite true. In particular, let $m=1$ and n be large. How many fixed points are there? The T_{ij} for $i \neq j$ are given by

$$T_{ij} = x_i x_j \qquad (11.2)$$

where $\boldsymbol{x} = (x_1, x_2, \cdots, x_n)$ is the random ± 1 n-vector. A ± 1 vector $\boldsymbol{y}$ is fixed if for every i, $1 \le i \le m$,

$$\operatorname{sgn} \sum_{\substack{j=1 \\ j\neq i}}^{n} x_i x_j y_j = y_i; \qquad (11.3)$$

that is, for $1 \le i \le n$,

$$x_i \operatorname{sgn} \sum_{j\neq i} x_j y_j = y_i. \qquad (11.4)$$

We see that $\boldsymbol{y} = \boldsymbol{x}$ and $\boldsymbol{y} = -\boldsymbol{x}$ are both fixed, so there are at least two fixed points when $m=1$, namely, $\boldsymbol{x}$ and $-\boldsymbol{x}$.

Now rewrite (11.4) as

$$x_i \operatorname{sgn}(\boldsymbol{x}\cdot\boldsymbol{y} - x_i y_i) = y_i, \qquad 1 \le i \le n. \qquad (11.5)$$

If $|\boldsymbol{x}\cdot\boldsymbol{y}| \ge 2$, then $\operatorname{sgn}(\boldsymbol{x}\cdot\boldsymbol{y} - x_i y_i)$ is independent of i, and $\boldsymbol{y} = \pm\boldsymbol{x}$. Using the convention $\operatorname{sgn} 0 = +$, as we have been when forced to make a choice, the same is true if $\boldsymbol{x}\cdot\boldsymbol{y} = +1$.

The only cases to worry about are $\boldsymbol{x}\cdot\boldsymbol{y} = 0$ and $\boldsymbol{x}\cdot\boldsymbol{y} = -1$. If $\boldsymbol{x}\cdot\boldsymbol{y} = 0$, then

$$x_i \operatorname{sgn}(-x_i y_i) = y_i, \qquad 1 \le i \le n$$

$$x_i y_i \operatorname{sgn}(-x_i y_i) = 1, \qquad 1 \le i \le n,$$

a contradiction because $z\operatorname{sgn}(-z) = -1$ if $z = \pm 1$. If $\boldsymbol{x}\cdot\boldsymbol{y} = -1$, then

$$x_i \operatorname{sgn}(-1 - x_i y_i) = y_i, \qquad 1 \le i \le n$$

$$x_i y_i \operatorname{sgn}(-1 - x_i y_i) = 1, \qquad 1 \le i \le n.$$

Here if $y_i = x_i$ for some i, then $\operatorname{sgn}(-2) = 1$, a contradiction, so $\boldsymbol{y} = -\boldsymbol{x}$ if $\boldsymbol{x}\cdot\boldsymbol{y} = -1$ (and $n=1$).

So there are only two fixed points when $m=2$. We expect that the number of fixed points F_n is asymptotic to a constant times 2 to another constant times n power, but that other constant is, we believe, *less* than the 0.2874 of (11.1) for m growing only like a constant times $n/\log n$. We have no idea yet as to how to proceed, other than perhaps to obtain lower bounds on the number of fixed points. With this class of problem we close the paper.

Acknowledgment

We thank A. Dembo for pointing out an error in a previous version of this paper.

References

[1] J. J. Hopfield, "Neural networks and physical systems with emergent collective computational abilities," *Proc. Nat. Acad. Sci. USA*, vol. 79, pp. 2554–2558, 1982.

[2] S. Grossberg, *Studies of Mind and Brain*. Boston: Reidel, 1982.

[3] ——, *The Adaptive Brain; Vol. I: Cognition, Learning, Reinforcement, and Rhythm; Vol. II: Vision, Speech, Language, and Motor Control*. Amsterdam, The Netherlands: North-Holland, 1986.

[4] G. E. Hinton and J. A. Anderson, eds., *Parallel Models of Associative Memory*, Hillsdale, NJ: Erlbaum, 1981.

[5] F. Tanaka and S. F. Edwards, "Analytical theory of the ground state properties of a spin glass: I. Ising spin glass," *J. Phys. F. Metal Phys.*, vol. 10, pp. 2769–2778, 1980.

[6] S. Wolfram, "Statistical mechanics of cellular automata," *Rev. Mod. Phys.*, vol. 55, pp. 601–644, 1983.

[7] D. O. Hebb, *The Organization of Behavior*. New York: Wiley, 1949.

[8] J. G. Eccles, *The Neurophysiological Basis of Mind*. Oxford: Clarendon, 1953.

[9] K. Nakano, "Associatron—A model of associative memory," *IEEE Trans. Syst. Man, Cybern.*, vol. SMC-2, pp. 380–388, 1972.

[10] T. Kohonen, *Associative Memory: A System-Theoretic Approach*. Berlin: Springer-Verlag, 1977.

[11] S. Amari, "Neural theory of association and concept formation," *Biol. Cybern.*, vol. 26, pp. 175–185, 1977.

[12] W. A. Little, "The existence of persistent states in the brain," *Math. Biosci.*, vol. 19, pp. 101–120, 1974.

[13] G. Palm, "On associative memory," *Biol. Cybern.*, vol. 36, pp. 19–31, 1980.

[14] J. J. Hopfield and D. W. Tank, "'Neural' computation of decisions in optimization problems," *Biol. Cybern.*, vol. 52, pp. 141–152, 1985.

[15] D. W. Tank and J. J. Hopfield, "Simple optimization networks: An A/D converter and a linear programming circuit," *IEEE Trans. Circuits Syst.*, vol. CAS-33, pp. 533–541, 1986.

[16] W. A. Little and G. L. Shaw, "Analytic study of the memory storage capacity of a neural network," *Math. Biosci.*, vol. 39, pp. 281–290, 1978.

[17] Y. S. Abu-Mostafa and J. St. Jacques, "Information capacity of the Hopfield Model," *IEEE Trans. Inform. Theory* vol. IT-31, pp. 461–464, 1985.

[18] S. S. Venkatesh, "Epsilon capacity of neural networks," to be published.

[19] S. S. Vankatesh and D. Psaltis, "Information storage and retrieval in two associative nets," submitted to *IEEE Trans. Inform. Theory.*

[20] W. Feller, *An Introduction to Probability Theory and Its Applications*, vol. I, 3rd ed. New York: Wiley, 1968.

[21] R. J. McEliece, *The Theory of Information and Coding*, vol. 3 of *Encyclopedia of Mathematics and Its Application*. Reading, MA: Addison-Wesley, 1977.

[22] J. M. Wozencraft and I. M. Jacobs, *Principles of Communication Engineering*. New York: Wiley, 1965.

[23] E. C. Posner and E. R. Rodemich, "Linear capacity in the Hopfield model," to be published.

[24] D. J. Gross and M. Mezard, "The simplest spin glass," *Nuclear Phys.*, vol. B 240 [FS12], pp. 431–452, 1984.

[25] R. J. McEliece and E. C. Posner, "The number of stable points of an infinite-range spin glass memory," Telecommunications and Data Acquisition Progress Report, vol. 42–83, July–Sept. 1985, Jet Propulsion Lab., California Inst. Technol. Pasadena, Nov. 15, 1985, pp. 209–215.

Reprinted from IEEE Transactions on Systems, Man, and Cybernetics 13(5), September/October 1983, pp. 851-57.

A Model of Human Associative Processor (HASP)

YUZO HIRAI, MEMBER, IEEE

***Abstract*—A model of an associative processor named HASP is proposed and described. The objective is to represent associative brain functions in terms of neural network structure. HASP is described with emphasis on its associative memory functions. HASP solved two critical problems which resided in associative memory models hitherto proposed: crosstalk noise elimination and multiple-match resolution. HASP eliminates crosstalk noise without complicated orthogonalizing methods. Both problems are solved by the same network structure. With the function of crosstalk noise elimination, the storage capacity increases, and an explosion of crosstalk noise, inevitable in a system such as mutually linked associative networks, can be avoided. With the function of multiple-match resolution, various operations of retrieving information from a memory organized in complicated data structures can be available.**

I. Introduction

ASSOCIATIVE processing is one of the most fundamental brain functions of our memory and thought processes. Various kinds of models have been proposed to represent the functional structure of associative processing. In its most abstract form, it is represented by a graph structure in which each item or concept is expressed by a single node and association is expressed by a labeled link between the nodes. Since the graph structure is realized by a list structure in a computer program, many attempts such as semantic networks have appeared in the cognitive psychology and AI literature [1], [2].

However, if we admit a notion that our memory is characterized by its associative, distributed, and content addressable structure, each item must be represented by a response pattern of a group of neural elements. Even a label which designates a specific relation between items must also be represented by such a pattern. According to this notion, many models have been proposed to represent associative memory in terms of neural network structure. An extensive list of references can be found in [3]. Since what a brain does when it functions should be intimately related to how it is constructed [4], perhaps what an abstract model can perform easily cannot be performed by a brain, and vice versa. Therefore, in understanding brain functions, describing them in terms of neural network structure is essential.

In this paper, a model of an associative processor named HASP is proposed, and its structure and performance are described in detail. In Section II, some problems resided in conventional associative memory models are pointed out, and the objective of this study is clarified. In Section III, the structure of HASP is fully described. In Section IV, the storage capacity is evaluated by computer simulation, and in Section V several operations of retrieving information from HASP are described. In Section VI, possible neural correlate of the proposed network is presented.

II. Problems in Associative Memory Models

Many models of associative memory hitherto proposed can be described in terms of correlation-matrix formalism [3] as follows. Let the kth pair of key vector P^k and associated vector Q^k be $P^k = (P_1^k, P_2^k, \cdots, P_m^k)$ and $Q^k = (q_1^k, q_2^k, \cdots, q_n^k)$, respectively. In the correlation-matrix formalism, association matrix M is defined by

$$M = \sum_k P^{kT} \cdot Q^k, \tag{1}$$

where T designates transposition of vector. The process of

Manuscript received August 12, 1982; revised March 28, 1983.
The author is with the Institute of Information Sciences and Electronics, University of Tsukuba, Sakura-mura, Niihari-gun, Ibaraki, Japan.

associative recollection is described as follows:

$$Q = P \cdot M = P \cdot \sum_k P^{kT} \cdot Q^k, \quad (2)$$

where P is a key input and Q is a recollected vector. If $P = P^k$, we have

$$Q = P^k \cdot P^{kT} \cdot Q^k + \sum_{l \neq k} P^k \cdot P^{lT} \cdot Q^l. \quad (3)$$

If the key vectors are mutually orthogonal, the inner products $P^k \cdot P^{lT}$ disappear and the associated vector Q^k appears in proportion to the inner product $P^k \cdot P^{kT}$. If the key vectors are not orthogonal, crosstalk noise Q^l $(l \neq k)$ appears in proportion to $P^k \cdot P^{lT}$. The author has already proposed a learning network which can orthogonalize any vectors composed of binary elements [5].

It should be noted, however, that even if keys are orthogonal, crosstalk will necessarily occur when one and the same key is associated with more than one item. The following simple question will illustrate how common and important the multiple-match resolution is in associative memory: "What is the color of a rose?" Probably you will answer as follows: "It can be red, yellow, white,... ." In this case, (3) becomes

$$Q = P^k \cdot P^{kT} \cdot (Q^{k1} + Q^{k2} + \cdots + Q^{kn}), \quad (4)$$

provided that "color of rose" is orthogonal to "color of daisy." No models exist, to my knowledge, which can resolve multiple-match situations. The author has already proposed a basic idea for that problem [6], and the idea is incorporated into HASP.

III. Structure of HASP

The structure of HASP is shown in Fig. 1. It consists of three components: heteroassociative networks, recurrent networks, and readout control units. Control signals to HASP are supposed to be supplied from a higher control center which includes recognition and decisionmaking systems.

A. Heteroassociative Networks

Input lines $K(x)$ and network elements $S(y)$ constitute a structure similar to that of conventional heteroassociative memory models. The strength of excitatory connection $WS(y, x)$ from $K(x)$ to $S(y)$, which is zero at first, is increased by the conjunctive activation of $K(x)$ and $T(y)$ in the following way:

1) if $T(y) \cdot K(x) > 0$, $WS(y, x)$ is strengthened to WS, and
2) if $T(y) \cdot K(x) = 0$, then $WS(y, x)$ is not changed,

where $K(x)$ and $T(y)$ constitute a pair of key and associated items, respectively. With this algorithm, these excitatory connections form an association matrix similar to the one proposed by Palm [7]. He introduced threshold into the corresponding element of $S(y)$ and showed that the threshold could eliminate crosstalk noise effectively. The network element IK, which has threshold θ, performs this

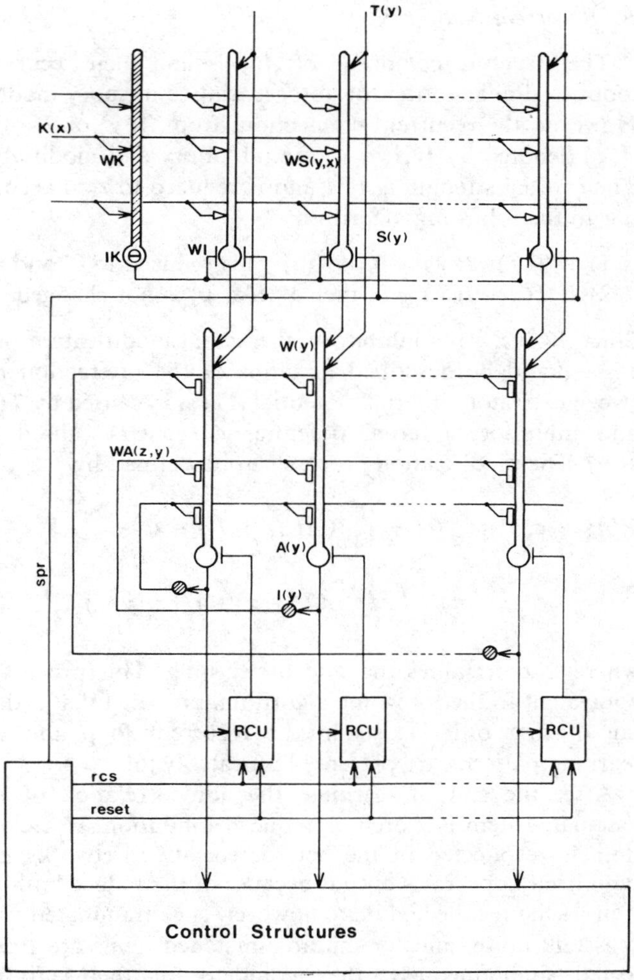

Fig. 1. Structure of HASP. RCU is Readout Control Unit; rcs is readout control signal; spr is output suppress signal. Hatched elements are inhibitory.

function in a more flexible way. It gathers activity of $K(x)$ through excitatory connection WK and inhibits the response of $S(y)$ through WI. Therefore, IK functions as a variable threshold. The element $S(y)$ receives another inhibitory signal (spr), which suppresses the output of HASP.

The output of $S(y)$ at time t is expressed by

$$S(y, t) = 1\left[\sum_x WS(y, x) \cdot K(x, t) - WI \cdot IK(t) - \mathrm{spr}(t)\right], \quad (5)$$

where

$$IK(t) = \varphi\left[\sum_x WK \cdot K(x, t) - \theta\right]. \quad (6)$$

The functions $1[\cdot]$ and $\varphi[\cdot]$ describe nonlinear transfer characteristics of the respective elements, and they are defined by

$$1[a] = \begin{cases} 1, & \text{if } a > 0 \\ 0, & \text{if } a \leqslant 0, \end{cases} \quad (7)$$

and

$$\varphi[a] = \begin{cases} a, & \text{if } a > 0 \\ 0, & \text{if } a \leqslant 0. \end{cases} \quad (8)$$

B. Recurrent Networks

The structure composed of $A(y)$'s and their recurrent loops is similar to that of autoassociative memory models. However, the recurrent connections from $A(y)$ or $I(y)$ to $A(z)$ denoted by $WA(z, y)$ are inhibitory and modifiable. Their initial strength is WA and is reduced to zero according to the following algorithm:

1) if $T(z) \cdot I(y) > 0$, $WA(z, y)$ is reduced to 0, and
2) if $T(z) \cdot I(y) = 0$, then $WA(z, y)$ is not changed.

Since $WA(z, y)$ is inhibitory, the actual modification process should be described in terms of the interaction between excitatory internal potential $AT(z, t)$ caused by $T(z)$ and inhibitory internal potential $AI(z, y, t)$ caused by $I(y)$. The modification process can be defined by

$$WA(z, y, T + \Delta T) = \varphi\left[WA(z, y, T) - C \cdot \int_{T}^{T+\Delta T} AT(z, t) \cdot AI(z, y, t)\, dt \right], \quad (9)$$

where C determines the rate of learning. This process is equivalent to the foregoing algorithm, provided that a time lag of first order exists in the recurrent loop and the learning patterns are presented repeatedly [6].

After the end of learning, the autocorrelation of the associated item is stored as reduced inhibition. If a clean item is recollected in the heteroassociative networks, the item itself appears as output because of the reduced inhibition. If the recollected item, however, is contaminated with crosstalk noise, and/or multiple-matched items are recollected simultaneously, they compete for their survival through the intact inhibition. By choosing network parameters appropriately, only one item wins the competition at a time. In order to recollect all the matched items, a readout controller which selects them one by one is necessary. The component denoted by a readout control unit (RCU) performs this function.

C. Readout Control Units

The structure of an RCU is shown in Fig. 2. RCU's are controlled by an externally supplied readout control signal (rcs) and weaken the competitive power of the currently selected item not to be chosen in further recollection. As shown in the figure, each RCU consists of three elements denoted by G, M, and R. The G element receives inputs from $A(y)$ and rcs. If $A(y)$ is active at the time when the rcs becomes active, the G element continues to pass the rcs as long as the rcs is active. The M element memorizes the gated rcs by a positive feedback loop. The R element receives inputs from the G and M elements and suppresses the output element $A(y)$.

D. Equations for Recurrent Networks and RCU

The output elements and R elements are analog threshold elements with a time lag of first order, and their structure is shown in Fig. 3. The other elements are assumed to pass

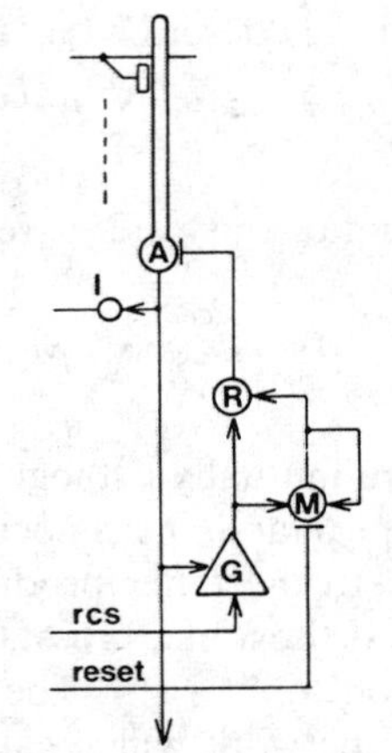

Fig. 2. Structure of RCU.

their inputs without time lag. The response of an output element at time t is expressed by

$$\mu_1 \cdot \frac{dA(y, t)}{dt} + A(y, t) = W(y) \cdot S(y, t) - \sum_z WA(y, z) \cdot \varphi[A(z, t)] - R(y, t), \quad (10)$$

where $W(y)$ is a connecting coefficient from $S(y)$ to $A(y)$ and the actual output is $\varphi[A(y, t)]$. Since $I(z)$ is only a relaying element, $\varphi[A(z, t)]$ is used instead of $I(z, t)$.

The response of the R element is expressed by

$$\mu_2 \cdot \frac{dR(y, t)}{dt} + R(y, t) = G(y, t) + \alpha \cdot M(y, t), \quad (11)$$

where α is a connecting coefficient from the M to the R element.

The response of the G and M elements are expressed by

$$G(y, t) = \text{rcs}(t) \cdot 1[A(y, t) + G(y, t)], \quad (12)$$

$$M(y, t) = 1[G(y, t) + M(y, t)] - \text{res}(t), \quad (13)$$

where $\text{res}(t)$ is a reset signal which clears all M elements. The behavior of this network was analyzed in detail in [6].

IV. Storage Capacity

In this section a set of conditions on which crosstalk noise cannot be eliminated are discussed. Since the storage capacity of HASP is limited by them, a series of simulation studies using binary random patterns have been carried out, and the capacity is evaluated under several situations.

A. Condition of Crosstalk Noise Occurrence

In the following discussions, key and associated items are assumed to be binary patterns, that is to say, each

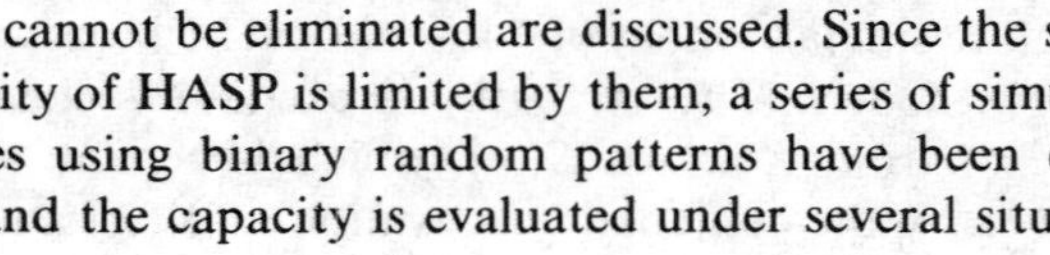

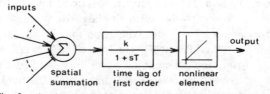

Fig. 3. Analog threshold element with time lag of first order.

TABLE I

RESULTS OF SIMULATION STUDIES FOR THE EVALUATION OF THE STORAGE CAPACITY OF HASP

Number of 1-elements (Total number of elements is 10×10)	Number of pairs of key and associated items	Number (ratio) of correct recollections	Number of recollections contaminated with cross-talk noise*	Total number of cross-talk noise*	Total number of eliminated cross-talk noise*
5	50	50 (1.0)	0	0	0
	100	100 (1.0)	8	11	11
	150	147 (0.98)	63	82	75
	200	193 (0.97)	146	299	281
	300	225 (0.75)	288	1295	860
10	50	50 (1.0)	2	2	2
	100	74 (0.74)	90	233	145
	150	24 (0.16)	150	1477	187

* Cross-talk noise appeared in the output of heteroassociative networks.

pattern element takes a value of one or zero randomly. Network parameters WK, WI, WS, and θ are set to 1.0. From (5) and (6), if $T(y)$ is a one-element of Q^k, the response of $S(y)$ to P^k becomes 1.0, regardless of the norm of P^k. Even if $T(y)$ is not a one-element of Q^k, however, the response to P^k appears at $S(y)$ if the following Condition 1 is satisfied [6].

Condition 1: For every one-element of P^k, a pair of P^l and Q^l $(l \neq k)$ exists in which the one-element is also a one-element of P^l and $T(y)$ is a one-element of Q^l, too.

Since HASP stores autocorrelation of Q^k as reduced inhibition, the crosstalk noise appeared at $S(y)$ cannot be eliminated if the following Condition 2 is satisfied.

Condition 2: For every one-element of Q^k, an item Q^l $(l \neq k)$ exists in which both of that one-element and $T(y)$ are one-elements of Q^l.

Therefore, crosstalk noise cannot be eliminated if both Conditions 1 and 2 are satisfied simultaneously.

B. Storage Capacity Evaluation

In order to evaluate the capability of crosstalk noise elimination and the storage capacity of HASP, a series of computer simulations has been performed.

Network parameters commonly used in the simulation are as follows. The time constants of $A(y)$ and R element, μ_1 and μ_2, are selected so that they correspond to ten steps and 20 steps of the time length used for numerical solutions, respectively. In order to avoid a state of mutual depression among competing items, the connecting coefficient $W(y)$ from $S(y)$ to $A(y)$ is set randomly to a value between 1.0 and 1.2. The initial strength of the recurrent inhibition WA is set to 1.5. The connecting coefficient α from M to R elements is set to 0.9. This means that the function of the M element is to weaken the competitive power of the previously selected items but not to suppress them completely. Therefore, an output element shared by several items in common can respond in the subsequent recollection process, and their complete patterns appear as outputs. Key and associated items are assumed to be two-dimensional arrays composed of 10 × 10 elements.

After the end of learning, all key items were applied one by one, and the number of recollections in which correct associated items appeared was counted. Since the correct item could not always appear at first, a sequential recollection under the control of rcs was performed until one of the following two conditions was met:

1) correct item appeared, or
2) previously recollected pattern appeared again.

The rcs was set to zero for the 300 steps of the time length used for numerical solutions and was set to 2.0 for the next 150 steps. The sequential recollection was performed by alternating these cycles, and the correctness of the response was judged at the 300th step of the off cycles.

From the results summarized in Table I, it can be concluded that if the number of one-elements is small and patterns are random, the storage capacity of HASP is more than those of associative memory models employing complicated orthogonalization procedures [8], [9]. It should be emphasized that, in addition, HASP has another crucial function, namely, the resolution of multiple-matched items as described in the next section.

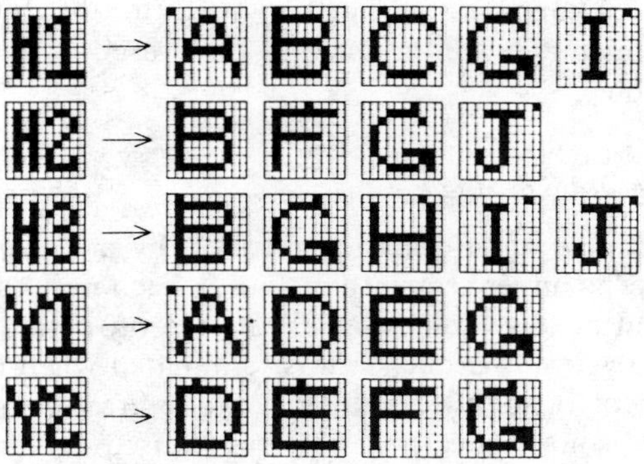

Fig. 4. Example of relation used in computer simulation.

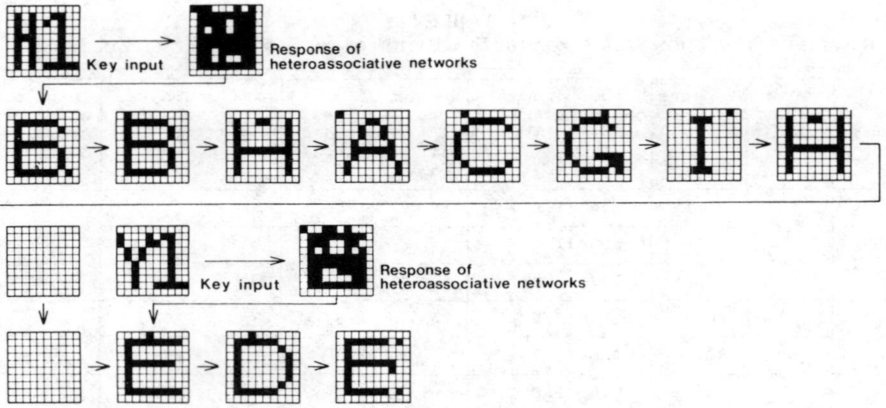

Fig. 5. Result showing information retrievals by such operations as single key (upper sequence only), OR, DIFFERENCE, and NEGATION.

V. Information Retrieval by HASP

In order to demonstrate the function of multiple-match resolution explicitly, it is shown next by simulation studies that HASP can perform set-theoretically defined key search operations. Key and associated items used in the simulation are shown in Fig. 4. This example may be interpreted as a relation between a course and students entered in it. Patterns in the leftmost column represent a set of course names, and they correspond to key items. Each arrow represents the relation "is taken by." Patterns shown on the right of the arrow represent students entered in the course, and they correspond to associated items. In order that any item can be recollected in any situation, a discrimination bit, which violates Condition 2 in the previous section, is added to the periphery of each associated pattern.

A process of retrieving information from associative memory is expressed by a function $V = R_A(k)$, where V, R_A, and k represent value, relation, and key, respectively. As shown in the example, the function is multiple-valued in general and V becomes a set of items: $\{D, E, F, G\} = R_A(Y1)$. In a computer program, a set-theoretically defined search operation such as $R_A(H1) \cap R_A(H2)$ is carried out by following all of the relevant items one by one. The results of the computer simulation show that HASP performs such an operation without following the items. It retrieves all items in a set-theoretically defined range at the same time as a superimposed pattern of them. Then the recurrent networks select them one by one under the control of rcs. The network parameters used in the following simulation studies are the same as those used in the previous section.

A. Retrieval by a Single Key

An example of information retrieval by a single key is shown in the upper sequence of Fig. 5. Each pattern shows stable and positive responses during the off-period of the rcs. The retrieving sequence was terminated when no output elements responded with magnitude greater than 0.9. Although some unlearned patterns caused by crosstalk noise appear in the sequence, all items associated with that key are retrieved. Since the retrieved item is not always the learned one, some recognition system should be responsible for the decision of whether the item is known or not. If overlappings among associated items are small, unknown patterns will not appear.

B. OR, DIFFERENCE, and NEGATION

These operations are performed by applying relevant keys one by one without resetting the M elements. In Fig. 5, another key $Y1$ preceded by a null input is applied after the end of the previous retrieval sequence. By applying a null input or activating spr, the next retrieval sequence can be started without influence from the previous response of the network.

All known items retrieved by $H1$ and $Y1$ constitute a set defined by $R_A(H1) \cup R_A(Y1)$, namely, OR. On the other hand, items retrieved by $Y1$ constitute a set defined by $R_A(Y1) - R_A(H1)$, namely, DIFFERENCE. This function is due to the M elements, which weaken the competitive power of the items retrieved before and perform the function of NEGATION.

C. AND Operation

By applying a superimposed pattern of relevant keys, only the items associated with all of those keys can be retrieved. An example is shown in Fig. 6, where a superposition of all keys is applied and only item G is retrieved. This function is due to the inhibition supplied by IK, because it suppresses the response of $S(y)$ receiving a total amount of excitation not greater than the norm of input minus the threshold of IK.

The AND operation can be formulated as follows. Let $M(\cdot)$ be an associative mapping function. A range speci-

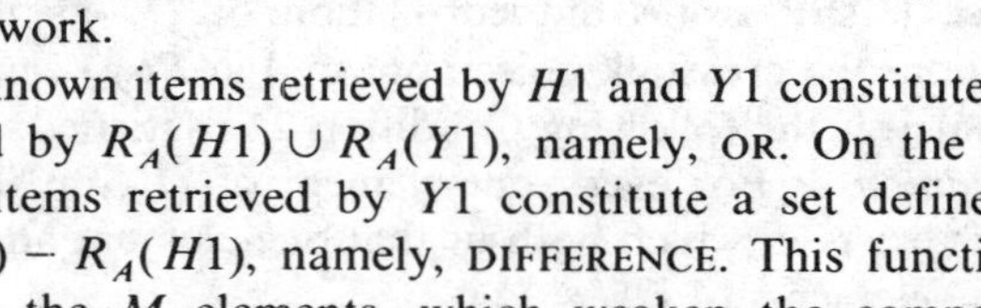

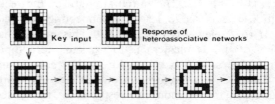

Fig. 6. Result of information retrieval by AND operation.

fied by an AND operation is expressed by $M(A) \cap M(B)$, where A and B represent associative input patterns. By virtue of the function of IK, HASP performs this operation as follows:

$$M(A) \cap M(B) = M(A \cup B), \tag{14}$$

and in general

$$\bigcap_i M(A_i) = M\Big(\bigcup_i A_i\Big), \tag{15}$$

where $A \cup B$ results in a superposition of the two patterns.

Since OR and DIFFERENCE operations are carried out sequentially, such a combination of operations as "OR's or DIFFERENCE's of AND operations" can be performed by HASP.

D. Miscellaneous Operations

By applying a part of the key pattern, all items associated with that part can be retrieved. In this case, the rest of the key becomes a "don't care" part. An example is shown in Fig. 7. Of course, the set-theoretically defined operations mentioned earlier can be performed with partial keys.

Another example of retrieval operation is shown in Fig. 8, where all key input lines are made active, but the response of IK is supposed to be suppressed by some other external signal. As seen in the result, all items stored in the network are retrieved.

VI. Possible Neural Correlate

A key structure of HASP lies in the recurrent networks with modifiable inhibitory connections, whose strength is reduced by learning. Although we have no direct evidence that this network exists in our brain, some recent neurological data [10] suggest that a functionally equivalent structure may exist in the linkage between cerebellum and cerebellar nucleus. Cells in the nucleus dentatus, which receive inhibitory inputs from Purkinje cells in the cerebellum, have been shown to return their outputs to the cerebellum as mossy fibers. Since the mossy fiber terminates to granule cells and each granule cell sends a parallel fiber to Purkinje cells with excitatory synapses, recurrent connections must exist from cerebellar nucleus to Purkunje cells. A speculative but possible structure is illustrated in Fig. 8. It should be pointed out that vast numbers of indirect recurrent loops to the cerebellar cortex exist other than the one just described.

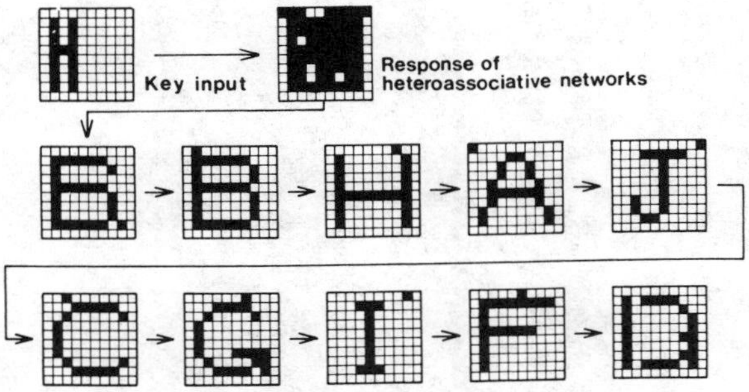

Fig. 7. Example of retrieval by partial key.

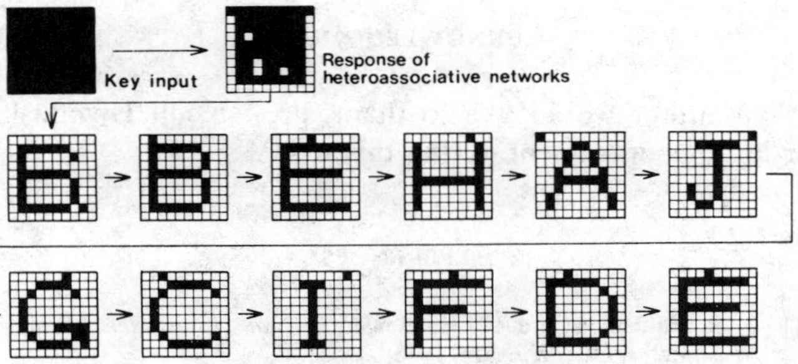

Fig. 8. Example of exhaustive readout of stored items.

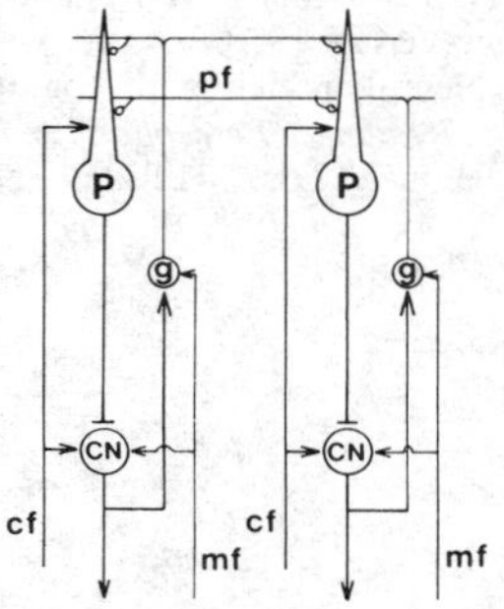

Fig. 9. Possible structure of cerebello–cerebellar nucleus linkage. cf: climbing fiber; P: Purkinje cell; CN: nucleus cell; g: granule cell; mf: mossy fiber; pf: parallel fiber. Inhibitory interneurons such as basket cells are not shown.

If cells in the cerebellar nucleus are mutually inhibited through the parallel fiber-Purkinje cell pathways as shown in the figure, the following two points are crucial.

1) Is the synapse between parallel fiber and Purkinje cell modifiable?
2) If modifiable, in which direction is the synaptic strength modified, increase or decrease?

Recently, it has been revealed [11] that the synapse is modifiable and the strength is reduced by conjunctive stimulation of parallel fiber and climbing fiber. Therefore, it is not unreasonable to assume that a functionally equivalent structure exists in our brain.

VII. Conclusion

In understanding brain functions, we should always keep in mind that our brain consists of neural networks, and what the brain can perform depends on the structure of the networks. Our memory is characterized by its associative, distributed, and content addressable structure. To represent associative brain functions in terms of such structures, a model of an associative processor named HASP is proposed, and its performance as associative memory is described.

HASP solved two critical problems in associative memory models hitherto proposed. They are crosstalk noise elimination and multiple-match resolution. The former function is necessary to avoid an explosion of crosstalk noise in such a structure as mutually linked associative networks. With the latter function, various operations can be available in retrieving information embedded in a memory with such a complicated data structure as a multilist.

Acknowledgment

The author would like to thank Prof. Kenji Hiwatashi for his encouragement during this work.

References

[1] J. R. Anderson and G. H. Bower, *Human Associative Memory*. Washington DC: Winston, 1973.

[2] N. V. Findler, Ed., *Associative Networks: Representation and Use of Knowledge by Computers*. New York: Academic, 1979

[3] T. Kohonen, *Associative Memory: A System-Theoretical Approach*. New York: Springer-Verlag, 1978.

[4] J. A. Anderson, "Neural models with cognitive implications," in *Basic Processes in Reading: Perception and Comprehension*, D. LaBerge and S. J. Samuels, Eds. Hillsdale, NJ: Erlbaum, 1977.

[5] Y. Hirai, "A template matching model for pattern recognition: Self-organization of template and template matching by a disinhibitory neural network," *Biol. Cybern.*, vol. 38, pp. 91–101, 1980.

[6] ____, "A learning network resolving multiple match in associative memory," in *Proc. 6th Int. Conf. Pattern Recognition*, 1982.

[7] G. Palm, "On associative memory," *Biol. Cybern.*, vol. 36, pp. 19–31, 1980.

[8] T. Kohonen and M. Ruohonen, "Representation of associated data by matrix operations," *IEEE Trans. Comput.*, vol. C-22, pp. 701–702, 1973.

[9] T. Kohonen and E. Oja, "Fast adaptive formation of orthogonalizing filters and associative memory in recurrent networks of neuron-like elements," *Biol. Cybern.*, vol. 21, pp. 85–95, 1976.

[10] V. Chan-Palay, *Cerebellar Dentate Nucleus: Organization, Cytology and Transmitters*. New York: Springer-Verlag, 1977.

[11] M. Ito, M. Sakurai, and P. Tongroach, "Climbing fiber induced depression of both mossy fiber responsiveness and gulutanate sensitivity of cerebellar Purkinje cells," *J. Physiol.*, vol. 324, pp. 113–134, 1982.

Reprinted from IEEE Transactions on Systems, Man, and Cybernetics 17(2), March/April 1987, pp. 326-31.

Electronic Implementation of Associative Memory Based on Neural Network Models

A. MOOPENN, JOHN LAMBE, AND A. P. THAKOOR

***Abstract*—An electronic embodiment of a neural network based associative memory in the form of a binary connection matrix is described. The nature of false memory errors, their effect on the information storage capacity of binary connection matrix memories, and a novel technique to eliminate such errors with the help of asymmetrical extra connections are discussed. The stability of the matrix memory system incorporating a unique local inhibition scheme is analyzed in terms of local minimization of an energy function. The memory's stability, dynamic behavior, and recall capability are investigated using a 32-"neuron" electronic neural network memory with a 1024-programmable binary connection matrix.**

I. Introduction

The search for new approaches to parallel computing and advanced information storage and retrieval has generated a high level of interest in neural networks. Neural networks have been studied extensively since the early influential work of McCulloch and Pitts [1] on neurons modeled as discrete decision-making elements with threshold logic output. In its simplest conception the neural network may be described as a collection of "neurons" which interact among themselves through a highly interconnected "synaptic" network. The most striking aspect of such a network is the highly distributed manner in which information is stored in it and the high degree of parallelism in which information is processed by the neurons. Current development of linear and nonlinear associative memory models [2]–[9] with modifiable synapses and McCulloch–Pitts-type neurons to describe the associative processing and self-organizing/learning properties associated with biological information processing systems has largely been stimulated by the early works of Rosenblatt [10], Widrow [11], and Steinbuch [12].

The associative recall ability and the information storage capacity of a neural network modeled as a nonlinear mapping matrix memory have been studied extensively [6], [13], [14]. Recently, Hopfield [15] hypothesized the nonlinearity and the asynchronous behavior of neurons modeled as electronic amplifiers and showed that the emergent collective properties of such an electronic neural network can serve as a basis for an associative or content-addressable memory with a unique capability to perform certain logical functions, such as pattern recognition, subject classification, and error correction. In a recent study Hopfield and Tank [16], [17] have examined some of the compu-

Manuscript received April 20, 1986; revised November 15, 1986. This work was supported in part by the Defense Advanced Research Projects Agency through an agreement with the National Aeronautics and Space Administration.

The authors are with the Jet Propulsion Laboratory, California Institute of Technology, MS 122-123, 4800 Oak Grove Drive, Pasadena, CA 91109, USA.

IEEE Log Number 8613028:

tational abilities of Hopfield's neural network model to solve a class of optimization problems, for example, the shortest path search for a traveling salesman.

In an electronic embodiment of an artificial neural network system the neurons correspond to thresholding nonlinear amplifiers, while the synapses become simple resistive feedback elements. Information is stored nonlocally in the resistive feedback network based on a distributive algorithm. The memory elements of the network are only passive two terminal resistors and can be extremely small (submicron) in size. Since such a resistive matrix could be fabricated in a thin-film form, an electronic associative memory based on such an architecture offers a potential of very high storage density (approaching $\sim 10^9$ bits/cm^2). The operational principles of an electronic neural network, its information storage capacity, error rate, and electronic device aspects for a hardware realization are discussed elsewhere [18], [19].

In this correspondence we describe an electronic implementation of a Hebbian-type neural network taking the form of a binary connection matrix with special emphasis on error correction to obtain a virtually error-free memory. In Section II, the binary matrix memory concepts are reviewed and a local form of inhibition scheme for dilute coding is described. The nature of false memory errors, their effect on information storage capacity, and an error-correction scheme for suppression of the false memories are discussed in Section III. In Section IV, an electronic embodiment of a binary connection matrix memory system is described and the stability of the memory system incorporating local inhibition is discussed in terms of an energy function. In Section V, a hardware realization of a programmable 1024 node (32 × 32) binary connection matrix memory is described and its "error-corrected" recall capability is discussed.

II. Binary Matrix Memory Concepts and Local Inhibition

The input and output information to and from the binary matrix memory may be represented in the form of binary vectors or words. Consider the set of R binary vectors $\{U^s, s = 1,\cdots, R\}$ of dimension N, with the ith component $U_i = 0$ or 1, for $i = 1,\cdots, N$. Suppose that each vector U^s is to be associated with or "mapped" to another binary vector V^s. Then this set of pair associations or mappings constitutes the information to be stored in the memory so that presenting the vector U^s to the memory input would evoke the output vector V^s. The mapping information is stored nonlocally in the form of an $N \times N$ "connection matrix" T with the connection strength T_{ij} taking on the value of 0 or 1. In a general sense, the storage prescription is a simplified construct of the Hebbian learning rule [20]; specifically, the binary matrix which will give the desired memory behavior is described [18] in terms of the sums of outer products and is given by the following algorithm:

$$T_{ij} = \begin{cases} 1, & \text{if } \sum_{s=1}^{R} V_i^s U_j^s > 0 \\ 0, & \text{otherwise} \end{cases} \tag{1}$$

Suppose U^t is the input vector to the memory; then the memory output is given by the matrix-vector product

$$V_i = \sum_{j=1}^{N} T_{ij} V_j^t \sim M V_i^t + f_i(V^t) \tag{2}$$

where M is the vector strength of U^t, i.e., the number of "ones" in the binary vector U^t, and f_i is the difference between $\Sigma T_{ij} U_j^t$ and MV_i^t. The first and second terms correspond to the memory output "signal" and "noise," respectively. The noise term arises from the mutual interference of the vectors. In particular, the level of interference is basically determined by the degree of overlap in Hamming space between the vectors. Provided the overlap between the vectors is not too severe, the magnitude of the noise term will generally be less than M. If the memory output is now thresholded at M, the correct association is obtained, i.e.,

$$V_i^t = \theta_M(V_i)$$

where θ_M is the step function

$$\theta_M(x) = \begin{cases} 1, & \text{if } x \geq M \\ 0, & \text{if } x < M \end{cases}.$$

However, if the noise term exceeds the threshold level, spurious ones will appear in the output vector, giving a retrieval error. The magnitude of the noise term can be reduced, in a statistical sense, by limiting the number of associated vector pairs to be memorized into the memory and/or by using dilute coding, in which case the input and output vectors are precoded binary vectors with $M \ll N$.

Two types of vector mappings exist that are of particular interest. First consider the case when an output vector (say V^s) is also treated as the next input vector (i.e., $V^s = U^{s+1}$) in a sequence. The memory then exhibits the interesting property that when an output is latched and fed back to the input, the next output word is delivered. By repeating the feedback process, the complete ordered sequence of vectors or words (a paragraph of a text or steps of a computer program) stored in the memory can be read out. This is referred to as the serial-associative mode of operation, or simply, the "tape recorder mode."

If, on the other hand, the input vector is mapped onto itself, i.e., $V^s = U^s$, then the memory functions in a self-addressing or auto-associative mode. A distinctive property of the matrix memory operating in this mode is that the connection pattern is always symmetrical about the matrix diagonal, i.e., $T_{ij} = T_{ji}$. Moreover, the memory can be viewed as a "pseudo-eigensystem" in a mathematical sense in that $(\theta_M T)V^s = V^s$, where T is the T_{ij} matrix. To be useful, the memory must operate in the "recurrent feedback" configuration so that given an input cue the memory would self-adjust and converge in an asynchronous manner to a stored vector compatible with the cue. A matrix memory operating in the auto-associative mode thus functions as a content-addressable memory.

It has been shown in the early works of Willshaw *et al.* [6], Willshaw [13], and the more recent work of Palm [14] that by limiting the vector strength of the input–output binary vectors to a small fraction of N, the retrieval error rate of binary matrix memories can be reduced significantly. Moreover, at the optimum vector strength $M_{\text{opt}} = \log_2 N$, the amount of information that can be retrieved from an $N \times N$ binary matrix memory in the limit of very large N approaches ($N^2 \times \ln 2$) bits or ~ 69 percent of the theoretical maximum possible in the case of a nonsymmetric binary matrix memory, and ($0.5\ N^2 \times \ln 2$) bits or ~ 35 percent for an auto-associative binary matrix memory. These results clearly confirm the need for dilute vector coding for optimal storage capacity and accurate retrieval.

In the following we consider one form of dilute coding which has a special property that the retrieval errors due to the appearance of spurious ones are intrinsically suppressed in an auto-associative binary matrix memory. This coding scheme is based on the idea of local inhibition which dictates that when one component of a binary vector takes the value one, some of the other components of the vector must take the value zero. One simple form of local inhibition consists of decomposing the vector into a certain number of groups in which only one component of each group has the value one. If all the input vectors are coded in this form, they would have the same vector strength equaling the number of groups. Let $V_{a,i}$ denote the ith component belonging to group a of a binary vector of vector strength M where $a = 1,\cdots, M$, $i = 1,\cdots, N_a$, and where N_a is the number of components in group a. For simplicity, we assume that each group has the same number of components, i.e., $N_a = N/M$. If R such vectors are stored, the connection matrix is then given by

$$T_{ai,bj} = \theta\left(\sum_{s=1}^{R} V_{ai}^s, V_{bj}^s\right). \tag{3}$$

The memory matrix T may be considered to consist of M^2 submatrices or blocks $T_{a,b}$ each with $N_a N_b$ or $(N/M)^2$ elements. Note particularly that with local inhibition, no off-diagonal connections exist in the diagonal blocks, i.e., $T_{ai,aj}$ is always zero for $i \neq j$. Consequently, this property of the diagonal blocks ensures that the noise term $f_i(U^t)$ in (2) is always less than M. The information content of a binary vector prescribing to this form of dilute coding is then $I_w = M \log_2 (N/M)$ bits. This may be compared with the information content of a general binary vector of length N and fixed strength M, given by $I'_w = \log_2 \binom{N}{M}$ bits, where $\binom{N}{M}$ is the combinatorial function. Evidently, $I_w/I'_w < 1$; however, for $M \ll N$, the ratio approaches $1 - (\log M/\log N) \cong 1$ in the limit of very large N. For example, for $N = 1000$ and $M = 10$, $I_w/I'_w = 0.8$. Although the use of local inhibition leads to a slight reduction in the information content per vector, this is more than compensated not only by the elimination of spurious ones but also by the ease with which information may be encoded in a dilute binary form.

III. False Memories

The information storage capacity of a binary matrix memory incorporating a local inhibition is still limited by another type of retrieval errors, namely, the appearance of false memories. These memories, like the spurious ones appearing in a distorted memory, arise as a result of the overlap among the originally prescribed vectors and correspond to all the other binary vectors V^f which satisfy $(\theta_M T)V^f = V^f(V^f \neq V^s)$. The false memories have the interesting property that for a given (ai, bi), $V_{ai}^f V_{bj}^f \neq 0$ always implies the existence of a stored vector V^s for which $V_{ai}^s V_{bj}^s \neq 0$. In a general sense, if the memory matrix is considered as a logic machine, the false memories may have a more important role as a set of additional logical statements which are consistent with the originally prescribed statements. However, as a content-addressable memory, the false memories must be considered spurious and should be suppressed.

To understand the effect of false memories on the storage capacity of a binary matrix memory, the dependence of the number of false memories F on the memory loading is examined. The memory loading is defined here to be $(R \times I_w/N^2)$ where R is the number of words stored. Fig. 1 shows the mean relative number of false memories (F/R) in the case of $N \cong 126$ for the vector strengths $M = 5$, 7, and 14. These false memory statistics were obtained from an optimized computer search program which identified all false memories generated when a set of random binary vectors was stored in the matrix memory. The rapid (nearly exponential) increase in the mean fraction of false memories with memory loading is evident, the rate of increase becoming much greater for the vector strength significantly larger than $M_{opt} = 7$. Moreover, at the optimum vector strength the false memories become quite appreciable $(F/R \gtrsim 0.1)$ for the memory loadings greater than 0.15. However, the false memory statistics tend to improve the increasing vector length N. This is seen in Fig. 2, which shows similar plots for $N = 126$, 256, and 513, with the vector strength near the optimum value in each case. When the false memories comprise a small fraction (< 0.10) of the number of stored vectors, their Hamming distance (defined as the number of different bits between two binary vectors), to a nearby stored vector is no more than two Hamming units. If one assumes that all false memories are of this nature, i.e., single-bit errors, the number of such errors may be calculated to a good approximation by taking into account the lowest order correlation due to two-component overlap between the prescribed memories. Details of the calculation are given in Appendix I; results

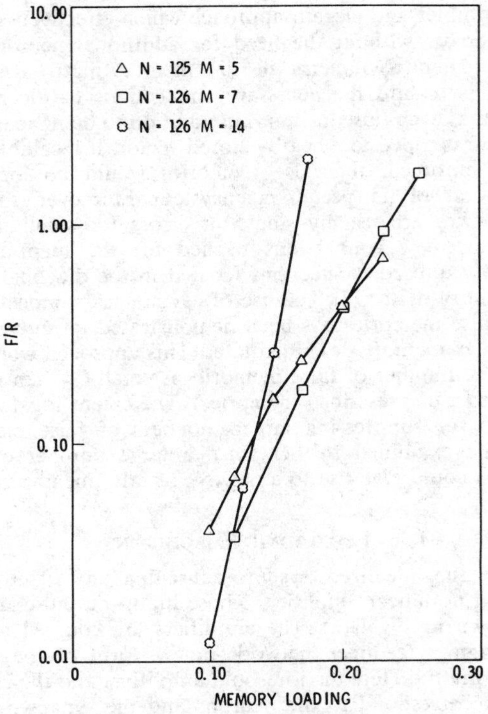

Fig. 1. False memory error rate curves for $N \cong 126$.

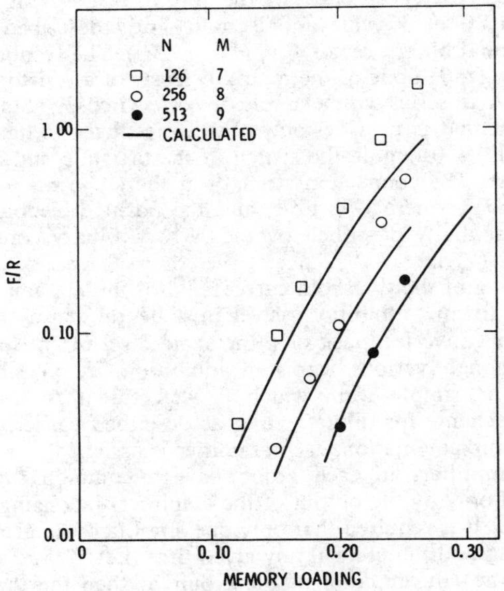

Fig. 2. False memory error rate curves for $N = 126, 256, 513$.

of the calculation are shown in Fig. 2. The observed and calculated number of false memories are in reasonable agreement for small memory loading. However, the smaller calculated number of false memories as compared to the statistical result, particularly for smaller N, is attributed to the assumption of single-bit error and the neglect of higher order correlation.

It is generally possible to suppress false memories using the dynamic error-correction algorithm of Widrow and Hoff [21]. However, the binary connection requirement and the nonlinearity of the memory system limit the applicability of the Widrow–Hoff method. Alternatively, an additional binary error correction matrix [19] can also suppress false memory errors but only with the help of an extra neuron (an active component) for each of these errors. A simpler and elegant approach which effectively corrects single-bit errors without the need for additional neurons is to introduce a slight asymmetry into the memory matrix itself. The basic idea is to add the necessary connections to the memory matrix so that each false memory, in addition to being mapped to itself, is also mapped to a nearby stored vector. If local inhibition is strictly enforced, the false memories would no longer be "eigenvectors" of the pseudo-eigensystem. Moreover, since the false memories are usually single-bit errors for small memory loadings, the new connections needed for the mappings are among those unused connections located in the diagonal blocks of the memory matrix T. The use of asymmetric connections to suppress false memories has been demonstrated in an electronic binary matrix memory described later. This approach works well provided the number of false memories is small (< ten percent of the number of prescribed memories). The extent to which it is well suited for suppressing larger numbers of false memories needs to be examined further since a large number of extra connections could give rise to a new set of false memories.

IV. Electronic Embodiment

Consider the idealized system consisting of a set of N thresholding nonlinear amplifiers whose input–output characteristic is shown in Fig. 3(a). The amplifiers are coupled to each other through a feedback network in the form of the binary connection matrix. Here the threshold amplifiers and the connection matrix correspond to the neurons and the synapses of the neural network, respectively. Fig. 3(b) shows a schematic representation of the electronic network system of N neurons. The state of the system is specified by the outputs of the N amplifiers having only 0 or 1 value and is more aptly described by an N-dimensional binary vector $V = (V_1, \cdots, V_n)$. The feedback element at the (i, j) node of the matrix consists of a resistor with a resistance R in series with a simple on/off switch T_{ij}. Since R is positive, the matrix provides only positive feedback to the amplifiers. Let $T_{ij} = 0$ denote the switch in the off state and $T_{ij} = 1$ the on state. The connection strength at the (i, j) node is then given by GT_{ij}, where $G = 1/R$, and the positive feedback network is essentially described by the $N \times N$ binary connection matrix $T = (T_{ij})$.

The setting of the threshold current I^{Th} of the ith amplifier is equivalent to an "inhibition" level in a neural sense and is a source of negative feedback or a threshold level in an electronic sense. Although various forms of inhibition are possible, we consider one simple form which is well suited to the local inhibition scheme for dilute coding as described earlier. In our electronic implementation, each amplifier is assigned to a group, and the amplifiers in each group have a common threshold determined only by the output of the amplifiers belonging to the same group. It is required that only one amplifier in a group can be in the high-output state at any given time. Let $V_{a,i}$ denote the output of the ith amplifier of the group a; then the threshold level is given by

$$I_{a,i}^{\mathrm{Th}} = I_a^{\mathrm{Th}} = B \sum_{i=1}^{N_a} V_{a,i} \tag{4}$$

where $a = 1, \cdots, M$; M is the number of groups, N_a is the number of amplifiers in group a, and B is an adjustable parameter.

For an appropriate choice of the connection matrix T, the interaction of the amplifiers through the positive feedback from the connection matrix, the negative feedback from the inhibition circuit, and the asynchronous updating of the amplifier outputs lead to a set of "stable states" of the system. Suppose the system is set to some initial state by an application of external input currents $I_{a,i}$ to the inputs of the amplifiers. The time evolution

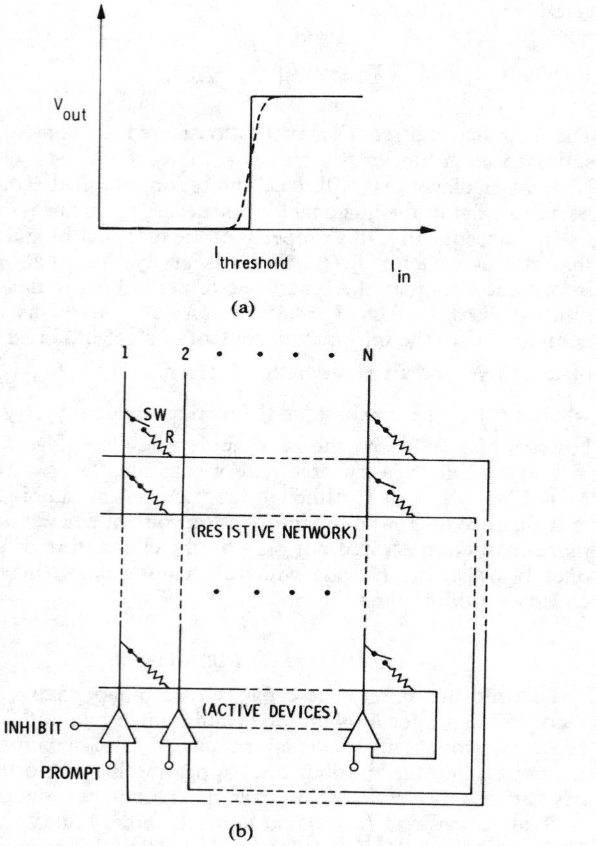

Fig. 3. (a) Input/output characteristics of neuron: (—) ideal and (- - -) nonideal (practical). (b) Schematic representation of $N \times N$ matrix memory.

of the system is then described by the following set of equations:

$$V_{a,i}(t + \Delta t) = \begin{cases} 1, & \text{if } \sum_{b=1}^{M} \sum_{j=1}^{N_b} T_{ai,bj} V_{b,j}(t) \\ & \quad - I_a^{\mathrm{Th}}(t) + I_{a,i}(t) \geq 0 \\ 0, & \text{otherwise} \end{cases}$$

where $I_{a,i}(t)$ is the external input current to the a, i amplifier. Upon removal of the external currents the system would "converge" to a stable state most compatible with (or "nearest" in Hamming distance to) the initial state. Thus information, when represented as binary vectors, may be "stored" in the system as prescribed stable states and evoked or retrieved as distinct stable states from appropriate memory cues.

Let V^s, $s = 1, \cdots, R$, be a set of R binary vectors which is to form the memories of the system. The connection matrix T which would render these vectors as stable states of the system is described by the storage algorithm given in (1) or (3). Using the concept of the energy function [15], we next examine the stability of the prescribed states of a binary matrix system with the positive feedback matrix given by (3) and an inhibition term described by (4). In Hopfield's theoretical study [16] of the collective behavior of the neural network system, he showed that for a symmetric network ($T_{ij} = T_{ji}$) the system always converges to a stable state. Moreover, an energy function for such a system can be defined in which stable states correspond to local energy minima. In its general form the energy function is described by

$$E = -1/2 \sum_{i=1}^{N} \sum_{j=1}^{N} T_{ij} V_i V_j - \sum_{i=1}^{N} V_i I_i \tag{5}$$

where I_i denotes the external current input to the ith amplifier

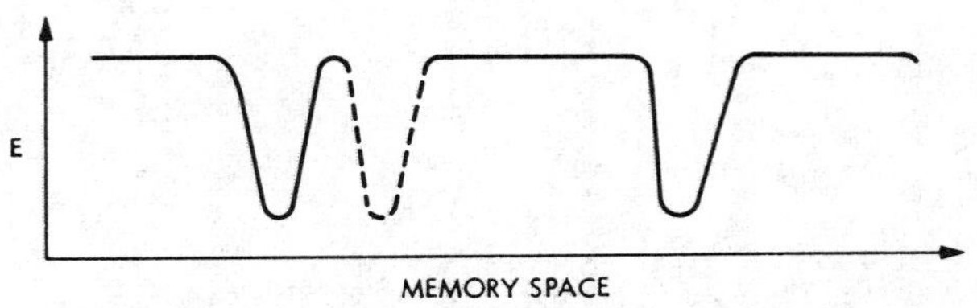

Fig. 4. Schematic representation of energy surface with local energy minima.

and T_{ij} is real and corresponds to the connection strength at the (i, j) node of a symmetric connection matrix T.

From (5) an energy function for a binary connection matrix system incorporating local inhibition may be constructed. Using the storage algorithm given by (3) to construct the connection matrix, it can be shown that prescribed states always correspond to the local energy minima of the energy function (see Appendix II).

The energy function may be interpreted geometrically as describing an energy surface with energy minima or wells of equal depth located at the corners of an N-dimensional hypercube defined by $V_i = 0$ or 1. These wells generally correspond to the stable states of the prescribed memories. This is shown schematically in Fig. 4. In addition, the spurious (satellite) minima of the same depth (shown as dashed wells in Fig. 4) correspond to the stable states of the false memories. As described in Section III, two approaches exist to suppressing the false memories in a binary connection matrix memory, by means of an error-correction matrix and the use of asymmetric connections. The addition of an error-correction matrix is equivalent to introducing a positive energy term to the energy function. This energy term in effect raises the energy of the satellite minima so that the false memories would no longer be energetically favorable. On the other hand, the addition of asymmetric connections to the T matrix does not alter the depth of the spurious energy wells but introduces slight distortions to the energy surface in the vicinity of the spurious and nearby energy wells so that the memory system tends to "move" away from such satellite minima toward the nearby local minima of the prescribed memories.

V. Electronic Hardware Implementation

To gain insight into how well a binary matrix system would function as a content-addressable memory, the dynamics and convergent behavior of the system were examined in this electronic implementation of a programmable binary matrix. The focus was on the recall capability, in terms of the system's ability to respond to incomplete and/or incorrect memory cues, and the memory retrieval time. The programmable binary connection matrix memory system was constructed from off-the-shelf electronic components.

The binary connection matrix consisted of a 32 × 32 array of CMOS (complementary metal oxide semiconductor) analog switches each in series with a positive-feedback resistor. The positive feedback resistance of 10^6 Ω was found to provide the appropriate signal level for interfacing to the threshold amplifiers. The high resistance clearly indicates that the connection strength in the "on" state can be very "weak." It is also worth noting that the use of weak connections (10^6 Ω) becomes necessary as a means for reducing the operating power level when the connection matrix increases in size (to ~ 1000 × 1000) and density (~ 10^8 connections/cm^2). The switches in the connection matrix were controlled by the parallel outputs of the serial-in shift registers connected in cascade. Programming of the switches (i.e., T_{ij}) was accomplished by sending a serial stream of the appropriate data bits to the shift registers from a minicomputer which was also used for memory cueing and readout. Each of the threshold amplifiers consisted of a current summing amplifier followed by a voltage comparator. A small inhibit offset was added to the inhibition signal so that the state with all $V_i = 0$, the "null" state, also became a stable state of the system.

The stability of the system was observed under the full dynamic threshold feedback conditions and local inhibition. A set of randomly generated binary vectors with length $N = 32$ and fixed vector strength was stored into the programmable connection matrix according to the storage algorithm given by (3). The system indeed exhibited the preselected stable states. When a memory prompt, which corresponded to one of the stored states, was applied to the external inputs of the amplifiers, the system converged and remained in that state when the prompt was removed. When the overlap between prescribed states was severe and/or the number of prescribed states became large, new stable states corresponding to induced or false memories appeared in the system.

As discussed in Section III, these false states could be "destabilized" by incorporating asymmetric connections to the binary matrix. Fig. 5 shows an example of false-state destabilization as demonstrated in the programmable 32 × 32 matrix memory system. The prescribed vectors assumed a specific form which was compatible with the local inhibition scheme. Each vector, of vector strength four, is described by four numbers, each specifying which of the eight components in a group takes the value 1. One such set of randomly chosen vectors and the corresponding T matrix are shown in Fig. 5(a) and Fig. 5(b), respectively. There are two false memories: (4118) and (4158). These were mapped to the prescribed vectors (4116) and (5158), respectively, according to (1). The new connection matrix which incorporates the additional mappings differs from the original matrix by the appearance of two new connections, one in the $T_{1,1}$ diagonal block resulting from the (4118) → (4116) mapping, and another in the $T_{4,4}$ block from the (4158) → (5158) mapping. Destabilization of the false memories was examined by applying various prompts to the memory system and observing the system's final state when the prompt was removed. False memories never appeared as final stable states. In fact, when a false memory was evoked as an intermediate state, it always converged to the prescribed memory it was mapped to upon the removal of the prompt.

The convergent properties of the binary connection matrix system were also investigated with the programmable 32 × 32 matrix hardware. The convergent behavior is best described by the mean radius of convergence, as it provides a quantitative measure of how "close" to a memory the initial system state needs to be for the system to converge to that memory. In a geometric sense, each memory word has a "region of attraction" in the Hamming space. The convergent behavior is examined by observing the system response to partial prompts and incorrect prompts. The prescribed states used in the convergence study are also of the form described earlier.

The convergence statistics of the 32 × 32 matrix system under local inhibition for various types of prompt conditions are summarized in Table I. The data were obtained with the inhibit gain and offset adjusted for maximum convergence. The memory prompts used also conformed to the format described earlier, i.e., no more than one amplifier in each group was driven to the high-output state from the external inputs. The various prompt conditions were distinguished according to the number of correctly and incorrectly driven amplifiers relative to the closest memory or memories in the sense of Hamming distance. For example, entry (1,2) in Table I shows the case for which the distance between the prompt and a nearest memory was three Hamming units away. Of the three amplifiers that were driven into the high-output state, only two of the high outputs correspond to those of the nearest memory. In this case the relative frequency of convergence to the nearest memory upon the removal of the prompt was 0.95. From Table I the relative frequency of convergence as a function of the minimum Hamming distance between the input prompt and a prescribed memory was obtained and is shown in Fig. 6. The mean radius of convergence R_c may be defined as the "area" under the frequency of conver-

STORED VECTORS:

    (1455),(4116),(3336),

    (2234),(8764),(4252),

    (7542),(4618),(5158),

    (7115),(3784),(6642)

INDUCED VECTORS:

    (4118),(4158)

VECTOR MAPPINGS:

    (4118)-->(4116)

    (4158)-->(5158)

(a)

(b)

Fig. 5. Destabilization of false memories using asymmetric connections. (a) List of prescribed and induced vectors. (b) Corresponding memory matrix. New asymmetric connections are denoted by "X".

TABLE I

MEAN RELATIVE FREQUENCY OF CONVERGENCE TO A NEAREST MEMORY UNDER VARIOUS PROMPT CONDITIONS

Number of Incorrectly Driven Amplifiers	Number of Correctly Driven Amplifiers				
	0	1	2	3	4
0	—	1.00	0.96	1.00	1.00
1	0.00	0.96	0.95	1.00	—
2	0.00	0.03	0.14	—	—
3	0.00	0.00	—	—	—
4	0.00	—	—	—	—

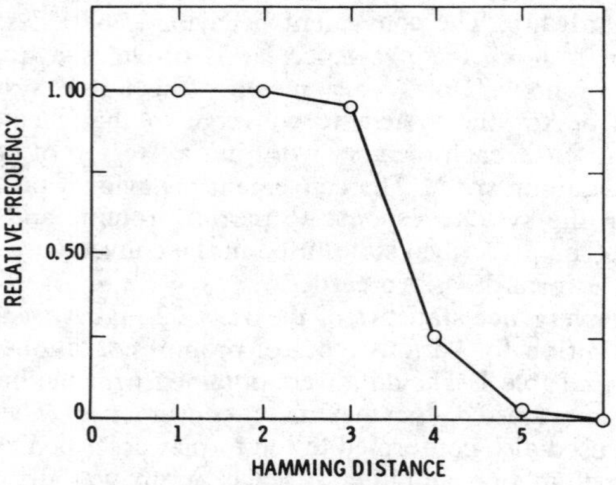

Fig. 6. Relative frequency of convergence versus Hamming distance between prompt and its nearest memory.

gence curve, in which case a value of 3.1 is obtained. Convergence statistics for several different sets of random memories were similarly obtained, and the R_c was observed to vary by less than ten percent from the foregoing value.

The system has the capability to discriminate against prompts with "excessive noise." From Table I it is seen that the system generally converged to the zero or null (i.e., "don't know") state when a poor match existed between a prompt and its nearest memories. When the system converged to a memory, it was always the same memory for a given prompt. When the prompt with some incorrectly driven amplifier was "ambiguous," i.e., it was equally distant to more than one memory, the system generally converged to one of the nearest memories. Moreover, when the prompt was fully ambiguous, i.e., no incorrectly driven amplifiers, the system always converged to one of the nearest memories. The system preference of one memory over others for ambiguous prompts was largely attributed to the slight variation in component characteristics and parasitic capacitance in the system's electronic circuitry.

The system converged to a memory in a single cycle without exhibiting any erratic wandering or oscillatory behavior. The cycle time for the 32×32 system with local inhibition was approximately 15 μs. The cycle time was insensitive to the Hamming distance between the prompt and the memory to which the system converged, but was primarily limited by the stray capacitance in the system and the speed of the threshold amplifiers.

VI. SUMMARY

In this correspondence we have described an electronic embodiment of a neural network model in which the synaptic network takes the form of a binary connection matrix. The associative recall properties of the binary matrix memory based on the outer-product storage algorithm have been examined. Memory retrieval errors corresponding to the appearance of extra ones in the memory output vectors were intrinsically eliminated by using a simple form of local inhibition for dilute vector coding in the auto-associative mode. Another type of retrieval errors, namely, the appearance of false memories, however, imposed a fundamental limitation on the information storage capacity of a binary connection memory. A near exponential growth in the number of false memories with memory loading was observed in a computer simulation study. However, for small memory loading (≤ 25 percent), the number of false memories was significantly reduced to a small fraction ($\leq$ ten percent) of the prescribed memories. The use of asymmetric connections to map false memories to nearby prescribed memories has been successfully implemented as a means for suppressing false memories without the need for an error-correction matrix.

The stability, dynamic behavior, and the convergent properties of binary connection matrix memories were investigated in an electronic hardware using a programmable 32×32 binary switch matrix memory system. The hardware system, with full dynamic feedback and local inhibition, has indeed demonstrated stability in accordance with the energy function formalism. In addition, the 32×32 system exhibited a high degree of content addressability, fault tolerance, as well as fast recall capability.

Appendix I

In this Appendix the number of false memories is calculated on the basis of the single-bit error approximation. In this approximation it is assumed that the false memories are single-bit errors; i.e., each false memory is two Hamming units away from a prescribed memory. This is a reasonable assumption provided the number of false memories is small compared to the number of prescribed memories.

In calculating the mean number of single-bit errors, first we ignore explicitly any overlap between the prescribed memories and determine directly from the connection density and probable number of single-bit errors arising from each prescribed memory. The density of ones in the off-diagonal blocks of the T matrix is given by

$$\rho = 1 - \left[1 - (M/N)^2\right]^R \cong 1 - \exp\left(RM^2/N^2\right)$$

so that the probability of a single-bit error is ρ^{M-1}. For each prescribed memory, $N - M$ ways exist for the error to occur; thus the total mean number of uncorrelated errors for R prescribed memories is $F_1 = R(N - M)_\rho^{M-1}$.

Next we calculate the number of correlated single-bit errors, taking into account explicitly the overlapping of the prescribed memories. For small memory loading the correlated errors are primarily due to single pair overlaps, i.e., two prescribed memories having two ones in common. The probability that such an overlap would generate a single-bit error is now $2(M-2)\rho^{M-3}$. The mean number of single pair overlaps is approximately given by

$$1/2(\rho' - \rho)\left[N^2(1 - 1/M)\right]$$

where $\rho' = RM^2/N^2$ is the connection density if no pair overlaps were among the prescribed memories. The quantity $(\rho' - \rho)/2$ is approximately equal to the density of pair overlaps, and the quantity in the square bracket is the number of connections available in the off-diagonal blocks. Thus the mean number of single-bit errors due to single pair-overlaps becomes

$$F_2 = (\rho' - \rho)\left[N^2(1 - 1/M)\right](M - 2)\rho^{M-3}.$$

One can similarly calculate higher order correlated single-bit errors due to triple-overlaps, quadruple-overlaps, etc. However, for small memory loading these higher order contributions may be neglected, and the mean number of single-bit errors may simply be taken to be $F \cong F_1 + F_2$.

Appendix II

In the following an energy function for a binary matrix memory with local inhibition is constructed. The prescribed states are then shown to always correspond to the local energy minima of the energy function.

From (3)–(5) the general form of the energy function for an $N \times N$ connection matrix memory with local inhibition becomes

$$E = -1/2 \sum_{a=1}^{M} \sum_{i=1}^{N_a} \sum_{b=1}^{M} \sum_{j=1}^{N_b} T_{ai,bj} V_{ai} V_{bj} - \sum_{a=1}^{M} \sum_{i=1}^{N_a} V_{ai} I_{ai}.$$

Let $I_{ai} \rightarrow I_{ai} + I_a^{\mathrm{Th}}$ where I_a^{Th} is given by (2). The energy function then becomes

$$E = -1/2 \sum_{a=1}^{M} \sum_{i=1}^{N_a} \sum_{b=1}^{M} \sum_{j=1}^{N_b} \left(T_{ai,bj} - B\delta_{a,b}\right) V_{ai} V_{bj} - \sum_{a=1}^{M} \sum_{i=1}^{N_a} V_{ai} I_{ai}$$

where

$$\delta_{a,b} = \begin{cases} 1, & \text{if } a = b, \\ 0, & \text{otherwise.} \end{cases}$$

Thus by comparing with (5), it is seen that a binary connection matrix system with local inhibition is equivalent to a nonbinary connection matrix system with positive and negative connection strengths given by $T'_{ai,bj} = T_{ai,bj} - B\delta_{a,b}$.

Suppose the state of the system corresponds to one of the prescribed states, i.e., $V_{a,i} = V_{a,i}^s$, with M amplifiers in the high-output state. The change in the energy function when $V_{ck} = V_{ck}^s = 0 \rightarrow 1$ is

$$\Delta E_{ck} = -\sum_{a=1}^{M} \sum_{i=1}^{N_a} \left(T_{ck,ai} - B\delta_{a,c}\right) V_{a,i}^s - 1/2\left(T_{ck,ck} - B\right).$$

If $B = M - \epsilon$, where ϵ is a small positive number,

$$\Delta E_{ck} = -\sum_{a=1}^{M} \sum_{i=1}^{N_a} T_{ck,ai} V_{ai}^s + 3M/2.$$

Since

$$\sum_{a=1}^{M} \sum_{i=1}^{N_a} T_{ck,ai} V_{ai}^s \leqslant M,$$

$$\Delta E_{ck} \sim M/2 > 0.$$

When $V_{ck} = V_{ck}^s = 1$ goes to zero, it can similarly be shown that $\Delta E_{ck} \sim M/2 > 0$. In the local inhibition scheme, the prescribed states always correspond to local minima and thus never appear as distorted stable states or memories.

Acknowledgment

The authors wish to thank Prof. J. Hopfield for many useful and interesting discussions.

References

[1] W. S. McCulloch and W. H. Pitts, "A logical calculus of ideas immanent in nervous activity," *Bull. Math. Biophys.*, vol. 5, pp. 115–133, 1943.

[2] S. I. Amari, "Neural theory association and concept-formation," *Biol. Cybern.*, vol. 26, pp. 175–185, 1977.

[3] T. Kohonen *et al.*, "A principle of neural associative memory," *Neurosci.*, vol. 2, pp. 1065–1076, 1977.

[4] K. Nakano, "Association—A model of associative memory," *IEEE Trans. Syst., Man, Cybern.*, vol. SMC-2, pp. 380–388, 1972.

[5] J. A. Anderson, J. W. Silverstein, S. A. Ritz, and R. S. Jones, "Distinctive features, categorical perceptions, and probability learning: Some application of a neural model," *Psych. Rev.*, vol. 84, pp. 413–451, 1977.

[6] D. J. Willshaw, O. P. Buneman, and H. C. Longuet-Higgins, "Non-holographic associative memory," *Nature*, vol. 222, pp. 960–962, 1969.

[7] J. A. Anderson and G. E. Hinton, Eds., *Parallel Models of Associative Memory*. Hillsdale, NJ: Erlbaum, 1981.

[8] T. Kohonen, *Self-Organization and Associative Memory*. Berlin: Springer-Verlag, 1984.

[9] A. C. Sanderson and Y. Y. Zeevi, Eds., "Special issue on neural and sensory information processing," *IEEE Trans. Syst., Man, Cybern.*, vol. SMC-13, 1983.

[10] F. Rosenblatt, *Principles of Neurodynamics*. Washington, DC: Spartan, 1961.

[11] B. Widrow, "Generalization and information storage in networks of adaline neurons," in *Self-Organizing Systems*, M. C. Yovits, G. T. Jacobi, and G. D. Goldstein, Eds. Washington, DC: Spartan, 1962, p. 435.

[12] K. Steinbuch and U. A. W. Piske, "Learning matrices and their applications," *IEEE Trans. Electron. Comput.*, vol. 12, p. 846, 1963.

[13] D. J. Willshaw, "Models of distributed associative memory," Thesis, Univ. Edinburgh, 1971.

[14] G. Palm, "On associative memory," *Biol. Cybern.*, vol. 36, pp. 19–31, 1980.

[15] J. J. Hopfield, "Neural networks and physical systems with emergent collective computational abilities," *Proc. Nat. Acad. Sci.*, vol. 79, pp. 2554–2558, 1982.

[16] J. J. Hopfield and D. W. Tank, "Neural computation of decision in optimization problems," *Biol. Cybern.*, vol. 52, pp. 141–152, 1985.

[17] D. W. Tank and J. J. Hopfield, "Simple neural optimization networks: An A/D converter, signal decision circuit, and a linear programming circuit," *IEEE Trans. Circuits Syst.*, vol. CAS-33, pp. 533–541, 1986.

[18] J. Lambe, A. Moopenn, and A. Thakoor, "Electronic device aspects of neural network memories," in *Proc. AIAA/ACM/NASA/IEEE Computers in Aerospace V Conf.*, 1985, pp. 160–165.

[19] J. Lambe, A. Thakoor, and A. Moopenn, "Content-addressable, high-density memories based on neural network models," Jet Propulsion Laboratory, Pasadena, CA, Tech. Rep. JPL (internal document) D-2875, Nov. 1985.

[20] D. O. Hebb, *Organization of Behavior*. New York: Wiley, 1949.

[21] B. Widrow and M. E. Hoff, "Adaptive switching circuit," in *1960 WESCON Conv. Rec.*, Part IV, 1960, pp. 96–104.

Reprinted from IEEE Transactions on Systems, Man, and Cybernetics 13(5), September/October 1983, pp. 826-34.

Neocognitron: A Neural Network Model for a Mechanism of Visual Pattern Recognition

KUNIHIKO FUKUSHIMA, SEI MIYAKE, AND TAKAYUKI ITO

Abstract—**A neural network model, called a "neocognitron," for a mechanism of visual pattern recognition was proposed earlier, and the result of computer simulation for a small-scale network was shown. A neocognitron with a larger-scale network is now simulated on a digital computer and is shown to have a great capability for visual pattern recognition: The neocognitron's ability to recognize handwritten Arabic numerals, even with considerable deformations in shape, is demonstrated. The neocognitron is a multilayered network consisting of a cascaded connection of many layers of cells. The information of the stimulus pattern given to the input layer is processed step by step in each stage of the multilayered network. A cell in a deeper layer generally has a tendency to respond selectively to a more complicated feature of the stimulus patterns and, at the same time, has a larger receptive field and is less sensitive to shifts in position of the stimulus patterns. Thus each cell of the deepest layer of the network responds selectively to a specific stimulus pattern and is not affected by the distortion in shape or the shift in position of the pattern. The synapses between the cells in the network are modifiable, and the neocognitron has a function of learning. A learning-with-a-teacher process is used to reinforce these modifiable synapses in the new model, instead of the learning-without-a-teacher process which was applied to the previous small-scale model.**

I. Introduction

THE NEURAL mechanism of visual pattern recognition in the brain is little known, and revealing it by conventional physiological experiments alone seems to be almost impossible. So, we take a slightly different approach to this problem. If we could make a neural network model which has the same capability for pattern recognition as a human being, it would give us a powerful clue to the understanding of the neural mechanism in the brain. In this paper, we discuss how to synthesize a neural network model in order to endow it with pattern recognition capability like that of a human being.

Several models were proposed with this intention [1]–[6]. In synthesizing such models, one of the most difficult problems is to design the networks so as to show position- and deformation-invariant responses. Some of these conventional models fail to recognize patterns which are shifted in position or deformed in shape. Although the four-layer perceptron [2] shows a kind of position-invariant responses, it works correctly only when the distance of shift is equal to one of the several specific values which are determined during the training of the network.

A few years ago, the authors [7], [8] proposed a multilayered neural network model, called a "neocognitron," which is capable of recognizing stimulus patterns correctly without being affected by any shift in position or even by considerable distortion in shape of the patterns. The result of computer simulation of a neocognitron with a small-scale network was reported there.

In this present paper, a neocognitron with a larger-scale network is simulated on a minicomputer PDP-11/34 and is shown to have a great capability for visual pattern recognition. The new model consists of nine layers of cells, while

Manuscript received August, 1, 1982; revised April 4, 1983.
The authors are with the NHK Broadcasting Science Research Laboratories, 1-10-11, Kinuta, Setagaya, Tokyo 157, Japan.

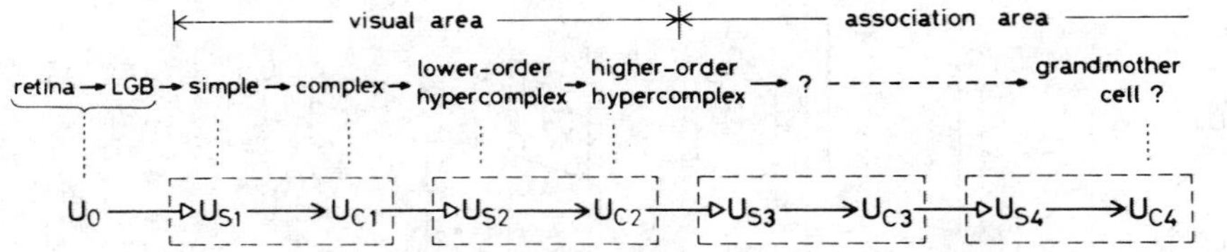

Fig. 1. Comparison between hierarchical model by Hubel and Wiesel and structure of neural network of neocognitron.

the previous model consisted of seven layers. We demonstrate that the new model can be trained to recognize handwritten Arabic numerals even with considerable deformations in shape.

We use a learning-with-a-teacher process for the reinforcement of the modifiable synapses in the new large-scale model, instead of the learning-without-a-teacher process applied to the previous model. In this paper, we focus on the mechanism for pattern recognition rather than that for self-organization.

II. Structure of the Network

The neocognition is a multilayered network with a hierarchical structure similar to the hierarchical model for the visual system proposed by Hubel and Wiesel [9], [10]. As shown in Fig. 1, the neocognitron is composed of a cascaded connection of a number of modular structures preceded by an input layer U_0 consisting of photoreceptor array. Each of the modular structures is composed of two layers of cells, namely, a layer U_S consisting of S cells, and a layer U_C consisting of C cells. The layers U_S and U_C in the lth module are denoted by U_{Sl} and U_{Cl}, respectively. An S cell has a response characteristic similar to a simple cell or a lower order hypercomplex cell according to the classification by Hubel and Wiesel, while a C cell resembles a complex cell or a higher order hypercomplex cells. In this network, a cell in a higher stage generally has a tendency to respond selectively to a more complicated feature of the stimulus pattern and, at the same time, has a larger receptive field and is more insensitive to the shift in position of the stimulus pattern.

Each S cell has modifiable input synapses which are reinforced with learning and acquires an ability to extract a specific stimulus feature. That is, an S cell comes to respond only to a specific stimulus feature and not to respond to other features.

Each C cell has afferent synapses leading from a group of S cells which have receptive fields of similar characteristics at approximately the same position on the input layer. This means that all of the presynaptic S cells are to extract almost the same stimulus feature but from slightly different positions on the input layer. The efficiencies of the synapses are determined in such a way that the C cell will be activated whenever at least one of its presynaptic S cells is active. Hence, even if a stimulus pattern which has elicited a large response from the C cell is shifted a little in position, the C cell will keep responding as before, because another presynaptic S cell will become active instead of the first one. In other words, a C cell responds to the same stimulus feature as its presynaptic S cells do but is less sensitive to the shift in position of the stimulus feature.

S cells or C cells in any single layer are sorted into subgroups according to the optimum stimulus features of their receptive fields. Since the cells in each subgroup are set in a two-dimensional array, we call the subgroup as a "cell plane." We will also use the terminology S plane and C plane to represent the cell planes consisting of S cells and C cells, respectively. All the cells in a single cell plane have input synapses of the same spatial distribution, and only the positions of the presynaptic cells are shifted in parallel depending on the position of the postsynaptic cells. Even in the process of learning, in which the efficiencies of the synapses are modified, the modification is performed always under this restriction.

Fig. 2 is a schematic diagram illustrating the synaptic connections between layers. Each tetragon drawn with heavy lines represents an S plane or a C plane, and each vertical tetragon drawn with thin lines, in which S planes or C planes are enclosed, represents an S layer or a C layer.

In Fig. 2, for the sake of simplicity, only one cell is shown in each cell plane. Each of these cells receives input synapses from the cells within the area enclosed by the ellipse in its preceding layer. All the other cells in the same cell plane have input synapses of the same spatial distribution, and only the positions of the presynaptic cells are shifted in parallel from cell to cell. Hence all the cells in a single cell plane have receptive fields of the same function but at different positions.

Since the cells in the network are interconnected in a cascade as shown in Fig. 2, the deeper the layer is, the larger becomes the receptive field of each cell of that layer. The density of the cells in each cell plane is so determined as to decrease in accordance with the increase of the size of the receptive fields. The number of cells in each layer is shown at the bottom of Fig. 2. In the deepest module, the receptive field of each C cell becomes so large as to cover the whole input layer, and each C plane is so determined as to have only one C cell. Fig. 3 illustrates concretely how the cells of each cell plane are interconnected to the cells of other cell planes.

S cells and C cells are excitatory cells. Although it is not shown in Figs. 2 and 3, we have inhibitory V_C cells in C layers.

Here, we will describe the outputs of these cells with numerical expressions. All the cells employed in the neocognitron are of analog type; that is, the input and output signals of the cells take nonnegative analog values proportional to the instantaneous firing frequencies of

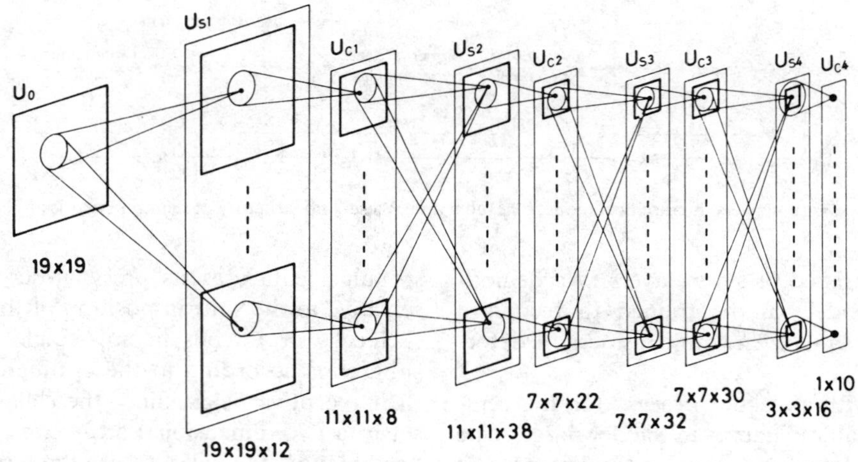

Fig. 2. Schematic diagram illustrating synaptic connections between layers in neocognitron.

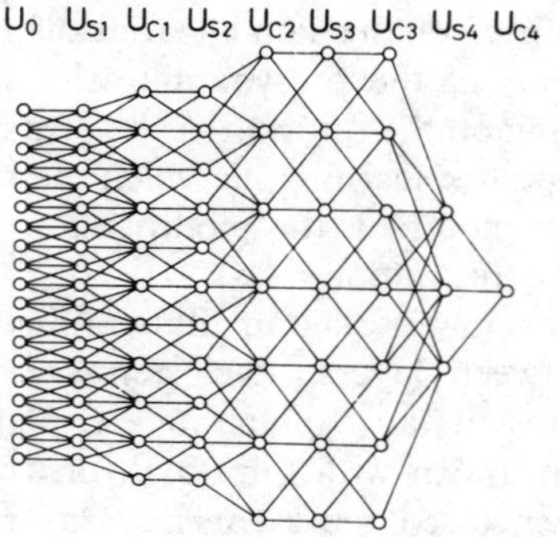

Fig. 3. One-dimensional view of interconnections between cells of different cell planes. Only one cell plane is drawn in each layer.

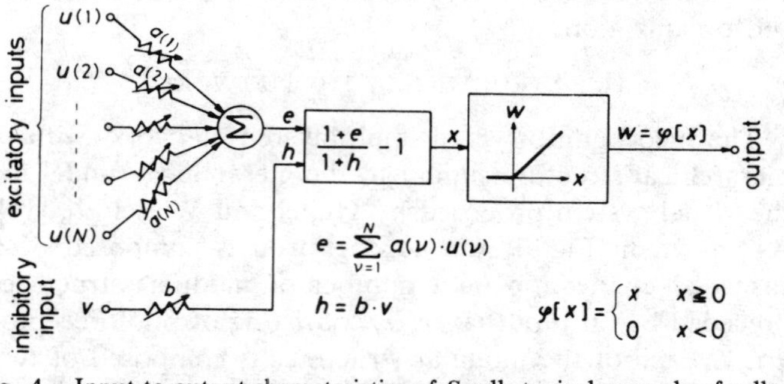

Fig. 4. Input-to-output characteristics of S cell: typical example of cells employed in neocognitron.

actual biological neurons. The output of a photoreceptor is denoted by $u_0(\boldsymbol{n})$ where $\boldsymbol{n}$ represents the two-dimensional coordinates indicating the location of the cell. We will use notations $U_{Sl}(k, \boldsymbol{n})$ to represent the output of an S cell in the kth S plane in the lth module, and $u_{Cl}(k, \boldsymbol{n})$ to represent the output of a C cell in the kth C plane in that module, where $\boldsymbol{n}$ is the two-dimensional coordinates representing the position of these cells' receptive fields on the input layer.

As shown in Fig. 4, S cells have inhibitory inputs with shunting mechanism. Incidentally, S cells have the same characteristics as the excitatory cells employed in the conventional cognitron [5], [6]. The output of an S cell of the kth S plane in the lth module is given by

$$U_{Sl}(k, \boldsymbol{n}) = r_l \cdot \phi\left(\frac{1 + \sum_{\kappa=1}^{K_{Cl-1}} \sum_{\boldsymbol{\nu} \in A_l} a_l(\kappa, \boldsymbol{\nu}, k) \cdot u_{Cl-1}(\kappa, \boldsymbol{n} + \boldsymbol{\nu})}{1 + \dfrac{r_l}{1 + r_l} \cdot b_l(k) \cdot v_{Cl-1}(\boldsymbol{n})} - 1\right), \quad k = 1, 2, \cdots, K_{Sl} \tag{1}$$

where $\phi[x] = \max(x, 0)$. In the case of $l = 1$ in (1), $u_{Cl-1}(\kappa, \boldsymbol{n})$ stands for $u_0(\boldsymbol{n})$, and we have $K_{Cl-1} = 1$.

Here, $a_l(\kappa, \boldsymbol{\nu}, k)$ and $b_l(k)$ represent the efficiencies of the excitatory and inhibitory modifiable synapses, respectively. As described before, all the S cells in the same S plane are assumed to have an identical set of afferent synapses. Hence $a_l(\kappa, \boldsymbol{\nu}, k)$ and $b_l(k)$ do not contain any argument representing the position $\boldsymbol{n}$ of the receptive field of cell $u_{Sl}(k, \boldsymbol{n})$.

Parameter r_l in (1) controls the intensity of the inhibition. The larger the value of r_l is, the more selective becomes the cell's response to its specific feature. Their values are $r_1 = 1.7$, $r_2 = 4.0$, $r_3 = 1.5$, and $r_4 = 1.0$. (A detailed discussion on the response of S cells will be given in Section III-B.)

The inhibitory cell $v_{Cl-1}(\boldsymbol{n})$, which is sending an inhibitory signal to cell $U_{Sl}(k, \boldsymbol{n})$, receives afferent synapses from the same group of cells as $u_{Sl}(k, \boldsymbol{n})$ does and yields an output proportional to the weighted root mean square of its inputs:

$$v_{Cl-1}(\boldsymbol{n}) = \sqrt{\sum_{\kappa=1}^{K_{Cl-1}} \sum_{\boldsymbol{\nu} \in A_l} c_{l-1}(\boldsymbol{\nu}) \cdot u_{Cl-1}^2(\kappa, \boldsymbol{n} + \boldsymbol{\nu})}\,. \tag{2}$$

The efficiencies of the unmodifiable synapses $c_{l-1}(\boldsymbol{\nu})$ are determined so as to decrease monotonically with respect to $|\boldsymbol{\nu}|$ and to satisfy

$$K_{Cl-1} \cdot \sum_{\boldsymbol{\nu} \in A_l} c_{l-1}(\boldsymbol{\nu}) = 1. \tag{3}$$

The size of the connection area A_l of these cells is set to be small in the first module and to increase with the depth l as illustrated in Fig. 3.

The output of a C cell of the kth C plane in the lth module is given by

$$u_{Cl}(k, \boldsymbol{n}) = \psi\left(\sum_{\kappa=1}^{K_{Sl}} j_l(\kappa, k) \sum_{\boldsymbol{\nu} \in D_l} d_l(\boldsymbol{\nu}, k) \cdot u_{Sl}(\kappa, \boldsymbol{n} + \boldsymbol{\nu}) \right), \cdot k = 1, 2, \cdots, K_{Cl}, \quad (4)$$

where

$$\psi[x] = \begin{cases} x/(\alpha_l + x), & (x \geqq 0); \\ 0, & (x < 0). \end{cases}$$

The parameter α_l is a positive constant which determines the degree of saturation of the output. Their values are $\alpha_1 = \alpha_2 = \alpha_3 = 0.25$, and $\alpha_4 = 1.0$.

In (4), $d_l(\boldsymbol{\nu}, k)$ represents the efficiencies of the excitatory synapses leading from S cells, and $j_l(\kappa, k)$ takes value one or zero depending on whether synaptic connections really exist from the κth S plane to the kth C plane. The value of $d_l(\boldsymbol{\nu}, k)$ is determined so as to decrease monotonically with respect to $|\boldsymbol{\nu}|$ and is independent of k except for $l = 1$. The size of the connection area D_l is set to be small in the first module and to increase with depth l as illustrated in Fig. 3.

The process of pattern recognition in this multilayered network can be briefly summarized as follows. The stimulus pattern is first observed within a narrow range by each of the S cells in the first module, and several features of the stimulus pattern are extracted. In the next module, these features are combined by observation over a little larger range, and higher order features are extracted. Operations of this kind are repeatedly applied through a cascaded connection of a number of modules. In each stage of these operations, a small amount of positional error is tolerated. The operation by which positional errors are tolerated little by little, not at a single stage, playes an important role in endowing the network with an ability to recognize even distorted patterns.

III. Synaptic Connections Between Cells

The synaptic connections in the new model of the neocognitron are reinforced by means of a supervised learning, that is, a learning-with-a-teacher process. During the training process, the network is presented with a set of training patterns to the input layer, together with the instructions which cells in the network should come to respond to each of the training patterns. This algorithm is different from that used in the previous model [7], [8]. In the new model, the algorithm for the reinforcement of synapses is determined from a standpoint of an engineering application to a design of a pattern recognizer rather than from that of pure biological modeling. That is, the algorithm is determined with the criterion of obtaining a better performance in handwritten character recognition.

A. Reinforcement of the Input Synapses of S Cells

The reinforcement of the synaptic connections are performed in sequence from the distal to the deeper layers. That is, the reinforcement of the input synapses of the lth layer is performed after completion of the reinforcement of up to the $(l-1)$th layer.

A number of cell planes are in an S layer. These cell planes are reinforced one at a time. In order to reinforce a cell plane, the "teacher" presents a training pattern to the input layer, and at the same time chooses one S cell which should work as the "representative" from that cell plane. The representative cell works like a seed in the crystal growth. The input synapses to the representative cell are reinforced depending on the stimuli given to these synapses. That is, only the synapses through which nonzero signals are coming are reinforced. As the result, the representative cell acquires a selective responsiveness to the training pattern which is now presented to the input layer. All the other cells in that cell plane have their input synapses reinforced in the identical manner as their representative.

This algorithm can be expressed as follows. Let cell $u_{Sl}(\hat{k}, \hat{\boldsymbol{n}})$ be the representative. The modifiable synapses $a_l(\kappa, \boldsymbol{\nu}, \hat{k})$ and $b_l(\hat{k})$, which are afferent to the S cells of this S plane, are reinforced by the amount shown below:

$$\Delta a_l(\kappa, \boldsymbol{\nu}, \hat{k}) = q_l \cdot c_{l-1}(\boldsymbol{\nu}) \cdot u_{Cl-1}(\kappa, \hat{\boldsymbol{n}} + \boldsymbol{\nu}), \quad (5)$$

$$\Delta b_l(\hat{k}) = q_l \cdot v_{Cl-1}(\hat{\boldsymbol{n}}), \quad (6)$$

where q_l is a positive constant which determines the amount of reinforcement. The initial values of these modifiable synapses are all zero.

We can choose any cell of a cell plane as the representative, and the choice of the representative does not have so much effect on the result of training, provided that the training pattern is presented at a proper position in the respective field of the representative. Hence, in the computer simulation discussed later, we always choose the cell situated at the center of each cell plane as the representative.

In the computer simulation, the number of training patterns given to each cell plane is from one to four, depending on the required allowance to the deformation of the stimulus features. (See the following section for more discussions.)

B. Analysis of the Response of an S Cell

In this section, we discuss how each S cell is trained to respond selectively to differences in stimulus patterns. Since the structure between two adjoining modules is similar in all parts of the network, we observe the response of an arbitrary S cell $U_{S1}(k, \boldsymbol{n})$ of layer U_{S1} as a typical example. Fig. 5 shows the synaptic connections converging to such a cell. For the sake of simplicity, we will omit the suffixes S, $l = 1$ and the arguments k, $\boldsymbol{n}$ and represent the response of this cell simply by u. Similarly, we will use the notation v for the output of the inhibitory cell $v_{C0}(\boldsymbol{n})$, which sends an

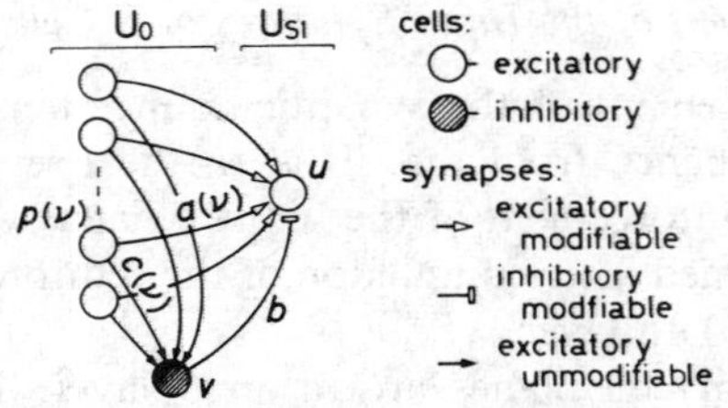

Fig. 5. Synaptic connections converging to S cell.

inhibitory signal to cell u. For the other variables, the arguments k and $\boldsymbol{n}$ and suffixes S, C, l, and $l-1$ will also be omitted.

Let $p(\boldsymbol{\nu})$ be the response of the cells of layer U_0 situated in the connection area of cell u, so that

$$p(\boldsymbol{\nu}) = u_0(\boldsymbol{n} + \boldsymbol{\nu}). \tag{7}$$

In other words, $p(\boldsymbol{\nu})$ is the stimulus pattern (or feature) presented to the receptive field of cell u.

With this notation, (1) and (2) can be written

$$u = r \cdot \phi\left(\frac{1 + \Sigma_{\nu} a(\boldsymbol{\nu}) \cdot p(\boldsymbol{\nu})}{1 + \dfrac{r}{1+r} \cdot b \cdot v} - 1\right) \tag{8}$$

$$v = \sqrt{\Sigma_{\nu} c(\boldsymbol{\nu}) \cdot p^2(\boldsymbol{\nu})}\,. \tag{9}$$

When cell u is chosen as the representative, the amounts of reinforcement of the modifiable synapses are derived from (5) and (6), that is,

$$\Delta a(\boldsymbol{\nu}) = q \cdot c(\boldsymbol{\nu}) \cdot p(\boldsymbol{\nu}), \tag{10}$$

$$\Delta b = q \cdot v. \tag{11}$$

Let s be defined by

$$s = \frac{\Sigma_{\nu} a(\boldsymbol{\nu}) \cdot p(\boldsymbol{\nu})}{b \cdot v}. \tag{12}$$

Then (8) reduces approximately to

$$u \simeq r \cdot \phi\left(\frac{r+1}{r} \cdot s - 1\right), \tag{13}$$

provided that $a(\boldsymbol{\nu})$ and b are sufficiently large.

Let a stimulus pattern $p(\boldsymbol{\nu}) = P(\boldsymbol{\nu})$ be presented, and let cell u be chosen as the representative. Then, from (5) and (6), we obtain

$$a(\boldsymbol{\nu}) = q \cdot c(\boldsymbol{\nu}) \cdot P(\boldsymbol{\nu}), \tag{14}$$

$$b = q\sqrt{\Sigma_{\nu} c(\boldsymbol{\nu}) \cdot P^2(\boldsymbol{\nu})}\,. \tag{15}$$

Substituting (9), (14), and (15) into (12), we obtain

$$s = \frac{\Sigma_{\nu} c(\boldsymbol{\nu}) \cdot P(\boldsymbol{\nu}) \cdot p(\boldsymbol{\nu})}{\sqrt{\Sigma_{\nu} c(\boldsymbol{\nu}) \cdot P^2(\boldsymbol{\nu})} \cdot \sqrt{\Sigma_{\nu} c(\boldsymbol{\nu}) \cdot p^2(\boldsymbol{\nu})}}. \tag{16}$$

If we regard $p(\boldsymbol{\nu})$ and $P(\boldsymbol{\nu})$ as vectors, (16) can be interpreted as the (weighted) inner product of the two vectors normalized by the norms of both vectors. In other words, s gives the cosine of the angle between the two vectors $p(\boldsymbol{\nu})$ and $P(\boldsymbol{\nu})$ in the multidimensional vector space. Therefore, we have $s = 1$ only when $p(\boldsymbol{\nu}) = P(\boldsymbol{\nu})$, and we have $s < 1$ for all patterns such as $p(\boldsymbol{\nu}) \neq P(\boldsymbol{\nu})$. This means that s becomes maximum for the training pattern and becomes smaller for any other patterns.

If parameter q is large enough, (13) holds. When an arbitrary pattern $p(\boldsymbol{\nu})$ is presented, and if it satisfies $s > r/(r+1)$, we have $u > 0$ by (13). Conversely, for a pattern which makes $s \leqq r/(r+1)$, cell u does not respond. We can interpret by saying that cell u judges the similarity between patterns $p(\boldsymbol{\nu})$ and $P(\boldsymbol{\nu})$ using the criterion defined by (16) and that it responds only to patterns judged to be similar to $P(\boldsymbol{\nu})$. Incidentally, if $p(\boldsymbol{\nu}) = P(\boldsymbol{\nu})$, we have $s = 1$ and consequently $u \simeq 1$.

Since the value $r/(r+1)$ tends to one with increase of r, a larger value of r makes the cell's response more selective to one specific pattern or feature. In other words, a large value of r endows the cell with a high ability to discriminate patterns of different classes. However, a higher selectivity of the cell's response is not always desirable, because it decreases the ability to tolerate the deformation of patterns. Hence the value of r should be determined at a point of compromise between these two contradictory conditions.

In the above analysis, we supposed that cell u is trained only for one particular pattern $P(\boldsymbol{\nu})$. When cell u has been trained to two patterns, say, to $P_1(\boldsymbol{\nu})$ and $P_2(\boldsymbol{\nu})$, $P(\boldsymbol{\nu})$ in the above discussions should be replaced with $\{P_1(\boldsymbol{\nu}) + P_2(\boldsymbol{\nu})\}$. Hence cell u acquires a tendency to respond equally to both $P_1(\boldsymbol{\nu})$ and $P_2(\boldsymbol{\nu})$. This, however, depends on the value of r, and also on the similarity between $P_1(\boldsymbol{\nu})$ and $P_2(\boldsymbol{\nu})$. If the difference between $P_1(\boldsymbol{\nu})$ and $P_2(\boldsymbol{\nu})$ is too large, or if the value of r is too large, cell u comes to respond neither to $P_1(\boldsymbol{\nu})$ nor $P_2(\boldsymbol{\nu})$.

The above discussion is not restricted to S cells of layer U_{S1}. Each S cell in succeeding modules shows a similar type of response, if we regard the response of the C cells in its connection area in the preceding layer as its input pattern.

C. Layers U_{S1} and U_{C1}

Layer U_{S1} has 12 cell planes, and each cell plane contains the same number of cells as layer U_0, that is, 19×19 (see Figs. 2 and 3). These S cells have their input synapses reinforced so as to acquire the ability to detect line components of various orientations.

The training patterns which are used for training the 12 cell planes are displayed in column a_1 in Fig. 6. This figure shows, for example, that the cells of the first cell plane are trained to detect a horizontal line component. We can also interpret this by saying that the patterns in column a_1 show the structure of the receptive fields of the cells of layer U_{S1}.

Since the spread of the excitatory input synapses $a_1(\kappa, \boldsymbol{\nu}, k)$ of each S cell (i.e., the connection area A_1 in (1) and (2)) is as small as 3×3, cases exist where two different cell planes should be prepared for detecting a line of a particular orientation. For example, in Fig. 6, the second and third cell planes of layer U_{S1} have the receptive fields of the same preferred orientation but of different structures. Hence the outputs from such pairs of cell planes are

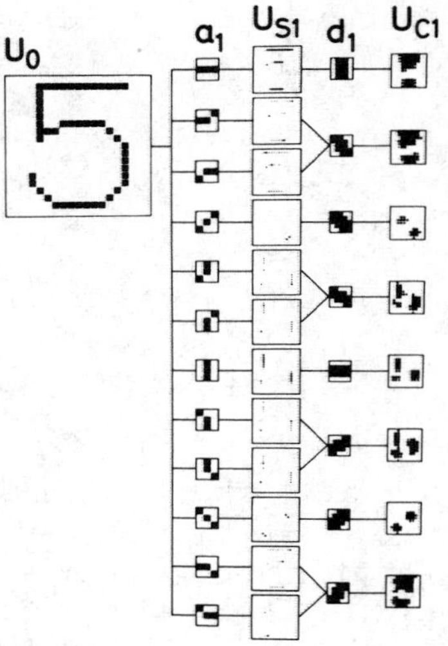

Fig. 6. Example of response of cells of layers U_0, U_{S1}, and U_{C1}, and synaptic connections between them.

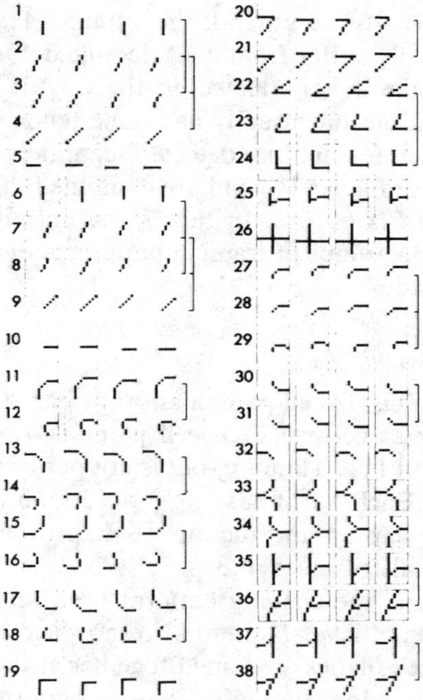

Fig. 7. Training patterns used to train 38 cell planes of layer U_{S2}. Way of joining at input stage of layer U_{C2} is also shown to right of each group of training patterns.

joined together at the input stage of layer U_{C1} as shown in Fig. 6. The parameter $j_1(\kappa, k)$ in (4) takes value one or zero, depending on this joining condition. For instance, $j_1(\kappa, 2) = 1$ for $\kappa = 2$ and 3, and $j_1(\kappa, 2) = 0$ for other κ. Because of this joining process, layer U_{C1} contains only eight cell planes.

Parameter r_1 in (1), which determines the selectivity of an S cell, is set at value of 1.7. Since the stimulus feature which is used for training an S cell contains three active elements, the S cell with $r_1 = 1.7$ yields nonzero output for a stimulus feature contaminated with up to two additive elements of noise, or one additive and one subtractive elements. However, it does not respond to a stimulus feature with two subtractive elements of noise or more. (These results can be obtained from the analysis in Section III-B as well as from the computer simulation.)

The spatial distribution of the input synapses $d_1(\nu, k)$ of a C cell (i.e., the connection area D_1 in (4)) is 5×5 in size, but all of these 5×5 synapses are not effective. As shown in Fig. 6, the effective part of the distribution is elongated to the direction perpendicular to its preferred orientation and is compressed in the direction of its preferred orientation.

Since each C cell receives excitatory signals from a number of S cells, it usually responds similarly as its neighboring C cells. Hence it is possible to reduce the number of C cells in each cell plane compared to that of S cells. The density of cells in each cell plane of layer U_{C1} are thinned out by two to one compared to that of layer U_{S1} both in horizontal and vertical directions. Thus as shown in Fig. 3, the number of cells in each cell plane is reduced to 11×11 in layer U_{C1}.

D. Layers U_{S2} and U_{C2}

Layer U_{S2} has 38 cell planes, and each cell plane contains 11×11 S cells. Layer U_{C2} has only 22 cell planes, because the outputs from some of the cell planes of layer U_{S2} are joined together at the input stage of layer U_{C2}. Each cell plane of layer U_{C2} contains 7×7 C cells because of the two to one thinning-out of the cell density as was shown in Fig. 3.

Each S cell of layer U_{S2} has modifiable excitatory input synapses of 3×3 spatial distribution. Since the preceding layer U_{C1} has eight cell planes, the total number of the excitatory input synapses to each S cell is $3 \times 3 \times 8$. All of these synapses are not reinforced by learning, but most of them usually stay at the initial value of zero. The input synapses to each C cell of layer U_{C2} have spatial distribution of 5×5.

Figure 7 shows the training patterns used for training the 38 cell planes of layer U_{S2}. Four training patterns, in which the same stimulus feature is shifted in parallel to each other by one element in both horizontal and vertical directions, are used to train each cell plane. The reason why the use of four patterns are necessary is discussed below.

Because the cells of this layer are thinned out by two to one compared to those of layer U_0 in both horizontal and vertical directions, each S cell should take charge of extracting a specific stimulus feature from four different positions on layer U_0. In this network, the two to one thinning-out of the cells is already made at the stage of layer U_{C1}, from which the relevant S cells receive synaptic connections. The effect of this thinning-out is not so small, and a somewhat different spatial response might appear in the preceding layer U_{C1} when the stimulus pattern is shifted in position by one element. Hence each cell-plane of layer U_{S2} should be trained with four different patterns beforehand so as to come to respond equally to them.

In this experiment, we intend to train the neocognitron so as to recognize handwritten Arabic numerals. When patterns are written by hand, the stimulus features in the patterns usually suffer from considerable deformations depending on the writers. However, the way of deformation is not at random but usually has some tendency. Some of such deformed features are detected separately in a number of cell planes of layer U_{S2} and are combined together at the input stage of layer U_{C2}. In Fig. 7, the lines drawn to the right of the 36 groups of training patterns indicate how this joining is made.

E. Layers U_{S3} and U_{C3}

Layer U_{S3} has 32 cell planes, and U_{C3} has 30 cell planes. The number of cells in each cell plane is 7×7 for both layers U_{S3} and U_{C3}. Thinning-out is not performed between these layers. Each S cell has $3 \times 3 \times 22$ modifiable excitatory input synapses, and the input synapses of each C cell have spatial distribution of 3×3.

Fig. 8 shows the training patterns used for training the 32 cell planes of layer U_{S3} and also shows how the outputs from these cell planes are joined together at the input stage of layer U_{C3}. Most of these training patterns consist of some parts of the standard numeral patterns which are to be taught to this network.

As is seen in Fig. 8, only two or three different patterns are used to train each cell plane of layer U_{S3}. They are deformed in shape or varied in size to each other. In the case of this layer, it is not necessary to present all of the deformed patterns which should be detected by the cell plane. Presentation of only a few number of typical patterns is enough for the training of each cell plane, because a considerable amount of deformation has already been absorbed before this stage.

F. Layers U_{S4} and U_{C4}

Layer U_{S4} has 16 cell planes, and each cell plane has 3×3 S cells. Each of these S cells has $5 \times 5 \times 30$ modifiable input synapses. Although the number of cells in each cell plane is reduced in layer U_{S4} from that in the preceding layer U_{C3}, no thinning out is made between these layers. Only the cells near the periphery of the cell planes of layer U_{S4} are omitted, because they are of little use for the recognition of the whole input pattern (see Fig. 3).

The 16 cell planes of layer U_{S4} are trained with the 16 sets of patterns as shown in Fig. 9 and are joined together into ten cell planes at layer U_{C4}. Each cell plane of layer U_{C4} has only one cell which has input synapses of 3×3 spatial distribution.

The ten cells of layer U_{C4} have one-to-one correspondence with ten Arabic numerals. In Figs. 10–12, which will be discussed later, they are arranged vertically from zero to nine in order at the rightmost column. Among these cells, a mechanism of lateral inhibition exists, although it is omitted in (4).

For some of the numerals, more than one quite different styles of writing are accustomed to be used. For each of these numerals, two S planes are prepared and are trained independently with two typical patterns of different styles

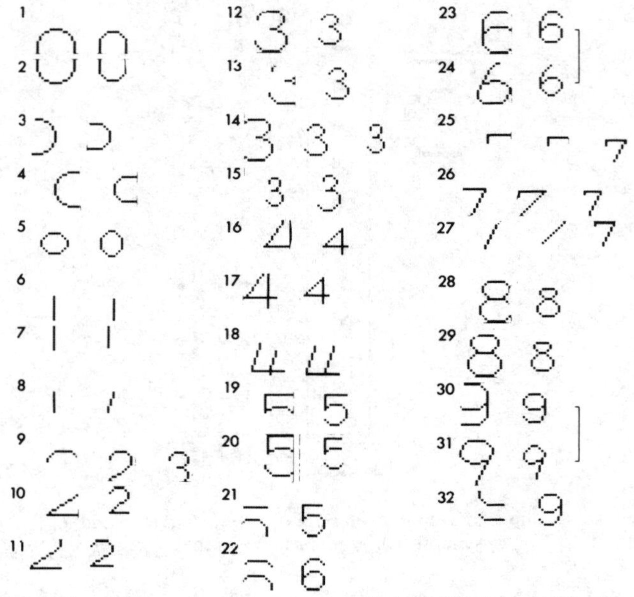

Fig. 8. Training patterns used to train 32 cell planes of layer U_{S3} and way of joining at input stage of layer U_{C3}.

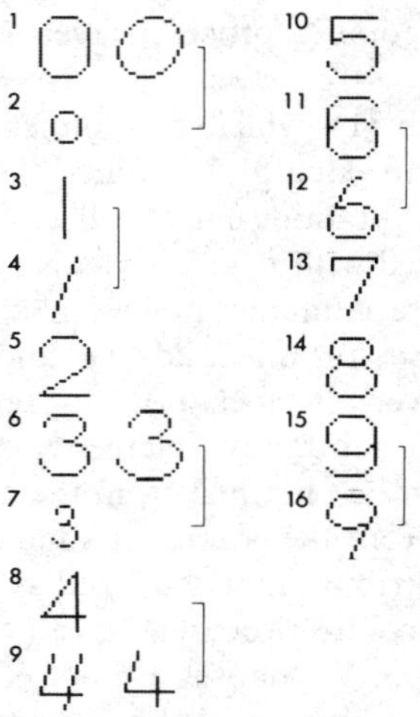

Fig. 9. Training patterns used to train 16 cell planes of layer U_{S4} and way of joining at input stage of layer U_{C4}.

as shown in Fig. 9, and their outputs are joined together at the input stage of layer U_{C4}.

IV. Response of the Network

The neocognitron, which has been trained with the procedure discussed in the previous chapter, is tested with various input patterns. Fig. 10 shows the response of the cells in the network to one of the patterns used for training the network. It is seen that only cell 2 of layer U_{C4} yields an output. This means that the neocognitron recognizes the input pattern correctly. Even if the input pattern is deformed from the training pattern as much as shown in Fig. 11, the neocognitron recognizes it correctly.

In the case of Fig. 12, two of the cells of layer U_{C4} respond; that is, a large output is obtained from cell 5 and

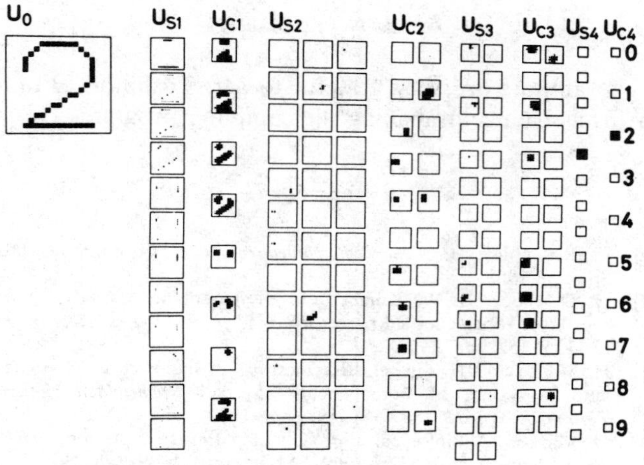

Fig. 10. Response of cells in network to one of training patterns "2."

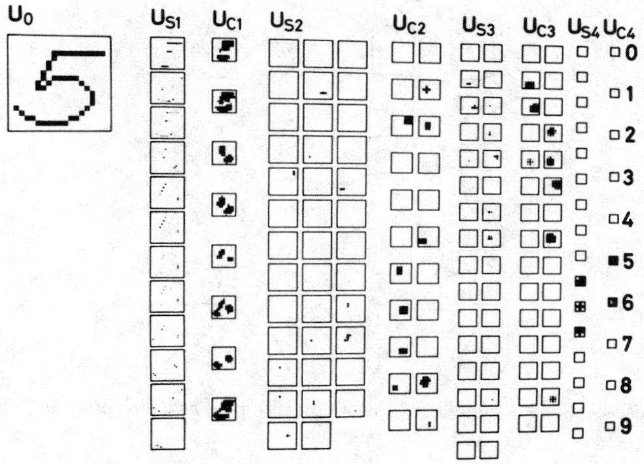

Fig. 12. Response of cells in network to deformed pattern, which elicits response from two cells of layer U_{C4}.

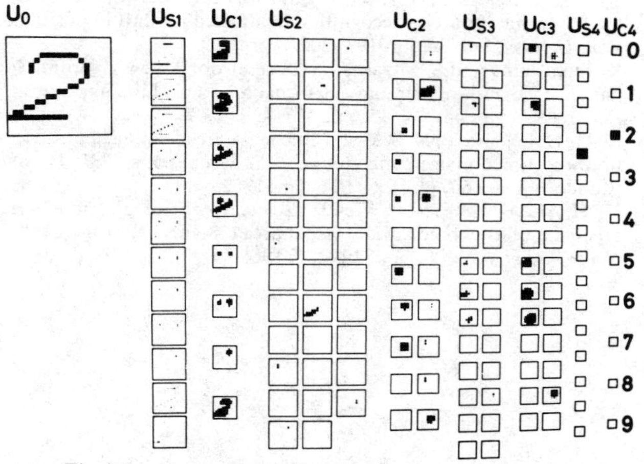

Fig. 11. Response of cells in network to deformed pattern.

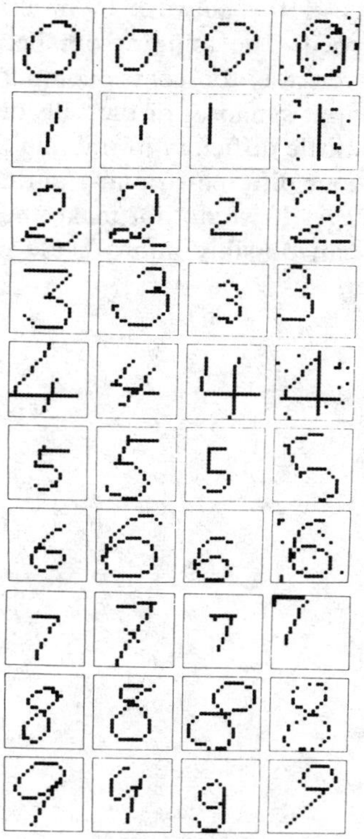

Fig. 13. Some examples of deformed numerals which neocognitron recognizes correctly.

a small output from cell 6. This means that the neocognitron correctly judges that the input pattern is 5, but also admits that the input pattern slightly resembles 6.

Fig. 13 shows some examples of the stimulus patterns which the neocognitron correctly recognizes. On the other hand, Fig. 14 shows some examples of the patterns which cannot be correctly recognized. Some of these patterns elicit no response from any of the cells of layer U_{C4}, and the others elicit responses from wrong cells of layer U_{C4}.

V. Discussion

We have demonstrated that the neocognitron recognizes handwritten numerals of various styles of penmanship correctly, even if they are considerably distorted in shape. Although the result is shown for the recognition of Arabic numerals, the neocognitron can be trained to recognize other set of patterns such as alphabet, geometrical shapes, or others.

The number of cell planes of each layer should be changed adaptively, depending on the set of patterns which the neocognitron should learn to recognize. The program for the computer simulation is made in such a way that the number of cell planes can be chosen freely and can readily be increased when necessary.

Although each S cell has a large number of modifiable input synapses, all of them are not generally reinforced by learning. On the contrary, most of them remain at the initial state in which their efficiencies are zero. Furthermore, the modifiable synapses tend to be reinforced in clusters. In the computer program, we made full use of these characteristics of the synapses and reduced the re-

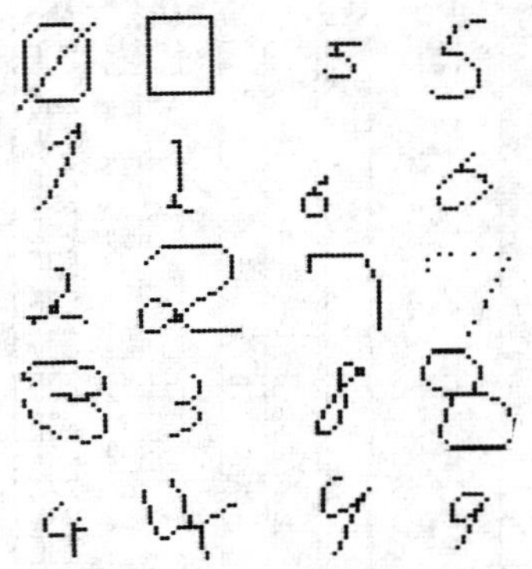

Fig. 14. Some examples of distorted patterns which are not correctly recognized.

quired memory capacity and increased the computation speed by eliminating unnecessary calculations.

In the simulated model, we made two to one thinning-out in several parts of the network in order to increase the computation speed. The thinning-out between layers U_{S1} and U_{C1}, however, was too coarse compared to the 5×5 spread of the input synapses of the cells of layer U_{C1}. As a result, we felt a little difficulty in training the network, and we had to use four different training patterns for each cell plane of layer U_{S2}. If we do not make the thinning-out at this stage, we can possibly improve the capability of the network further.

Acknowledgment

The authors are very grateful to Mr. Toshinori Hirano for his assistance in making the computer program.

References

[1] F. Rosenblatt, *Principles of Neurodynamics*. Washington, DC: Spartan, 1962.

[2] H. D. Block, B. W. Knight, and F. Rosenblatt, "Analysis of a four-layer series-coupled perceptron. II," *Rev. Mod. Phys.*, vol. 34, pp. 135–152, Jan. 1962.

[3] H. Marko and H. Giebel, "Recognition of handwritten characters with a system of homogeneous layers," *Nachrichtentechnische Zeitschrift*, vol. 23, pp. 455–459, Sept. 1970.

[4] H. Marko, "A biological approach to pattern recognition," *IEEE Trans. Syst., Man, Cybern.*, vol. SMC-4, pp. 34–39, Jan. 1974.

[5] K. Fukushima, "Cognitron: A self-organizing mulitlayered neural network," *Biol. Cybern.*, vol. 20, pp. 121–136, Nov. 1975.

[6] ——, "Cognitron: A self-organizing multilayered neural network model," NHK Tech. Monograph, no. 30, Jan. 1981.

[7] ——, "Neocognitron: A self-organizing neural network model for a mechanism of pattern recognition unaffected by shift in position," *Biol. Cybern.*, vol. 36, pp. 193–202, Apr. 1980.

[8] K. Fukushima and S. Miyake, "Neocognitron: A new algorithm for pattern recognition tolerant of deformations and shifts in position," *Pattern Recognition*, vol. 15, pp. 455–469, 1982.

[9] D. H. Hubel and T. N. Wiesel, "Receptive fields, binocular interaction and functional architecture in cat's visual cortex," *J. Physiol.* (London), vol. 160, pp. 106–154, Jan. 1962.

[10] D. H. Hubel and T. N. Wiesel, "Receptive fields and functional architecture in two nonstriate visual area (18 and 19) of the cat," *J. Neurophysiol.*, vol. 28, pp. 229–289, 1965.

About the Author

V. ("Rao") Vemuri is a professor of applied science at the University of California, Davis-Livermore and also an engineer at the Lawrence Livermore National Laboratories. His research interests include artificial neural networks, high performance architectures, and modeling/simulation of distributed parameter systems.

Vemuri has served the Computer Society in various capacities. He was the secretary, vice-chair, and chair of the Binghamton (NY) Chapter. He was a member of the committee that drafted the Model Program in Computer Science and Engineering. He is now an editor for the Computer Society Press Technology Series.

Vemuri received his Ph.D. degree from UCLA in 1968. He received his M.S. from the University of Detroit and B.E. from Andhra University. His address is Department of Applied Science, P.O. Box 808, L-794, University of California, Livermore, CA 94550.

IEEE Computer Society

Offices of the IEEE Computer Society

Headquarters Office
1730 Massachusetts Avenue, NW
Washington, DC 20036-1903
Phone: (202) 371-0101
Fax: (202) 728-9614

Publications Office
P.O. Box 3014
10662 Los Vaqueros Circle
Los Alamitos, CA 90720-1264
Membership and General Information: (714) 821-8380
Publication Orders: (800) 272-6657
Fax: (714) 821-4010

European Office
13, avenue de l'Aquilon
B-1200 Brussels, BELGIUM
Phone: 32-2-770-21-98
Fax: 32-3-770-8505

Asian Office
Ooshima Building
2-19-1 Minami-Aoyama, Minato-ku
Tokyo 107, JAPAN
Phone: 81-3-408-3118

IEEE Computer Society Press Publications

Monographs: A monograph is an authored book consisting of 100% original material.

Tutorials: A tutorial is a collection of original materials prepared by the editors and reprints of the best articles published in a subject area. They must contain at least five percent original material (15 to 20 percent original material is recommended).

Reprint Books: A reprint book is a collection of reprints divided into sections with a preface, table of contents, and section introductions that discuss the reprints and why they were selected. It contains less than five percent original material.

Technology Series: Each technology series is a collection of anthologies of reprints, each with a narrow focus on a subset of a particular discipline, such as networks, architecture, software, robotics, etc.

Submission of proposals: For guidelines on preparing CS Press Books, write Editor-in-Chief, IEEE Computer Society, P.O. Box 3014, 10662 Los Vaqueros Circle, Los Alamitos, CA 90720-1264 (or telephone 714-821-8380).

Purpose

The IEEE Computer Society advances the theory and practice of computer science and engineering, promotes the exchange of technical information among 100,000 members worldwide, and provides a wide range of services to members and nonmembers.

Membership

Members receive the acclaimed monthly magazine IEEE Computer, discounts, and opportunities to serve (all activities are led by volunteer members). Membership is open to all IEEE members, affiliate society members, and others seriously interested in the computer field.

Publications and Activities

IEEE Computer. An authoritative, easy-to-read magazine containing tutorials and in-depth articles on topics across the computer field, plus news, conferences, calendars, interviews, and new products.

Periodicals. The society publishes six magazines and four research transactions. Refer to membership application or request information as noted above.

Conference Proceedings, Tutorial Texts, Standards Documents. The IEEE Computer Society Press publishes more than 100 titles every year.

Standards Working Groups. Over 100 of these groups produce IEEE standards used throughout the industrial world.

Technical Committees. Over 30 TCs publish newsletters, provide interaction with peers in specialty areas, and directly influence standards, conferences, and education.

Conferences/Education. The society holds about 100 conferences each year and sponsors many educational activities, including computing science accreditation.

Chapters. Regular and student chapters worldwide provide the opportunity to interact with colleagues, hear technical experts, and serve the local professional community.

Other IEEE Computer Society Press Titles

Monographs

Analyzing Computer Architectures
Written by J.C. Huck and M.J. Flynn
(ISBN 0-8186-8857-2); 206 pages

Desktop Publishing for the Writer: Designing, Writing, and Developing
Written by Richard Ziegfeld and John Tarp
(ISBN 0-8186-8840-8); 380 pages

Digital Image Warping
Written by George Wolberg
(ISBN 0-8186-8944-7); 340 pages

Integrating Design and Test—CAE Tools for ATE Programming
Written by K.P. Parker
(ISBN 0-8186-8788-6); 160 pages

JSP and JSD—The Jackson Approach to Software Development (Second Edition)
Written by J.R. Cameron
(ISBN 0-8186-8858-0); 560 pages

National Computer Policies
Written by Ben G. Matley and Thomas A. McDannold
(ISBN 0-8186-8784-3); 192 pages

Physical Level Interfaces and Protocols
Written by Uyless Black
(ISBN 0-8186-8824-2); 240 pages

Protecting Your Proprietary Rights in Computer and Hi-Tech Industries
Written by Tobey B. Marzook, Esq.
(ISBN 0-8186-8754-1); 224 pages

Tutorials

Ada Programming Language
Edited by S.H. Saib and R.E. Fritz
(ISBN 0-8186-0456-5); 548 pages

Advanced Computer Architecture
Edited by D.P. Agrawal
(ISBN 0-8186-0667-3); 400 pages

Advanced Microprocessors and Hi-Level Language Computer Architectures
Edited by V. Mulutinovic
(ISBN 0-8186-0623-1); 608 pages

Advances in Distributed System Reliability
Edited by Suresh Rai an Dharma P. Agrawal
(ISBN 0-8186-8907-2); 352 pages

Computer Architecture
Edited by D.D. Gajski, V.M. Multinovic, H. Siegel, and B.P. Furht
(ISBN 0-8186-0704-1); 602 pages

Computer Arithmetic I
Edited by Earl E. Swartzlander, Jr.
(ISBN 0-8186-8931-5); 398 pages

Computer Arithmetic II
Edited by Earl E. Swartzlander, Jr.
(ISBN 0-8186-8945-5); 412 pages

Computer Communications: Architectures, Protocols and Standards (Second Edition)
Edited by William Stallings
(ISBN 0-8186-0790-4); 448 pages

Computer Graphics (Second Edition)
Edited by J.C. Beatty and K.S. Booth
(ISBN 0-8186-0425-5); 576 pages

Computer Graphics Hardware: Image Generation and Display
Edited by H.K. Reghbati and A.Y.C. Lee
(ISBN 0-8186-0753-X); 384 pages

Computer Graphics: Image Synthesis
Edited by Kenneth Joy, Max Nelson, Charles Grant, and Lansing Hatfield
(ISBN 0-8186-8854-8); 380.4 pages

Computer and Network Security
Edited by M.D. Abrams and H.J. Podell
(ISBN 0-8186-0756-4); 448 pages

Computer Networks (Fourth Edition)
Edited by M.D. Abrams and I.W. Cotton
(ISBN 0-8186-0568-5); 512 pages

Computer Text Recognition and Error Correction
Edited by S.N. Srihari
(ISBN 0-8186-0579-0); 364 pages

Computers for Artificial Intelligence Applications
Edited by B. Wah and G.J. Li
(ISBN 0-8186-0706-8); 656 pages

Database Management
Edited by J.A. Larson
(ISBN 0-8186-0714-9); 448 pages

Digital Image Processing and Analysis: Vol 1—Digital Image Processing
Edited by R. Chellappa and A.A. Sawchuk
(ISBN 0-8186-0665-7); 736 pages

Digital Image Processing and Analysis: Vol 2—Digital Image Analysis
Edited by H.A. Freeman and K.J. Thurber
(ISBN 0-8186-0605-3); 384 pages

Local Network Technology (Third Edition)
Edited by William Stallings
(ISBN 0-8186-0825-0); 512 pages

Microprogramming and Firmware Engineering
Edited by V. Milutinovic
(ISBN 0-8186-0839-0); 416 pages

Modeling and Control of Automated Manufacturing Systems
Edited by A. A. Desrochers
(ISBN 0-8186-8916-1); 384 pages

Modern Design and Analysis of Discrete-Event Computer Simulation
Edited by E.J. Dudewicz and Z. Karian
(ISBN 0-8186-0597-9); 486 pages

Nearest Neighbor Pattern Classification Techniques
Edited by Belur V. Dasarathy
(ISBN 0-8186-8930-); 500 pages

New Paradigms for Software Development
Edited by William Agresti
(ISBN 0-8186-0707-6); 304 pages

Object-Oriented Computing, Vol. 1: Concepts
Edited by Gerald E. Petersen
(ISBN 0-8186-0821-8); 214 pages

Object-Oriented Computing, Vol. 2: Implementations
Edited by Gerald E. Petersen
(ISBN 0-8186-0822-6); 324 pages

Office Automation Systems (Second Edition)
Edited by H.A. Freeman and K.J. Thurber
(ISBN 0-8186-0711-4); 324 pages

Parallel Architectures for Database Systems
Edited by A.R. Hurson, L.L. Miller, and S.H. Pakzad
(ISBN 0-8186-8838-6); 478 pages

Programming Productivity: Issues for '80s (Second Edition)
Edited by C. Jones
(ISBN 0-8186-0681-9); 472 pages

Recent Advances in Distributed Database Management
Edited by C. Mohan
(ISBN 0-8186-0571-5); 500 pages

Reduced Instruction Set Computers (RISC) (Second Edition)
Edited by William Stallings
(ISBN 0-8186-8943-9); 448 pages

Reliable Distributed System Software
Edited by J.A. Stankovic
(ISBN 0-8186-0570-7); 400 pages

Robotics (Second Edition)
Edited by C.S.G. Lee, R.C. Gonzalez, and K.S. Fu
(ISBN 0-8186-0570-7); 630 pages

Software Design Techniques (Fourth Edition)
Edited by P. Freeman and A.I. Wasserman
(ISBN 0-8186-0514-6); 736 pages

Software Engineering Project Management
Edited by R. Thayer
(ISBN 0-8186-0751-3); 512 pages

Software Maintenance and Computers
Edited by D.H. Longstreet
(ISBN 0-8186-8898-X); 304 pages

Software Management (Third Edition)
Edited by D.J. Reifer
(ISBN 0-8186-0678-9); 526 pages

Software-Oriented Computer Architecture
Edited by E. Fernandez and T.J. Lang
(ISBN 0-8186-0708-4); 376 pages

Software Quality Assurance: A Practical Approach
Edited by T.S. Chow
(ISBN 0-8186-0569-3); 506 pages

Software Restructuring
Edited by R.S. Arnold
(ISBN 0-8186-0680-0); 376 pages

Software Reusability
Edited by Peter Freeman
(ISBN 0-8186-0750-5); 304 pages

Software Reuse—Emerging Technology
Edited by Will Tracz
(ISBN 0-8186-0846-3); 400 pages

Software Risk Management
Edited by B.W. Boehm
(ISBN 0-8186-8906-4); 508 pages

Standards, Guidelines and Examples: System and Software Requirements Engineering
Edited by Merlin Dorfman and Richard H. Thayer
(ISBN 0-8186-8922-6); 626 pages

System and Software Requirements Engineering
Edited by Richard H. Thayer and Merlin Dorfman
(ISBN 0-8186-8921-8); 740 pages

Test Access Port and Boundary-Scan Architecture
Edited by C. M. Maunder and R. E. Tulloss
(ISBN 0-8186-9070-4); 400 pages

Test Generation for VLSI Chips
Edited by V.D. Agrawal and S.C. Seth
(ISBN 0-8186-8786-X); 416 pages

Visual Programming Environments: Paradigms and Systems
Edited by Ephraim Glinert
(ISBN 0-8186-8973-0); 680 pages

Visual Programming Environments: Applications and Issues
Edited by Ephraim Glinert
(ISBN 0-8186-8974-9); 704 pages

Visualization in Scientific Computing
Edited by G.M. Nielson, B. Shriver, and L. Rosenblum
(ISBN 0-8186-1979-1); 304 pages

VLSI Support Technologies: Computer-Aided Design
Edited by Rex Rice
(ISBN 0-8186-0386-1); 464 pages

VLSI Testing and Validation Techniques
Edited by H. Reghbati
(ISBN 0-8186-0668-1); 616 pages

Volume Visualization
Edited by Arie Kaufman
(ISBN 0-8186-9020-8); 494 pages

Reprint Collections

Dataflow and Reduction Architectures
Edited by S.S. Thakkar
(ISBN 0-8186-0759-9); 460 pages

Expert Systems: A Software Methodology for Modern Applications
Edited by Peter Raeth
(ISBN 0-8186-8904-8); 476 pages

Logic Design for Testability
Edited by C.C. Timoc
(ISBN 0-8186-0573-1); 324 pages

Milestones in Software Evolution
Edited by Paul W. Oman and Ted G. Lewis
(ISBN 0-8186-9033-X); 332 pages

Software (Third Edition)
Edited by M.V. Zelkowitz
(ISBN 0-8186-0789-0); 440 pages

Validation and Verification of Knowledge-Based Systems
Edited by Uma G. Gupta
(ISBN 0-8186-8995-1); 400 pages

VLSI Technologies and Computer Graphics
Edited by H. Fuchs
(ISBN 0-8186-0491-3); 490 pages

Artificial Neural Networks Technology Series

Artificial Neural Networks—Concept Learning
Edited by Joachim Diederich
(ISBN 0-8186-2015-3); 160 pages

Artificial Neural Networks—Electronic Implementation
Edited by Nelson Morgan
(ISBN 0-8186-2029-3); 144 pages

Artificial Neural Networks—Theoretical Concepts
Edited by V. Vemuri
(ISBN 0-8186-0855-2); 160 pages

Software Technology Series

Computer-Aided Software Engineering (CASE)
Edited by E.J. Chikofsky
(ISBN 0-8186-1917-1); 110 pages

Communications Technology Series

Multicast Communication in Distributed Systems
Edited by Mustaque Ahamad
(ISBN 0-8186-1970-8); 110 pages

Robotic Technology Series

Multirobot Systems
Edited by Rajiv Mehrotra and Murali R. Varanasi
(ISBN 0-8186-1977-5); 122 pages